W9-BZJ-337

The Social Logic of Politics

Personal Networks as Contexts
for Political Behavior

Released from
Samford University Library

The Social Logic of Politics

Personal Networks as Contexts for Political Behavior

Edited by

ALAN S. ZUCKERMAN

TEMPLE UNIVERSITY PRESS
Philadelphia

Samford University Library

Temple University Press
1601 North Broad Street
Philadelphia PA 19122
www.temple.edu/tempress

Copyright © 2005 by Temple University
All rights reserved
Published 2005
Printed in the United States of America

☺ The paper used in this publication meets the requirements of the American
National Standard for Information Sciences—Permanence of Paper for Printed
Library Materials, ANSI Z39.48-1992

Library of Congress Cataloging-in-Publication Data

The social logic of politics : personal networks as contexts for political behavior /
    edited by Alan S. Zuckerman.
        p.   cm.
    Includes bibliographical references and index.
    ISBN 1-59213-147-6 (cloth : alk. paper) — ISBN 1-59213-148-4 (pbk. :
alk. paper)
    1. Political sociology.   2. Political socialization.   3. Social networks—
Political aspects.   4. Political participation.   5. Voting.   I. Zuckerman,
Alan S., 1945–

JA76.S6222 2005
306.2–dc22   2004049819

2   4   6   8   9   7   5   3   1

JA
76
.S6222
2005

To my grandchildren,

Jack, Nina, Gabriel, Jesse, Eli, and Adi

As I wish for their parents, may they too know the blessings of Psalm 128

And may they also know the wisdom of Maimonides

Contents

III. THE SOCIAL LOGIC OF POLITICS: LOOKING AHEAD

List of Tables and Figures

FIGURES

Preface and Acknowledgments

Happy is the man, who has not followed the counsel of the wicked, or taken the path of sinners, or joined the company of the insolent; rather his concern is the teaching of the Lord, and he recites that teaching day and night.

—Psalms 1:1

He who walks with the wise will become wise, And he who gathers with the fools will become bad.

—Proverbs 13:20

God always pairs off like with like.

—*The Iliad,* XVII, 1:218

STUDENTS OF POLITICS have always known that the immediate social circumstances of people's lives affect their political preferences and behavior. This principle derives from a more fundamental claim about all perception, cognition, and action: human life is social. As persons interact and anticipate interactions, each influences what the others perceive, value, and do. When persons make decisions, they take into account the cues, knowledge, values, and expectations of their spouse, parents, children, friends, work-mates, and others around them—those who matter in their lives. When they associate with others, they look for persons like themselves. As the epigraphs to this chapter highlight, the sources for this theoretical position go back to the Bible and Greek wisdom.

As elements of general wisdom, it is not surprising, therefore, that these principles are embedded in the founding works of social science and the behavioral revolution in political science. What is surprising is how they alternately disappear and recur. As the authors of the chapters in the volume apply the theoretical principles to the study of politics, they repeat calls made five decades ago. Consider Robert Merton's observations in *Social Theory and Social Action* (1957):

> In his inventory of sociological concepts in 1932, Earle E. Eubank could muster thirty-nine distinct classifications of groups. . . . And in view of what I have described as the "recent rediscovery of the primary group," consider what Eubank had to say about the publication of B. Warren Brown's book, *Social Groups*, in 1926: "This little volume is a tangible evidence of the fact that the group has been discovered, or more accurately, *re*-discovered during recent years. In its new role and with its new implications it becomes . . . the central concept of Sociology as a whole. . . ." With the experience, if not necessarily the wisdom gained through hindsight, it can only be hoped that the more recent rediscovery will prove more productive and sequential than the one which was enthusiastically hailed by Eubank a generation ago. (pp. 308–9)

Writing at about the same time, Edward Shils (1951) too describes a "renaissance" in the study of primary groups, and Elihu Katz and Paul Lazarsfeld open their classic *Personal Influence* (1955) with the same observations. Citing Shils, Katz, and Lazarsfeld among others, Sidney Verba also draws attention to the importance of small groups for the study of politics (1961, 18). In this volume, scholars of politics reaffirm the importance of social context for the analysis of political preferences, choices, and behavior. Once again, social scientists put quotation marks around rediscovery and return to the logic of social politics.

EXPLANATORY MECHANISMS

Research on the social logic of politics coheres around a set of related explanatory propositions. At the most general level, individuals make political decisions, like other choices, by taking into account cues from other persons. These decisions cover political preferences, electoral ballots, and the selection of allies and associates in political groups. Persons follow some of their associates, ignore others, and choose to do the opposite of what some others do. They vary, as well, in the extent to which they take cues from anyone. The relationship between a person's choices and actions and the messages he or she obtains is a variable, not a determined certainty.

From whom do persons take political cues? The social logic of politics offers a set of answers. Individuals are especially likely to follow those persons from whom they take other cues, those on whom they depend, whom they trust, with whom they regularly interact, and whom they perceive as like themselves. They are especially likely to reject the political cues of people whom they perceive as different from themselves, whom they do not trust, and who are strangers to them. The clearer are the political cues offered and the more frequent and consistent, the more likely are they to serve as reference points. The greater is the level of interdependence, trust, interaction, and perceived similarity, the more likely are these persons to form a political association. More concretely, parents and spouses or life partners are the most frequent sources of cues, but persons also follow their relatives, friends, work-mates, and neighbors.

These propositions may be rephrased and extended to apply to sets of people. Given the probabilistic nature of cue giving and taking and the complex web of social ties, those who share any particular social criteria vary in the extent to which they display political cohesion—display the same political values, perceptions, understandings, and preferences, vote for candidates of the same party, and join together in other forms of political action. The greater is the level of interdependence, trust, and interaction among a set of persons, the greater is their level of political cohesion. The greater is the level of political discussion among a set of persons, the greater is their level of political cohesion.

PRECURSORS AND SOURCES

The social logic of politics has an ancient pedigree. Relevant stories, principles, themes, and statements abound in the Bible, Greek classics, and foundational works of the medieval period. The Bible opens with stories—of Adam and Eve,

Cain and Abel, Noah and his family, Abraham, Sarah, and Hagar, Abraham and the binding of Isaac, the search for wives for Isaac and Jacob, the conflicts among Abraham, Sarah, and Hagar and among Isaac, Rebecca, Jacob, and Esau, among Joseph and his brothers—and as it does so, it centers the principles of human life around the family. In more abstract terms, Aristotle defines the family as the nucleus of the polity, a claim that resonates through centuries of Christian political thought. Even a cursory look at these literatures finds the family at the heart of personal and collective life.

More directly linked to the task at hand, these literatures recognize that people live their lives by learning from those around them. Ancient proverbs are presented as analytical truths and behavioral rules that lead one to a good life. One set of principles involves the benefits obtained from good friends and the need to avoid bad associates. Another set involves the selection of colleagues: similar persons associate with each other; but sometimes they repel each other, and different people may find themselves drawn together as well.

Here I present Aristotle's views, highlighting critical statements and propositions. As I note in the epigraph to this Preface, the Hebrew Bible and the *Iliad* too offer similar principles for the good life.[1] Aristotle explores the importance of friends in the following passage from the *Nicomechean Ethics*:

> No one would choose to live without friends, even if he had all other goods. . . . Friends help young men avoid error; to older people they give the care and help needed to supplement the failing powers of actions which infirmity brings in its train; and to those in their prime they give the opportunity to perform noble actions. . . . Friends enhance our ability to think and to act. . . . There are, however, several controversial points about friendship. Some people define it as a kind of likeness, and say that friends are those like us; hence according to them, the proverb: "Like to like," "Birds of a feather flock together." Others, on the contrary, hold that all similar individuals are mutually opposed. (Aristotle, *Nicomechean Ethics* 1155a: 214–16)

> The friendship of base people becomes wicked, because unsteady as they are, they share in base pursuits, and by becoming like one another they become wicked. But the friendship of good men is good, and it increases with [the frequency] of meetings. Also, it seems, they become better as they are active together and correct one another: from the mould of the other each takes the imprints of the traits he likes, whence the saying: "Noble things from noble people." (Ibid., 1172a: 271–72)

These proverbs did not originate with Aristotle. Rather, he cites Homer (see the chapter's epigraph), Empedocles, Euripides, and Heraclitus. Indeed, these proverbs indicate that even Aristotle considered the aphorisms "like to like," "birds of a feather flock together," and "opposites attract" to be the wisdom of the ancients.[2]

During the Middle Ages, Maimonides and Aquinas develop these principles:

> It is natural to man to be influenced by the beliefs and practices of his friends and neighbors and to behave like the practices of his community. Therefore, a man should attach himself to the righteous and sit always among the wise, so that he may learn from their deeds. He should also stay away from evil people who walk in darkness, so as not to learn from them. (Maimonides, *Mishnah Torah*, 6:1; my translation)

> Friends become better by working together and loving each other. For one receives from the other an example of virtuous work which is at the same time pleasing to

him. Hence it is proverbial that man adopts noble deeds from noble men. (Aquinas, *Commentary on the Nicomechean Ethics*, 2:5)

Are friends necessary for happiness? *Response*: If the question refers to the happiness of the present life then, as the Philosopher says, the happy man needs friends, not because they are useful, since he is able to get along without help, nor for the enjoyment, since the activity of virtue furnishes him with complete joy, but for good activity, that is so that he may do good to them and delight in seeing them do good and be helped by them in doing his own good deeds. For, in order to do well, whether in the works of the active life or in the activity of the contemplative life, man needs the help of friends. (Aquinas, *Treatise on Happiness*, 12)

The Bible, Greek wisdom, and the sources that develop and bring them together highlight a basic understanding of social life. Persons need and rely on each other; they learn from each other, and they enable each other to live well. As important, people usually associate with others like themselves, but they sometimes avoid their similars, choosing instead to bond with their opposites. The ancients understood the selection of associates as inherently probabilistic.

Among the principles offered by the founders of modern social science too, it is easy to find statements that affirm the propositions of the social logic of politics. Tocqueville conceptualizes individualism without a distinction between person and primary group (1969, 508), and, he argues, in democracies people take their political views from those around them (1969, 643). Marx maintains that as individuals interact with others who share the same relationship to the means of production and, therefore, the same social circumstances, they will come to share the same perceptions, understandings, values, and political action. As these processes unfold, these persons form a social class—a political association in opposition to the other social class, which takes on ontological reality. (For the appropriate passages in Marx, consult, for example, Bottomore and Rubel 1956; and for useful analyses, see Katznelson 1986 and Zuckerman 1989.) Max Weber replaces the deterministic nature of Marx's analysis with probabilistic relationships. (See, for example, Roth and Wittich 1978, 2:928–30). As important, Weber also places the inherent sociality of people's lives at the heart of his social science (ibid., 1:4). For Émile Durkheim, the interactions of persons in groups define their essential humanity (Durkheim 1964, 26), and Gaetano Mosca refers "to mimetism . . . the great psychological force whereby every individual is wont to adopt the ideas, the beliefs, the sentiments that are most current in the environment in which he has grown up" (Mosca 1939, 26). Georg Simmel uses networks of social interaction to explore the tension between persons and groups (Simmel 1955, 140, 141, 151). Differences appear among the titans of social science. Marx and Durkheim depict groups as part of the social ontology. Tocqueville, Weber, Mosca, and Simmel examine interactions among persons, maintaining analytical space for individuals and groups. The founders of social science offer theoretical and conceptual reasoning and some empirical evidence for the social logic of politics.

In this volume, we return to these ancient and foundational principles of social and political life. Persons are necessarily tied to others; they learn from, assist, and constrain each other. Persons do not exist—think, reason, assess, value—independent of other persons. Similarly, social groups do not swallow individuals. Thus the essays insist that explanations in social science demand social mechanisms that include the characteristics of both individuals and their social contexts and that link these two levels of analysis. (See the essays in Hedström and Swedberg 1998 for an elaboration of this position, especially the chapter by Hernes.)

THE AUTHORS OF the various chapters come to this theoretical stance from different routes: some from research on social and political networks; some from political socialization; others from geography; and yet others from additional sources. I started on this path as a graduate student at Princeton under the tutelage of Harry Eckstein. Harry introduced me to Weber and Mosca, as well as his own focus on authority patterns in social units. Our scholarship moved along different paths. Eckstein's research expanded to focus on culturalist themes, and I have narrowed my gaze to explore the influence of intimate social ties on political behavior. I have followed work on social networks and engaged in secondary survey analysis to link the abstractions of social collectivities to the analysis of electoral choice. In recent years I have been examining exceptionally rich panel surveys that interview all persons over the age of fifteen in each household. These allow me, working with Jennifer Fitzgerald and Josip Dasović, to get very close to the immediate social context of political choices, and together with Jennifer and Josip I present some of this research in the volume's fourth chapter. I also have thought again about fundamental theoretical and conceptual issues. I returned to the work of Paul Lazarsfeld, the leader of the Columbia school of electoral sociologists, whose scholarship dominated the study of political behavior until it was swept aside by the Michigan school's emphasis on the survey respondent and rational choice theory's rational and self-interested individual. I reread Herbert Simon's classic *Administrative Behavior* and followed his efforts to establish the principles of bounded rationality along with those of scholars of decision theory in political science and cognitive science who would extend his work. And I turned back as well to Leon Festinger and Kurt Lewin. Reflections on these matters provide the material for the volume's first chapter, where I also introduce the other essays.

Even if it is patently obvious that a collected volume is the product of many persons' efforts, I still want to thank them and to recognize the others who have helped us. Many of the essays in this book were first presented at the conference "The Social Context of Politics," held at Brown University in June 2002, funding for which came from the Watson Institute for International Studies and the Office of the Dean of the Faculty. And so I offer thanks to Thomas Biersteker and his colleagues at the Watson Institute and to Mary Fennell, the Dean of the Faculty. Patti Gardner, department manager of the Department of Political Science, Brown University, administered the conference just as she takes care of the department: with efficiency, grace, good sense, and good humor. It is a pleasure to thank her publicly. This is also an appropriate point to praise Robert Zimmer and Ruth Simmons, Brown's provost and president respectively. Bob Huckfeldt, Kent Jennings, and Sid Verba have provided wise counsel at critical junctures as the project moved from idea to conference to published volume, and Jennifer Fitzgerald has been a wonderful partner in the editorial work. In two long meetings in Jerusalem, Elihu Katz helped me to understand better the intellectual history of the Columbia school of social and political analysis. In many enormously pleasurable conversations, my son Ezra Zuckerman, an economic sociologist, has shown me how this approach bridges our respective disciplines. I want especially to acknowledge the assistance of Lucas Swaine, who led me to the sources in Aristotle, and Thomas O'Meara, OP, who aided my understanding of the passages in Aquinas. I have sought out the names of some of the anonymous reviewers of the book manuscript, so that I can publicly recognize their contributions. Susan Herbst, Jan Leighley, Robert Shapiro, and Katherine Cramer Walsh offered the most incisive and most encouraging set of reviews that I have ever received. Alex Holzman is a wonderful editor, friend, and fellow Yankee fan, and it was a kick to join him at the last game of the 2003 World Series, even if our team lost (that time). I am honored that this volume will be among the first to be published under his directorship of Temple University Press. All these persons have helped to make this book as good as it is, and it is a pleasure as well as an obligation to thank them.

And now for the most immediate social circumstances of my life: my wife Ricki (sometimes called Roberta), our children, their spouses, and their children: Greg, Michelle, Gabriel, and Eli; Ezra, Lisa, Jack, Nina, and Jesse; Shara, Igal, and Adi. Ricki and I have been best friends, and more, for more than forty-three years. I have long ago given up trying to know where I end and she begins. We began in Brooklyn (really Boro Park and Williamsburgh/Greenpoint) and have spent more years than we could ever have supposed in Providence, leavening that with extended stays in California (Palo Alto), Italy (Florence, Milan, Potenza, and Rome), England (Colchester and Wivenhoe), and of course Israel (Jerusalem, Tel-Aviv, and Netanyah). Ricki has received her namesake Rebecca's blessing, and we now have children and grandchildren. Together we have tasted life's joys and sorrows. If that were all, it would suffice.

I dedicated my first book to my parents, Edith and Jack Zuckerman, and subsequent books to Ricki and to our children. It is a pleasure to dedicate this one to our grandchildren.

About the Contributors

CHRISTOPHER J. ANDERSON is Professor of Political Science, the Maxwell School of Citizenship and Public Affairs, Syracuse University, Syracuse, New York.

NANCY BURNS is Henry Simmons Frieze Professor, Department of Political Science and Center for Political Studies, University of Michigan, Ann Arbor, Michigan.

JOSIP DASOVIĆ is a doctoral student, Department of Political Science, Brown University, Providence, Rhode Island.

JENNIFER FITZGERALD is a doctoral student, Department of Political Science, Brown University, Providence, Rhode Island.

JAMES H. FOWLER is Assistant Professor, Department of Political Science, University of California at Davis, Davis, California.

JAMES G. GIMPEL is Professor, Department of Government, the University of Maryland, College Park, Maryland.

ROBERT HUCKFELDT is Distinguished Professor, Department of Political Science, University of California at Davis, Davis, California.

M. KENT JENNINGS is Professor of Political Science, University of California at Santa Barbara, Santa Barbara, California, and Professor Emeritus, University of Michigan, Ann Arbor, Michigan.

PAUL E. JOHNSON is Associate Professor of Political Science, University of Kansas, Lawrence, Kansas.

RON J. JOHNSTON is Professor, School of Geographical Sciences, University of Bristol, Bristol, England.

ULRICH KOHLER is a research scholar at the Wissenschaftszentrum, Berlin, Germany.

LAURENCE KOTLER-BERKOWITZ is Research Director, National Jewish Population Survey 2000–01, United Jewish Communities, New York, New York.

J. CELESTE LAY is Assistant Professor of Political Science, Tulane University, New Orleans, Louisiana.

JEFFREY LEVINE is Director of the Center for Public Interest Polling at the Eagleton Institute of Politics, Rutgers University, New Brunswick, New Jersey.

ANN CHIH LIN is Associate Professor, Ford School of Public Policy and Department of Political Science, University of Michigan, Ann Arbor, Michigan.

AIDA PASKEVICIUTE is a doctoral student, Department of Political Science, Binghamton University (SUNY), Binghamton, New York.

CHARLES J. PATTIE is Professor and Head, Department of Geography, Sheffield University, Sheffield, England.

KAY LEHMAN SCHLOZMAN is the J. Joseph Moakley Professor of Political Science, Boston College, Chestnut Hill, Massachusetts.

JOHN SPRAGUE is the Sidney W. Souers Professor of Government, Emeritus, Washington University in St. Louis, St. Louis, Missouri.

LAURA STOKER is Associate Professor of Political Science, University of California, Berkeley, Berkeley, California.

SIDNEY VERBA is Carl H. Pforzheimer University Professor and Professor of Government, and Director, the Harvard University Library, Harvard University, Cambridge, Massachusetts.

ALAN S. ZUCKERMAN is Professor and Chair, Department of Political Science, Brown University, Providence, Rhode Island, and Research Professor, DIW–German Institute for Economic Research, Berlin, Germany.

Introduction

Theoretical and Methodological Context

ALAN S. ZUCKERMAN

1 Returning to the Social Logic of Political Behavior

IN POLITICAL SCIENCE, the study of political choice and behavior—the focus of this collection of essays—has had a complex relationship with the social logic of politics. It is both obvious and well known that the immediate social circumstances of people's lives influence what they believe and do about politics. Even so, relatively few political scientists incorporate these principles into their analyses. The founders of the behavioral revolution in political science—Angus Campbell, Philip Converse, Warren Miller, and Donald Stokes, Anthony Downs, Heinz Eulau, V. O. Key, Robert Lane, and Sidney Verba—those intellectual visionaries who set the agenda for more than half a century of scholarship—understood and accepted these theoretical principles. Even so, they directed research away from them. Driven primarily by issues of data and survey methodology, Campbell, Converse, Miller, and Stokes changed direction, first in small steps and then in leaps and bounds. Explicit theoretical needs moved others like Key and Downs to blaze new paths. None, I will argue, offered compelling reasons for the change of course. Furthermore, recent advances in theory and methods support a return to the social logic of political behavior.

This chapter offers an intellectual history. I present the critical texts that helped to define the research orientation. Passages, statements, and long quotations stand as the data for this analysis. Here I set out the story of the social logic of politics in the behavioral revolution in political science, and I give reasons for political scientists and others who study political choice and behavior to return to this social logic.

THE SOCIAL LOGIC OF POLITICS IN THE BEHAVIORAL REVOLUTION IN POLITICAL SCIENCE

Returning to the foundational texts of the behavioral revolution in political science highlights the fundamental importance of the social logic of politics. I begin with a selection from *The American Voter* (Campbell, Converse, Miller, and Stokes 1960). This volume raised the flag of the Michigan school of electoral analysis, as it institutionalized the research agenda for electoral studies in the United States and other established democracies. It spawned as well the American National Election Surveys and parallel studies elsewhere. This research has provided the lion's share of evidence for the study of political behavior during the past fifty years.

Campbell, Converse, Miller, and Stokes recognized the power of immediate social circles on the ways that persons perceive and act in politics:

> Not only does the individual absorb from his primary groups the attitudes that guide his behavior; he often behaves politically as a self-conscious member of these groups, and his perception of their preferences can be of great importance for his own voting act. Our interviews suggest that the dynamics of these face-to-face associations

are capable of generating forces that may negate the force of the individual's own evaluations of the elements of politics. Probably this happens most often in the relations of husband and wife . . . (p. 76)

Knowledge of social processes may add much to our understanding of the fact that party allegiances not only remain stable but grow stronger over time. In addition to intra-psychic mechanisms that act in this direction, social communication in a congenial primary group may constitute a potent extra-psychic process leading to the same end. The ambiguity of the merits of political objects and events is such that people are dependent upon "social reality" to support and justify their political opinions. When primary groups engage in political discussions and are homogeneous in basic member viewpoints, the attitudes of the individual must be continually reinforced as he sees similar opinions echoed in the social group. (p. 293)

Here the founders of the Michigan school presented principles for the analysis of political behavior that were held by the other leaders of the behavioral revolution. Consider too the views of their colleagues, beginning with Robert Lane:

Political participation for an individual increases with (a) the political consciousness and participation of his associates, (b) the frequency and harmony of his interpersonal contacts and group membership, and (c) the salience and unambiguity of his group references. (Lane 1959, 189)

Groups orient a person in a political direction specifically by (a) redefining what is public and private in their lives, (b) providing new grounds for partisanship . . . (Ibid., 195)

Even V. O. Key, who was among the first to argue against the principles of the social logic of politics, accepted its importance. "Probably it is correct to picture the political system as one in which a complex network of [primary] group relations fixes and maintains opinions in some systematic relation to the larger components of the system, such as political parties" (1961, 69–70). Sidney Verba underlined the importance of small groups in the analysis of political processes as well as the behavior of individuals:

If we are to understand the political process, greater consideration must be given to the role of face-to-face contacts. Primary groups of all sorts mediate political relationships at strategic points in the political process. They are the locus of most political decision-making, they are important transmission points in political communications, and they exercise a major influence on the political beliefs and attitudes of their members. (1961, 4)

It is well known that the face-to-face groups to which an individual belongs exert a powerful influence over him; that he will accept the norms and standards of the group. . . . [This] is one of the best documented generalizations in the small group literature. (Ibid., 22–23)

And finally, note as well Heinz Eulau's general principles:

Just as the significant environment of the individual is another individual, so the significant environment of the group is another group. (1962, 91–92)

Political behavior is likely to vary with the type of groups in which the individual is involved. (1986, 38)

The behavioral revolution in political science began with the principles of the social logic of politics.

Every revolution draws on, negates, and transforms what precedes it. The transformation of political science is no exception to this rule. Political scientists drew on several sets of theoretical and empirical sources. Of direct and powerful relevance was a group of electoral sociologists at Columbia University, led by Paul Lazarsfeld and Bernard Berelson. Robert Merton and Edward Shils offered more general theoretical statements. At the same time, Campbell, Converse, Miller, and Stokes reinterpreted Karl Lewin's social psychology in order to reformulate the understanding of the relationship between the group and the individual. Political scientists accepted as well Leon Festinger's analysis of the relationship between the individual and the political reality portrayed by his or her peers. All of these sources accepted, applied, and developed the principles of the social logic of politics. And so the behavioral revolution in the study of political behavior transformed these intellectual sources.

Sources in Sociology

Paul Lazarsfeld and his colleagues at Columbia University, Bernard Berelson, Hazel Gaudet, and William McPhee, were the first to apply the social logic of politics to the study of electoral choice. *The People's Choice: How the Voter Makes Up His Mind in a Presidential Campaign* (Lazarsfeld, Berelson, and Gaudet 1968) and *Voting: A Study of Opinion Formation in a Presidential Campaign* (Berelson, Lazarsfeld, and McPhee 1954) introduced mass surveys into the analysis of political preferences. These studies interview respondents several times during an electoral campaign, offering the first panel surveys of electoral behavior. Several sets of questions ask respondents for information on the members of their immediate social circles, family, friends, work-mates, and neighbors. These colleagues examined evidence drawn from single communities, Elmira, New York, and Erie County, Pennsylvania, not a nationally representative sample of the electorate. These electoral sociologists initiated a research path, which Campbell, Converse, Miller, Stokes, Key, Eulau, and other political scientists followed and then redirected.

How important is the research of the electoral sociologists for the behavioral revolution in political science? Here are the opening words of *The American Voter:*

> In the contemporary world the activity of voting is rivaled only by the market as a means of reaching collective decisions from individual choices. . . . Indeed, anyone who reads the literature of voting research must be impressed by its proliferation in recent years. The report of one major study lists 209 hypotheses about voting in political elections, which recent work has tended to confirm. (1960, 3)

The volume's first footnote cites Berelson, Lazarsfeld, and McPhee's *Voting,* published in 1954, six years earlier. Similarly, the first sentence of Key and Munger's classic article cites *The People's Choice,* as they frame their presentation in opposition to Lazarsfeld and his colleagues: "The style set in the Erie County study of voting, *The People's Choice,* threatens to take the politics out of the study of electoral behavior" (Key and Munger 1959, 281). Heinz Eulau's first book also begins by echoing Key and Munger's point, citing the same passage from *The People's Choice* and declaring his opposition to social determinism (1962, 1). The leaders of the behavioral revolution in political science first observed electoral choice through the lenses of electoral sociology.

As a result, they began with the principles of the social logic of political behavior. How did Lazarsfeld, Berelson, Gaudet, and McPhee enunciate those explanatory mechanisms? What were the leaders of the behavioral revolution in political science reading? And to what precisely did they react? Consider some critical themes in *The People's Choice:*

> While the individual preserves his security by sealing himself off from the propaganda which threatens his attitudes, he finds these attitudes reinforced in his contacts with other members of the group. Because of their common group membership, they will share similar attitudes and will exhibit similar selective tendencies. But this does not mean that all of the members of group will expose themselves to exactly the same bits of propaganda or that they will be influenced by precisely the same aspects of common experiences. (1968, xxxii)

The boldest version of this statement sounds like social determinism, and, as I will show below, it provides a point of attack for the political scientists:

> There is a familiar adage in American folklore to the effect that a person is only what he thinks he is, an adage which reflects the typically American notion of unlimited opportunity, the tendency toward self-betterment, etc. Now we find that the reverse of the adage is true: a person thinks, politically, as he is, socially. Social characteristics determine political preference. (1968, 27)

It is clear, however, that the last line only highlights the general stance; it is not a theoretical principle. The volume abounds in statements and evidence, which maintain that the effects of social context on political preferences vary. For example:

> People who work or play together *are likely to* vote for the same candidates. (Ibid., 137; emphasis added)

> The political homogeneity of social groups *is promoted by* personal relationships among the same kind of people. . . . In comparison with the formal media of communication, personal relationships are potentially *more influential* for two reasons: their coverage is greater and they have certain psychological advantages. (Ibid., 150; emphases added)

The study demonstrates how personal contacts affect the electoral choices of undecided citizens. Several factors drive the process: the power of the two-step flow of communications, in which information flows through opinion leaders; personal contacts need have no particular purpose; flexibility when encountering resistance; rewards of compliance; greater level of trust in the source, and persuasion without conviction (Ibid.,150–57):

> In short, personal influence, with all its overtones of personal affection and loyalty, can bring to the polls votes that would otherwise not be cast or would be cast for the opposing party just as readily if some other friend had insisted. (Ibid., 157).

In a footnote in the book's last chapter, Lazarsfeld, Berelson, Gaudet, and McPhee sketched a research project that would examine variations in the political homogeneity of social groups:

The statement that people vote in groups is not very satisfactory. People belong to a variety of groups and therefore further research is necessary on the question: with *which group* are they most likely to vote? (Ibid., 170)

The complexity of social ties affects the political cohesion of social groups.

Berelson, Lazarsfeld, and McPhee (1954) developed this perspective. They expected, and their research finds, high levels of political homogeneity in primary groups (1954, 88–118). During an election campaign, intention responds directly to a combination of cues and requests from members of discussion circles, families, friends, and co-workers (pp. 118–49).

[B]y the very process of talking to one another, the vague dispositions which people have are crystallized, step by step, into specific attitudes, acts, or votes. (Ibid., 300)

In turn, they disagreed with those who view casting a ballot as a rational act:

The upshot of this is that the usual analogy between the voting "decision" and the more or less carefully calculated decisions of consumers or businessmen or courts, incidentally, may be quite incorrect. . . . In short, it appears that a sense of fitness is a more striking feature of political preference than reason and calculation. (Ibid., 311)

Finally, they added that the logic of democracy works at the aggregate level, not the individual level:

True, the individual casts his own personal ballot. But as we have tried to indicate throughout this volume, that is perhaps the most individualized action he takes in an election. His vote is formed in the midst of his fellows in a sort of group decision— if indeed, it may be called a decision at all—and the total information and knowledge possessed in the group's present and past generations can be made available for the group's choice. Here is where opinion-leading relationships, for example, play an active role.

    Second, and probably more important, the individual voter may not have a great deal of detailed information, but he usually has picked up the crucial *general* information as part of his social learning. (Ibid., 320–21; emphasis in original)

Working with Elihu Katz, Lazarsfeld presented a broader analysis of the process by which people form attitudes, preferences, and values. Consider the following propositions taken from Katz and Lazarsfeld's *Personal Influence* (1955):

As far as "communications *within* the group" are concerned two major sets of findings current in small group research are of considerable relevance:

(a) Ostensibly private opinions and attitudes are often generated and/or reinforced in small intimate groups of family, friends, co-workers. . . .
(b) Families, friendships, work-groups and the like are interpersonal communications networks through which influences flow in patterned ways. (p. 8)

The way in which people influence each other is not only affected by the primary groups within which they live; it is co-determined by the broad institutional setting of the American scene. (Ibid., 9)

[I]nterpersonal relations "intervene" [in the process of mass communication] by inducing *resistance* to those influences that go counter to those ideas that individuals share with others they hold in esteem; and, on the other hand, we found that when individuals share norms which are in harmony with an outside influence or when they are willing to incorporate a proposed change to group norms, then interpersonal relations may act as *facilitators* of change. (Ibid., 81)

Lazarsfeld, Berelson, Gaudet, McPhee, and Katz articulated the principles of the social context of politics as testable hypotheses. They examined panel surveys of particular communities in order to test and demonstrate the power of this theoretical perspective.

These sociologists draw directly on Simmel's and Weber's social science. They echoed as well the sociological wisdom of their own era. As noted in the Preface to this volume, Robert Merton highlighted the centrality of primary groups as he developed the concepts of reference group theory. He maintained that the Elmira election studies confirm the theoretical, normative, and empirical claims of pluralist theory:

[I]t is not "individuals," tacitly conceived as "sand heap [*sic!*] of disconnected particles of humanity," who are protected in their liberties by the associations which stand between them and the sovereign state, but "persons," diversely engaged in primary groups, such as the family, companionships, and local groups. That figment of the truly isolated individual, which was so powerfully conceived in ... Hobbes' *Leviathan*, and which was since caught up in the assumptions of the liberal pluralists, is a fiction which present-day sociology has shown, beyond all reasonable doubt, to be both untrue and superfluous. . . .

[E]ven the primary groups in which persons are in some measure involved do not have uniform effects upon the orientations of their members. . . . Moreover, when conflicting value-orientations obtain in the primary-groups, and the modal orientations of the larger social environment are pronounced, the mediating role of the primary group becomes lessened or even negligible, and the influence of the larger society becomes more binding. (1957, 334–35)

Again, we find the general principles: people depend on each other, and there is a complex relationship among individuals, primary groups, and the broader society.

This perspective extends beyond Merton, Lazarsfeld, and their colleagues at Columbia University. It appears in Edward Shils's classic essay on primary groups (1951, 69) and David Riesman's *The Lonely Crowd* (1961, 23). The founders of contemporary sociology refurbished and transmitted the principles that began with the ancients and were presented again by Tocqueville, Marx, Weber, Durkheim, Mosca, and Simmel. The sociologists offered their colleagues in political science a choice: follow us or blaze your own path.

Sources in Social Psychology and Organizational Theory

Social psychologists—especially Kurt Lewin and Leon Festinger—provided another source for ideas that guided the behavioral revolution in political science. The authors of *The American Voter* modeled their "funnel of causality" on Lewin's field theory. This analytical approach applies a large set of immediately relevant explanatory factors (Campbell, Converse, Miller, and Stokes 1960, 33). Key (1961, 62) and Verba (1961, 23) explained the tendency toward conformity in political preferences among members of primary groups by referring to Festinger's work on cognitive dissonance, and Campbell and his colleagues also drew on Festinger to raise questions about using respondents' reports to describe their immediate social circles. As the political scientists analyzed political preferences, they again utilized the principles of the social logic of politics.

Lewin's social psychology argues for the utility of examining groups as collectives, defined by the interdependence of members:

> Conceiving of a group as a dynamic whole should include a definition of group which is based on interdependence of the members. . . . A group, on the other hand, need not consist of members which show great similarity. . . . Not similarity but a certain interdependence of members constitutes a group. . . .
>
> [E]ven a definition by "equality of goal or equality of an enemy is still a definition by similarity. The same holds for the definition of a group by the feeling of loyalty or of belongingness of their members. (1964, 146–47)

Abstract categories like social class, ethnicity, or religion, therefore, do not define social groups. Similarly, sharing identification with a political party does not define a group. Indeed, psychological attachment provides the weakest form on which to base a group. It applies because it might constitute "a certain kind of interdependence, because there might be interdependence established by the feeling" (Lewin 1964, 146–54, and see also Lewin 1948, 84ff.). Analyzing an individual, Lewin maintained, requires examining the person's "life-space," which is defined as anything that might affect the person. One segment includes the individual's perceptions; another examines members of a person's immediate social circle (see Lewin 1964, xii). Here, too, the immediate social circumstances of people's lives affect their perceptions, choices, and actions.

Leon Festinger offered a tripartite analysis of the individual and the social group. Opinions, preferences, and beliefs are a joint function of how "real" the matter is, the views held by the members of a person's group(s), and the person's own conception(s):

> Validity of opinion depends on what others around him say: "An opinion, a belief, an attitude is 'correct,' 'valid,' and 'proper' to the extent that it is anchored in a group of people with similar beliefs, opinions, and attitudes." (Schachter and Gazzaniga 1989, 119)

In turn, Festinger recognized a fundamental tension in the set of explanatory mechanisms. Persons are influenced by members of their groups, and they join groups whose views conform to their own:

> It is to some extent inherently circular since an appropriate reference group tends to be a group which does share a person's opinions and attitudes, and people do locomote *into* such groups and *out* of such groups which do not agree with them. (Ibid.,19)

Drawing on the results of his own and other studies, Festinger noted a strong tendency for members of groups to adopt similar views: "Belonging to the same group tends to produce changes in opinions and attitudes in the direction of establishing uniformity within the group." Furthermore, the amount of change toward uniformity is a function of how attractive belonging to the group is to its members (ibid., 161).

Festinger's most frequently cited contribution, the theory of cognitive dissonance, combines these ideas into three core principles:

1. There may exist dissonant or "nonfitting" relations among cognitive elements.
2. The existence of dissonance gives rise to pressures to reduce the dissonance and to avoid increases in dissonance.
3. Manifestations of the operation of these pressures include behavior changes, changes of cognition, and circumspect exposure to new information and opinions (Ibid., 225).

Any of these outcomes may appear at any time.

Like the electoral sociologists, Festinger and Levin articulated theoretical principles in line with the social logic of politics, and not surprisingly both also drew on Simmel's and Weber's social science. As the political scientists who led their discipline's revolution applied this scholarship to the study of political behavior, they reaffirmed these principles. As they carved their own intellectual path, they moved away from the social logic of politics.

Parallel developments in the study of political organizations echoed these theoretical principles. Writing at about the same time, Herbert Simon also emphasized the centrality of social context for understanding people's decisions. Consider a passage from the introduction to his classic *Administrative Behavior: A Study of Decision-Making Processes in Administrative Organization* (1965):

> Organization is important, first, because in our society, where men spend most of their waking adult lives in organizations, this environment provides much of the force that molds and develops personal qualities and habits. (p. xv)

> In the pages of this book, the term *organization* refers to the complex pattern of communications and other relations in a group of human beings. This pattern provides to each member of the group much of the information, assumptions, goals, and attitudes that enter into his decisions, and provides him also with a set of stable and comprehensible expectations as to what the other members of the group are doing and how they will react to what he says and does. The sociologist calls this pattern a "role system"; to most of us it is more familiarly known as "organization." (p. xvi)

In Simon's presentation, social context especially affects the initial decision, preference, or social action:

> Two principal sets of mechanisms may be distinguished: (1) those that cause behavior to persist in a particular direction once it has been turned in that direction, and (2) those that initiate behavior in a particular direction. The former are for the most part—though by no means entirely—internal. Their situs is in the human mind. . . . Behavior-initiating mechanisms, on the other hand, are largely external to the individual, although they usually imply his sensitivity to particular stimuli. Being external, they can be interpersonal—they can be invoked by someone other than the person they are intended to influence. (Ibid., 95)

In *Administrative Behavior* and *The American Voter*, immediate social circumstances are the source of a person's initial political preferences. In both works, social circles provide stability for political preferences. Simon's approach to the analysis of decisions emphasizes the context in which choices are made and the cognitive factors that limit people's ability to behave in ways consistent with rational choice theory.

THE TURN AWAY FROM THE SOCIAL LOGIC OF POLITICS

Notwithstanding their initial theoretical stance, the founders of the behavioral analysis of political preferences and electoral choices institutionalized a research agenda that departed from the social logic of politics. They conducted surveys that examine individuals but ignore the members of their social circles, and they transformed social groups into objects of individual identification. In the analysis of electoral decisions, they focused on political attitudes, perceptions of the candidates, and policy preferences. In *The American Voter*, social contexts provide background factors. As the American National Election Surveys became the primary source of data on electoral behavior for political scientists, they framed research around party identification and the issues and perceptions of the candidates in particular elections. As this model traveled across oceans, it structured electoral research in other democracies. As Key and Anthony Downs introduced rational choice theory into this subject matter, they left behind the principles of the social logic of politics. As debates have raged between the Michigan school and proponents of rational choice theory, scholarly attention has focused on the individual level of analysis. The social logic of politics lost scholarly prominence.

Several factors help to explain this change in direction. One set derives from the joint decision to use national sample surveys as the exclusive source of empirical evidence for political behavior and to analyze the information with statistical techniques. Designed to explain the outcome of elections as much as they were to account for electoral decisions, the surveys emphasize factors that may vary systematically at the national level during election campaigns. Policy issues and perceptions of the candidates stand as the classic examples. Just as important, those who designed the first national surveys denied the reliability of respondents' reports about the political preferences and behavior of their social intimates. Furthermore, the available statistical techniques could apply only to respondents who are independent of each other, a principle violated when members of social circles are included in the same survey. As a result, these surveys ask almost no questions that might provide direct information on the social context of politics.[1]

Issues of theory offer another set of explanations for the turn away from the social logic of politics. The political scientists exaggerated the social determinism in the work of Lazarsfeld and his colleagues and then rejected the distorted image. They insisted that the electoral sociologists could neither explain electoral decisions nor the outcome of elections. Key and Downs denied what they saw as the approach's presentation of nonrational or even irrational voters. Key argued that this conceptualization does not mesh with the core assumptions of democratic theory, while Downs maintained that it violated the principles of rational choice theory. As a result, the political scientists moved to the analytical foreground the immediate determinants of vote choice: attitudes and calculations.

Once again, I will sustain these points with statements taken from the critical books and articles. Consider first arguments about the effects of using national sample surveys, the absence of direct responses by social intimates, and the assumptions of the statistical techniques applied to the data.

> The structure of small groups has been successfully investigated by sociometric techniques but sociometry is difficult, if not impossible, to apply to large systems

like nations. The macro-study of individuals was greatly aided by the development of the sample survey technique. But those who make most use of it—sociologists and social psychologists—are more interested in the behavior of individuals as individuals than in the structure and functioning of those large systems in which the political scientist is interested. (Eulau 1962, 134–35)

[D]ifficulties in securing pertinent data have obstructed research on politically salient dyadic interactions as the building blocks for a sociological (rather than a psychological) understanding of individual-on-individual political effects. (Eulau 1986, 516)

The assumptions of most statistical studies provide another reason for the shift away from the analysis of the immediate social context of politics. Here the point comes from a recent general criticism of research in social psychology:

Dyadic relationships form the core element of our social lives. They also form the core unit of study by relationship researchers. Then why (to paraphrase Woody Allen) do so many analyses in this area focus on only one consenting adult at a time? The reason, we suspect, has to do with the rather austere authority figures of our early professional development: statistics professors who conveyed the cherished assumption of independent sampling. . . . How do we capture the psychology of interdependence with the statistics of independence?

Unfortunately for the development of interpersonal relations theory, the patterns laid down by the imprinting period of graduate statistics classes tend to dominate the rest of one's professional life. Interdependence in one's data is typically viewed as a nuisance and so dyadic researchers have developed strategies to sweep interdependence under the rug. (Gonzalez and Griffin 2000, 181–82)

The data and methods moved analysis away from the principles of the social context of politics.

The shift derived as well from theoretical considerations. The Michigan school reformulated and the rationalists transformed the core explanatory principles for the analysis of political preferences. Together they moved the study of political behavior away from the social logic of politics.

Consider first the flow of the argument in *The American Voter.* The opening chapter justifies the move away from community studies to a survey of the national electorate:

In one important respect the research in Erie County and Elmira is only a partial account of the behavior of the American voter. Each of these studies has examined voting behavior within a single community. (Campbell, Converse, Miller, and Stokes 1960, 15)

The volume then describes the National Opinion Research Center's first nationwide study of this sort, a survey of the 1944 presidential election:

This study was prompted at least in part by the desire to extend beyond the bounds of a single community some of the generalizations suggested by the study of Erie County. (Ibid., 15–16)

Next it details the national surveys conducted for the elections of 1948 and 1952:

The project represented a shift in emphasis from explanation in sociological terms to the exploration of political attitudes that orient the individual voter's behavior in an immediate sense. (Ibid., 16)

More fundamentally, *The American Voter* seeks to link the analysis of electoral choice to the outcome of particular elections:

> This approach differed sharply from earlier sociological explanations and was intended to remedy some of the weaker aspects of these explanations. For example, the distribution of social characteristics in a population varies but slowly over a period of time. Yet crucial fluctuations in the national vote occur from election to election. . . . The attitudinal approach directed more attention to political objects of orientation, such as the candidates and issues, which do shift in the short term. (Ibid., 17; and see p. 65, where the authors cite Key and Munger [1959] on this point)

Attitudinal variables stand close to the vote in the authors' "funnel of causality" (ibid., 24–32). They merit, therefore, analytical priority.

Campbell, Converse, Miller, and Stokes also maintained that it is not appropriate to use respondents' reports to characterize the political views and behavior of the members of their social circles:

> Important as primary group influence may be in forming or contradicting partisan attitude, an interview survey of widely separated individuals is not well suited to its study. The small group setting of attitude and behavior is one of great significance, but estimates in survey studies of its importance in voting have had to depend on what respondents tell about the partisan preferences of their family, work, and friendship groups. (Ibid., 76)

Echoing one of Festinger's principles (and ignoring others) and noting a point, which Converse would elaborate in a later work (Newcomb, Turner, and Converse 1964, 126), the authors feared that people would impute their own political views to the members of their immediate social circle. Hence, these data are tainted by problems of unreliability. Only questions relevant to the study of political socialization and descriptions of objective social characteristics escape this decision.

Campbell, Converse, Miller, and Stokes did not, however, break completely with the social logic of politics. Even as they denied the reliability of respondents' reports, they affirmed the theoretical importance of these perceptions:

> Yet this difficulty does not lessen our qualitative sense of the importance of the small group setting of partisan attitude and the partisan choice. And it does not obscure the finding from an analysis of errors of prediction that primary group associations may in the exceptional case introduce forces in the individual's psychological field that are of sufficient strength to produce behavior that contradicts his evaluations of political objects. (Ibid., 76–77)

Alas, they recognized, data problems inhibited their ability to follow their theoretical preferences.

The authors of *The American Voter* offered an ingenious—if fundamentally flawed—solution to the conflict between a theoretical need to include information on social contexts in the face of inadequate data. They altered the definition of the social group, conceptualizing it according to a person's perceptions, and they referred to Kurt Lewin for support.[2]

> [T]he distinctive behavior of group members was too obvious to leave unanalyzed. After a time the psychologist, Kurt Lewin, suggested a convincing resolution to the problem of the "group mind." "Groups are real," he said, "if they have real effects."

> Groups are real because they are *psychologically* real, and thereby affect the way in which we behave. . . . Groups have influence, then, because we tend to think of them as wholes, and come to respond positively or negatively to them in that form. . . . Groups can become reference points for the formation of attitudes and decisions about behavior; we speak of them as *positive* or *negative reference groups.* (Ibid., 296)

In their interpretation of Lewin's analysis, Campbell, Converse, Miller, and Stokes defined groups not by patterns of interdependence or interaction but by a shared perception of a reference object. Note how far they moved from Lewin's definition of groups presented above. Campbell and his colleagues shifted the definition of social group and altered its role in the analysis of political preferences.

This step justifies the conceptualization of party identification as a psychological identification (Ibid., 121) or attachment (Ibid., 122). Strength of partisanship refers not to actions as much as feelings of intensity with regard to the reference group. (See, for example, 122 for the initial formulation of the measure.) In this conceptualization, people vary as well in the extent to which they identify with particular groups.

> [T]he concept of group identification and psychological membership remains extremely valuable. Individuals, all of whom are nominal group members, vary in *degree* of membership, in a psychological sense. . . . (Ibid., 297)

> Let us think of the group as a psychological reality that exerts greater or lesser attractive force upon its members. (Ibid., 306)

And so, Campbell, Converse, Miller, and Stokes constructed a survey question to assess how close the respondent feels to members of a group in order to measure group identification. This leads to their guiding hypothesis on the relationship between social context and political preferences:

> *[T]he higher the identification of the individual with the group, the higher is the probability that he will think and behave in ways which distinguish members of the group from non-members.* (Ibid., 307; emphasis in original)

The conceptualization implies a set of related concepts and their measures. Cohesive groups have intensely loyal members (Ibid., 309), and the extent to which members "feel set apart" from others defines cohesiveness (Ibid., 310). "The political party may be treated, then, as a special case of a more general group-influence phenomenon" (Ibid., 331). *The American Voter* offers two measures of social context: objective indicators such as education and occupation, and subjective measures of identifications and feelings of strength or closeness. Except for questions about the respondent's parents, it offers no information on the voters' immediate social circles. Subjective perceptions of social and political objects and reference groups replace patterns of trust, interdependence, and interaction among members of primary groups.

V. O. Key and Anthony Downs offered a more dramatic break with the social logic of politics. Both derived political choices from reasoned calculations about political objects. Key set aside the importance of members of social circles on political preferences, and Downs suggested that they play only a limited role. Both took giant leaps of theory.

Consider first the development of Key's position. As I note above, Key and Munger began their article by criticizing *The People's Choice*. This volume, they feared,

> threatens to take the politics out of the study of electoral behavior. The theoretical heart of *The People's Choice* rests on the contention that "social characteristics determine political preference. . . ." [Even though Lazarsfeld qualifies the statement] [t]he focus of analysis . . . comes to rest broadly on the capacity of the "nonpolitical group" to induce conformity to its political standards by the individual voter. . . .
>
> The study of electoral behavior then becomes only a special case of the more general problem of group inducement of individual behavior in accord with group norms. As such it does not invariably throw much light on the broad nature of the electoral decision in the sense of decisions by the electorate as a whole. (1959, 281–82)

> A major burden of the argument has been that the isolation of the electorate from the total governing process and its subjection to microscopic analysis tends to make electoral study a nonpolitical endeavor. . . . Hence, all studies of so-called "political behavior" do not add impressively to our comprehension of the awesome process by which the community or nation makes decisions at the ballot box. (Ibid., 297)

V. O. Key's final work, *The Responsible Electorate* (1966, 7–8), extends the criticism beyond the research of Lazarsfeld and his colleagues to include *The American Voter* as well. Even as Key accepted the findings of Lazarsfeld's research (see above, as well as numerous generalizations in the work with Munger [1959] and in *Public Opinion and American Democracy* [1961]), he rejected the conceptual and theoretical implications for the understanding of the democratic citizen.

In *An Economic Theory of Democracy* (1957), Anthony Downs reinforced this break with the social logic of politics. Offering a perspective that defines rationality solely in political or economic terms, he maintained that members of intimate social circles provide no more than time-saving sources of information to calculating citizens. The effects of the immediate social contexts on people's preferences are well known, he conceded, but they stand in the way of a rational-choice analysis of political behavior.

Downs (1957) began his analysis by insisting that not every decision may be defined as rational. He examined, therefore, only the economic and political goals of persons and groups:

> Admittedly, separation of these goals from the many others which men pursue is quite arbitrary. . . . Nevertheless, this study is a study of economic and political rationality, not of psychology. . . .
>
> Our approach to elections illustrates how this narrow definition of rationality works. The political function of elections in a democracy, we assume, is to select a government. Therefore rational behavior in connection with elections is behavior oriented toward this end and no other. Let us assume a certain man prefers Party A for political reasons, but his wife has a tantrum whenever he fails to vote for Party B. It is perfectly rational *personally* for this man to vote for Party B if preventing his wife's tantrums is more important to him than having A win instead of B. Nevertheless, in our model such behavior is considered irrational because it employs a political device for a nonpolitical purpose.
>
> Thus we do not take into consideration the whole personality of each individual when we discuss what behavior is rational for him. . . . Rather we borrow from traditional economic theory the idea of the rational consumer. . . . [O]ur *homo politicus* is the "average man" in the electorate, the "rational citizen" of our model democracy. (p. 7; emphasis in original)

Undoubtedly, the fact that our model world is inhabited by such artificial men limits the comparability of behavior to behavior in the real world. In the latter, some men *do* cast votes to please their wives—and vice versa—rather than to express their political preferences. And such behavior is highly rational in terms of the domestic situations in which it occurs. Empirical studies are almost unanimous in their conclusion that adjustment in primary groups is far more crucial to nearly every individual than more remote considerations of economic or political welfare. [Here, Downs cites Katz and Lazarsfeld 1955.]

Nevertheless, we must assume that men orient their behavior chiefly toward the latter in our world; otherwise all analysis of either economics or politics turns into a mere adjunct of primary-group sociology. (Ibid., 8)

Downs offered a theoretical postulate in order to reject the well-founded observation that husbands and wives influence each other's political preferences. Claims for theoretical pay-off justify this move, although he also offers an empirical observation (Ibid., 8).

Note as well that Downs—like Key and Campbell, Converse, Miller, and Stokes—retained a place for the principles of the social logic of politics. Toward the end of the book, he addressed the issue of the relationship between rational citizens and the costs of information. As citizens economize on time, they delegate the accumulation of information to others. Indeed, he maintained, people obtain information from others who share their views, again citing the work of Katz and Lazarsfeld and Lazarsfeld, Berelson and Gaudet (Ibid., 228–29).

Even as the behavioral revolution in political science began by demonstrating the power of the primary group to explain political choices and action, it set off in another direction. Even though the Michigan school took incremental steps and Key and Downs took leaps of theory, the final result is the same. Subsequent research has moved along a path that pays little attention to dyadic relations, other intimate social circles, or workplaces and neighborhoods. Isolated respondents aggregated into nationally representative sample surveys provide the locus of study. Attitudes about candidates, policies, and issues proximate to the vote obtain theoretical primacy. Calculations about asocial self-interest predominate. The explanatory principles of the social logic of politics recede into the analytical distance.

THE RETURN (AGAIN) TO THE SOCIAL LOGIC OF POLITICS

And yet the chapters in this volume demonstrate that the social logic of politics has not disappeared; indeed it continues to offer powerful theoretical principles for the analysis of political behavior. The essays offer analyses of turnout, partisanship, policy preferences, voter choice, and political discussions and participation. Several expand the frames of reference by examining multiple levels of analysis and by presenting political events and structures as part of explanatory schema. Several focus on the bases of political agreement among members of immediate social circles. They address the problems of data and methods by examining new sources of evidence and new analytical techniques. They reformulate and sharpen core theoretical issues and principles. These essays build on earlier studies of the social logic of politics as they strive to advance this research agenda.

Consider first the treatment of political preferences and behavior. Huckfeldt, Johnson, and Sprague (Chapter 2) examine voter choice, as do Levine (Chapter 8),

Johnston and Pattie (Chapter 10), and Fowler (Chapter 14). The analysis of partisanship appears in the chapters authored by Stoker and Jennings (Chapter 3), Kohler (Chapter 6), and Huckfeldt, Johnson, and Sprague (Chapter 2), as well as Zuckerman, Fitzgerald, and Dasović (Chapter 4). Verba, Schlozman, and Burns (Chapter 5) along with Kotler-Berkowitz (Chapter 7) and Lin (Chapter 9) study political participation. Even as some of the essays take political discussion as an explanatory variable, Gimpel and Lay (Chapter 11) and Anderson and Paskeviciute (Chapter 12) frame this mode of political activity as a dependent variable. In turn, Stoker and Jennings (Chapter 3) and Gimpel and Lay (Chapter 11) examine policy preferences and psychological stances toward political action as well. These chapters jointly apply the social logic of politics to the classic questions in the study of political behavior.

Several of the essays bring new data and analytical techniques to address the bases for agreement among sets of persons. Stoker and Jennings (Chapter 3) focus attention on variations in the level of political similarity between husbands and wives, as I do in my essay with Fitzgerald and Dasović (Chapter 4). Both chapters look at associative mating—Homer's and Aristotle's "like to like." The chapters by Huckfeldt, Johnson, and Sprague (Chapter 2), Levine (Chapter 8), and Fowler (Chapter 14) examine agreement among discussion partners and members of social networks. All three underline the recurrent presence of diverse political preferences among members of social networks. These chapters explore the extent to which sets of persons display political agreement.

In addition, Verba, Schlozman, and Burns (Chapter 5) maintain that exogenous political events and structures—such as the American Civil Rights movement in the 1960s—have powerful explanatory impacts on political participation. This theme returns in the chapters by Gimpel and Lay (Chapter 11, neighborhood and county political climate), Johnston and Pattie (Chapter 10, party activity during campaigns), and Anderson and Paskeviciute (Chapter 12, the aggregate distribution of political preferences at the national level). These essays move beyond the traditional questions and answers that frame analyses of political choice.

Several chapters show as well that classic "Michigan" surveys may be used to study the role of immediate social circles on political choice and behavior. First and most obvious, Huckfeldt, Johnson, and Sprague (Chapter 2), Levine (Chapter 8), and Anderson and Paskeviciute (Chapter 12) use questions on political discussants that appear in surveys intimately linked to the American National Election Surveys: the 2000 American National Election Surveys, the 1992 Cross-National Election Survey, and the World Values Survey (1993–95). Notwithstanding the worries of Campbell, Converse, Miller, Stokes, and Eulau, surveys may be designed to account for the results of national elections and to gather information on families, friends, and discussion partners. Similarly, Chapter 3 by Stoker and Jennings draws on Jennings's well-developed research on political socialization (see, for example, Jennings and Niemi 1974, 1981), which flows from the Michigan research tradition. So does the Civic Participation Study, which provides the data for Verba, Schlozman, and Burns's chapter as well as their recent studies of political participation (Verba, Schlozman, and Brady 1995; Burns, Schlozman and Verba 2001). Johnston and Pattie (Chapter 10) apply information on neighborhoods taken from the British Election Study of 1997, no matter that these surveys originated in collaborative work led by Donald Stokes (Butler and

Stokes 1969, 1974).[3] There are no fundamental difficulties in examining data taken from mainstream studies of partisan choice and political participation in order to explore hypotheses drawn from the social logic of politics.

The scholarship presented here benefits as well from new sources of data. My chapter with Fitzgerald and Dasović (on Britain and Germany) and Kohler's analysis (Germany) examine surveys (the British Household Panel Survey and the German Socioeconomic Panel Study) that cover many years and interview all persons in a household over the age of fifteen.[4] Designed by labor and health economists and demographers, they offer insights into the place of politics in the daily lives of Britons and Germans. Kotler-Berkowitz (Chapter 7) explores the Social Capital Benchmark Study (2000). Gimpel and Lay (Chapter 11) gather their own data on high schools and counties in the regions around Baltimore and Washington, D.C. Drawing on her extensive interviews with Arab immigrants in the Detroit metropolitan area, Lin (Chapter 9) demonstrates the utility of qualitative methodologies applied to the social logic of politics. Fowler (Chapter 14) too examines locally circumscribed areas, as he uses Huckfeldt and Sprague's studies of the St. Louis and South Bend areas.

The data permit multiple levels of analysis. Stoker and Jennings (Chapter 3) relate individuals to their households and then to the aggregate distribution of political preferences across the United States. Fitzgerald, Dasović, and I (Chapter 4) and Kohler (Chapter 6) contrast individuals, their household partners, and their more general social class and religious circumstances. Levine (Chapter 8) and Kotler-Berkowitz (Chapter 7) show that no matter a person's own characteristics, friendship ties affect vote choice and political participation. Johnston and Pattie (Chapter 10) offer a parallel argument as they demonstrate that neighborhood characteristics influence voting decisions in Britain, apart from the social characteristics of the respondents. Similarly, Gimpel and Lay (Chapter 11) study how the political characteristics of communities affect the acquisition of norms encouraging political participation. In two related essays, Huckfeldt and Johnson (Chapter 13, and joined in Chapter 2 with Sprague) show the autoregressive nature of discussant effects: the ability of discussion partners to influence each other depends on the preferences of others in the relevant social networks. Anderson and Paskeviciute (Chapter 12) link individual propensities to talk about politics to the aggregate distribution of political views at the national level of fifteen democracies. Finally, Fowler (Chapter 14) shows how decisions to cast a ballot influence others in a person's social network, finding a "turnout cascade." These essays approach the study of political behavior from several levels of analysis.

New statistical techniques enable researchers to address these complex data sets—the respondent, the immediate social circle, work-mates, neighbors, and more distant social and political structures (see especially Gonzalez and Griffin 2000). Interdependence among respondents no longer stands in the way of solid scholarship. The chapters employ diverse techniques, not only the relatively familiar Ordinary Least Squares regression, logit, or ordered logit models. Stoker and Jennings (Chapter 3) apply structural equation models to the problem of distinguishing the mutual effects of household partners; Levine (Chapter 8) parses the difference by offering instrumental variables as well as alternative models; and Fitzgerald, Dasović, and I (Chapter 4) lag the impact of one partner on the other. Kohler (Chapter 6) uses a fixed-effects panel logit model to study change in partisanship. Gimpel and Lay (Chapter 11) use hierarchical linear models to study the relationship between adolescents and their towns and cities, and these same models appear again. Anderson and Paskeviciute (Chapter 12) study the combined impact of personal and national-level phenomena to explain cross-national variations in political discussions. In turn, Johnson and Huckfeldt (Chapter 13) offer agent-based modeling to explore the relationship between discussants and opinion change, one of the cardinal principles of the social logic. Finally, Fowler (Chapter 14) applies formal mathematical models to explore how each person's decision to cast a ballot influences those in the immediate social circle.

Put simply, researchers need no longer choose between evidence on discussion networks and evidence that applies to the national level of politics. They need no longer choose between Elmira and America (or Wivenhoe and Britain, or Freiburg and Germany)! Scholars of political behavior are no longer limited by statistical techniques that force them to assume that persons are atoms, with no necessary ties to each other. Gone are the impediments that turned Campbell, Converse, Miller, Stokes, Verba, and Eulau away from the social logic of politics.

Similarly, the contributors to this volume are not constrained by the theoretical concerns that induced Key and Downs to carve a new theoretical path. Huckfeldt's essays with Johnson and Sprague (Chapters 2 and 13) show the benefits of merging this perspective with Downs's recognition that individuals learn from each other. Fowler (Chapter 14) too retains the core principles of rational choice theory as he explores the impact of social interactions on turnout and vote choice. These essays as well as Levine's Chapter 8 speak directly to questions of democratic deliberation. Indeed, as Stoker and Jennings (Chapter 3) and Fitzgerald, Dasović, and I (Chapter 4) study political agreement between husbands and wives, we too look at the flow of influence between persons. The social logic of politics does not stand in contradiction with the claims about reasoning voters or citizens. It implies no social determinism.

Like the founders of the behavioral revolution in politics, many of the chapter authors recognize that the social logic of politics draws on an established body of scholarship (though we were all surprised to see some of its principles in a footnote in Aristotle!). References to Lazarsfeld, Berelson, Gaudet, and McPhee abound in the volume. As sociologists extend this tradition beyond electoral decisions (see, for example, Burt 1992, Granovetter 1973, and Knoke 1990), their research helps to frame many of the studies in this volume. Fowler (Chapter 14), Huckfeldt, Johnson, and Sprague (Chapter 2), Johnson and Huckfeldt (Chapter 13), Kotler-Berkowitz (Chapter 7), Levine (Chapter 8), and Lin (Chapter 9) draw directly on this literature's distinction between strong and weak ties. The theme of network density appears too. In turn, several of the chapters explore the hypotheses that sets of interacting persons will come to share the same political views. While Huckfeldt, Johnson, and Sprague (Chapters 2 and 13) do so directly, Stoker and Jennings (Chapter 3), Fitzgerald, Dasović, and I (Chapter 4), Verba, Schlozman, and Burns (Chapter 5), Kotler-Berkowitz (Chapter 7), Kohler (Chapter 6), and Lin (Chapter 9) also apply and examine this principle. Scholarship from sociology continues to underpin analyses that draw on the social logic of politics.

Finally, and perhaps most importantly, the chapters in this volume use this perspective to demonstrate what would not be known with another approach to the analysis of political behavior. Each chapter presents at least one finding that denies, clarifies, refines, or extends accepted understandings. Huckfeldt, Johnson, and Sprague (Chapter 2) show that discussion networks affect electoral choices among persons who identify with a political party, and they also link the impact of one discussion partner on the distribution of preferences in the social network. Stoker and Jennings (Chapter 3) indicate that political agreement within marital households is a primary source of the narrowing of the gender gap in American politics. Fitzgerald, Dasović, and I (Chapter 4) point to the direct impact of household partners on each other's partisanship, no matter their level of political interest and other social characteristics. Verba, Schlozman, and Burns (Chapter 5) show that political discussions in households affect the future level of political participation by persons raised there, even after controlling for personal level of education. Kohler shows that interactions between personal political interest and the preferences of discussion partners activate the association between social class and partisanship. Friendship diversity, argues Kotler-Berkowitz (Chapter 7), affects political participation, even after controlling for the long-established importance of level of education. Similarly, Levine shows (Chapter 8) the importance of discussant effects on electoral choice, after controlling for a host of personal political characteristics, and Johnston and Pattie (Chapter 10) present these findings for the effects of neighborhoods. In Lin's essay (Chapter 9), various forms of political participation and perceptions flow from different kinds of social ties. In different ways, Gimpel and Lay (Chapter 11) and Anderson and Paskeviciute (Chapter 12) link variations in the rate of political discussion to the political context, not only individual-level factors. The volume's final essays are the most ambitious, as each addresses a long-standing theoretical puzzle. Johnson and Huckfeldt (Chapter 13) deny claims made by Axelrod and others by showing that the autoregressive natures of discussant effects ensures that sets of persons who interact with each other need never reach unanimous political views. Fowler (Chapter 14) shows that turnout cascades offer a creative solution to the problem of electoral turnout in rational choice theory. Applying the social logic of politics does more than reframe analysis; it advances knowledge of political behavior.

As these chapters move research forward, they also return to the classic themes of the social logic of politics. Stoker and Jennings (Chapter 3), and Fitzgerald, Dasović, and I (Chapter 4) give reason to doubt the venerable principles of associative mating ("like to like"), at least with regard to political preferences. At the same time, the essays show that the longer couples stay together, the more likely they are to hold the same political preferences. And while the chapters note the enormous impact of spouses on each other when compared with other social ties, they also demonstrate that husbands and wives do not share precisely the same politics. Even in this most intimate social relationship, political agreement is a variable. Friends matter too. Indeed, Kotler-Berkowitz (Chapter 7), Levine (Chapter 8), and Lin (Chapter 9) offer complementary demonstrations of the importance of weak and diverse friendship ties for political choices and participation. Here, close ties seem not to matter much at all. Neighbors also matter, as Johnston and Pattie (Chapter 10), Gimpel and Lay (Chapter 11), and Fowler (Chapter 14) demonstrate. And so we return (once again) to the concerns of Homer, Aristotle, and the Bible.

ROBERT HUCKFELDT, PAUL E. JOHNSON, AND JOHN SPRAGUE

2   Individuals, Dyads, and Networks

Autoregressive Patterns of Political Influence

POLITICAL INTERDEPENDENCE AND communication among citizens has little consequence if individuals reside in self-contained, politically homogeneous groups. In settings such as these, new information cannot easily penetrate the social barriers that surround the individual. If you are a liberal Democrat and all your friends are liberal Democrats, the odds are very high that you will never hear one of your friends make a passionately convincing argument in favor of tax cuts. Conversely, if you are a conservative Republican and all your friends are conservative Republicans, the odds are similarly high that you will never hear a friend make a passionately convincing case for eliminating restrictions on abortion. When networks of communication are populated by individuals who share the same political viewpoints and orientations, the information that individuals receive will correspond quite closely to the information they convey, and the information conveyed through one exchange will correspond to the information that is conveyed through every other exchange.

In contrast, if citizens are located in communication networks characterized by political heterogeneity, the exchange of information is likely to take on heightened political consequence. As McPhee (1963) recognized, political disagreement gives rise to opportunities for political change. When individuals encounter preferences that are different from their own, they often find it difficult to ignore the event. Either they construct a counter argument to overcome the disagreement, or they discredit the message by dismissing its source, or they reconsider their own position in light of the disagreement. In each of these instances, disagreement forces individuals to engage in a critical examination—to think more deeply and attend more carefully to the substance of the political disagreement. Even when citizens reject the disagreeable preference, they are forced to reconsider the justification for their own position, and in this way political change can be seen to occur regardless of the manner in which disagreement is resolved (Kotler-Berkowitz, in this volume).

This potential for micro-level change carries important macro-level consequences. To the extent that citizens are socially insulated from disagreement, the opportunity for collective deliberation is reduced, as is the opportunity and occasion for political influence. Hence, political change at both the micro and macro levels becomes disembodied from communication among citizens. Indeed, absent communication among citizens with diverse viewpoints, it becomes difficult to offer a compelling account of the role played by communication among citizens in the process of political change.

This chapter addresses a number of issues related to these problems: First, to what extent are citizens located in politically homogeneous networks of political communication? Second, how is disagreement resolved within these networks? Third, how does disagreement affect the flow of information and influence? In order to address these questions, we construct a set of arguments regarding the manner in which disagreement within dyads is filtered through larger networks of association. These questions and arguments are evaluated in the context of data taken from the 2000 National Election Study.[1]

NETWORK THEORIES OF POLITICAL INFLUENCE

Any effort to address informational interdependence among citizens in democratic politics necessarily builds on the foundational work of the Columbia sociologists—work that began with Paul Lazarsfeld's arrival in New York City in the 1930s. In particular, the 1940 election study conducted in Elmira by Lazarsfeld, Berelson, and Gaudet (1944), as well as the 1948 study conducted in Erie County, Ohio, by Berelson, Lazarsfeld, and McPhee (1954), serve as defining moments in the study of political influence and electoral politics. These efforts were extended and elaborated in the work of Katz and Lazarsfeld (1955), Katz (1957), McPhee (1963), and many others.

A primary and enduring message of these studies is that people do not act as isolated individuals when they confront the complex tasks of citizenship. Quite the opposite: The Columbia sociologists demonstrate that politics is a social experience in which individuals share information and viewpoints in arriving at individual decisions, and hence the individual voter is usefully seen within a particular social setting.

This framework produces a compelling account of the dynamic consequences that arise due to election campaigns. Berelson, Lazarsfeld, and McPhee (1954, chapter 7) argue that political preferences are likely to become individually idiosyncratic as political communication among citizens becomes less frequent during the time between election campaigns. In response to the stimulus of the election, the frequency of political communication increases, idiosyncratic preferences become socially visible, and hence individuals are brought into conformity with micro-environmental surroundings (Huckfeldt and Sprague 1995).

This argument is quite persuasive, and carried to its extreme, the logic of group conformity would seem to suggest that political disagreement should disappear within networks of social relations. Pressures toward conformity might drive out disagreement in several ways (Festinger 1957; Huckfeldt and Sprague 1995). First, the discomfort of disagreement might encourage people to modify their patterns of social relations so as to exclude those with whom they disagree. Second, people might avoid political discussion with associates who hold politically divergent preferences, or they might engage in self-censorship to avoid political disagreement (MacKuen 1990). Third, and partially as a consequence of discussion avoidance, people might incorrectly perceive agreement among those with whom they actually disagree. Finally, and perhaps most importantly, individuals might bring their own preferences into correspondence with the preferences that they encounter within their networks of social relations. (See Stoker and Jennings and Zuckerman, Fitzgerald, and Dasović in this volume for parallel findings.)

In fact, the Columbia studies never suggested that disagreement would disappear, and a major part of their effort was directed toward understanding the consequences of disagreement and cross pressures. Taken together, these analyses constitute an explicit recognition that the dynamic underlying political influence is frequently self-limiting (see McPhee 1963), in part due to the complex webs of association that lie behind the two-step flow of communication (Katz 1957).

The irony is that, among many political scientists, the work has been taken to suggest that citizens reside in homogeneous social settings, that they select their associates to avoid disagreement, and hence the information they obtain is a direct reflection of their own political biases. Such a view has strong appeal among those who would argue that cognitive dissonance serves to extinguish disagreement. It is also in keeping with Downs's (1957) argument that, in order to minimize information costs, rational individuals obtain information from other individuals who share their own political viewpoints.

As compelling as these various arguments regarding group conformity may be, they suffer from a major empirical weakness: campaigns do *not* extinguish disagreement within networks of social relations. At the end of the 1984 presidential election campaign, Huckfeldt and Sprague (1995) interviewed discussion partners who had been identified by a sample of respondents from South Bend, Indiana. And at the end of the 1992 election campaign, Huckfeldt et al. (1995) interviewed discussion partners who had been identified by a nationally drawn sample of respondents. In both instances, no more than two-thirds of the discussion partners held a presidential candidate preference that coincided with the main respondent who named them.

Moreover, these findings understate the levels of disagreement within the networks in which citizens are situated. These measures are based on dyads rather than networks. If the probability of dyadic agreement within a network is .7, and if these probabilities are independent across the dyads within a network, then the probability of agreement across all the relationships within a three-discussant network drops to $.7^3$ or .34. In other words, the presence of heterogeneous preferences is likely to be the rule rather than the exception within the micro-environments surrounding individual citizens.

The frequency of disagreement within communication networks stimulates a reassessment of the implications that arise for patterns of agreement and disagreement. The advances of the early Columbia school occurred before the development of network concepts, and one of the important disjunctures between traditional efforts at small-group research and social-network studies is the problematic nature of links within networks. In particular, an individual's political communication network may or may not constitute a self-contained small group, and whether it does is a direct consequence of network construction.

The major differences between groups and networks come in two forms. First, the density of relations within networks is variable, and hence two friends may never encounter the friends of *their* friends. Even though Tom and Dick may frequently engage in political discussions, Tom may also engage in frequent discussions with individuals who are unknown to Dick. The contributions of Granovetter (1973) and Burt (1992) demonstrate the importance of network density for the flow of information within and between networks, and their efforts are relevant for the survival of disagreement as well (Huckfeldt, Johnson, and Sprague 2002, 2004). Second, relationships in communication networks may be asymmetric and nonreciprocal. Tom may be a source of information for Dick, but that does not mean that Dick is a source of information for Tom. We argue that both of these factors mean that the structure of networks may sustain rather than eliminate disagreement among citizens. But first we address heterogeneity and influence within citizen networks during the 2000 presidential election campaign. (For consideration of other consequences of network construction, see Fowler, in this volume.)

HETEROGENEITY AND INFLUENCE WITHIN NETWORKS

The political influence that develops through patterns of communication among citizens is a fact of life in democratic politics. Citizens depend on one another for information and guidance, and this interdependence gives rise to persuasion and shared political preferences. Evidence in support of this assertion is readily available, and we will document the circumstances that inhibit and enhance influence in the pages that follow. But the reality of interdependence and influence raises an important question: To what extent do citizens reside in cozy groups of like-minded associates? Does persuasion overwhelm disagreement so as to create political homogeneity within networks of political communication?

We address these issues in Table 2.1 by examining the distribution of political preferences within networks of political communication. Each respondent to the post-election survey of the National Election Study was asked to provide the first names of the people with whom they discussed government, elections, and politics. In a subsequent battery of questions, they were asked to make a judgment regarding the presidential candidates for whom each of these discussants voted. Seventy-four percent of the post-election respondents were able to provide at least one name, and Table 2.1 is based on these respondents.

In Parts A and B of Table 2.1, the partisan distribution within networks is contingent on the partisan identifications of the respondents. Both contingent distributions show clear evidence of political clustering among the respondents. More than 70 percent of strong Republicans fail to report a single discussant who supports Gore, and nearly 70 percent of the strong Democrats fail to report a single discussant who supports Bush. In contrast, only 9.3 percent of the strong Republicans and 17.3 percent of the strong Democrats fail to report a discussant who supports their own party's candidate. Thus, Parts A and B offer compelling evidence that a clustering of political preferences is produced within communication networks.

At the same time, neither Part A nor Part B offers evidence of overwhelming homogeneity within the discussion networks. Nearly 45 percent of the strong Democrats report that all their discussants voted for Gore, but this means that more than half report at least one discussant who did something other than vote for Gore. Approximately 54 percent of the strong Republicans report that all their discussants voted for Bush, but this means that nearly half report at least one discussant who did not vote for Bush.

Moreover, the levels of disagreement and heterogeneity are even higher among respondents who report intermediate levels of partisan attachment. For example,

TABLE 2.1. Level of Diversity within Political Communication Networks

	SD	WD	ID	I	IR	WR	SR
A. PERCENTAGE OF NETWORK VOTING FOR GORE BY RESPONDENT'S PARTISANSHIP							
None	17.3	24.8	30.7	52.6	58.8	57.8	71.5
Some	38.0	40.9	43.9	32.8	30.8	31.1	24.2
All	44.7	34.3	25.4	14.6	10.4	11.0	4.3
Actual N	220	158	174	89	162	143	186
Weighted N	211.5	156.0	168.3	88.5	160.1	134.7	173.2
B. PERCENTAGE OF NETWORK VOTING FOR BUSH BY RESPONDENT'S PARTISANSHIP							
None	67.7	60.9	54.7	43.7	19.8	23.3	9.3
Some	26.6	31.0	36.0	39.3	50.4	35.2	36.6
All	5.7	8.0	9.3	17.0	29.8	41.4	54.1
Actual N	220	158	174	89	62	143	186
Weighted N	211.5	156.0	168.3	88.5	160.1	134.7	173.2

	Gore	Neither	Bush
C. PERCENTAGE OF NETWORK VOTING FOR GORE BY RESPONDENT'S VOTE			
None	14.2	58.2	64.3
Some	44.3	29.3	28.5
All	41.5	12.5	7.2
Actual N	473	244	430
Weighted N	436.3	268.5	398.8
D. PERCENTAGE OF NETWORK VOTING FOR BUSH BY RESPONDENT'S VOTE			
None	63.1	46.7	12.6
Some	32.3	36.2	39.9
All	4.5	17.0	47.5
Actual N	473	244	430
Weighted N	436.3	268.5	398.8

Source: 2000 National Election Study; unit of analysis is respondent; weighted data.
SD = strong Democrat, WD = weak Democrat, ID = independent leaning toward Democrat, I = independent, IR = independent leaning toward Republican, WR = weak Republican, SR = strong Republican.

only 25.4 percent of the independents who lean toward the Democrats report that all their discussants support Gore, and more than 45 percent report at least one discussant who supports Bush. Similarly, less than 30 percent of the Republican-leaning independents report that all their discussants support Bush, and more than 40 percent report that at least one discussant supports Gore.

The same patterns of clustering and heterogeneity are present in Parts C and D of Table 2.1, where partisan distributions within networks are contingent on the respondents' reported vote choice. While more than 64 percent of the Bush voters and more than 63 percent of the Gore voters report that none of their discussants supports the opposite party's candidate, this means that more than one-third of the two-party voters report at least one discussant who supports the opposite party's candidate. Approximately 42 percent of Gore voters and 48 percent of

Bush voters report that all their discussants share the same preference, but this means that more than half the respondents perceive that they reside in politically heterogeneous networks.

Table 2.1 presents a tale of glasses that are both half empty *and* half full. On one hand, the partisan loyalties and vote choices of respondents are clearly interdependent with the partisan distributions within networks. We do not bother to calculate chi-square measures for the various parts of Table 2.1, but each of them would confirm that we can safely reject the null hypothesis of independence among the columns in each section of the table. On the other hand, these patterns of interdependence are far from complete. Indeed, the evidence of disagreement is as noteworthy as the evidence of agreement.

Moreover, the figures shown in Table 2.1 inevitably include modest biases that underestimate levels of diversity. While the 2000 National Election Study did not include interviews with the discussants of the main respondents, other studies have incorporated snowball designs that pursue interviews with members of the networks named by the respondents (Huckfeldt and Sprague 1987; Huckfeldt et al. 1998; Huckfeldt, Sprague, and Levine 2000). These other studies use the discussant's self-reported vote as the baseline criterion against which to judge the presence of systematic biases in the respondent's perception of political preferences in the network. In general, these studies show that respondents are reasonably accurate in their perceptions of discussant preferences. Nevertheless, these studies also demonstrate a number of factors that enhance and attenuate the accuracy of discussant preferences.

Most notably for present purposes, respondents are less likely to recognize the preferences of discussants with whom they disagree. One possible explanation for these results is that disagreement produces cognitive dissonance, and respondents avoid dissonance by selectively misperceiving the signals and messages conveyed by others in their networks. The problem with this interpretation is that, as Table 2.1 makes abundantly clear, a great many respondents are perfectly able to recognize the existence of disagreement within their networks of political communication!

Other explanations for these patterns of perceptual bias point in different directions. As MacKuen suggests (1990), in order to avoid social discomfort, citizens may dissemble when confronted with disagreement, thereby sending a fuzzy signal that is more likely to be misperceived.

Finally, citizens may generalize on the basis of their own experience in reaching a perceptual judgment regarding the politics of an associate (Huckfeldt et al. 1998). In many instances, the political preference of an associate may be ambiguous, and individuals may resort to a representativeness heuristic in reaching a judgment regarding another individual's preference. A simple version of such a heuristic would be: If in doubt, assume that the discussant shares your own preference. A more complicated heuristic would be: If in doubt, assume that the discussant shares the preference that is most common among the other people you know.

In any event, the tendency for individuals to underestimate the extent of disagreement means that Table 2.1 underestimates the extent to which individuals disagree with others in their communication networks. Our best guess is that only about one-third of the respondents who voted for Bush or Gore are located in politically homogeneous networks where all the discussants share the same vote choice.

Thus it becomes quite clear that political preferences are interdependent within communication networks—that the probability of agreement is higher among individuals who are located in the same network than between people who belong to different networks. At the same time, it is equally clear that high levels of political heterogeneity persist within communication networks. How should we account for these patterns of agreement and disagreement within networks?

One explanation is that agreement is the natural outcome of association, and the presence of disagreement among associates thus signifies an explanatory failure. That is not the position that we take. Our goal is to construct an explanation for social interaction that takes account of both agreement and disagreement as the potentially systematic outcomes of social influence. We begin by considering factors that might lead to disagreement before turning to an explanation that accounts for both agreement and disagreement within communication networks.

POINTS OF INTERSECTION BETWEEN INDIVIDUALS AND AGGREGATES

When individuals are confronted with political choices, they use various devices at their disposal as sources of political guidance. Some of these devices are based on individual predispositions and attitudes. Indeed, the heuristic utility of political attitudes is that they serve to summarize an individual's political experience, as well as the lessons drawn from that experience. In this way, when individuals confront a choice, they are guided by attitudes and orientations that possess an experiential base. Hence, the experience of the Great Depression and the New Deal convinced several generations of Americans to develop positive attitudes and orientations toward the Democratic Party, and these served as the bases for subsequent political choices. In a similar manner, the civil rights movement reinforced those positive orientations among some, at the same time that it led to an erosion of those orientations among others (Huckfeldt and Kohfeld 1989). In this way, political attitudes are anchored in information gained through political experience.

The precise manner in which these attitudes and orientations change and respond to experience is a matter of fundamental theoretical concern, and scholars have come to understand that process more completely in the context of serially occurring events and individual judgments regarding those events (Fiorina 1981; Lodge 1995). Political economists and political psychologists agree that attitudes are not immune to experience. Rather, they are inherently dynamic, formulated at the point of intersection between individual citizens and their experience of the events and dramas of politics.

But attitudes and orientations are not the only points of intersection between individuals and their experience of political events. Individuals also obtain information through channels and networks of social communication. And as we have seen, the political content of messages conveyed through these networks does not simply replicate the orientations of the individuals who populate the networks. These networks of political communication are frequently characterized by high levels of political heterogeneity, and hence individuals often find themselves in situations where their own political orientations point in one direction while the messages received from others point in opposite directions. How do citizens respond to politically diverse messages?

Part A of Table 2.2 provides a baseline characterization of the relationship between partisan identification and voting in the 2000 election. Nearly 84 percent of strong Democrats report a vote for Gore, but less than 1 percent of strong Republicans do the same. Nearly 91 percent of strong Republicans report a vote for Bush, but only 3.3 percent of strong Democrats do the same. The table also shows a pronounced relationship to levels of support for the major party candidates. The share who vote for neither of the major party candidates is 12.9 percent among strong Democrats and 8.7 percent among strong Republicans, but this increases to 54.9 percent among the independents.

The results of Table 2.2(A) come as no surprise: The strong association between partisan identification and presidential vote choice has historically been a staple of political behavior research (Campbell, Converse, Miller, and Stokes 1960). Against this baseline pattern, consider Parts B through D of Table 2.2. First, notice

TABLE 2.2. Respondent Vote by Aggregate Characteristics of Network (Percentage)

	SD	WD	ID	I	IR	WR	SR
A. Respondent Vote by Respondent Partisanship							
Gore	83.8	70.9	53.2	24.4	9.9	13.4	.4
Neither	12.9	20.0	33.0	54.9	32.0	22.5	8.7
Bush	3.3	9.0	13.8	20.7	58.1	64.0	90.9
Actual N	221	161	174	89	162	143	186
Weighted N	212.0	160.1	168.3	88.0	160.1	134.7	173.2
B. Respondent Vote by Respondent Partisanship in Homogeneous Gore Networks							
Gore	89.4	82.2	72.8	44.5	49.8	46.2	0.0
Neither	10.6	9.8	17.8	43.2	7.8	17.6	15.4
Bush	0.0	8.0	9.4	12.3	42.4	36.3	84.6
Actual N	101	51	48	14	17	16	8
Weighted N	94.6	53.5	42.8	12.9	16.6	14.9	7.5
C. Respondent Vote by Respondent Partisanship in Networks That Are Not Unanimously in Support of Either Major Candidate							
Gore	82.3	69.6	49.2	23.5	6.6	14.8	.5
Neither	15.6	22.3	39.9	59.1	40.8	27.9	12.7
Bush	2.1	8.1	10.9	17.4	52.6	57.3	86.8
Actual N	108	96	107	59	97	70	79
Weighted N	105.4	94.0	109.9	60.1	95.8	64.0	72.1
D. Respondent Vote by Respondent Partisanship in Homogeneous Bush Networks							
Gore	52.7	32.9	27.7	10.9	2.7	3.2	.4
Neither	7.2	46.4	25.3	48.0	22.6	17.7	5.0
Bush	40.1	20.7	47.0	41.2	74.8	79.1	94.6
Actual N	12	14	19	16	48	57	99
Weighted N	12.0	12.6	15.6	15.0	47.7	55.8	93.6

Source: 2000 National Election Study.
Unit of analysis is respondent; weighted data.

that the vast majority of strong partisans are located either in homogeneously partisan networks that support their own orientations or in heterogeneous networks. Only 5.7 percent of strong Democrats (based on a weighted count of 12 out of 212) are located in networks that are unanimous in support of Bush, and only 4.3 percent of strong Republicans (based on a weighted count of 7.5 out of 173.2) are located in networks that are unanimous in supporting Gore. A similar but less pronounced pattern occurs among the weak partisans—very few weak Democrats are located in homogeneous Bush networks, and very few weak Republicans are located in homogeneous Gore networks. Indeed, even the independent partisans—self-proclaimed independents who lean toward one of the major parties—are quite unlikely to be located in networks that unanimously support the opposite party's presidential candidate.

Hence, while individual partisan orientations are outstanding predictors of vote choice, they are often quite difficult to separate from the political composition of the surrounding communication network. Partisans may associate with others who are politically sympathetic, or strong partisanship may be unable to survive in a politically hostile micro-environment, or some combination of both processes may be at work. In any event, we seldom observe self-proclaimed Democrats in a network full of Bush supporters, or self-proclaimed Republicans in a network full of Gore supporters.

At the same time, nearly half of the strong partisans are located in politically heterogeneous networks, and clear majorities of the weak partisans are located in politically heterogeneous networks. What difference does this make? Among the strong partisans, it would appear to make very little difference. Strong Democrats are likely to vote for Gore and strong Republicans for Bush, regardless of whether they inhabit heterogeneous networks or networks that unanimously support their own point of political orientation. A very different pattern exists among the weak and independent partisans: they are substantially more likely to support their party's candidate if they are located in a network characterized by homogeneous support for that candidate, and their support declines in politically heterogeneous networks.

Perhaps the most pronounced pattern of association occurs among the independents. A clear majority of independents are located in heterogeneous networks—networks that are not unanimous in support of either candidate. In these networks, a clear majority of independents fail to support either of the major party candidates: 23.5 percent support Gore and 17.4 percent support Bush. In contrast, 44.5 percent report supporting Gore if they are located in networks that unanimously support Gore. In networks that unanimously support Bush, 41.2 percent of the independents report voting for Bush.

The socially heroic partisan is a rare species in democratic politics—very few party loyalists reside in communication networks that are unanimously oriented in the opposite political direction. In contrast, a great many partisans are located in politically heterogeneous networks: Strong, weak, and independent partisans frequently find themselves in communication networks where their own points of political orientation are not held by everyone they encounter. The theoretical question thus becomes, How are we to understand the flow of information and influence in politically heterogeneous environments?

SOCIAL INFLUENCE IN POLITICALLY
HETEROGENEOUS ENVIRONMENTS

We begin with an informal characterization of the manner in which social interaction occurs through time. Several ingredients are crucial to this characterization.
First, citizens do not experience their social setting as a whole. They do not consume their diet of information in a single bite, or even at a single meal. Rather, to
pursue the metaphor, they consume socially supplied political information through
a series of snacks and meals. In this way they obtain the information in a serial,
cumulative fashion as a collection of responses, unsolicited opinions, offhand comments, and occasional heated arguments. In short, the process of social communication regarding politics constitutes a virtually endless series of discrete encounters between individuals and the associates with whom they share a social space.

This means, in turn, that citizens never experience the central tendency of their
political micro-environment directly. Rather, they experience the environment in
bits and pieces that accumulate into something that may or may not resemble a
central tendency. It only *resembles* a central tendency because the citizens are not
in the business of producing representative random samples. Rather, their goal is
to make sense out of politics—to employ the information at their disposal to construct a meaningful version of political events that will guide them in making
political choices (Sniderman, Brody, and Tetlock 1991). As a consequence, they
inevitably weigh some pieces of information more heavily than others. Hence, even
if social interaction is random within a defined social space, some interactions will
be weighted more heavily than others.

What are the factors that go into these weights? One set is related to the perceived expertise of the information source. People pay more attention to individuals whom they perceive to be politically expert. Moreover, their judgments regarding political expertise are not lost in a cloud of misperception: They are fully
capable of taking into account the objectively defined expertise of others (Huckfeldt 2001).

Another set of factors is even more directly related to the characteristics of the
discussant. Some discussants spend a great deal of time talking about politics,
while others talk more frequently about fly-fishing and the Chicago Bears. Some
discussants are strong partisans with unambiguous preferences that are unam-
biguously articulated. Others are ambivalent in their political preferences and hes-
itant in their political judgments. Empirical investigations have repeatedly demonstrated the importance of the *discussants'* characteristics in affecting the flow of
information (Huckfeldt et al. 1998; Huckfeldt, Sprague, and Levine 2000). In this
way, we might even say that the preferences of discussants are self-weighting.

In short, the central political tendency of a particular setting is never experienced directly; rather it is reconstructed on the basis of fragmented experiences
that are differentially weighted in ways that are idiosyncratic both to the recipient
and to the source of the information. This view marks an extension and a departure from a rich tradition of contextual studies in which individuals are seen as
responding, more or less directly, to the political climate within which they reside
(Berelson et al. 1954; Huckfeldt 1986; Lazarsfeld et al. 1944; Miller 1956; Putnam 1966).

Second, each information exchange is imbedded within the cumulative (but decaying) effect of every other information exchange. Citizens do not obtain information in a vacuum. Rather, they judge each new piece of information within the context of the information they have previously obtained. This is another way of saying that political influence is spatially autoregressive (Anselin 1988). Within a social space that is defined relative to a particular citizen, the impact of every social encounter depends on the cumulative social impact of all other social encounters. Hence, if we predict individual behavior on the basis of any single encounter or piece of information, our average error in prediction is likely to be correlated with the other sources of information that an individual employs in the given social space.

At the same time, working memory is finite. Any individual is capable of simultaneously considering only a small set of informational elements at any given moment. Hence, information is stored in long-term memory and accessed through an activation process that depends on the strength of association among memory elements (Fazio 1995). Lodge and Taber (2000) offer a provocative view of political judgment in which people form summary judgments based on particular political objects that are being continually updated as new information becomes available. This "on-line tally" is readily accessible from long-term memory, even though the information on which the judgments are based is not. In short, people form opinions that serve as summary judgments based on a continuing series of incoming information. Hence, these summary judgments are continually being updated as new information becomes available, but the new information is not viewed in a neutral fashion. Rather, it is understood and evaluated within the context of the existing summary judgment (Lodge and Taber 2000).

What are the implications for judgments based on political information that is obtained through social interaction? Individuals who encounter a friend wearing a Bush for President lapel pin may have quite different responses depending on their past interactions. If the lapel-pin episode is the first time that our individual has ever encountered a positive sentiment regarding Bush, the information received through the interaction might well be discounted. On the other hand, if our individual has multiple encounters with individuals who are favorably disposed toward Bush, the cumulative impact of the repeated messages may be quite compelling.

In short, the viewpoints of discussants are not only weighted (or self-weighted) by the expertise and interest of the discussants. These viewpoints are also weighted by the degree to which they resonate with other information that an individual is receiving with respect to a particular political object. Information is not evaluated in an objective fashion. Rather, it is evaluated in a political context with respect to the information that is dominant within the setting.

The important point is that individuals do not simply formulate judgments based on the last piece of information they obtain. Because the veracity of information and information sources is judged relative to stored information, individuals are quite capable of resisting the information that is supplied in any particular exchange. Hence, it is not uncommon to find persistent disagreement within networks of political information. Indeed, the autoregressive influence of social communication makes it possible for individuals to *resist* socially supplied information with which they disagree.

Dramatic evidence in support of this assertion comes from the work of Solomon Asch (1963). In his famous series of experiments, each of eight individuals in a small group was asked to identify which of three comparison lines was the same length as a given standard line. All the individuals except one, the subject, were provided with a predetermined script of responses, and in some cases they were instructed to identify the wrong line. Hence, the uninformed subjects were confronted with situations in which socially supplied information—the other group members' judgments—conflicted with their own sensory perceptions.

Two features of the Asch experiments are especially noteworthy for present purposes. First, while he did not intend to suggest that individuals are mindless automatons (Ross 1990), Asch demonstrated that a majority is capable of producing important distortion effects on individual judgments. Nearly three-fourths of the subjects denied their own sensory perceptions in at least one instance, adjusting their own judgments to agree with incorrect majority judgments. About one-fourth of the subjects never compromised their own individual judgments, and approximately one-fourth compromised their judgments in at least half of the instances involving mistaken majority judgments. Overall, the subjects embraced majority opinion in about one third of the instances involving a mistaken majority judgment.

An equally important aspect of the Asch experiment is that if only *one other member* was instructed to diverge from the group's mistaken judgment by consistently providing a correct report, the majority opinion was effectively nullified. Hence, in this particular instance, an individual judgment based on sensory evidence consistently survives the challenge of majority disagreement if one other individual supports the subject's judgment. Once again, the influence of particular information sources must be judged not only relative to the individual's own viewpoint but also relative to the distribution of viewpoints provided by alternative information sources.

Third, social space is separate from physical location, even though it is constructed on the basis of social proximity. How should we conceive the relevant social space? In another departure from the tradition of contextual analysis, we do not define social space as coinciding with geographical boundaries. This is not to say that geography is irrelevant; indeed geographical location goes a long way in helping to explain the particular configuration of the social space that is relevant to a particular citizen (Baybeck and Huckfeldt 2002b). Social space is an overlay on physical, geographically defined location, but it is idiosyncratic to the geographical locales of particular individuals.

For example, an individual who resides in south St. Louis County may work at a bank in the central business district of the city. His cubicle may be next to another individual who resides in west St. Louis County, and their homes may be more than twenty miles apart. Our south county citizen may also play racquetball at a sports club on his way home from work with an individual who commutes from the Illinois side of the Mississippi River.

What is the relevant social space for this individual? Such a space must be defined idiosyncratically, relative to the particular construction of his or her network of social contacts. Is geography relevant to the construction of this network?

The answer is quite obvious: It would be impossible to understand the construction of an individual's network without reference to the spatial dimension of social engagement (see Johnston and Pattie, and Gimpel and Lay, in this volume). At the same time, an individual's social setting is not coincident with any particular spatial setting, and the configuration of that person's network of contacts is most easily understood with respect to the multiple spatial settings in which he or she interacts.

The end result is that social space is defined in terms of the communication network within which an individual is imbedded. While geography and physical location play a central role in the creation of the network, social space is not the same thing as physical space. Individuals who live next door to one another may share the same geographically defined neighborhood, but they may also inhabit networks without a single overlapping node. Hence, while they share the same physical space, their social spaces may be independent. And such independence may only become apparent during an election campaign, when yard signs pop up on their front lawns.

REPRESENTATIONS OF CONTEXTUAL EFFECTS ON SOCIAL COMMUNICATION

This discussion becomes more helpful if we translate these ideas into several simply defined mathematical formulations that occur in the literatures on contextual and network effects on individual behavior. We begin with a contextual representation that is explicated most fully in the work of Boyd and Iversen (1979):

$$Y_{ij} = a_j + b_j X_{ij},$$

where:

Y_{ij} = support for the Democratic candidate on the part of the ith individual in the jth context;

X_{ij} = a relevant characteristic, say income, on the part of the ith individual in the jth context;

$a_j = a' + a''X_{.j}$;

$b_j = b' + b''X_{.j}$; and

$X_{.j}$ = the mean of the relevant social characteristic summed across all the individuals in the jth context.

This model suggests that the individual level of support for the Democratic candidate depends on the presence or absence of an individual characteristic (X_{ij}) as well as the incidence of that characteristic in the surrounding population ($X_{.j}$). Moreover, the translation of the individual characteristic into a factor influencing individual behavior also depends on the incidence of this characteristic in the surrounding population. And this correspondingly means that the translation of the aggregate distribution of the individual behaviors also depends on the individual-level presence of the characteristic. These contingent effects are perhaps seen more directly if the model is put into a single equation form:

$$Y_{ij} = a' + b'X_{ij} + a''X_{.j} + b''X_{ij}X_{.j}$$

This representation suggests that individual behavior depends on the presence of an individual trait as well as the incidence of that trait in the surrounding population. Moreover, the relationship between the individual trait and the individual possession of the trait also responds to the central tendency. This formulation portrays some complex, multi-level, hierarchical effects (Huckfeldt 1986; Huckfeldt and Sprague 1995). Employing the model for purposes of data analysis produces important implications for the structure of error terms that are addressed, either directly or indirectly, by Boyd and Iversen (1979), Bryk and Raudenbush (1992), Gelman et al. (1995), and Gill (2002). While this model produces a powerful analytic framework for understanding multi-level effects, it is poorly suited to pursue some of the issues we have introduced above. Hence, we proceed to consider a parallel but separate literature regarding network effects on individual behavior.

REPRESENTATIONS OF NETWORK EFFECTS ON SOCIAL COMMUNICATION

An alternative formulation is summarized in matrix form by Marsden and Friedkin as

$$y = \alpha Wy + X\beta + e.$$

Absent the term that includes the W matrix, this equation looks much like a standard least-squares regression model. X is a $(N \times K)$ matrix of individually based explanatory variables, y is a $(N \times 1)$ vector of individually based response variables, and e is a $(N \times 1)$ vector of errors, where the $(K \times 1)$ β vector is the vector of coefficients that measures the effect of the exogenous explanatory variables that are included in the X matrix.

The innovation of this model lies in the formulation of the endogenous network effects on individual behavior, αWy. The W matrix is a $(N \times N)$ matrix of influence coefficients such that each of the elements is greater than or equal to zero, and the sum of the coefficients for any individual is unity ($\Sigma w_{ij} = 1$, summed across j for any i). Finally, α is a weight operating on endogenous influence within the model. Hence, if α is zero, individual behavior is wholly a function of the exogenous factors and errors.

If, in fact, this is an appropriate characterization of the population in question, omitting the term with the W matrix produces a model with autocorrelated error terms (Anselin 1988; Marsden and Friedkin 1994):

$$Y = X\beta + \epsilon, \quad \text{where } \epsilon = \rho W\epsilon + \nu.$$

These formulations produce a number of advantages in the present context. First, rather than conceiving a contextual effect in which the central tendency of a population produces a direct effect, these models explicitly recognize that social influence comes in bits and pieces, in fits and starts, in a process where individuals typically encounter the other individuals within their network in serial fashion.

Second, this network formulation creates a social space that is not *necessarily* defined in terms of physical or geographic location. A variety of populations might be analyzed in the context of these models. One might employ the models to consider network effects among colleagues in an academic department, policy makers in a set of governmental institutions, members of a religious congregation, residents of a neighborhood, and more. In short, while the population might be defined in terms of physical location, and while geography might play an important role in the definition of the network, this need not be the case.

A final advantage is that the model is formulated to consider network effects that arise through behavioral interdependence. The modern tradition of contextual effects was originally articulated by Blau (1960) and Davis, Spaeth, and Huson (1961) to consider more general milieu effects. So, one might ask, how do the political consequences of being a member of the Chilean working class compare to the political consequences of being located *among* the other members of the Chilean working class (Langton and Rapoport 1975)?

As originally conceived, these contextual effects might be conceptualized in terms of social interaction effects (or network effects) within the surrounding population, but they might also be seen more diffusely in terms of effects on social identities. The contextual-effects literature is vulnerable to the criticism offered by Erbring and Young (1979), in which a contextual effect becomes a matter of "social telepathy"—an instance in which some general population characteristic mysteriously becomes a factor affecting individual behavior. The Marsden and Friedkin formulation is less vulnerable because it explicitly makes individual behavior contingent on the behavior of others. At the same time, making individual behavior dependent on behavioral distributions within the network creates some challenging endogeneity problems if one's goal is to isolate asymmetric individual-level causal effects.

Dyads, Networks, and Social Communication

While the network-effects model demonstrates some important advantages, it also has limitations. Most importantly for present purposes, we are not studying political influence within a self-contained population. Rather, we are examining patterns of influence in the entire United States population during a presidential election campaign. In this setting, and in most other settings that are of interest to students of voting, elections, and public opinion, the populations are not usefully seen as being self-contained. (See Anderson and Paskeviciute, Kohler, and Levine, in this volume.) In particular, the W matrix becomes enormous for anything other than small, self-contained populations, and nearly all the entries are zero. What do we need instead?

Rather than mapping the network of relationships for an entire self-contained population, we are interested in the networks that are defined with respect to particular individuals within a larger and more extensive population. (Within the specialized study of social networks, these are known as egocentric networks.) Hence, we might define the network as: $N_i = \Sigma w_k d_k$ where N_i is the ith individual's communication network. Each network includes the k discussants with whom the particular individual regularly communicates, and the w_k are the complex undefined weights operating on communication patterns within the network.

While it is possible that one discussant (one d_k) might serve as such for more than one individual, the probability is extremely low for any random sample taken from a large population. And indeed, in addressing a random sample of American citizens, we might judge this probability to be zero.

Where does this formulation lead us with respect to our theoretical and substantive goals? First, rather than focusing on the individual's preference, we shift the focus to consider whether an individual's preference corresponds to the preferences of particular discussants within the network—to consider the probability that an individual agrees with any particular discussant in the network. Second, we address the flow of information and influence among and between the members of the network, and consider the flow of information within dyads as being contingent on the flow of information and influence within the larger network. In particular, we begin with the ith individual and her kth discussant. The probability of agreement depends on two general factors: (1) the distance between the discussant's preference and the political orientation of the respondent and (2) the preference of the *particular* discussant with respect to the distribution of preferences in the remainder of the individual's network. Beginning with the first factor, the probability of agreement between the ith individual and her kth discussant is portrayed as:

$$P(A_{ik}) = 1/(1 + \exp(-(\beta_0 + \beta_1 P_k + \beta_2 O_i + \beta_3 P_k O_i))),$$

where $P(A_{ik})$ is the probability of agreement within a dyad between the ith individual and her kth discussant, O_i is the ith individual's political orientation, and P_k is the political preference of the kth discussant in the dyad, measured in terms of the individual's perception. This formulation says that the probability of agreement between an individual and any one of her discussants is a consequence of the discussant's preference, her own political orientation, and the interaction between the two.

Our argument is that an individual will consider the information obtained from any particular discussant within the context of the information taken from all other discussants. In order to incorporate this argument, the model for the probability of agreement between the ith individual and the kth discussant is expanded to become:

$$P(A_{ik}) = 1/(1 = \exp(-(\beta_0 + \beta_1 P_k + \beta_2 O_i + \beta_3 P_k O_i + \beta_4 P_{.-k} + \beta_5 P_k P_{.-k}))),$$

where $P_{.-k}$ is the distribution of discussant preferences in the residual network: the remaining discussants absent the kth discussant included in the dyad. Hence, this formulation expands the model to suggest that not only does agreement depend on the political distance between discussion partners within a dyad but it also depends on the political distance between the particular discussant and the remainder of the individual's communication network.

The same logic applies to each of the dyadic relationships within the network. Hence the same individual would also consider information taken from the second discussant within the context of information provided by the first and third discussants, as well as information taken from the third discussant within the context of information taken from the first and second discussants.

If this argument is correct, what would be the consequence of ignoring the fact that information taken from a single source is contingent on information taken from other sources? The slope operating on P_k becomes $\beta_1 + \beta_3 O_i + \beta_5 P_{.-k}$, and hence the discussant's preference is contingent on the distribution of preferences in the residual network. A model that ignores this contingency produces "spatially" autocorrelated errors within the social space where individuals reside. In particular, we are likely to overestimate the effects of discussants who hold minority preferences within networks and underestimate the influence of discussants who hold majority preferences within networks.

Hence, for these purposes, information taken from the environment is not easily summed across the network. Rather than characterizing the individual's correspondence with the central tendency of the network, we consider the level of correspondence within each dyad. Each observation within the resulting data matrix represents a dyad, and each individual's appearance in the matrix is multiplied by the size of her network. Hence, if she has four discussants, she is represented within four different dyads within the matrix. This means that we are clustering within networks, and agreement with the same individual appears as the regressand within multiple rows of the matrix. Clustering produces a situation in which the size of the matrix overstates the amount of information that is carried by the matrix, and thus we employ a procedure that takes account of the clustering and produces robust estimates for the standard errors (Rogers 1993).

Our argument is not simply that predicting individual behavior on the basis of individual characteristics produces individual errors that are correlated among associated individuals. Rather, we are arguing that *the consequences of dyadic information flows are conditioned on the remainder of the individual's network*. Hence, we imbed dyadic communication within the context of the larger network in order to avoid autocorrelation among the dyads within the same network.

DYADS, NETWORKS, AND THE 2000 ELECTION

How do individuals respond to political heterogeneity within their communication networks? Our argument is that the views of individuals are discounted if they run counter to the dominant view within the network. In this way, the message conveyed by any particular discussant is weighted by the distribution of preferences in the remainder of the network (Huckfeldt, Johnson, and Sprague 2002, 2004). Hence, we would expect agreement within dyads to depend not only on the political distance between the discussant's candidate preference and the respondent's political orientation but also on the distance between the discussant's preference and the distribution of preferences in the remainder of the network.

We employ this model in analyzing the consequence of dyadic information flows within the networks of the respondents to the 2000 National Election Study. Recall that, in the post-election survey, interviewers asked each individual respondent to identify people with whom they discussed government, elections, and politics. As many as four discussants were identified for each respondent, and interviewers asked the respondents to provide information regarding each of the discussants, including their judgment regarding the discussant's presidential vote choice in the immediately preceding election.

Hence, the discussant's political preference is defined in terms of the individual respondent's perception. The individual respondent's own political preference is defined in terms of the respondent's self-report of his own behavior, and the respondent's political orientation is defined as his partisan self-identification. Finally, the measure for the residual network is the proportion of the remaining discussants perceived by the individual respondent to hold the same preference as the discussant being considered within the particular dyad.

The presence or absence of agreement within each of the identified dyads is considered in terms of this argument, based on the logit models in Table 2.3. In each of the dyads analyzed in the first model, the respondent perceives that the discussant voted for Bush, and hence agreement is defined as an instance in which the respondent also reported voting for Bush. Similarly in the second model, the respondent perceives that each of the discussants supported Gore, and agreement exists if the respondent also reports voting for Gore. Finally, in the third model, respondents perceive these discussants as having voted neither for Bush nor Gore, and agreement exists if the respondent reports voting for neither candidate. (Based on these measurement procedures, the participants in 60 percent of all dyads in the sample hold the same political preferences.)

Several explanatory variables are included in the models: the respondent's partisanship, as well as the numbers of discussants in the remaining network whom the respondent perceived as voting for Bush, Gore, and neither. In the models for discussants who are perceived to support Gore and Bush, respondent partisanship is measured on the traditional 7-point scale, where -3 is strong Democrat and 3 is strong Republican. In the model for discussants who support neither candidate, respondent partisanship is measured as strength absent direction—as the absolute value of the party identification measure. Recall that a maximum of four discussants is recorded for each respondent, and hence the maximum number of discussants in the residual network is three.

These models allow us to address the conditions that enhance and diminish the probability of agreement within particular dyads. The models consistently produce statistically discernible coefficients for respondent partisanship. Strong Democrats are more likely to agree with Gore voters and less likely to agree with Bush voters. Correspondingly, strong Republicans are more likely to agree with Bush voters and less likely to agree with Gore voters. Strong partisans of either variety are less likely to agree with voters who support neither of the major party candidates.

The preference distributions within the residual networks produce more complex (and perhaps more interesting) results. Support for Bush in the residual network enhances the probability of agreeing with a discussant who supports Bush and attenuates the probability of agreeing with a discussant who supports neither of the major party candidates. Similarly, support for Gore enhances the probability of agreement with a discussant who supports Gore and diminishes the probability of agreement with a discussant who supports neither candidate. In addition, increased Gore support attenuates the probability of agreeing with a discussant who voted for Bush. Finally, the number of discussants who support neither candidate fails to produce a discernible coefficient in any of the three models.

The magnitudes and implications of these patterns of relationships are seen most readily in Figure 2.1, which displays the estimated probabilities of agreement within dyads for respondents who identify as political independents. The independent respondents are more likely to agree with discussants who voted for Bush to the extent that support for Bush occurs in the remainder of their networks. Similarly, they are more likely to agree with Gore-voting discussants to the extent that Gore voting is more common in the remainder of their networks. In both instances,

TABLE 2.3. Respondent Agreement with Discussants Who Support Bush, Gore, and Neither Candidate by Partisanship of the Respondent and Distribution of Preferences in the Residual Network (Logit Models)

	Respondent Agreement with a Discussant Who Supports		
	Bush	Gore	Neither
Constant	−.49	−.27	1.65
	(1.82)	(.98)	(4.45)
Party identification		.81	−.77
		(10.03)	(8.14)
Partisan strength			−.71
			(4.64)
Residual network support for:			
Bush	.65	−.18	−.65
	(3.21)	1.32)	(3.63)
Gore	−.35	.64	−.93
	(2.15)	(2.81)	(4.50)
Neither	−.18	−.30	.04
	(.98)	(1.64)	(.20)
N (clusters)	1,183 (665)	1,071 (649)	545 (395)
$\chi^2/df/p$	125/4/.00	86/4/.00	43/4/.00

Source: 2000 National Election Study.
Unit of analysis is dyad; data are weighted; standard errors are corrected for clustering.
Respondent agreement within dyad: 1 = respondent perceives that the discussant supports their own candidate choice, 0 = other.
Party identification: seven-point scale ranging from −3 (strong Democrat) to 3 (strong Republican).
Partisan strength: four-point scale ranging from 0 (independent) to 3 (strong partisan).
Residual network support for Bush: number of discussants in remainder of network that are perceived to support Bush.
Residual network support for Gore: number of discussants in remainder of network that are perceived to support Gore.
Residual network support for neither: number of discussants in remainder of network that are perceived to support neither candidate.

the agreement probability is only modestly attenuated by the distribution of other preferences or nonpreferences. Finally, and in contrast, the probability of agreement with a discussant who supports neither candidate is not enhanced by the presence of other nonsupporters in the remainder of the network, but is diminished by the presence of either Bush or Gore voters.

Figures 2.2 and 2.3 replicate Figure 2.1, but for respondents who identify as strong Republicans and strong Democrats respectively. These figures demonstrate the strong bias toward (1) agreement with discussants whose vote preferences correspond with the respondents' partisan loyalties and (2) disagreement with discussants whose vote preferences run counter to the respondents' partisan loyalties. The pattern of agreement and disagreement that depends on preference distributions in the residual network is also present in these figures, but its magnitude is greatly reduced.

In summary, this analysis yields several results. First, a strong partisan is highly likely to agree with a discussant who supports her own party's candidate—and to

A. Discussant Is Bush Supporter

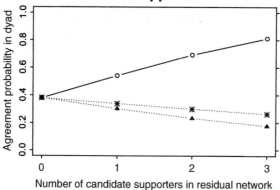

o Bush support
▲ Gore support
✳ Support for neither

B. Discussant Is Gore Supporter

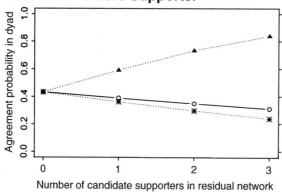

C. Discussant Supports Neither Candidate

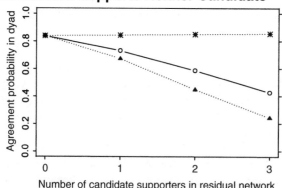

FIGURE 2.1. Contingent Probability of Agreement within Network Dyads, by the Candidate Preference of the Discussant in the Dyad and the Levels of Candidate Support in the Remainder of the Network (All respondents are Independents.)

Source: Table 2.3 estimates.

Note: When the level of support for a particular candidate preference in the residual network is held constant at 0, 1, 2, or 3 discussants, support for the other preferences is held constant at 0.

A. Discussant Is Bush Supporter

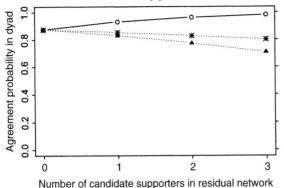

B. Discussant Is Gore Supporter

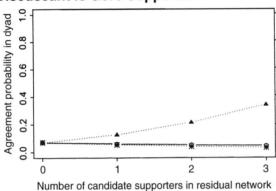

C. Discussant Supports Neither Candidate

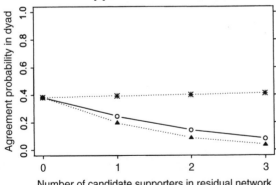

FIGURE 2.2. Contingent Probability of Agreement within Network Dyads, by the Candidate Preference of the Discussant in the Dyad and the Levels of Candidate Support in the Remainder of the Network (All respondents are strong Republicans.)

Source: Table 2.3 estimates.

Note: When the level of support for a particular candidate preference in the residual network is held constant at 0, 1, 2, or 3 discussants, support for the other preferences is held constant at 0.

A. Discussant Is Bush Supporter

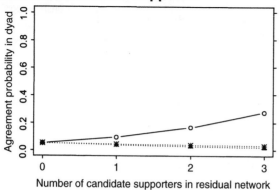

○ Bush support
▲ Gore support
✳ Support for neither

B. Discussant Is Gore Supporter

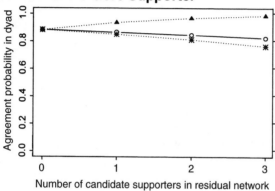

C. Discussant Supports Neither Candidate

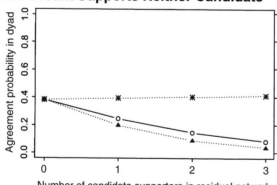

FIGURE 2.3. Contingent Probability of Agreement within Network Dyads, by the Candidate Preference of the Discussant in the Dyad and the Levels of Candidate Support in the Remainder of the Network (All respondents are strong Democrats.)

Source: Table 2.3 estimates.

Note: When the level of support for a particular candidate preference in the residual network is held constant at 0, 1, 2, or 3 discussants, support for the other preferences is held constant at 0.

disagree with a discussant who supports the opposite party's candidate—regardless of the partisan division in the remainder of the network.

Second, as the strength of partisanship decreases, the probability that individuals will agree or disagree with a discussant who supports either candidate increasingly becomes contingent on the distribution of candidate preferences in the remainder of the communication network. In particular, the probability of agreement is enhanced by the presence of other discussants who hold the same political preference.

Third, the probability of agreeing or disagreeing with a discussant who supports *neither* of the major party candidates is also contingent on preference distributions in the remainder of the network. While the probability is not enhanced by the presence of other discussants who support neither candidate, it is dramatically diminished by the presence of discussants who support either of the candidates.

What do these results suggest? Agreement within dyads is typically sustained by larger networks of communication that simultaneously support the preferences of both individuals within the dyad. Hence, disagreement is also socially sustained, but by politically divergent networks that serve to pull the two members of the dyad in politically opposite directions (Huckfeldt, Johnson, and Sprague 2004; Johnson and Huckfeldt, in this volume). In short, the survival of disagreement within dyads is profitably seen within larger patterns of association and communication that occur at the intersection between the networks that surround individual citizens.

HETEROGENEITY WITHIN PREFERENCE CATEGORIES: OPINIONS REGARDING CANDIDATES

Thus far we have seen that the correspondence in vote choice between a respondent and a particular discussant is often contingent on the distribution of candidate support in the remainder of the network. At the same time, these patterns of relationships depend on the individual respondent's partisanship in some interesting and important ways. In particular, strong partisans appear to be less influenced by the flow of information in their networks: They are unlikely to agree with a discussant who supports the opposite party's candidate, regardless of the distribution of candidate preferences in the remainder of the network.

Do these same patterns persist for opinions regarding the candidates? That is, do we see the same patterns of effects for respondents' candidate evaluations as we do for their ultimate vote choices? This is an important issue that is directly related to the nature of the informational effects we are observing. One interpretation, based on the results in Table 2.3, is that strong partisans are much less likely to be affected by socially communicated information. In particular, Figures 2.2 and 2.3 suggest that it is very difficult to convince a strong partisan to vote for the other party's candidate.

An alternative interpretation suggests that, in such instances, the effects of socially communicated information are still present. The fact that strong partisans do not cross over to vote for the opposite party's candidate is not evidence that social communication is lacking in influence but rather that the information effect is overwhelmed by partisan loyalty. If the strong Democrat of 2000 resembles the "yellow dog" Democrat of an earlier era, she might indeed vote for a yellow dog rather than a Republican. But if her Republican associates convince her that the Democrat is indeed a yellow dog, it seems mistaken to suggest that partisans are insulated from socially communicated information. In other words, strong partisans may be *loyal* to their parties' candidates, but that is not the same thing as saying that they are *enthusiastic* supporters of their parties' candidates.

In this section, we give attention to opinion dynamics during the campaign. In particular, what are the consequences of network preference distributions for changes in the respondents' evaluations of George Bush and Al Gore during the campaign? One of the most compelling results from the early Columbia studies was the manner in which volatility was produced in situations where individual preferences ran contrary to the dominant opinions within networks (Berelson et al. 1954; Huckfeldt and Sprague 1995; Lazarsfeld et al. 1944; McPhee 1963). We explore that issue here by comparing respondents' pre- and post-election feeling thermometer scores for the candidates.

The dependent variable in Part A of Table 2.4 is the individual change in the feeling thermometer over the course of the campaign: the post-election thermometer measure minus the pre-election thermometer measure. The resulting difference measure is regressed on two sets of variables: (1) the respondent's party identification, the discussant's vote, and their interaction, as well as (2) the percentage of the residual network that agrees with the discussant and its interaction with the discussant's vote. (The pre-election thermometer score is also included as a control variable.) As the results show, three explanatory variables produce consistently discernible coefficients: the control variable for the pre-election thermometer score, individual partisanship, and the interaction between the discussant's vote and the remainder of the network that shares the discussant's vote.

How are these effects interpreted? First, partisans are likely to become more favorable toward the candidate of their own party and less favorable toward the candidate of the opposite party. For example, the thermometer score for Gore is likely to increase by more than 10 points across the general election campaign among strong Democrats (-3×-3.86), and it is likely to decrease by more than 10 points among strong Republicans (3×-3.86). These effects are wholly in keeping with the insights of the Columbia studies: Election campaigns have the effect of increasing the differences in preference distributions among politically relevant groups (Berelson, Lazarsfeld, and McPhee 1954).

Second, respondents are likely to become more favorably disposed toward the candidates supported by their discussants, but only when the discussant's preference is widespread within the remainder of the network. Indeed, if the discussant is the sole supporter of a candidate within a network, the results for both feeling thermometers suggest that respondent's preference demonstrates *no* discernible correspondence with the discussant's preference. In contrast, if the discussant's preference is shared throughout the network, the Gore discussant's preference produces a 4.95 point increase in the main respondent's feeling thermometer score toward Gore, and the Bush discussant's preference produces a 6.75 point increase in the feeling thermometer score toward Bush. These results suggest that the events of the campaign are not only filtered through the prism of individual partisanship but also through the partisan networks within which individuals are located. Moreover,

TABLE 2.4. Change in Feeling Thermometers toward Candidates by Respondent Party Identification, Discussant Vote, the Percentage of the Residual Network That Agrees with the Discussant, and Initial Feeling Thermometer Score

	Bush feeling thermometer		Gore feeling thermometer	
	Coefficient	t-value	Coefficient	t-value
A. DIFFERENCE IN THERMOMETERS: POST-ELECTION MINUS PRE-ELECTION. LEAST SQUARES				
Constant	25.00	9.08	24.34	7.74
Party identification	3.51	7.44	−3.86	7.45
Discussant vote	−.78	1.48	−.52	.96
Party id. × discussant vote	.79	2.60	−.31	1.17
Percent in residual net agreeing with discussant	−1.03	.63	−.09	.06
Residual net agreement × discussant vote	6.75	3.99	−4.95	2.90
Pre-election feeling thermometer	−.44	9.74	−.48	10.04
N (number of clusters)	2,493 (831)	2,484 (828)		
R^2	.23	.24		
Standard error of estimate	16.81	17.39		
B. DIRECTION OF CHANGE: INCREASE, STAY THE SAME. DECREASE. ORDERED LOGIT				
Party identification	.38	7.68	−.31	5.74
Discussant vote	−.032	.53	−.057	1.02
Party id. × discussant vote	.062	2.04	−.061	1.93
Percent in residual net agreeing with discussant	−.12	.71	.10	.57
Residual net agreement × discussant vote	.50	2.75	−.31	1.77
Pre-election feeling thermometer	−.040	9.71	−.038	9.25
First threshold	−3.26	s = .29	−2.82	s = .28
Second threshold	−1.49	s = .27	−1.00	s = .26
N (number of clusters)	2,493 (831)	2,484 (828)		
$\chi^2/df/p$	123/6/.00	94/6/.00		

Source: 2000 National Election Study.
Unit of analysis is dyad; data are weighted; standard errors are corrected for clustering.
Direction of change: 1 = thermometer increased more than 5 points, 0 = change in thermometer is 5 points or less, −1 = thermometer decreased more than 5 points.
Discussant vote (as perceived by respondent): −1 = Gore, 1 = Bush, 0 = other or no vote.

the information coming from any single discussant would appear to be filtered through information coming from the remainder of the network.

In order to assess the mediating impact of partisanship on these information flows, we employ a nonlinear ordered logit model to consider the probability that the individual's level of support for Gore and Bush either increased, decreased, or stayed the same. Increases and decreases in support constitute individual-level differences in the pre- and post-election feeling thermometers of more than five points in the appropriate direction, and a lack of change is an instance in which the two feeling thermometer ratings are within five points of each other. Based on these definitions, 40 percent of the respondents did not change their Bush evaluations and 39 percent did not change their Gore evaluations; 30 percent reported decreased levels of support for Bush and 36 percent reported decreased levels of support for Gore; 30 percent reported increased levels of support for Bush while 25 percent reported increased levels of support for Gore.

The ordered logit model is nonlinear, with the effect of each explanatory variable depending on the effect of every other explanatory variable. Hence the model incorporates contingent effects among the explanatory variables by virtue of its construction, allowing us to see whether network effects persist across partisan categories.

In Part B of Table 2.4, the resulting measures of individual change in Bush and Gore support are regressed on the same explanatory variables as in Part A, and the pattern of t-values for the coefficients is very similar to the earlier results. In order to assess the magnitude of network effects across individual partisan categories, we vary the respondent's partisanship across its range while varying network and discussant variables across their ranges. This strategy allows a comparison of discussant and network effects across partisan categories as well as a comparison of partisan effects across discussant and network categories.

As Figure 2.4 shows, the presence of a Bush discussant enhances the probability of increased favorability toward Bush, and the presence of a Gore discussant diminishes the probability, but only to the extent that the remainder of the network supports the discussant's candidate preference. The effects are somewhat larger among independents, but the differences are not dramatic. A similar pattern of effects is present, but not shown here, when we consider changes in favorability toward Gore. Hence, it would appear that strong partisans are not immune to the political messages that are filtered through networks of political communication.

CONCLUSION

This chapter's analysis suggests that disagreement was a common event among citizens during the 2000 presidential election campaign, even within close networks of political communication. At the end of the lengthy campaign, heterogeneous preferences persisted among people who interact on a regular basis. Indeed, it seems clear that political homogeneity within communication networks does not constitute an equilibrium condition in democratic politics. Hence the question naturally arises, If socially communicated political information is influential, how is disagreement able to persist?

A central part of the answer to this question relates to the low-density characteristics of political communication networks. In networks characterized by "weak ties" (Granovetter 1973) and "structural holes" (Burt 1992), associated individuals are frequently located in networks that intersect but do not correspond. Regardless of the fact that two individuals communicate with each other on a regular basis, their remaining lists of contacts may be nonoverlapping. That is, Tom and Dick may regularly eat lunch together at work, but neither of them may associate with the other's non-workplace acquaintances (see Fuchs 1955).

These sorts of low-density networks create a high potential for accommodating and even sustaining disagreement. Suppose that Tom is a strong Democrat and Dick is a strong Republican. They regularly disagree about politics, but when Tom goes home at night and undertakes his other activities, he is regularly surrounded

A. Respondent Is Strong Democrat

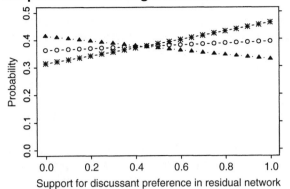

▲ Discussant is
Gore voter

✳ Discussant is
Bush voter

○ Discussant is
neither

B. Respondent Is Strong Republican

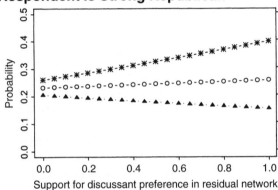

C. Respondent Is Independent

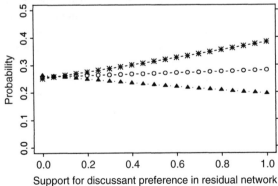

FIGURE 2.4. Predicted Probability of Increased Favorability toward Bush from Pre-election to Post-election

Source: Table 2.4B estimates.

Note: The pre-election Bush feeling thermometer is held constant at the pre-election mean for the partisan category: 80 for strong Republicans, 55 for independents, and 39 for strong Democrats.

by other strong Democrats. Correspondingly, when Dick leaves work he is regularly located among other strong Republicans. Neither of them is persuaded by their lunchtime discussions because they discount the information communicated within the dyad based on information communicated through the remainder of the network. (See Stoker and Jennings, Verba, Schlozman, and Burns, and Zuckerman, Fitzgerald, and Dasović, in this volume.)

In short, the political dynamic within dyads is contingent on the political dynamic within the remainder of each individual's network. This means, in turn, that the influence of particular discussants is "spatially" autocorrelated within networks. Not only do individually based models of political preference generate autocorrelated errors by failing to take account of interdependence among individuals within the same network, but dyadic models of communication also produce autocorrelated error by failing to locate dyads within the larger preference distributions that are present within networks. Correspondingly, models of communication and influence that rely on the central tendencies within networks and contexts do not capture the nonlinear systems of weights that operate on patterns of communication within those settings.

How do Tom and Dick manage to maintain the relationship in the face of disagreement? The answer depends on the particulars of the individuals and the relationship. For some individuals, politics is simply not at the center of the relationship. Tom and Dick may spend most of their time talking about baseball or fly-fishing.

Other individuals may not be particularly troubled by disagreement because they have suitable idiosyncratic explanations for their lunch partner's wrong-headed views. As Ross and his colleagues suggest (1976), the powers of social-conformity pressures are inversely proportional to the explanations available to account for disagreement. If Tom thinks that Dick is a Republican because he is unduly influenced by his rich uncle, it becomes much easier to dismiss his views.

The management of political disagreement within a dyad depends on the circumstances of the individuals within the relationships. The important point for our analysis is that the structure of a given network may actually sustain disagreement. Hence we might say that both agreement and disagreement are capable of being socially sustained by the structural details of particular settings. And the persistence of political heterogeneity within networks of political communication is not, by itself, evidence of either a social-influence failure or a lack of interdependence among citizens.

PART I

FAMILIES AS SOURCES OF STRONG POLITICAL TIES

3   Political Similarity and Influence between Husbands and Wives

WHILE IT HAS long been recognized that primary groups are important in shaping, reinforcing, and modifying political beliefs, the formalization of these understandings through social-context and social-network theories is of more recent origin (e.g., Eulau 1986; Huckfeldt and Sprague 1987; Weatherford 1982; Zuckerman, Kotler-Berkowitz, and Swaine 1998). Curiously absent from most of this literature, until recently (Beck 1991; Hays and Bean 1992, 1994; Kenney 1994; Straits 1991; Zuckerman and Kotler-Berkowitz 1998; Zuckerman, Fitzgerald, and Dasović, in this volume), is the context and mini-network that figures so prominently in the lives of most people: the family. Of course, the family has been a focus of attention in the study of political socialization, and various socioeconomic traits of the familial household are used to help account for adult attitudes and behaviors. It is also true that an implicit interest in the family has accompanied study of the gender gap (e.g., Norrander 1997; Sapiro 2002), and the so-called marriage gap (e.g., Plutzer and McBurnett 1991; Weisberg 1987). Nevertheless, there are few treatments of adult family members as sources of political information for each other, as instigators of change and preservers of the status quo, and as targets and recipients of political influence. If political communication networks built up of neighbors, co-workers, and volunteer organization co-members are important in helping us understand the dynamics of political attitudes, then surely the more intimate one of family is also.

In this chapter we consider the central adult actors in the nuclear family, namely, marital (or cohabiting) partners. Despite the prevalence of divorce and single heads of households in the United States, the great majority of Americans will marry at least once in their lifetimes. Marriage constitutes for most adults the most intimate of environments and the spouse the most intimate of conversation partners. It would be surprising if this intimacy was devoid of all political content for the political, even in the narrow sense, penetrates into every home and affects every couple.

Our goals are to illuminate how marriage shapes the lifelong development of political attitudes and to probe the implications of that process for the gender gap in political attitudes in the United States. We begin by addressing two related questions about marriage and political-attitude change: First, to what extent do husbands and wives become politically more similar as their marriages age? Second, do husbands and wives exert political influence upon each other? And if so, is the influence mutual, with each partner contributing to the resolution of differences? Or is it one-sided, with one partner doing most of the accommodating? Although these two questions are related, their relationship is inexact. On one hand, increasing couple similarity could result from selection processes and shared experiences (homophily) rather than interpersonal influence. On the other hand, marital partners may influence each other even if they do not become more similar over time. That would be the case if the forces working to produce differences between them overwhelm, or at least counterbalance, the influence processes at work.

In the last section of the chapter, we turn to the macro-level implications of these micro-level marital dynamics. Because partners to a marriage undergo experiences, including mutual influence, that bring them together politically, marriage has important consequences for the character of the gender gap that has emerged in the United States. As we demonstrate, marriage significantly shapes and limits the political differences between women and men.

A LONGITUDINAL STUDY OF HUSBAND-WIFE PAIRS

Our analysis takes advantage of a long-term study of political socialization that began in 1965 with a national probability sample survey of 1,669 high school seniors located in ninety-seven schools, public and private. Subsequent interviews of the same individuals were attempted in 1973, 1982, and 1997, yielding a four-wave panel of 935 individuals who matured in age from eighteen to fifty years old over the course of the study.[1] In 1973, 1982, and 1997 data were also collected from the partners of primary respondents who were married or cohabiting with someone. Spouses who were at home were asked to complete a self-administered questionnaire while the primary respondent was being interviewed; those not at home were requested to fill it out later and mail it in. The response rates, based on all potential spouses, were quite respectable: 60 percent ($N = 556$) in 1973, 60 percent again in 1982 ($N = 515$), and 65 percent in 1997 ($N = 469$).

We combined these spouse data with the matching primary-respondent data to form three cross-sectional, couple-level datasets. Although these cross-sectional pair sets can be useful for addressing some questions about marriage and politics, longitudinal data are superior for addressing the questions at hand. Consequently, we constructed three panel datasets involving husband-wife pairs from whom we had gathered information in two or more waves. One dataset consisted of pairs from the 1973 and 1982 waves, a second involved pairs from the 1982 and 1997 waves, and a third involved pairs from all three waves. After discarding pairs in which a remarriage had occurred during the panel period (thus involving data from at least two different spouses), we retained 257 intact pairs from the 1973–1982 panel, 248 from the 1982–1997 panel, and 150 from the three-wave panel. Considering the varied ways in which attrition could have occurred in this special instance—separation, divorce, and widowhood in addition to the usual sources of nonresponse—these are very satisfactory response rates.

To check for bias in the cross-sectional pair samples, we compared those primary respondents whose spouses completed the questionnaire with those whose spouses did not. Virtually no significant differences emerged with respect to the key attitudinal and behavioral variables of interest to us. We also checked the primary respondents' descriptions of their spouses' party identification, education, employment, and occupational status, as well as the couple's length of marriage. Again, scarcely any differences correlated with spousal response or nonresponse. Based on these two tests, the amount of bias appears to be negligible.

As noted above, two different forms of survey administration were used. Most of the primary respondents were interviewed face to face (or by phone for about half the 1997 respondents), whereas their spouses completed a self-administered questionnaire. The latter was considerably shorter than the version given to the primary respondent and consisted primarily of closed-ended questions. Although mode of administration is known to generate some differences in the amount and quality of responses, and to impose limitations on the types of questions than can be asked (see, e.g., Bradburn 1983; Singer and Presser 1989), these issues do not pose serious problems in the present case for two reasons. First, a comparison between modes of administration in terms of the amount of missing data produced, the distribution of the responses, and the degree of attitudinal constraint revealed only small differences, much in accord with evidence from other systematic investigations (e.g., De Leeuw 1992; Hippler and Schwarz 1987). Second, whatever distortion might have occurred as a result of mode differences is eased by the fact that we were as much or more interested in the patterns and relative positioning of results than in the absolute values themselves.

ATTITUDINAL CONGRUENCE AND LENGTH OF MARRIAGE

There are three major reasons for hypothesizing that marital partners will resemble each other politically. First, while Americans seldom use politics as a criterion for mate selection, assortative mating based on factors related to politics (such as class, religion, and race) will inevitably produce some initial congruence and pave the way for further convergence. Then, after marriage, each partner is exposed to an enormous number of common experiences, all the way from living in the same neighborhood and sharing the same children to being exposed to the same media entering the household. These similarities of exposure would be expected to push the partners closer together, other things being equal. Finally, the increasing volume of shared experiences and interactions with each other could be expected to elevate concordance. Marital partners talk to each other, frequently in fragments, side comments, and casual observations as well as in more sustained conversations. Spouses, in fact, tend to be one another's major discussion partner for matters in general (Marsden 1987) and for politics in particular (Beck 1991; Zuckerman 1998; Zuckerman, Fitzgerald, and Dasović, in this volume). Moreover, couples put some value on developing harmony. Politics is not usually uppermost in the everyday lives of individuals, and marital partners are subject to other influences that may work to push them apart. Nevertheless it is reasonable to expect that accommodation and influence processes would work over time to increase the level of political homogeneity among couples.[2]

For most of what follows we analyze the data provided by each marital partner. The advantage to this is that projection and subjectivity are reduced inasmuch as the respondents were presumably making no effort either to make themselves match or to differ from their spouses. We utilize eleven measures based on responses from each of the marriage partners, ten tapping political orientations and, for comparison, one concerning religiosity. The political measures range from the very general to the more specific, tap several different attitudinal domains, are based on varying question formats, are reasonably reliable, and are commonly judged to lie along a liberal-to-conservative continuum. Most of these measures employ questions used in the National Election Studies (NES). Each is described in more detail in the chapter Appendix.

Party identification, assessed in the conventional NES fashion, and presidential vote choice, based on votes cast in the two most recent elections, comprise the partisan measures. Self-location on a seven-point liberal-to-conservative scale serves as a general marker of ideology. Preferences regarding several long-standing public policy issues were ascertained in several ways. Attitudes concerning the legalization of marijuana and federal assistance with respect to ensuring jobs were measured by seven-point scales, while those concerning abortion and school prayer were based on responses to forced-choice questions. Preferences concerning racial policy were indexed by a forced-choice question concerning school integration and a seven-point scale concerning federal aid to minorities. Attitudes toward two institutional rivals in American politics, big business and labor unions, were assessed by questions about their level of political influence. The measure of attitudes toward gender equality combined judgments about the political influence of women as well as self-location on a seven-point scale concerning gender roles. Finally, a religiosity measure combined responses concerning frequency of church attendance and belief in the inerrancy of the Bible.

Gender Differences

In order to provide a vital backdrop for the analysis of marital pairs we begin by presenting the distribution of these measures over time for the husbands and wives in our sample. Doing so conveys a sense of the secular trends captured by the three surveys as well as differences by gender. Table 3.1 presents the findings for the intact three-wave couples.[3]

Not surprisingly, a gender gap in political attitudes emerged over time. With one exception (legalization of marijuana), men and women in the aggregate did not differ at statistically significant levels in 1973. Yet over time, men became more conservative (or less liberal) relative to women, so much so that by 1997 they differed from them on six of the ten political measures. A gap emerged on the three more global indicators of political attitudes—party identification, vote choice, and liberal/conservative ideology—as well as on attitudes concerning gender equality, government job assistance, and legalization of marijuana. In some ways the most striking change concerns the marijuana issue, where significant differences exist at all three points but where the *direction* of the relationship changes. By contrast, a gender gap in terms of religiosity is evident at each point in time, with women tending to be more religious than men.

Further scrutiny of Table 3.1 implicates the 1973–1982 period as a critical one for the development of the gap. Most of the differences had appeared by 1982, and are very similar to those found for 1997. In this respect our findings, though derived from a single cohort, bear a distinct resemblance to findings based on larger, national samples (Chaney, Alvarez, and Nagler 1998; Shapiro and Mahajan 1986).

Pair Similarities

Given the findings about emerging gender differences over time, an initial expectation would be one of increasing dissimilarity between marriage partners over time

TABLE 3.1. Gender Gap in Spousal Political Orientations over Time:
Three-wave Panel Pairs

	1973	1982	1997
Party identification			
Husband	.47	.50	.54
Wife	.45	.47	.46
Gap	.02	.03	.08***
Vote choice			
Husband	.58	.62	.54
Wife	.54	.50	.46
Gap	.04	.12***	.08**
Ideology			
Husband	.46	.57	.61
Wife	.47	.55	.56
Gap	−.01	.02	.05**
Race policy			
Husband	.52	.68	.58
Wife	.49	.64	.58
Gap	.03	.04	.00
Gender equality			
Husband	.35	.28	.27
Wife	.32	.23	.22
Gap	.03	.05**	.05*
Business vs. labor			
Husband	.44	.45	.34
Wife	.40	.40	.34
Gap	.04	.05*	.00
Government job assistance			
Husband	.60	.70	.67
Wife	.58	.63	.60
Gap	.02	.07**	.07**
Abortion			
Husband		.32	.28
Wife	na	.34	.32
Gap		−.02	−.04
School prayer			
Husband	.73	.68	.66
Wife	.68	.69	.65
Gap	.05	−.01	.01
Legalization of marijuana			
Husband	.50	.60	.60
Wife	.59	.67	.55
Gap	−.09**	−.07*	.05*
Religiosity			
Husband	.61	.64	.61
Wife	.65	.74	.69
Gap	−.04*	−.10***	−.08***

Note: Entries are averages. Each variable was scored to range from 0 to 1. All variables were scored so
that the more conservative/religious responses received higher scores. Base n = 150.
    *p < .05, **p < .01, ***p < .001.

as well. After all, we are talking about the same respondents. Recall, however, that the foregoing analysis was based on aggregate trends among husbands and wives taken separately as the units of analysis. What happened at that level may or may not reflect developments when marital *pairs* become the units of analysis. Indeed, there is no necessary statistical relationship between what is transpiring at these two levels.

Table 3.2 presents the longitudinal findings for the three-wave panel couples, using the intraclass correlation coefficient to index similarity.[4] Although our main focus is the consequences of marital longevity, the range of couple concordance across attitude objects also merits attention. Couples are obviously much more alike than unlike, with substantial variation depending upon the nature of the attitude object. Long-standing, central, and salient objects such as the political parties and electoral choice command high consonance. The same tends to be true for political topics heavily charged with religious and moral content, such as abortion and marijuana control, and for level of religiosity itself.

Considering the effects of marital duration, we should note that the column headings of years in Table 3.2 represent, in effect, marital longevity. The couples had been married for an average of four years by 1973, thirteen years by 1982, and twenty-eight years by 1997. If the duration hypothesis is to be supported, pair agreement should increase over time. At a bare minimum, agreement should not decrease. Evidence from the three-wave panel offers strong support for either continuity or increasing convergence over time. Only one of the political measures, legalization of marijuana, exhibits less similarity in 1997 than in 1973. Similarity is also reduced on levels of religiosity. Conversely, the measures representing party identification, vote choice, ideology, racial policy, and government job assistance show strong gains while the other measures show essentially no change.[5]

In general, congruence increased substantially more in the second panel period than in the first. In fact, more decreases than increases occurred in the first panel

TABLE 3.2. Husband-Wife Similarity in Political Attitudes over Time: Three-wave Panel Pairs

	1973	1982	1997
Party identification	.34	.47	.54
Vote choice	.59	.52	.69
Ideology	.22	.33	.41
Race policy	.22	.27	.38
Gender equality	.15	.49	.14
Business vs. labor	.33	.31	.31
Government job assistance	.11	.23	.21
Abortion	na	.51	.50
School prayer	.44	.46	.47
Legalization of marijuana	.46	.34	.37
Religiosity	.72	.67	.53

Note: Entries are intraclass correlation coefficients (ICC). An ICC of 0.0 indicates no within-couple homogeneity, and an ICC of 1.0 indicates perfect within-couple agreement. Base $n = 150$. All coefficients but two are statistically different from 0 at $p < .01$ or better. The exceptions are government job assistance in 1973 ($p = .10$) and gender equality in 1997 ($p = .09$).

period, although most of the decreases are very small. There are two likely explanations for these differences across time. One is that the marriages are on average considerably older by the end of the later panel (twenty-eight years) than by the end of the earlier one (thirteen years). Couples have had even more time to accommodate to each other through various mechanisms, including interpersonal influence, as we show below. A second explanation focuses on the social and political currents at work during the earlier (1973–1982) period. Differential responses by men and women to Watergate and the aftermath of the Vietnam War are possible candidates. More likely would be differential responses to the cresting of the women's movement and the emergence of a gender gap in voting behavior.[6]

On balance, then, marital longevity works to heighten pair concordance. These results run counter to what might have been expected based on the aggregate comparisons between husbands and wives. Long-term trends pointing toward growing differences, in general, between husbands and wives on a number of key political attitudes are not reflected in growing marital disharmony.

SPOUSAL INFLUENCE AND ACCOMMODATION

As noted earlier, increased couple similarity may arise over time even if the marriage partners are not influencing each other; they may simply be reacting to common experiences and shared influences. Similarly, even if husbands and wives are not becoming more similar over time in the aggregate, it is still possible that mutual socialization is taking place within the marriage. Consequently, the results we have seen so far leave open the question of whether husbands and wives are influencing each other. Panel data on marital partners provide an excellent resource for addressing this issue.

A Subjective View

It is instructive first to view the dynamics of influence and accommodation as the participants themselves see them. Our interviews with the 1973 youth generation shed considerable light on the experience of political conflict within marriage and its resolution. In addition to asking the interviewed respondents about the frequency and nature of their current political disagreements, we also asked whether they had had disagreements with their spouses when they were first married and, if so, what were the outcomes of these differences. The lead question directed the respondents to think back to when they were first married (a short time for most of them) and recall if they had ever disagreed about public affairs and politics. About one-fourth acknowledged there were such disagreements.[7]

To no one's surprise, the early dissonance centered on two subject areas: political parties, elections, and politicians; and issues involving morality and civil rights. What were the outcomes of these early disagreements? According to their own perceptions, many young couples seemed to agree to disagree about politics. Disagreements remained in place for nearly one-half of the couples (44 percent). However, in the remaining 56 percent one partner yielded to the other. Overall, both accommodation and resistance are common patterns in the early years of a marriage.

Equally significant are the reports as to which partner yielded.[8] By tradition, political conflict in a marriage is resolved with the husband's viewpoint prevailing, at least in the arena of partisanship (Beck and Jennings 1975). Some expected this pattern to erode with the advent of the second-wave women's movement and its accompanying changes in gender roles. Nevertheless, the evidence shows the traditional pattern prevailing in 1973. A breakdown by sex of the respondent shows that only 9 percent of the husbands acknowledged yielding to their wives, while 49 percent claimed that their wives capitulated. Nor does this impressive gap merely reflect a virile exercise of the male ego, for 58 percent of the wives admitted to moving in the husband's direction while only 14 percent said their husbands sided with them. The balance of responses, for both sexes, fell into the "both changed" category, instances where more than one divisive issue existed or where each partner conceded a bit on a given issue.

The same questions, but restricted to contemporary political disagreements, were put to the respondents in 1997. A massive change had occurred since 1973, one that probably reflects the effects of marital longevity as well as secular forces at work. Roughly twice as many respondents as in 1973 reported that both partners changed their minds (73 percent in 1997, versus 35 percent in 1973), an increase found among both men and women.[9] Among those who said that one partner yielded, husbands designated themselves about as often as they designated their spouses (58 percent versus 42 percent); wives, however, still designated themselves much more often (86 percent versus 14 percent). Traces of the earlier pronounced male advantage thus prevailed along with a strong movement toward mutual change. These changes in conflict resolution as seen by subjective appraisals presage those based on revealed changes, to which we now turn.

A Dynamic Analysis

If, when political disagreements exist, one or both marriage partners successfully exert influence upon the other, this should be evident in the patterning of change we observe in the attitudes of each marital partner. In this section we develop and estimate a dynamic, simultaneous-influence panel model to trace these influence flows.[10]

Figure 3.1 depicts the two-wave model of reciprocal influence that we employ here. The model first takes into account the opinion each respondent expressed at Time 1 (T1): paths B1 (for beta) and B2. As such, it controls for those background factors that explain differences of opinion at T1, as well as any husband/wife similarity already in place at that time. The remaining variables are introduced to help account for the change in respondents' political orientations occurring between Time 1 and Time 2 (T2). For present purposes, the most important of these explanatory variables is the opinion of the spouse as expressed at T2—paths G1 (for gamma) and G2. The other variables in this model, while of less interest to us, help guard against the possibility that the reciprocal influence effects we observe are being driven by other circumstances and experiences producing change. These other variables can be grouped into four separate categories, as follows.

(1) *Shared experiences*. Some between-waves changes in the lives of these respondents occurred to each member of the couple and were shared by virtue of the marital relationship. These would include, for example, the birth of a child or changes in the couple's family income. Such experiences may have political consequences, and those consequences may be different for wives and husbands; but they are shared experiences among married couples nonetheless. If such experiences

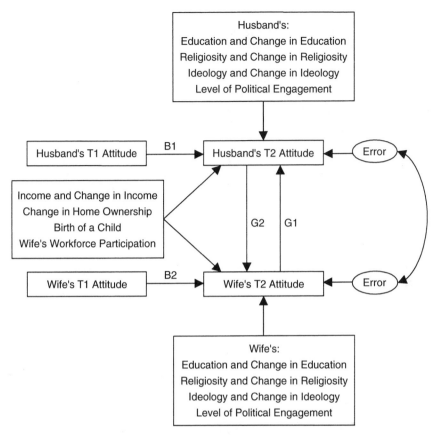

FIGURE 3.1. Two-wave Model of Spousal Influence

do affect each marital partner similarly, we would expect to observe a consonant pattern of change in the political attitudes of both husbands and wives. Rather than reflecting a process of interpersonal influence, however, the growing consonance would be driven by shared experiences that themselves have political consequences. Our model includes a number of such "couple-level" variables in order to help guard against the possibility that our estimates of reciprocal influence will be inflated in this fashion: T1–T2 change in family income, T1–T2 change in homeowner status, and whether the couple had a child between T1 and T2.

(2) *Individual experiences.* Although much of their lives are shared, each partner to the marriage will also undergo unique experiences of direct consequence for his or her political outlook. One partner may go back to school to earn an advanced degree, for example, or become more religiously involved. Though such experiences may directly affect one's own political views, any impact on one's spouse should be indirect, operating through the exchange of information and opinion to which those experiences give rise.[11] In this category of explanatory variables, our model incorporates the respondent's T1–T2 change in educational attainment, T1–T2 change in religiosity, and T1–T2 change in ideological identification.[12]

(3) *Experiences that are both individual and shared.* Some changes experienced by one partner will appreciably alter the circumstances of the couple's shared life, and thus are appropriately classified neither as simply "shared" nor as simply "individual." An exemplar in this respect is the wife's movement into or out of the workforce. When a working wife becomes a homemaker, or vice versa, the couple's daily routines and interactions usually undergo substantial change. These changes may have direct effects on the political orientations of each of the partners, quite apart from any indirect effects that may arise as a result of interpersonal influence. While we might expect changes in one partner's labor force participation to directly affect the political outlook of each marriage partner, we would also expect those effects to be different because of the different set of experiences that this variable summarizes. Our model incorporates changes in the wife's labor force participation,[13] conceiving of this as having direct effects upon the political attitudes of each marital partner.

(4) *Prior characteristics mediating change.* All of the potential change-inducing factors that we have discussed thus far refer to the respondents' changing circumstances or experiences between Time 1 and Time 2. Yet prior states may have lagged effects, or may modify the experiences that come with the passage of time, and thus also be sources of change. High income, for example, may itself engender conservative attitude change over time. Or a person who identifies as conservative at T1 may be more likely than a person who identifies as a liberal at T1 to move in a conservative direction in response to new issues and events. Similarly, arguments based on continued political learning emphasize the key role of political awareness or attentiveness in mediating attitude change in response to external events and elite opinion (McClosky, Zaller, and Chong 1985; Zaller 1992). The most politically aware should be most likely to respond to the dominant political messages of the day, evidencing greater change than those who are less attuned to contemporary political events. In order to reflect these possibilities, our model includes a number of explanatory variables tapping prior (T1) characteristics. Specifically, we include the respondent's T1 educational attainment, T1 income, T1 level of religiosity, and T1 partisan and/or ideological identification. We also include an indicator of the respondent's level of political engagement between T1 and T2.

In sum, the model we employ to assess interpersonal influence in the marital context allows for continuity in political orientations over time, as well as for changes arising either from shared or from individual experiences, experiences that in either case might have gender-specific effects. It explicitly recognizes the possibility that, quite apart from any mutual socialization that might occur, partners to a marriage are subject to many forces promoting change throughout their lifespan. We then place the question of spousal influence within this larger perspective on political continuity and change.[14]

For any given political issue, one of three different patterns of influence might emerge. First, there might be no signs of interpersonal influence, no evidence that married people adjust their views in light of the positions taken by their spouses (G1 and G2 equal zero). This would accord with the view that husband/wife similarity first arises from a process of assortative mating that tends to produce politically like-minded couples. Any similarity in their patterns of change across time is driven not by a process of interpersonal influence but by the changing life circumstances and experiences that they share.

Second, a pattern of mutual influence might emerge, wherein men and women are equally responsive to the opinions expressed by their spouses (G1 and G2 are positive and equal). Such findings would suggest that spouses exert significant influence upon each other through the course of their marriage, quite apart from the similarities or differences that are intact when their marriage begins and quite apart from the other forces that generate continuity and change over time. Accommodation and adjustment are taking place within the marriage, with each partner contributing to the resolution of differences.

Finally, there might be a pattern of dominance by husbands or by wives, of asymmetry in influence (G1 : G2, or G1 < G2). Such findings would again favor the thesis that socialization within the marriage occurs over time. But one partner would be dominant in exerting influence upon the other, accommodation being a relatively one-sided affair. Our findings about perceptions concerning the resolution of disagreements, taken together with conventional wisdom and the scant other research on this subject, suggests that any asymmetry in influence would be to the husband's advantage. Even at the twentieth century's end, we may find husbands exerting more influence upon their wives than vice versa.

We estimated the two-wave model for both the 1973–82 panel pairs and the 1982–97 panel pairs, using full-information maximum likelihood.[15] We also estimated a three-wave version of the model for the 1973–1982–1997 panel pairs. Because the three-wave results are so similar to those obtained from the two two-wave panels, we focus on the two-wave results here. Further, because our interest lies in understanding how influence patterns vary across political attitudes and across time, we report and focus on the findings pertaining to reciprocal influence rather than those for the entire model of change. Table 3.3 summarizes these results. The coefficients indicate the extent to which the respondent's T2 attitude was contingent on his or her spouse's T2 attitude, net of the other explanatory variables in the model.

To illustrate, consider the 1973–1982 findings for party identification. Each party identification variable was coded on a 0–1 scale. Anchoring one end was the strong Democratic position (score 0) and anchoring the other end was the strong Republican position (score 1). The coefficient representing the husband's influence on his wife, .33, indicates the extent of adjustment made by the wife, from her T1 position, in light of a complete discrepancy between that position and the T2 position taken by her husband. Illustratively, if the wife was a strong Democrat at time 1, and her husband was a strong Republican at time 2, she is predicted to have moved .33 units in her husband's direction from Time 1 to Time 2. Another way to think about this is to compare what would happen to our strong Democrat (T1) wife if her husband was a strong Democrat at T2 (which is that her predicted T2 score would be unaffected [.33 × husband score of 0]) with what would happen if her husband was a strong Republican at T2 (which is that her predicted T2 score would increase by .33 [.33 × husband score of 1]). The coefficient representing the wife's influence on the husband has a comparable interpretation, as do the coefficients on the rest of the variables in the table. Each of these other variables were

TABLE 3.3. Husband-wife Interpersonal Influence: Two-wave Panel Analysis

	1982 estimates (1973–1982 panel)		1997 estimates (1982–1997 panel)	
	Husband's influence on wife	Wife's influence on husband	Husband's influence on wife	Wife's influence on husband
Party identification	.33*** (4.92)	.27** (3.30)	.21*** (3.10)	.32*** (4.27)
Vote choice	.40*** (4.16)	.29** (3.54)	.33*** (5.59)	.19*** (3.10)
Ideology	.02 (.17)	.23** (2.00)	.19** (2.34)	.02 (.22)
Race policy	.62*** (3.53)	.09 (.67)	.48*** (4.14)	.31* (2.22)
Gender equality	.57*** (4.02)	−.06 (−.38)	.08 (.63)	.04 (.27)
Business vs. labor	.71*** (4.85)	.43* (1.99)	.76*** (4.10)	−.10 (−.32)
Government job assistance	.06 (.52)	.20 (1.49)	.09 (.76)	.15 (1.61)
Abortion	na	na	.36*** (3.47)	.17* (1.83)
School prayer	.37*** (4.43)	.12 (1.06)	.34*** (3.71)	.49*** (4.41)
Legalization of marijuana	.14 (1.46)	.37** (3.07)	.48*** (4.29)	.48*** (3.29)
Religiosity	.22* (2.07)	.44*** (3.78)	.36*** (4.15)	.41*** (4.41)

Note: Entries are unstandardized regression coefficients with t ratios in parentheses below. See text for further details. The 1973–1982 panel $n = 257$. The 1982–1997 panel $n = 248$.
$*p < .05$, $**p < .01$, $***p < .001$.

scored so that 0 represents the most extreme liberal position available, and 1 represents the most extreme conservative (or religious) position available.[16]

As discussed above, these results bear on two partially separable questions: (1) How much influence do husbands and wives exert on each other? and (2) Is the influence process reciprocal or asymmetric, with either husbands or wives tending to dominate? The short answer to the first question is: a lot! At least one influence coefficient is substantively and statistically significant in nineteen of the twenty-two models estimated (the exception being attitudes about government job assistance in both panel periods and about gender equality in the second panel period). There is some, but not a great deal, of variation across political attitudes. Mutual socialization—with each spouse exerting influence upon the other—is the norm with respect to party identification, vote choice, and religiosity. The influence coefficients are sizeable (in the .20 to .45 range) and statistically significant for each spouse and in each panel period. On all of the other attitude items influence is either slight or one-sided in one or both panel periods. Still, attitudes on issues with a strong moral component—those concerning race and gender, abortion, the legalization of marijuana, and school prayer—show strong traces of spousal influence, as do attitudes concerning business and labor.

In order to help assess differences in the magnitude of influence across time, we averaged the coefficients for husbands and wives found in Table 3.3, which are summarized under the "Average Direct Effects" heading in Table 3.4. For the most part, influence levels are relatively stable across the two panel periods. In two cases, however, influence declines. In one, the case concerning attitudes toward gender equality, the husband is influential in the first panel period, but neither spouse is influential in the second. In the second case, that concerning attitudes toward business and labor, it is the wife's influence in the first period that evaporates by the second. We see no obvious explanation for this pattern.

More intriguing are the cases that show an uptick in influence. These include attitudes toward school prayer and the legalization of marijuana and, to a lesser extent, religiosity. The increases in these cases are even more noticeable when considering the total effects summarized in the last two columns of Table 3.4. Total effect estimates take into account the feedback loops entailed by the reciprocal model. When influence flows increase, and especially when they rise for both partners, mutual reinforcement takes place and total effects can rise quite dramatically. For the issues just named, not only did the average influence flows rise in the second period but they also tended to equalize across the partners and hence to spur the process of mutual reinforcement. Thus, for example, while the direct effects for legalization of marijuana went from an average of .25 (.37 and .12) to an average of .48 (.48 and .48), the total effects went from an average of .26 to an average of .67.

Why would these influence flows increase over time? One likely explanation involves marital duration. The average length of the marriage in the first panel is thirteen years compared with twenty-six years for the second panel.

TABLE 3.4. Estimating Spousal Influence

	Average direct effects[a]		Average total effects[b]	
	1982	1997	1982	1997
Party identification	.30	.27	.33	.28
Vote choice	.35	.26	.39	.28
Ideology	.13	.10	.13	.10
Race policy	.36	.39	.38	.46
Gender equality	.26	.06	.25	.06
Business vs. labor	.57	.33	.82	.30
Government job assistance	.13	.12	.13	.12
Abortion	na	.26	na	.28
School prayer	.25	.41	.26	.53
Legalization of marijuana	.25	.48	.27	.67
Religiosity	.33	.39	.36	.45

[a]Entries are the average of the spousal influence coefficients given in Table 3.3.

[b]Entries are the average of (a) the total effect of the husband's position on the wife's position, and (b) the total effect of the wife's position on the husband's position. These are drawn from the same analyses producing the direct effects, and differ from the direct effects because of the feedback loops involved in the nonrecursive model.

Spouses could become more influential over time for three distinct reasons. First, they could assume more importance simply by default, as the partners enter the more settled period of middle age and are subject to fewer new external influences while continuing to interact as a couple. Related to that, spouses could exert more political influence later in the life of the marriage because they have become personally more important in the lives of their partner. Individuals in marriages of this duration are obviously in them for the long haul. Even though politics are not of paramount concern in most marriages, political compromise may increase in long-lived marriage as a way of maintaining harmony. Lastly, spouses could become more influential because the attitudes they hold are mature and more meaningful than the political views they articulated in young adulthood. As research has shown, attitudinal stability increases substantially between the mid-twenties and mid-thirties (Jennings and Stoker 1999). Consistent cue-giving and more successful influence attempts could be one outcome of those gains in stability.

A second explanation focuses on compositional differences in the couple cohorts. Rather than spouses becoming more important later in the marriage, it could be that spouses assume importance only in marriages destined to *survive*. Conceivably, the lower levels of influence found in the first panel period could be due to weaknesses in the marriages of those couples. Based on the reports of the primary respondents from the 1973–1982 panel pairs who survived into the 1997 wave, one-fifth of those marriages later failed. Some portion of the marriages in the second panel may yet fail, but with an average duration of twenty-six years, the prospects for survival are high. Influence flows in long-lived marriages may exceed those found in short-lived marriages simply because weak partnerships have been weeded out.[17]

Turning to the question of dominance requires focusing attention on the relative size of the husbands' and wives' influence coefficients. To assist in this comparison, we have summarized the coefficient differences in Table 3.5. Several general patterns are evident in these results. Most generally, husbands appear to exert more influence on their wives than vice versa. In the first panel period, for example, asymmetries in influence are evident in six cases, and husbands are more influential in four of them.[18] Men have the influence edge on issues concerning race ($p < .01$), gender ($p < .01$), business versus labor ($p < .10$), and school prayer ($p < .05$). They have a slight edge on party identification and vote choice as well, but the differences are not statistically significant. However, women have the influence edge on religiosity and the legalization of marijuana (each at $p < .10$).

Even so, male dominance is more pronounced in the first panel period than in the second. Of the four attitudes where husbands tend to dominate in the first period, only one—that concerning business versus labor—shows clear husband dominance in the later period. On the other three, the husbands' influence coefficients average .52 in the first period, compared to .05 for the wives, while those averages are .30 and .29 respectively in the second panel period. Hence mutual socialization, with each partner contributing to the resolution of political differences, is more evident in the older marriages than in younger ones. Reciprocal

TABLE 3.5. Relative Influence of Husbands and Wives

	Direct effects	
	1982	1997
Party identification	.06	−.11
	(.57)	(−1.13)
Vote choice	.11	.15*
	(.87)	(1.67)
Ideology	−.21	.17
	(−1.29)	(1.40)
Race policy	.53**	.18
	(2.49)	(1.06)
Gender equality	.63**	.04
	(3.05)	(.24)
Business vs. labor	.32	.86**
	(1.35)	(2.46)
Government job assistance	−.14	−.06
	(−.75)	(−.37)
Abortion	na	.19
		(1.45)
School prayer	.25*	−.15
	(1.88)	(−1.15)
Legalization of marijuana	−.23	.00
	(−1.59)	(.02)
Religiosity	−.22	−.05
	(−1.53)	(−.44)

Note: Entries are the (husband-wife) differences in the spousal influence coefficients given in Table 3.3. A positive score indicates husband dominance, a negative score indicates wife dominance, and 0 indicates parity in influence. *T* ratios for testing whether the difference is statistically significant are given below each coefficient, and significance levels are starred.

*$p < .05$, **$p < .01$.

influence is evident in seven out of eleven cases in the second panel period, by contrast with three of the ten cases in the earlier panel period. Still, husbands in the later panel show signs of being more influential than their wives on vote choice ($p < .05$), ideology ($p < .10$), and abortion ($p < .10$), in addition to business versus labor.

In sum, both mutual socialization and parity in influence become more evident in longer-lasting marriages. Support for this conclusion comes not only from the results based on the dynamic analysis but from the respondents' own portrayals of political conflict and its resolution within their marriages. Yet even in this generation, whose members came of age in the late 1960s and early 1970s, wives go along with their husbands somewhat more than vice versa. Early asymmetry may later turn into balance, but its effects will still be felt. At the same time, it would be wrong to characterize the husband's influence advantage too starkly. As our results reveal, wives have their say as well.[19]

SPOUSAL INFLUENCE, COUPLE HOMOGENEITY, AND THE GENDER GAP

It is now clear that spousal influence is, at least in part, responsible for the increasing couple homogeneity we reported in Table 3.2. Indeed, the highest levels of couple homogeneity are found for party identification, vote choice, and religiosity, precisely where mutual spousal influence is most evident. Interpersonal influence between married partners can produce this kind of similarity as long as it is not overridden by other forces working to push the partners apart. If we think of individuals as less susceptible to outside influences as they age, while remaining vulnerable to their spouses, the levels of similarity we see in Table 3.2 are likely to rise even higher as these couples grow old.

These findings also have great significance for the presence and magnitude of any gender gap in political attitudes or voting behavior. The implication is straightforward: spousal influence will work to reduce or eliminate any gap. We have seen that a gender gap did, in fact, emerge among the married couples we studied (Table 3.1). That development echoes what has transpired more generally in the United States over the past twenty or so years, especially with respect to electoral politics. Assuming our reasoning is correct, we would expect the gender gap to be greatly diminished relative to the gap that would exist were men and women *not* married to each other and *not* exerting influence upon each other. Evidence in support of this counterfactual claim appears in Table 3.6, which depicts the 1997 gender gap in opinion for two sets of respondents: (1) those who have been single across their adult lives thus far, and (2) those who were married to the same per-

TABLE 3.6. The Gender Gap in 1997, by Marital History

	Unmarried, 1973–1997 ($n = 82$)	Married, 1973–1997 ($n = 391$)	Difference
Party identification	.22***	.05*	.17**
Vote choice	.41***	.06	.35***
Ideology	.14**	.03	.11*
Race policy	.25***	.00	.25**
Gender equality	.13*	−.02	.15*
Business vs. labor	.08	−.03	.11
Government job assistance	−.05	.04*	−.09
Abortion	−.08	−.02	−.06
School prayer	−.08	.05	−.12
Legalization of marijuana	−.09	.00	−.09
Religiosity	−.20***	−.10***	−.09

Note: In the first two columns, entries are the average gender difference on the row variable for respondents unmarried across the period (column 1) and those married across the period (column 2). Positive scores indicate that males were more conservative/religious than females, on average. Negative scores indicate that females were relatively more conservative/religious. The third column reports the difference in the gender gap across the unmarried/married groups. Entries and significance tests were drawn from OLS regression analyses using sex, marital status, and the interaction of sex and marital status as predictors of 1997 attitudes.

$*p < .05$, $**p < .01$, $***p < .001$.

son for most of their adult lives, twenty-five years or more.[20] The former group represents our counterfactual world, where women and men developed and changed their attitudes without the operation of spousal influence. In the latter group, by contrast, spousal influence processes have been working for decades. Importantly, both represent the same cohort, identical in age and identical in the larger political environment that characterized their coming of age.[21]

The results are striking. With one exception (government job assistance), a marked gender gap divides the unmarried while almost no gap appears for the married. Among those who remained unmarried across their young adult and middle years, men were substantially more Republican than were women, more conservative ideologically, and more conservative in matters concerning race and gender. The gender gap in voting is most dramatic, where single men were 41 percent more likely to vote Republican than were single women. All of these differences drop to almost nothing in the married comparison group.

Although these results confirm what we would expect to see due to the operation of spousal influence, it is also possible that the varying gender gaps reflect political differences that were in place much earlier in life, or differences in life circumstances—for example, in economic situation—between single and married men and women. To help rule out this possibility, we also estimated panel models that examined the extent to which the gender gap that emerged across the 1973–1997 period varied across these two groups. The 1973–1997 change in each attitude served as the dependent variable. The explanatory variables included a dummy variable for marital history over the period (unmarried versus married), sex, the interaction of sex and marital history, controls for 1973 education and 1973–1997 change in education, 1973 income and 1973–1997 change in income, 1973 religiosity and 1973–1997 change in religiosity (except for the equation using religiosity as a dependent variable), race, and, to control for floor and ceiling effects, the 1973 attitude score. Table 3.7 reports the 1973–1997 change in the gender gap for each attribute, for both unmarried and married groups, as estimated by the regression analyses.

These findings reinforce what Table 3.6 demonstrated. The gender gap that emerged between 1973 and 1997 for party identification, vote choice, ideology, and attitudes toward race and gender was dramatic among those who were unmarried across the period, and sharply attenuated, though not always nonexistent, among the married. Considering party identification, for example, the gender gap grew by .25 among the single group, but only by .07 among the married group.

So far we have argued that the aggregate gender gap is attenuated by the individual- and couple-level processes working to bring husbands and wives together. This leaves gender differences more pronounced among single than among married folk, and smaller overall than they would be were men and women not married to each other. But these micro-level processes have other implications for the character of the divide that separates married and single men and women. Specifically, if spousal influence is reciprocal, then married men and women should express (similar) political views that are in between those expressed by single men and single women. Alternatively, if males dominate the influence

TABLE 3.7. Change in the Gender Gap, 1973–1997, by Marital History

	Unmarried, 1973–1997	Married, 1973–1997	Difference
Party identification	.25***	.07*	.18**
Vote choice	.47***	.14**	.34**
Ideology	.16***	.04*	.12*
Race policy	.28***	−.04	.32***
Gender equality	.22**	.00	.22**
Business vs. labor	.10	.01	.09
Government job assistance	.01	.08**	−.07
Abortion	.04	.05*	−.01
School prayer	.10	.12**	−.02
Legalization of marijuana	−.01	.08*	−.09
Religiosity	−.07	−.04	−.03

Note: In the first two columns, entries are the average 1973–1997 change in the gender gap on the row variable for respondents unmarried across the period (column 1) and those married across the period (column 2). Positive scores indicate that the males were becoming more conservative/religious than females, on average. Negative scores indicate that females were becoming relatively more conservative/religious. The third column reports the difference in the gender gap change across the unmarried/married groups. Entries and significance tests were derived from panel analyses that regressed 1973–1997 changes in each row variable on the 1973 value of the row variable, sex, marital status, the interaction of sex and marital status, income in 1973, 1973–1997 change in income, education in 1973, 1973–1997 change in education, and race. All equations except that for change in religiosity (last row) also included religiosity in 1973 and 1973–1997 change in religiosity as explanatory variables. The sample included respondents either unmarried across the period ($n = 82$) or married across the period ($n = 391$) who also had valid data on all variables in the analysis.

$*p < .05$, $**p < .01$, $***p < .001$.

process, then the difference between single and married males should be small relative to the difference between single and married females. In the face of disagreements, married women would be more likely to move toward their (relatively conservative) husbands than married men would be to move toward their (relatively liberal) wives.

Not surprisingly given the evidence of husband dominance already discussed, the reciprocal model is not supported. Figure 3.2 shows the average score for single and married men and women for each of the five political traits on which the gender gap varies by marital history (party identification, vote choice, ideology, racial policy, and attitudes about gender equality). In each case single and married women vary substantially, while single and married men vary hardly at all. The upshot is that married women look, on average, very much like married men as well as like single men. This is precisely what one would expect to find if asymmetric influence processes are operating within marriage to draw women toward the right-leaning perspectives of men.

When one is working with cohort-specific data like that we have been analyzing, it is always possible that the findings do not generalize to other cohorts or to Americans in general. Yet the aggregate patterns observed in our data mirror closely what is seen in representative samples. To illustrate, Figure 3.3 uses National Election Studies (NES) data to map the gender gap in party identification over time for two groups: those who identify themselves as married (or living

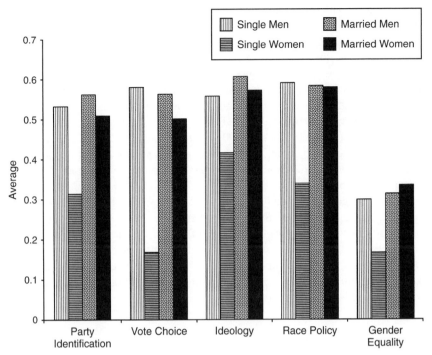

FIGURE 3.2. Political Attitudes in 1997, by Gender and Marital History
Note: The higher the average score, the more conservative the attitude.

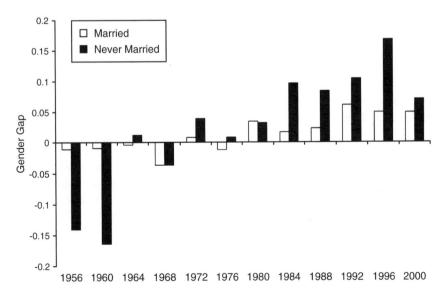

FIGURE 3.3. Gender Gap in Party Identification over Time
Source: American National Election Studies (1956–2000)

with a partner), and those who identify themselves as never married. As before, party identification is coded to range from 0–1; positive gaps indicate that men are more Republican, and negative gaps indicate that women are more Republican.[22] There are two distinct periods in which gender gaps are evident— 1956–1960, when women had a more Republican cast, and 1984–2000, when men had a more Republican cast. More importantly, in each period the gender gap is noticeably larger, and usually statistically significant, among the "never married" than among the married respondents.[23] In addition, it is the single women who end up as distinctive; in the 1980s and 1990s, they are substantially more Democratic than the cluster of single men, married men, and married women (not shown).[24] Thus, an analysis of NES data reinforces the conclusions drawn from the three-wave panel of couples.

In sum, the gender gap that has emerged among married men and women in our data, and in the United States more generally, has been constrained and shaped by ongoing processes of spousal influence. Marriage, with its characteristically strong ties, mutes gender differences that would otherwise be present. By contrast, it is quite conceivable that weak ties (see Levine, this volume) exert substantial influence on single men and women, though pushing them in different directions.

CONCLUSION

Not only does marriage shape the everyday lives of most Americans but it also shapes the way their political attitudes develop and change. Spouses tend toward like-mindedness because of the selection processes that bring them together in the first place. After marriage, mutual socialization also works to produce commonalities in political outlook over time. Because of this process, and in both a relative and an absolute sense, husbands and wives really do begin to look more alike as the marriage ages. Over the past few decades divorces and remarriages and delayed age of first marriages have all worked to shorten the expected duration of marriages. That being so, it is possible that the net influence of this intimate environment may diminish. For now, however, it remains an important interpersonal source of attitudinal change and stability, a unique dyadic network.

Because reciprocal influence between husbands and wives works to erase their political differences, it has important implications for how gender becomes politicized in the electoral arena. Among married men and women, aggregate gender gaps in political preferences surface only when forces working outside the marriage to produce them overwhelm the strong forces operating within marriage to reduce them. While these external forces may be sufficient to produce at least some aggregate gender divisions among the married, as they were within the couples we studied, the marital divisions are likely to be dwarfed by the divisions found between men and women less embedded, so to speak, in marriage. In the society as a whole there will inevitably be divisions within each gender according to marital history.

How these influence processes play out in the aggregate should depend both upon the degree to which husbands and wives are successfully influencing each other and upon the presence or absence of gender asymmetries in influence. When husbands are more influential, opinions in the aggregate should drift one way; whereas when women are more influential, opinions in the aggregate should shift the other way. As shown by an analysis of the class of 1965, men and women do not appear to exert political equal influence within the family. Although both marital partners were influential, husbands nevertheless had the edge. As a result, the political attitudes of the married women we analyzed developed a relatively conservative cast.

In light of the substantial variations in influence patterns that we have seen in these results—variation by issue domain, by gender, and across time—the question of whether influence is taking place must be succeeded by questions about the circumstances that facilitate or inhibit spousal influence, and those under which the husband or the wife come to dominate. Any number of factors might be at work here. They include patently political features such as the levels of political engagement by each partner and the importance of particular issues for them; such marriage-related factors as marital satisfaction, power differentials within the couple, and partner differences in nonpolitical arenas; and such social structure characteristics as class, religion, and race and ethnicity. Our understanding of how couples navigate their way through political waters will be enriched by including these sorts of features in our future investigations.

APPENDIX: QUESTION WORDING AND INDEX CONSTRUCTION

The majority of the measures discussed in this chapter are found in the National Election Studies (NES) series. The exact wordings can readily be located in the codebooks provided by the Inter-University Consortium for Social and Political Research (ICPSR). Here we present abbreviated descriptions except for items not ordinarily found in the NES studies. All variables were ultimately coded to range from 0 to 1, where 0 represented the most liberal/Democratic/secular position and 1 represented the most conservative/Republican/religious position.

Party Identification and Change in Party Identification: The traditional seven-point subjective identification measure was restricted to five points because the spouse questionnaire did not differentiate between "leaning" independents and pure independents. Change in Party Identification was the simple difference score across waves.

Presidential Vote: This was the averaged reported vote for the two presidential elections preceding each wave of interviews. Valid responses on both variables were required. In the 1968 election, Wallace voters were coded with Nixon voters. In the 1980 election, John Anderson voters were coded between Jimmy Carter and Ronald Reagan voters. In the 1992 and 1996 elections, Perot voters were coded in the middle. In the 1972 and 1976 elections, only votes or preferences for the major party nominees were coded as valid. The pairwise correlation for the two components going into each variable, averaged across waves and across genders, was .47 for the three-wave panel pairs, .37 for the 1973–1982 panel pairs, and .51 for the 1982–1997 panel pairs.

Ideology and Change in Ideology: Ideology measured self-location on the traditional seven-point scale, anchored at one end by "extremely liberal" and at the other by "extremely conservative." Change in Ideology was the simple difference score across waves.

Race Policy: This averaged responses to two component variables, School Integration and Aid to Minorities, described below. Each variable was first coded on a 0–1 scale before averaging, and valid responses on both variables were required. The pairwise correlation for the two components going into each variable, averaged across waves and across genders, was .38 for the three-wave panel pairs, .29 for the 1973–1982 panel pairs, and .39 for the 1982–1997 panel pairs.

School Integration: This variable consisted of a forced-choice response to the statement, "Some people say that the government in Washington should see to it that white and black children are allowed to go the same schools. Others claim that this is not the government's business." Respondents were asked which position most closely expressed their own views.

Aid to Blacks: Respondents indicated their own location on a seven-point scale anchored by polar alternatives: "The government in Washington should make every possible effort to improve the social and economic position of blacks and other minority groups," versus "The government should not make any special effort to help minorities because they should help themselves."

Gender Equality: This averaged responses to two component variables, Gender Roles and Women's Influence, described below. Each variable was first coded on a 0–1 scale before averaging, and valid responses on both variables were required. The pairwise correlation for the two components going into each variable, averaged across waves and across genders, was .39 for the three-wave panel pairs, .39 for the 1973–1982 panel pairs, and .40 for the 1982–1997 panel pairs.

Gender Roles: Respondents indicated their own location on a seven-point scale anchored by polar alternatives: "Women should have an equal role with men in running business, industry, and government," versus "Women's place is in the home."

Women's Influence: This consisted of a forced-choice response to a question asking whether women have "too much influence in American life and politics," "just about the right amount of influence," or "not as much influence as they deserve."

Business versus Labor: This measure was built from two component variables, Labor Union Influence and Big Business Influence, described below. At one end (coded 1) are those who feel that labor has too much influence relative to big business; these people had higher scores on the labor component variable than on the big-business component variable. At the other end (coded 0) are those who feel that labor has too little influence relative to big business; these people had lower scores on the labor component variable than on the big-business component variable. Other respondents are coded at the midpoint.

Labor Union Influence: This variable represented a forced-choice response to a question asking whether labor unions have "too much influence in American life and politics," "just about the right amount of influence," or "not as much influence as they deserve." People who selected "too much" were coded 1, while the "right amount" and "not as much as they deserve" categories were coded 0. These categories were collapsed because of the tiny number of respondents selecting the latter option.

Big Business Influence: This variable represented a forced-choice response to a question asking whether big business has "too much influence in American life and politics," "just about the right amount of influence," or "not as much influence as they deserve." People who selected "too much" were coded 1, while the "right amount" and "not as much as they deserve" categories were coded 0. These categories were collapsed because of the tiny number of respondents selecting the latter option.

Government Job Assistance: Respondents indicated their own self-location on a seven-point scale anchored by polar alternatives: "The government in Washington should see to it that every person has a job and a good standard of living" versus "the government should let each person get ahead on his or her own."

Abortion: Forced-choice responses were given to these four alternatives: "By law, abortion should never be permitted"; "The law should permit abortion *only* in the case of rape, incest, or when the woman's life is in danger"; "The law should permit abortion for reasons *other than* rape, incest, or danger to the mother's life, but only after the need for the abortion has been clearly established"; and "By law, a woman should always be able to obtain an abortion as a matter of personal choice."

Legalization of Marijuana: Respondents indicated their own location on a seven-point scale anchored by polar alternatives: "The use of marijuana should be made legal," versus "The penalties for using marijuana should be set higher than they are now."

School Prayer: This variable represented a forced-choice response to the statement, "Some people think it is all right for public schools to start each day with a prayer. Others feel that religion does not belong in the schools but should be taken care of by the family and church." Respondents were asked which position most closely expressed their own views.

Religiosity and Change in Religiosity: This was based on two component variables, Bible Beliefs and Frequency of Church Attendance, described below. Each variable was first coded on a 0–1 scale before averaging, and valid responses on both variables were required. The pairwise correlation for the two components going into each variable, averaged across waves and across genders, was .38 for the three-wave panel pairs, .38 for the 1973–1982 panel pairs, and .38 for the 1982–1997 panel pairs. Change in Religiosity was the simple difference score across waves.

   Bible Beliefs: This consisted of a forced-choice response to four possible options: "The Bible is God's word and all it says is true"; "The Bible was written by men inspired by God, but it contains some human errors"; "The Bible is a good book because it was written by wise men, but God had nothing to do with it"; and "The Bible was written by men who lived so long ago that it is worth very little today."

   Frequency of Church Attendance: Respondents had five choices in answering, "How often do you go to [church/synagogue]? Do you go every week, almost every week, once or twice a month, a few times a year, or never?"

Education Level and Change in Education: Education level was coded into a three-point scale, distinguishing those with a high school degree only, those with some college education, and those with a college degree. Change in Education was the simple difference score across waves.

Political Engagement: This variable consisted of the average number of "yes" responses to six questions about political participation, including: working for a party, issue, or candidate; attempting to persuade others during election campaigns; attending meetings, rallies, or dinners; displaying campaign buttons or stickers; giving money for campaigns; and voting in the most recent presidential election. Although it is well known that political-information questions yield a better measure of political awareness than do items involving interest and activism such as these (Zaller 1992), we were not able to gauge political-information levels for the spouses due to the self-administered questionnaire mode of interview.

Income and Change in Income: At each wave, Income was coded into twenty or so categories. The codes varied across waves, as inflation changed Americans' income levels. The Change in Income variable was the simple difference between income variables at each wave, each first recoded on a 0–1 interval. This measure captures relative, but not absolute, income change.

Change in Home Ownership: At each wave, we recorded whether the primary respondent owned his or her own home. Change in Home Ownership is the simple difference score across waves.

Wife's Work Status and Change in Work Status: The wife's labor-force status was represented with three dummy variables: worked outside the home at both waves, moved into the workforce between waves, or moved out of the workforce between waves. Nonworker at both waves represented the baseline category.

Birth of a Child: At each wave we ascertained whether the couple had had a child since the previous wave. In 1982 most of those saying yes had their first child during the 1973–1982 period. In 1997 most of those saying yes were expanding their family. Each variable was coded in dummy-variable fashion.

ALAN S. ZUCKERMAN, JENNIFER FITZGERALD, AND
JOSIP DASOVIĆ

4 Do Couples Support the Same Political Parties? Sometimes

Evidence from British and German Household Panel Surveys

COUPLES SOMETIMES SUPPORT the same political party. How frequently? They do so less than half the time, during a ten to fifteen year period in the two countries analyzed here. How frequently do the partners support opposing parties? Hardly ever. The political preferences of persons who live together vary in systematic ways. These variations reflect two primary factors: hardly anyone offers consistent responses over time, and persons who reside in the same household influence each other. In this chapter, we account for the occasions when partners prefer the same political party and we specify how the partners influence each other. As we do this, we detail the relationships among elements of immediate social contexts and networks and partisanship.

Families stand as the primary social units and households as the first and most recurrent location for social interactions. Here questions about the political dimensions of national societies enter the personal space of each citizen (see, for example, Glaser 1959–60; Hays 1992; March 1953–54; Stoker and Jennings 1995; Verba, Schlozman, and Burns in this volume; and Zuckerman and Kotler-Berkowitz 1998). Indeed, there is good reason to maintain that households are the primary locus of political discussions. In 1987 more than 75 percent of all Britons report that the person with whom they most frequently discuss politics is a family member who lives in their household; 66 percent of the British single out their spouse or live-in partner as that person; 30 percent engage in political discussion with no one but family members, and fewer than 5 percent do not include a family member among the two persons with whom they most frequently discuss politics (Zuckerman, Kotler-Berkowitz, and Swaine 1998). In households, too, groans, smiles, grimaces, shouts, and poker faces also convey political preferences. As persons who live together exchange ideas and opinions, they state, test, reinforce, and reformulate their political preferences.

This analysis builds on our study of the dynamics of partisanship for individuals (Zuckerman, Dasović, Fitzgerald, and Brynin 2002; Zuckerman, Fitzgerald, and Dasović 2003 analyzes cohabiting parents and children). In Britain and Germany, we find, most everyone is negatively disposed toward one or the other of the major parties while supporting its main rival at varying rates. The year-to-year consistency with which a person selects a party varies according to specific social contexts—namely, social class and religion—and level of political interest. Relatively few people behave as if their preferences derive from a psychological attachment to a political party. Even fewer seem to view the parties as alternative choices in a defined political set. We also locate strong evidence that parents influence the party preferences of their children. These findings provide the baseline for the analysis of the dynamics of partisanship between spouses and others who live together.

Our study of couples reports the analysis of ten years of annual choices in Britain (1991–2000) as found in the British Household Panel Survey (BHPS) and fourteen survey waves in Germany (1985–98, taken from the German Socioeconomic Panel Study, GSOEP). In both countries, household partners are much more likely than two randomly chosen persons to share partisanship, but they do not move in lockstep. Instead, British and German husbands and wives stay near each other, remaining on the same side of the national political divide: usually picking the same party, jointly preferring none of the parties, or moving between one or the other of the major parties and no partisan preference. While couples are not single units, they choose singular paths; almost all couples move along routes that no other set of partners follows, even as none display the patterns of partisanship that characterize the national electorates taken as an aggregated whole. Members of households chart their own political paths while each of them stays away from one of the major political options.

Household partners influence each other's partisan choices. Their political similarity derives in part from their interactions over time. Political preferences do not form a component of marital homophily—"like to like," and "birds of a feather flock together" (to recall the passages from Aristotle cited in this volume's Preface)—the tendency for similar persons to marry each other. Instead, the greater the number of years that members of a household are together, the more likely they are to share partisanship. Three factors influence the rate at which couples share partisanship: (1) variations in the level of political interest—a personal characteristic; (2) generalized social contexts such as social class and religious locations; and (3) immediate social contexts, including the number of years that they have been a couple and the party preferences of their mates. Combining these variables allows us to predict with statistical certainty when people who live together will support the same political party and when they will not. As our analysis proceeds, it demonstrates that partisanship responds strongly to people's immediate social circumstances.

BHPS and GSOEP as Sources for the Analysis of Party Support in Households

The two data sets provide information for a fine-grained analysis of partisanship in British and German households.[1] Both survey large numbers of persons who live together during all the years of the surveys. In Britain 1,428 couples respond each year between 1991 and 2000, and 1,033 German pairs[2] answer questions in each year between 1985 and 1998.[3] Both sets offer representative samples of couples in each country. The BHPS and GSOEP provide an extensive and detailed array of data for the exploration of the dynamics of partisanship between husbands and wives and other domestic partners.

The surveys are especially valuable sources to study the processes of partisanship. No other panel survey encompasses so many years, and all others contain smaller samples. (See Schickler and Green 1997 for a review of nine relevant examples.) Because BHPS and GSOEP regularly tap party choices throughout and between electoral cycles, political campaigns do not much influence the responses. These large-scale panel surveys facilitate the study of the micro dynamics of partisan support, which are invisible in long-term macro analyses.

The measures of partisanship display internal validity. Each offers a multidimensional assessment of the concept.

- Here are the BHPS questions: "Generally speaking do you think of yourself as a supporter of any one political party?" If the answer is "no," the survey then asks, "Do you think of yourself as a little closer to one political party than to the others?" Those who answer "yes" to either question are then asked, "Which one?" and they volunteer the party's name. These persons are defined as supporting a party.
- The English-language translation of the GSOEP question reads, "Many people in the Federal Republic of West Germany [Germany, after 1990] are inclined to a certain political party, although from time to time they vote for another political party. What about you: Are you inclined—generally speaking—to a particular party?" Those who respond "yes"—party supporters—are then asked, "Which one?" and are shown a card that lists all parties with seats in the Bundestag with a request to point to their preference.[4]

Note the value of these measures. The surveys include each question in each wave. Because the parties are not named until the respondent affirms a partisan preference, they avoid problems of instrumentation that are associated with the traditional measure.[5] Both also ask the respondents to describe their support, without prejudging the issue of psychological attachment. As with other questions in BHPS and GSOEP, the political questions offer the appropriate "country specific" measures. These are reliable measures of partisan support.

The data contain evidence for various theoretical perspectives on party support: information about age, social class (measures of occupation, education, and subjective identification), religion (identification and attendance at services), economic perceptions and concerns, membership and activity in trade unions. Both data sets also include a measure that describes levels of political interest, general political values in both countries, and policy preferences. Potential problems of endogeneity keep us from relating the dynamics of party preferences to patterns of change in policy goals and political values.

Inasmuch as the two surveys provide information on many of the same phenomena, they enable us to offer parallel analyses of partisanship in the two nations. At the same time, the very different histories of democratic rule in Britain and Germany offer contrasting loci for the study of partisanship in established democracies. Furthermore, during the years of the surveys, political power in Britain moved from the Conservatives (victors in 1992) to Labour (which returned to power in 1997). In Germany the Christian Democratic Union/Christian Social Union (CDU/CSU) controlled the national government for all but the last year of the panel survey, when the Social Democratic Party (SPD) rose to the top. Also, German reunification occurred in 1990, allowing the analysis to examine the effects of this transformation on partisan preferences. BHPS and GSOEP provide an exceptionally useful set of information for a paired comparison of Britain and Germany.

HOW FREQUENTLY DO COUPLES SUPPORT THE
SAME POLITICAL PARTY?

What is the precise level of agreement on the choice of a party over time? BHPS surveys 1,428 couples in each and all of the ten years, providing 14,280 couple-opportunities with regard to partisan preferences. The partners pick the same party 43 percent of the time. In Germany, there are 14,462 couple opportunities (1,033 couples over fourteen waves), and the partners select the same party in 42 percent of these chances.[6] Slightly fewer than half the couples agree on the same major party during the years of the panel surveys. The analytical task, to which we return in the next section, is to account for the party choices and the number of times that choice is made during the years of the surveys.

Consider, as well, the rate by which couples find themselves on different sides of national politics. In Britain one partner reports supporting the Conservatives while the other favors Labour on just 4 percent of the opportunities. In Germany the rate is 3 percent for couples supporting both the CDU/CSU and the Social Democrats. In each country, 10 percent of the pairs have one member who picks both of the major parties, at different times. In sum, hardly anyone who ever chooses one of the major parties lives with someone who ever supports the other. Rather, each partner moves between picking the same major party or picking no party; very few are enticed to move across to the other major party. Put differently, household partners typically share an aversion to one of the major parties and a variable preference for the other, but they almost never report clashing party preferences. In this respect we find, and will show repeatedly, that there are no substantive distinctions between the two countries, notwithstanding their very different political histories.

Figures 4.1 and 4.2 focus on the selection of each of the major parties, summarizing the choices made by the British and German couples during the years of the survey. The British data show that the responses for the Tories and Labour are remarkably similar; it is barely possible to perceive the patterns of two distinct lines. To elaborate: 65 percent of the households are characterized by both partners never jointly supporting the Conservatives, and in 60 percent both never support Labour at any one point in time. Figure 4.2 displays very similar lines for Germany. Here too, couples jointly eschew one of the dominant parties and vary their joint support for the other. Note that among those partners who ever pick a party, they are equally likely to come back to it an inconsistent number of times—that is, one, two, three, four, or any number of years in the surveys.

"Sometimes" is also the appropriate answer to the question, "Do couples claim the same class or religious identity?" In Britain questions about each of these items appear three times: in 1991, 1996, and 1999 for social class, and in 1991, 1997, and 2000 for religion. 57 percent of the couples in the sample choose the same social class identification every time, and 40 percent pick the same religion. This compares to 41 percent who jointly name the same major party during those three years. GSOEP asks about religious identification in 1990 and 1997, and never about class. What portion of our sample jointly picks the same religion in both of those two years? The answer is 68 percent, more than those who share support for the same party in those two years (43 percent). Couples vary in the extent to which they share social-class and religious identification as well as partisanship.

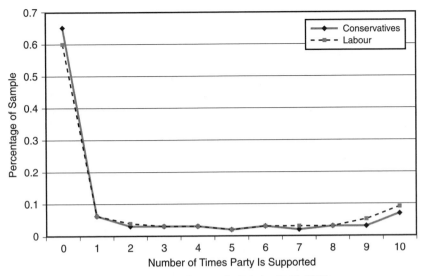

FIGURE 4.1. Frequency of Joint Party Support in Britain, 1991–2000

Couples are about as likely as sets of persons defined by more generalized social criteria to support the same political party over time. Here we examine person-opportunities to pick a party in 1991, 1996, and 2000.[7] As we have seen, couples support the same major party slightly more than 40 percent of the time. The same portion of those persons who report a middle-class identification in those three years choose the appropriate political party, the Tories, 42 percent of the opportunities. The rate of Labour partisanship among those who persistently claim working-class identification is 48 percent. Continued religious identification shows similar patterns: Persistent Anglicans and persistent Catholics share partisanship

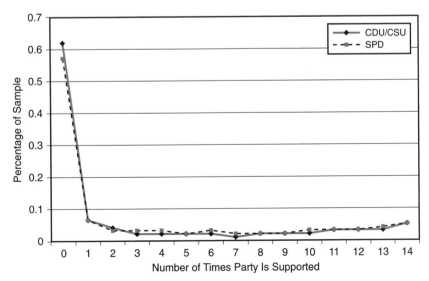

FIGURE 4.2. Frequency of Joint Party Support in Germany, 1985–1998

at rates of 38 percent and 48 percent for the respective political parties. Very few persons claim to be union members during all ten years of the BHPS survey, and so we examine the rate of jointly picking Labour among those who are members more than six times. Here, the rate is 47 percent. Again, the German patterns are very similar. Those who report that they are Catholics in both years claim a Christian Democratic a partisanship rate of 36 percent, and those who are always Protestants select the Social Democrats 31 percent of the time. Union members in Germany support the SPD 53 percent of the opportunities. These findings indicate that with regard to partisanship, living with someone is at least as important as sharing the same social class or religious identifications with another set of persons.

Further examination of the data also shows that at each point in time, less than half the couples jointly pick the same major party. Because they almost never support the opposing major parties, there is a relatively high level of *negative* agreement in the households. Table 4.1 displays the results for both countries. Again and again, the partners almost never pick both of the different major parties; most of the time they select the same party, or one announces a preference for one of the major parties and the other for no party. The Intra-Class Correlation (ICC) corrects for the particular and general distributions of the results and is an alternative

TABLE 4.1. Partisan Agreement between Household Partners

Year	% agree		% disagree	
	Major party	No party	Major/no party	Major parties
		BRITAIN		
1991	42.4	11.2	23.1	4.6
1992	49.4	9.1	19.9	4.1
1993	44.4	11.6	18.9	3.8
1994	42.2	13.5	22.7	3.6
1995	45.3	7.8	22.4	3.2
1996	42.8	12.4	23.5	4.6
1997	47.7	10.2	21.6	3.9
1998	41.6	13.0	25.0	3.9
1999	43.0	12.8	23.2	3.7
2000	39.9	17.0	23.9	3.4
		GERMANY		
1985	42.3	22.6	21.2	3.8
1986	45.0	21.2	20.1	3.7
1987	49.2	19.7	14.9	3.5
1988	47.1	20.5	18.5	3.7
1989	44.1	22.6	18.2	3.7
1990	48.8	19.3	18.0	3.6
1991	47.2	20.8	18.4	2.4
1992	38.9	26.3	21.4	2.9
1993	33.2	33.4	20.1	1.6
1994	37.5	29.2	21.2	2.3
1995	41.0	24.4	21.4	2.8
1996	38.2	28.1	21.6	2.7
1997	37.5	29.7	21.9	2.7
1998	38.4	28.5	21.2	3.0

Note: For Britain, $N = 1,428$ couples; for Germany, $N = 1,033$ couples.

TABLE 4.2. Partisan Agreement between Household Partners (Intra-Class Correlations)

Year	ICC	Year	ICC	Year	ICC	Year	ICC
				BRITAIN			
1991	0.75	1994	0.78	1997	0.79	1999	0.77
1992	0.80	1995	0.80	1998	0.75	2000	0.77
1993	0.80	1996	0.75				
				GERMANY			
1985	0.79	1989	0.81	1993	0.80	1996	0.80
1986	0.81	1990	0.83	1994	0.81	1997	0.80
1987	0.84	1991	0.85	1995	0.81	1998	0.80
1988	0.82	1992	0.79				

Note: For Britain, $N = 1,428$ couples; for Germany, $N = 1,033$ couples.

measure of association for couples. (See Stoker and Jennings in this volume and the references cited there; Robinson 1957 is the classic source.) Table 4.2 displays the very high ICC scores for both countries for each of the survey years, offering results very similar to those obtained by Stoker and Jennings for the United States, in this volume. Because our measures do not use interval scales, the scores suggest but do not precisely detail the level of agreement.[8] The summary results presented in Table 4.2 are best understood as highlighting the very strong tendency of household partners to avoid one side or the other of the national political divide.

Couples select unique paths through the political options open to them. Displaying the responses in a columnar report enables us to observe their selections during the years of the panel surveys.[9] How many unique trails can be observed? In Britain there are 1,100 routes, indicating 1.3 couples per path. In Germany there are 879 trails, 1.2 couples per trail. In both cases, eliminating those sets in which both partners always offer the same responses (almost always uniform support for one of the parties) reduces the number of paths to barely more than one per couple (1.08 in Britain and 1.06 in Germany). As is true for individuals, no couple moves on a track that mimics the relative strength of the parties over time aggregated to the level of each nation. Just as important, and notwithstanding the large-scale issues that characterize national politics, each pair responds to them in ways that distinguish it from all the others. In this regard at least, each couple is its own political universe.

Persons who live together usually jointly support the same party or split between one of the major parties and no partisan preference. Partisan agreement within households is a variable, and so the analysis seeks to account for partisan choice and the frequency of that selection over time.

What accounts for the variation? The Michigan school's focus on partisan identification offers the analytical point of departure. In this perspective, partisan agreement between household partners derives from the presence of shared individual-level factors, such as religion or class, or policy and issue preferences.[10] Most studies of partisanship in Britain and Germany focus on the relative importance of personal characteristics and generalized social contexts, especially social class and religion. (For a very useful collection of essays see Evans 1999.) Alternatively, studies drawing on the literature of social networks would expect increasing levels of agreement as the partners interact with and rely upon each other on a host of other issues.[11] Studies of conversations are the most common explorations of the effects of immediate social contexts on political preferences. (In addition to the studies in this volume, see Conover, Searing, and Crewe 2002; Huckfeldt and Sprague 1995; Pattie and Johnston 1999, 2000, 2001; Zuckerman and Kotler-Berkowitz 1998; Zuckerman, Kotler-Berkowitz, and Swaine 1998; and Zuckerman, Valentino, and Zuckerman 1994.) The literature on marital homophily specifies the networks-based approach. (For classic sources, see Katz and Lazarsfeld 1955 and Merton 1957.) The general principle of "like to like" expects couples to exhibit relatively high levels of partisan agreement at the start of their marriage and for those levels to increase over time. Our analysis shows that interactions within households, as measured by years married, influence the rate of agreement between the partners. Indeed, newlyweds are consistently less likely to agree on partisan choice than are older couples. We will also demonstrate that marital partners have a very strong effect on each other's political preferences, even after controlling for other variables that affect partisan choices.

LIVING TOGETHER AND PARTISAN AGREEMENT

This portion of the analysis unfolds in two steps. First, we contrast the political choices of newlyweds with other couples. Then we specify a model that combines the number of years that a couple has been together with variables that we know from our previous analysis to influence the dynamics of partisan consistency. Both sections show that the longer partners live together, the higher is the level of partisan consistency in a household.

Evidence from both the BHPS and GSOEP tells the same story about the partisanship of newlyweds: they are less likely than other couples to pick the same political party in any one year. We define a couple as newlywed when they have been married or lived together for no more than one year. Six percent of the British couples who respond in all waves of the survey ($n = 91$) and 7 percent of the German couples ($n = 73$) fit this category. The analysis examines the rate by which the partners in the two types of couples both support one of the major political parties in each year of the panels' waves. In Britain young couples are usually less likely to support the same major party, and in Germany they are always less likely to do so. Table 4.3 displays the results for each country. It contains a difference measure, in which the percentage of newlyweds who support the same party is subtracted from the percentage of all other couples who share a party choice. Table 4.3 also presents two measures of statistical association for ordinal measures (gamma and tau-b) and the level of statistical significance for each year in each country. Note this is not at all surprising because newlyweds are usually young and young persons are most likely to claim to support no party. Newlyweds are less likely than other couples to pick the same political party.

We further explore the general theme of marital homophily with regard to class identification in Britain and religion in both countries. Here we do not find the same results in both countries. New British couples are no less likely to share religious and class identifications than older couples. Indeed in the final wave of the survey, they are more likely to identify with the same religion. In Germany newlyweds are considerably less likely than older couples to claim the same religious

TABLE 4.3. Partisan Agreement: Newlyweds and Other Couples Compared

Year	Difference score	Gamma	Tau-*b*
	BRITAIN		
1991	8.9	−0.19	−0.04*
1992	9.3	−0.19	−0.05*
1993	13.3	−0.28	−0.07**
1994	2.8	−0.06	−0.01
1995	6.2	−0.13	−0.03
1996	8.1	−0.17	−0.04
1997	3.9	−0.18	−0.02
1998	9.3	−0.20	−0.05*
1999	3.6	−0.07	−0.02
2000	15.6	−0.34	−0.08**
	GERMANY		
1985	27.8	−0.60	−0.14***
1986	20.4	−0.42	−0.11**
1987	11.6	−0.23	−0.06*
1988	9.4	−0.19	−0.05
1989	13.6	−0.28	−0.07**
1990	15.7	−0.31	−0.08**
1991	18.4	−0.37	−0.09**
1992	13.9	−0.31	−0.07**
1993	16.6	−0.41	−0.09**
1994	18.2	−0.42	−0.10**
1995	70.7	−0.28	−0.07**
1996	19.0	−0.43	−0.10**
1997	4.9	−0.11	−0.03
1998	10.4	−0.23	−0.05*

Note: For Britain, N = 91 couples; for Germany, N = 73 newlywed couples.
*.051 $< p <$ .10, **.00 $< p <$.05, ***p = .000.

identification. In Britain class and religious identifications, but not partisanship, are associated with the initial decision to form a couple. In Germany neither religion nor political preference is associated with initial bonding. Again, we find no evidence to support the claim that "like marries like" on these dimensions.

Furthermore, multivariate regression analyses provide strong evidence that the more years a couple stays together the higher is the rate by which they support the same political party. Because we seek to account for the joint selection of a major party during the years covered by our surveys, we examine two dependent variables in each of our models: whether the partners ever jointly pick the party and the number of times they do so over the length of each panel. Note the structure of these variables: they are all non-negative integers (where possible values range from zero to ten in Britain and zero to fourteen in Germany). They are not continuous variables because they cannot take any real value from negative infinity to positive infinity. As a result, we use count models rather than the standard OLS regression analysis.

The Poisson model is generally considered to be the standard for analyzing count data. This model, however, imposes the restrictive assumption of equality between the mean and variance of the dependent variable. This assumption frequently does not apply to real-world social processes, and, indeed, it does not hold for our data, which are over-dispersed (i.e., the variance is greater than the mean). Therefore, we move beyond the simple Poisson model to a count model that incorporates a dispersion parameter. The negative binomial model is not only a simple generalization of the Poisson model; unlike the Poisson model, it incorporates and allows for over-dispersion of the dependent variable.

There is a final substantive consideration with respect to selection of the appropriate statistical model, which requires us to move beyond the negative binomial model. Recall that most couples never jointly choose one or the other of the dominant parties. In fact, for each of our analyses we find that there are more "zero" values in the distribution of the dependent variable than would be expected given the distribution of the remaining (i.e., nonzero) counts (see Figures 4.1 and 4.2.). We need, therefore, to account for this "excess of zeros" in the distribution of the dependent variable.

An appropriate statistical model, given the considerations listed above, is the zero-inflated negative binomial (ZINB; see Winkelmann 2000). This formulation has the additional advantage of being able to explain the phenomena of interest. Recall that our descriptive analysis implies the operation of two processes: (1) the decision to support jointly (or not) one of the major political parties, and (2) decisions to support together a party over many points in time. This is a two-step decision-making process, each step of which could have different causes. Because ZINB explicitly models each of these separate steps, it is a better choice than alternatives (Winkelmann 2000). The statistical program Stata (version 7) allows us to perform ZINB analyses and provides separate parameter estimates for both of these processes (labeled the "inflated" and "count" portions of the regression analysis respectively in Tables 4.4A and 4.4B). ZINB offers the appropriate statistical model.

The analysis determines the significance of each of the hypothesized explanatory variables on each of the two parts of the model: (1) the "inflated" portion (which is modeled as the likelihood of an individual remaining at zero), and (2) the "count" portion (which determines the number of times a couple has chosen a party over the years, given that it has determined to support it). We perform four separate analyses: for the Conservatives and Labour in Britain, and CDU/CSU and Social Democrats in Germany. Using the parameter estimates, we apply post-estimation techniques to predict the number of times a couple would support a particular political party given the chosen values of the predictor variables. ZINB, therefore, offers a powerful examination of the absolute and relative ability of critical variables to predict the rate of party support.

In our study of partisanship at the individual level, several factors help to predict the frequency and consistency of support for each of the major political parties: level of political interest; social class, as measured by occupation, education, union membership, and, in Britain, class identification; and religious identification (Zuckerman, Dasović, Fitzgerald, and Brynin 2002). We employ these results as the analytical baseline. The predictor variables are the total level of political interest the partners display during the years of the survey, the number of times that each claims a union membership, and the appropriate social class (in Britain) and religious identification.[12] We use measures of middle class or no union membership and Church of England/Roman Catholic identification in order to predict support for the Conservatives/Christian Democrats and measures of working-class identification and union membership as well as Catholic identification for Labour and union membership and Protestant identification for the Social Democrats. To this list of variables we add the number of years married so as to show the additional impact of this variable on the rate of shared partisanship.

The results are displayed in four zero-inflated negative binomial count models (Table 4.4), each with an inflate portion and a count portion, with attendant graphs showing the attendant probability statements. The results are remarkably consistent for each party in each country and across the two countries. The measures of personal political interest and class and religion again show that they influence party choice. The inflate portion of the table details which variables move a couple ever to select one of the parties at the same time. Here, negative signs indicate that the couple does *not* remain zero—that is, that there is a positive effect. The more frequently that each partner claims a specified social class or religious identification, the more likely they are to choose one of the parties. Here the findings are as would be expected from the literature on the relationship between social and political divisions in Britain and Germany. In Britain, middle class and Church of England identifications are linked with the Conservative Party, and working-class and Catholic identification point to the Labour Party. In Germany, not being a member of a trade union and a Catholic identification are associated with a preference for the CDU/CSU, and membership in a trade union and a Protestant identification implies a Social Democratic choice. The count portion of the table shows the variable's effect on the number of times the party is chosen. Here measures of social class and religious identification retain the expected associations with the dependent variables. As we found earlier, variations in political interest by the two partners influence the number of times they jointly support a party: The greater each partner's interest in politics, the more times they jointly offer the same partisan choice. Note here that the number of years that a couple is married or lives together also influences their level of persistent partisan support, but not the party chosen. With regard to three of the parties, the models display a strong and powerful effect in the length of time that the couple has been together on the rate of partisan agreement; the exception is support for the SPD in Germany. As Stoker and Jennings show for the United States (in this volume), the longer that a couple lives together, the higher is the rate by which they prefer the same political party.

Probability statements permit a direct interpretation of these results, and we present them as graphs in Figures 4.3 and 4.4. In order to display the effects of living together in their most striking form, we set the impact of the variables that measure social class, religion, and political interest to their highest levels. Then we include the measure of years of marriage at its minimal level—that is, among newlyweds—and follow that with the same variable at its maximal level. These are virtual couples, in that no couples are characterized by maximum scores on the measures of class, religion, and political interest and maximum or minimum years married. Each figure also displays a mean level of agreement for the population of couples in the sample. The figures display the analytical impact on partisan agreement, as they are drawn from the results shown in Table 4.4.

TABLE 4.4. Multivariate Regression Analyses of Joint Party Support (Zero-Inflated Negative Binomial Model)

Predictor variable	Inflate model		Count model			Inflate model		Count model		
	Coeff.	z-score	Coeff.	z-score	Min→max	Coeff.	z-score	Coeff.	z-score	Min→max
A. Britain (1991–2000)	Conservatives					Labour				
Years married (in 1991)	−0.001	−0.21	0.006	2.62**	0.76	−0.009	−2.01**	0.008	3.68***	1.8
Total political interest household	−0.004	−0.40	0.024	4.07***	1.51	−0.049	−4.49***	0.028	5.94***	4.1
Total middle class household	−0.252	−8.31***	0.053	3.55***	2.36					
Total working class household						−0.280	−9.46***	0.055	4.17***	2.9
Total Church of England household	−0.146	−5.26***	0.048	3.44**	1.56					
Total Roman Catholic household						−0.142	−3.27**	−0	−0.26	1.0
Total trade union household	0.074	4.42***	−0.017	−1.94*	−1.53	−0.086	−5.56***	0.011	2.00**	2.7
B. Germany	CDU/CSU					SPD				
Years married (in 1985)	−0.015	−2.41**	0.012	3.01**	2.96	−0.056	−0.90	0.005	1.48	1.24
Total political interest household	−0.007	−1.33	0.021	5.72***	6.53	−0.010	−1.91*	0.011	4.08***	4.59
Total Catholic household	−0.270	−6.53***	0.071	3.02**	2.28					
Total Protestant household						−0.207	−4.95***	0.022	1.00	1.63
Total trade union household	0.244	6.00***	−0.028	−1.07	−2.44	−0.298	−7.71***	0.034	1.99**	4.88

Note: For Britain, $N = 1,363$ couples; for Germany, $N = 994$ couples.
*.051 < p < .10, **.00 < p < .05, ***p = .000.

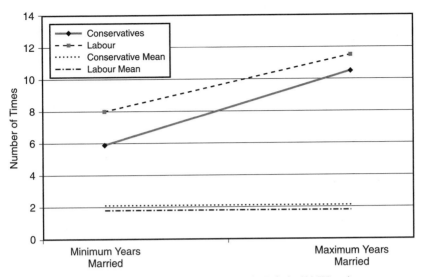

FIGURE 4.3. Predicted Count of Joint Party Support in Britain (10 Waves)

Both figures show that even for couples whose partners display maximum levels of the appropriate mix of social class, religious, and political interest characteristics, living together directly affects the frequency by which they both choose the same party. At maximum levels on the first set of variables, many years of marriage make the recurrent choice of the same party a virtual certainty. Conversely, among newlyweds the level of joint partisanship drops below the level predicted by the social and political measures alone. This result meshes with Huckfeldt, Johnson, and Sprague's hypothesis (see their chapter in this volume) that political agreement between members of a

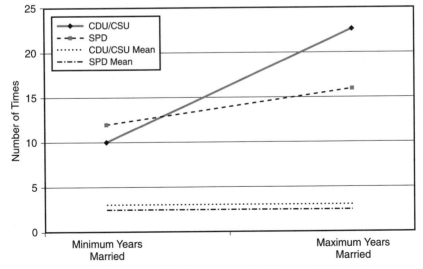

FIGURE 4.4. Predicted Count of Joint Party Support in Germany (14 Waves)

dyad rests on the extent to which other members of their relevant social networks share the same political views (i.e., agreement is autoregressive). It is important, however, not to exaggerate the impact of living together on the probability that couples will jointly support the same political party. It takes more than twenty years of marriage in Britain (in 1991) and more than nineteen years in Germany (as of 1985) for the couple to exceed the sample mean. Another decade needs to pass for both of them to pick the same party all the time, holding all the other variables at the sample means. Ever so slowly, but inevitably, couples become more politically homogeneous.

POLITICAL INFLUENCE BETWEEN HOUSEHOLD PARTNERS

Our analysis of the BHPS and GSOEP data also provides direct evidence that household members influence each other's party preferences. Each serves as a pole of attraction, keeping the partner away from one side of the national political divide. While this may not be the source of the individual's proclivity not to move between the major parties, it certainly reinforces it. The immediate social circumstance of the household combines with each person's level of political interest and his or her union membership, social class, and religious identification to account for partisan choices in any one year.

This portion of the research displays the results of models that seek to explain the partisan choice of each partner in a single year. Here the dependent variable is the selection of one of the major parties in a particular year. Again we use our previous work as the analytic baseline. Persons at the maximum levels of political interest joined with the appropriate social class and religious identifications have a .5 probability of choosing each party, double the mean (Zuckerman, Dasović, Fitzgerald and Brynin 2002). We now add the partisan characteristics of the respondent's partner as an additional predictor variable of partisan choice. Because we expect each member of the couple to influence the other, we may not use the partner's partisanship at T in order to predict the respondent's choice in that year. And so we use the partner's partisanship in the previous year, T-1, as the predictor, thereby obviating problems of endogeneity.[13]

The models are logistic regressions for each partner's choice for each year in which there is appropriate information on political interest, union membership, social class, and/or religious identification (though where necessary we use a measure of a predictor variable from the previous year). We also include information on the partner's partisanship at t_{-1}. As a result, we specify models for three years for each party with two equations for the different characterizations of the other half of the couple, twelve for each country, and twenty-four all told. Because the results hardly differ across the analyses, Tables 4.5 and 4.6 present four models for each country for the first year for which there is appropriate data.[14] Here we display the partisan choice of the women and men in the households for each of the two major parties in each country.

The results sustain the basic argument: political interest, the appropriate social class, and religious contexts and identifications, as well as the partisanship of the significant other, all have substantively and statistically significant relationships with party choice in each year. An examination of the z-scores shows that partisanship of the respondent's partner has the strongest impact on the party selected. Indeed, this variable has a greater influence on the dependent variables than do the

TABLE 4.5. Effects of Partner's Party Support on Individual Party Choice, Britain (Logit Analyses)

Predictor variable	Wives		Husbands	
	Coeff.	z-score	Coeff.	z-score
BRITAIN: CONSERVATIVE SUPPORT, 1992				
Maximum political interest	0.498	5.27***	0.143	1.63
Middle class identification (T-1)	0.454	3.18**	0.437	3.11**
Church of England (T-1)	0.661	4.62***	0.433	3.05**
Trade union member	−0.851	−2.34**	−0.646	−2.22**
Partner Conservative support (T-1)	2.580	13.80***	2.626	13.69***
Partner no party support (T-1)	0.999	4.36***	0.796	3.62***
Constant	−4.309	−13.47***	−3.172	−10.04***
BRITAIN: LABOUR PARTY SUPPORT, 1992				
Maximum political interest	0.214	2.6**	0.399	5.01***
Working class identification (T-1)	0.299	2.26**	0.55	4.25***
Catholic identification (T-1)	0.441	2.13**	0.689	2.99**
Trade union member	0.398	1.51	0.614	2.79**
Partner Labour support (T-1)	2.306	15.04***	2.285	14.00***
Partner no party support (T-1)	0.780	4.36***	1.190	7.62***
Constant	−2.616	−10.56***	−3.166	−11.84***
	$\chi^2 = 315.91$***		$\chi^2 = 331.46$***	
	Pseudo R^2 = .181		Pseudo R^2 = .182	

Note: N = 1,425 couples.
*.051 < p < .10, **.00 < p <.05, ***p = .000.

measures of personal political interest and generalized social context of the respondent. This pattern appears again and again in each of the twenty-four equations.

Figures 4.5–4.8 display the appropriate probability statements for each of the models. Because the results are so similar and because again we want to minimize the number of figures in this chapter, we offer only the results taken from the first years: 1992 in Britain and 1990 in Germany. Each figure shows separate curves for men and women. As we did in Figures 4.3 and 4.4, we present the results of post-model estimations, where we manipulate the values of key explanatory variables in order to predict scores on the outcome variables. Each time, we set the values for political interest and social class and religious circumstances to their maximum levels (relative to each political party) and all other variables to their means. Then we vary the party support of the respondent's partner at T-1. In Figure 4.5 for example, we predict the likelihood of the respondent supporting the Conservative Party in 1992. Partners vary among supporting Labour in 1991 (for whom the predicted likelihood is .14 for men and .17 for women), preferring no party (.29 for men and .39 for women), and choosing the Tories in the previous year (.79 for men and .89 for women). The means in the figures represent the predicted likelihood of support for the party, holding all of the respondents' characteristics at their means.

The results are strong, consistent, and very clear. As we found in the individual-level analysis (Zuckerman, Dasović, Fitzgerald, and Brynin 2002), persons with the appropriate personal and generalized social characteristics are more than twice as

TABLE 4.6. Effects of Partner's Party Support on Individual Party Choice, Germany (Logit Analyses)

	Wives		Husbands	
Predictor variable	Coeff.	z-score	Coeff.	z-score
GERMANY: CDU/CSU SUPPORT, 1990				
Maximum political interest	0.282	2.35**	0.250	2.30**
Catholic	0.547	3.20**	0.614	3.52***
Trade union member (T-1)	−0.726	−1.85**	−0.670	−3.36**
Partner CDU/CSU support (T-1)	2.808	13.58***	3.033	13.91***
Partner no party support (T-1)	0.694	3.10**	0.537	2.50**
Constant	−2.785	−11.20***	−2.575	−9.49***
	$\chi^2 = 295.96$***		$\chi^2 = 363.34$***	
	Pseudo $R^2 = .249$		Pseudo $R^2 = .291$	
GERMANY: SPD SUPPORT, 1990				
Maximum political interest	0.814	6.42***	0.327	3.24**
Protestant	0.438	2.50**	0.010	0.61
Trade union member (T-1)	0.568	1.81*	0.855	5.05***
Partner SPD support (T-1)	3.412	14.57***	3.230	14.90***
Partner no party support (T-1)	0.565	2.15**	1.013	5.00***
Constant	−3.694	−12.63***	−2.823	110.75***
	$\chi^2 = 473.14$***		$\chi^2 = 395.97$***	
	Pseudo $R^2 = .359$		Pseudo $R^2 = .290$	

Note: $N = 1,030$ couples.
*.051 $< p <$ .10, **.00 $< p <$.05, ***$p = .000$.

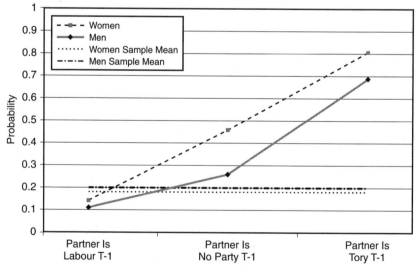

FIGURE 4.5. Contexts of Conservative Support in Britain, 1992

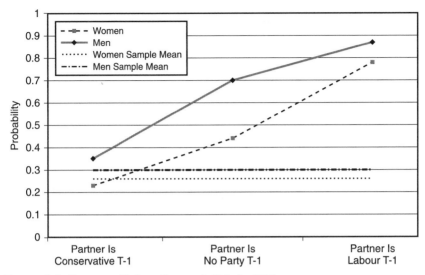

FIGURE 4.6. Contexts of Labour Support in Britain, 1992

likely as the mean respondent to support the party. When the household mate also picks that party, the probability of support approaches statistical certainty. When the mate chooses the *other* party, the probability of support drops to or below the general mean.[15] The story is simple: people respond directly to the partisanship of their spouses and partners. Family members provide important determinants of partisan choice. These variables interact with factors associated with individual-level characteristics as well as those of more generalized social circumstances.

Note that the figures also shed light on the differences as well as the similarities between the men and women in households. In both countries, the mean sample

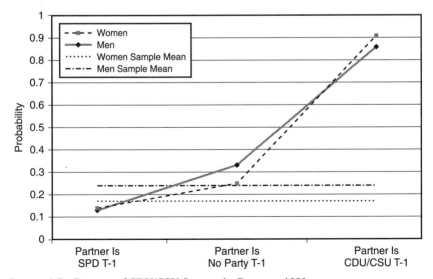

FIGURE 4.7. Contexts of CDU/CSU Support in Germany, 1990

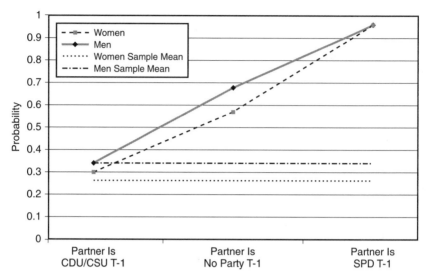

FIGURE 4.8. Contexts of SPD Support in Germany, 1990

scores indicate that men are more likely to support the left party and women the party of the political right, a well-established descriptive generalization. In Britain these differences affect the probability of supporting each of the parties, but in Germany they do not. In the figures for the CDU/CSU and the SPD, the two lines are barely distinguishable. Most important, the effects of personal political interest, generalized social context, and immediate social context are essentially the same for both partners.

This analysis, like the previous one, underscores the extent to which immediate social contexts influence political choices. Household partners influence each other, usually keeping one another on the same side of the national political divide and occasionally pulling over the fence persons who would not be expected to be there. This relationship is stronger than is the association between the measures of social class, religious identification, political interest, and partisanship.

SUMMARY AND IMPLICATIONS

People make political choices that reflect their intimate social circumstances as well as their generalized social attachments and locations and their personal political characteristics. With regard to partisanship, couples are much more than just two persons who happen to live together; they influence each other. At the same time, they are not a single political unit.

With regard to the intimate social relationship that is the couple, the marriage, or the household, our research underscores several generalizations:

- The more interested that each of them is in politics and the more they share the social context of union membership and the social identities of class and religion, the more frequently they support the same political party. (See also Huckfeldt, Johnson, and Sprague, in this volume.)
- The more years they live together, the more likely they are to support the same political party recurrently. Shared party preferences do not initially bring cou-

ples together. Instead, they become more alike as they share their lives. As they live together, they offer political cues to each other and usually accept them.

- Couples share generalized and particular locations on the political maps of their nations. They almost always refuse support for one of the major parties, but this does not translate into the obverse: consistent support for the other party. Rather, household partners vary their picks between one of the parties and no party preference.
- They also follow unique paths over time. Hardly any two couples offer the same views of the political parties. None resembles the aggregate distribution of partisanship over time. Rather, each set represents a distinct set of political choices.

There is little reason to be surprised by the finding that partners influence each other's party preferences. After all, households provide the primary locus of affection, trust, comradeship, and political discussion for their members. Additional evidence taken from the BHPS underscores this general point. In four years—1993, 1995, 1997, and 1999—the survey asked the respondents to identify their closest friends, offering options that included partners/spouses, various relatives, and friends. How frequently do domestic partners pick each other as their closest friends? The rate is 65 percent for the men and 55 percent for the women and, given the distribution of the sample, a total of slightly less than 60 percent of all respondents. Recall too that British couples are more likely to talk about politics with each other than with anyone else. None of this is surprising, but it does underscore the extent to which there is reason to expect persons who live together to take political cues from each other.[16]

May we generalize from these British and German findings to other established democracies? We have found many strong similarities between the two countries, despite their very different political histories. Hence, there is some reason to suppose that couples in other well-established democracies display similar partisan preferences. However, differences in party systems, and not just historical pasts, may be associated with different partisan dynamics between household partners. In both Britain and Germany, contests between the same two dominant parties have structured electoral competition for decades. More than 80 percent of the citizens never support one of the smaller parties. Will the findings that we located in these two countries appear in other party systems? Will they apply to persons and couples in a political system with several parties of relatively equal size, or one in which there is a single large party and multiple smaller parties? We close this chapter with reasoned answers to these questions, knowing that more definitive responses await the availability of panel data like the BHPS and GSOEP for other democracies.

The patterns that we uncovered in Britain and Germany will apply to other established democracies if our empirical generalizations rest on two theoretical principles: (1) people take political cues from members of their households, and (2) they frame their choices into stark alternatives, enabling them to reject one and support the other a varying number of times. The first principle follows from the nature of marriage and other long-term relationships. The second works best when the number of choices approaches one on each side of the political divide. Because so many people apply the left-right metaphor applied to party preferences, it increases the probability that this mechanism of choice will apply. As it simplifies, it induces a decision to reject one location and accept the other.

- We would expect our findings to characterize couples in other established democracies that feature two dominant parties, such as the United States.
- In the case of one large party on side A of the political spectrum and several relatively equal parties on side B, we would expect persons who locate themselves on side A (1) to reject the other set, never supporting any of them, and (2) to vary their selections between their party and no party preference. Another large group of citizens will move among the choices on side B (including no party) but never choose the large party on the other side of the political fence.
- Where there are many relatively small parties, we would expect people to frame their choices into two blocs and then to vary their support among the parties located in one of the two divisions (or no party).
- Household partners will influence each other, and the longer they live together the stronger will be the impact of each on the other and the more likely they will be to choose the same party at any given time and over time.

APPENDIX

Measures for the BHPS Data

The following question measures religion: "Do you regard yourself as belonging to any particular religion? If Yes, which? Church of England; Other Protestant; Roman Catholic; Jewish, Muslim, Other [which we collapsed into one category], and None."

The social-class questions first ask about identity: "Do you think of yourself as belonging to a particular social class? A second question offers seven options, which we collapsed into two: working and middle class. In both instances, we count the number of times that respondents claim these identifications.

A positive answer to "Are you currently a member of a Trades Union?" labels a person as a union member.

The following question taps respondents' level of political interest: "How interested would you say you are in politics? Would you say you are: Very interested, fairly interested, not very interested, not at all interested?" The measure awards points for the level of political interest: three for very interested, two for fairly interested, one for not very interested, and none for not at all interested.

Newlyweds are persons in their first year of marriage or of a shared living arrangement.

Closeness of the relationship is measured by the response to: "Is there anyone you can count on to offer comfort? What is this person's relationship to you? partner, child, sibling, parent, grandparent, grandchild, aunt, uncle, cousin, other relative?"

Measures for the GSOEP Data

Political interest is tapped by this question: "First of all in general: How interested are you in politics?" Respondents are offered the following choices: "Very interested [three points], fairly interested [two points], not very interested [one point], and not interested [zero points]."

Religion is measured by a question that asks about "membership in a church or denomination." It allows for five options: Roman Catholic, Protestant, Other Christian, non-Christian, and no religion.

Union membership derives from two related questions: "Are you a member of a workplace union/of any union?"

Newlyweds are persons in their first year of marriage or of a shared living arrangement.

SIDNEY VERBA, KAY LEHMAN SCHLOZMAN, AND
NANCY BURNS

5   Family Ties

*Understanding the Intergenerational Transmission of
Political Participation*

THE FAMILY IS, perhaps, the universal social institution—present throughout history in widely ranging cultural settings. Although often difficult to specify, its influence is indisputable. Thus, any enterprise seeking to understand the place of primary institutions in political life must come to terms with the family. In general, the understanding of how families shape future members of the political community has drawn from a learning model: in the family children absorb explicit and implicit lessons about politics and the rights and responsibilities of citizens. In this chapter, we consider the impact of the families in which we are reared on our political activity as adults and seek to clarify how the family operates to influence future political participation. We argue that, when it comes to political participation, as important as the political learning that takes place in families is the set of opportunities bequeathed by the socioeconomic status (SES) of the family of origin, in particular, the opportunity for educational attainment. Those whose parents are advantaged in terms of SES are not only likely to come of age in a politically rich environment, and thus to learn lessons germane to future political activity, but are likely themselves to attain high levels of education, which, in turn, enhances the likelihood of acquiring many other attributes that foster political participation.

TAKING FAMILY SERIOUSLY:
THE LITERATURE ON POLITICAL SOCIALIZATION

Although observers of public life since the Greeks have considered the role of the family in creating future citizens, the family does not figure especially importantly in contemporary political science. Nonetheless, it once had greater prominence among the concerns of empirical political scientists. During the 1960s and 1970s, students of political socialization focused on the family as part of a broader concern with the institutions that shape the political orientations, attitudes, and behaviors of the young.[1] While studies of political socialization inevitably dealt with the family, there was no consensus on its role. On one hand, Stanley Renshon (1973, 31) referred to the family as "the most important agent in the socialization process," and James C. Davies (1970, 108) maintained that "most of the individual's political personality—his tendencies to think and act politically in particular ways—have been determined at home." On the other hand, Robert Hess and Judith Torney (1968, 120) maintained that "the public school appears to be the most important and effective instrument of political socialization in the United States." Taking a position between these two, M. Kent Jennings and Richard Niemi (1981, 76) concluded that "although our research left the role of the family quite strong relative to the other agents examined, both the direct and indirect effects of the family appeared to be markedly lower and more variable than had been assumed."

Whether or not the family truly has the primacy among the agents of socialization that is sometimes taken as axiomatic, there is no doubt that various family characteristics influence the political development of the young. Perhaps most important among these is social class. Children and adolescents with higher socioeconomic backgrounds, or whose parents had high levels of formal education, have been found to have higher levels of political information and understanding (Greenstein 1965, 100; Jennings and Niemi 1974, 109–10), to be more politically interested and efficacious (Hess and Torney 1968, 168–79), more tolerant (Jennings and Niemi 1974, 69), and more politically active (Hess and Torney 1968, 189–90; Sigel and Hosken 1981, 141–51).

With respect to the *way* that family matters (and, therefore, that family SES matters) for future political life, the dominant understanding in the socialization literature is a learning model. Hess and Torney (1968, 110–11) specified three mechanisms by which the young absorb political lessons. First, according to the Accumulation Model, is the kind of explicit learning that takes place when "parents transmit attitudes which they consider valuable for their child to hold." Second, the Identification Model posits that "the family also presents examples that children may emulate." Third, the Interpersonal Transfer Model specifies a much more implicit learning process in which "expectations formed from experience in family relationships are later generalized to political objects."[2] In general, the socialization literature emphasizes correspondence between the generations with respect to the content of political attitudes and commitments—in particular, partisanship—rather than the transmission of orientations and skills that encourage later political activity.[3] Nevertheless, the learning model helps us to understand the empirical findings in the socialization literature about the association between parental SES and the participatory orientations and behaviors of offspring. Adults who are advantaged in terms of SES are more likely to have high levels of political knowledge, interest, efficacy, and tolerance; to engage in political discussion; to be politically active; and to encourage their children to become independent and to express themselves fully in family discussions. What such parents teach out loud, and teach by example, helps us to understand the political differences among socioeconomic groups in the next generation.

The socialization literature contains hints of an alternative to the learning model, a different mechanism for the translation of socioeconomic advantage into participatory advantage across generations. Jennings and Niemi (1974, 22) argue that the "social stratification system [that] operates in the nation . . . bequeaths to people of different strata differential access to resources most useful in the political process." They point out that, among other advantages, "the middle class child goes to 'better' schools, interacts with children with greater social competence, [and] has access to more varied learning encounters." In a similar vein, Renshon (1975, 48) notes that socioeconomic status is "a shorthand for a whole range of life and developmental experiences, attitudes, and life-styles" and that a child who is born into a family with high SES has the advantage of an "expanding choice system."[4]

Neither Jennings and Niemi nor Renshon pursues this fruitful lead. One reason that Jennings and Niemi (1974, 22) do not focus more centrally on socioeconomic status is that, as they point out, "the major difficulty with the social stratification approach is that it deals with causes at a second or third remove." That is, because social groups differ in so many ways, SES functions as a surrogate for a variety of attributes and practices with potential consequences for political socialization. It is, therefore, difficult to isolate the mechanisms through which the socioeconomic characteristics of the family of origin shape later political life.

In this chapter, we take up the challenge. Although we are unable to consider all aspects of socioeconomic status that might influence political socialization, we do specify two paths that link parents' SES to the adult political participation of their offspring. We demonstrate that, as expected, parents with higher levels of social and economic resources are more likely to participate in politics themselves and to create households in which there is political discussion, both of which contribute to the political learning of their children. In addition, the advantages conferred by growing up in such families—in particular, the opportunity to achieve high levels of education—are crucial for the cultivation of future citizens.[5] Indeed, when it comes to political participation, such resource advantages make a bigger difference than having parents who are politically active and engaged and who function as role models.

Linking Parents' SES to Political Participation: An Overview

Why are some people more active in politics than others? Systematic research has repeatedly demonstrated the strong links between socioeconomic status—occupation, income, and especially education—and citizen political participation.[6] The Civic Voluntarism Model points to three sets of factors that foster participation: resources, motivation, and location in recruitment networks.[7] In other words, those who are able to take part, who want to take part, and who are asked to take part are more likely to do so. Among the determinants of SES, educational attainment has a particular primacy. Not only does education have a direct impact on political activity but level of education affects the acquisition of factors that facilitate participation. The well-educated are more likely to earn high incomes; to develop civic skills at work, in nonpolitical organizations, and, to a lesser extent, in church; to be in social networks through which requests for political activity are mediated; and to be politically interested and knowledgeable. Furthermore, we shall see that each of these factors is affected by the legacy of the families in which we are raised. Those whose parents were advantaged in terms of SES are more likely, as adults, to have the resources to be active, to be in networks through which requests for activity are mediated, and to be motivated to take part in political life.

The socialization literature demonstrates a political connection between parents' social status and future political activity. High-SES parents are more likely to create a politically rich home environment—in which there are frequent political discussions, and politically active parents serve as role models—and children who grow up in such an environment are distinctive in their political orientations. Presumably, the lessons that are absorbed in a politically stimulating home would carry on into adulthood, creating citizens who are motivated to take part: who are politically interested, informed, and efficacious. Adults who are psychologically engaged with politics are more likely to take part.

However, being raised in an advantaged home is politically enabling in another way, one that is less explicitly political and that has had much less attention in the literature on political socialization. Parents' SES affects the ultimate socioeconomic position of their children—including their educations, the jobs they get as adults, and the incomes they earn. Position in the socioeconomic hierarchy, in turn, affects the acquisition of civic skills in school and in adult settings as well as participation in networks through which recruitment to political activity takes place. Because of the multiplicity and power of its direct and indirect effects upon participation, we focus, in particular, on education as the engine for the transmission of political activity from generation to generation, drawing out the consequences of the link between parents' education and the education of their offspring.[8] Well-educated parents produce well-educated children who enjoy opportunities that permit them to enhance their stockpile of virtually all the factors that facilitate political activity.

Figure 5.1 illustrates two different paths by which parental SES influences political activity. One path operates through the education of the child, which then affects all three of the participatory factors: resources, recruitment, and motivation. That is, parental education channels the members of the next generation into life circumstances—including, most prominently, educational attainment—that are conducive to the accumulation of political resources and placement into social networks from which they may be recruited to politics and that shape psychological orientations to politics. Another path operates through the political stimulation provided at home, which then influences motivation. That is, beginning at the same place, the educational level of parents influences the political richness of the home environment, which in turn affects political activity through increased psychological engagement with politics. Though these paths intertwine, they will be shown to have differing consequences for cross-generational political inequality.

We hasten to add two qualifications to the paths sketched out in Figure 5.1. First, we make no claim that these are the sole mechanisms by which parents' SES has an impact on their offspring's future political participation. We expect that the legacy of parents' education operates in other ways about which, because we use recall data

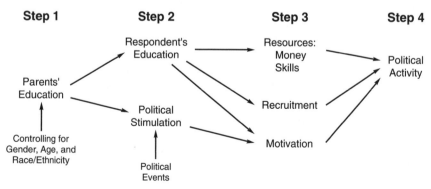

FIGURE 5.1. The Four Steps to Political Activity

collected from adults, we were unable to ask. For example, all things equal, having parents who were politically and socially well connected or who filled the house with books, newspapers, and periodicals would, presumably, have consequences for future activity. Moreover, unmeasured aspects of child-rearing that are discussed in the literature on socialization—for example, emphasis on obedience or encouragement of autonomy and independence—might influence future political activity. Second, the links between parents' education and the amount of education or political stimulation received by their children are anything but ironclad. Many people who do not enjoy socioeconomic advantage as children go on—by dint of luck, pluck, or scholarship aid—to enjoy high levels of education, income, and occupational prestige. Moreover, family SES does not determine the extent to which a home is politically stimulating; in fact, political stimulation can derive from other sources—including, most importantly, politics itself. Later on, we show an example in which the political climate in which the individual comes of age can modify the relationship between parental SES and the political participation of children.

From Generation to Generation: Some Preliminary Data

We begin our analysis with basic descriptive data.[9] The first part of Figure 5.2 shows that respondents who benefited from growing up in a politically stimulating home are more likely to be politically active.[10] When respondents are stratified on the basis of the political richness of the original home environment, we find that 43 percent of respondents in the lowest quartile of the scale undertake some political activity other than voting, in contrast to 69 percent of the respondents in the highest quartile. The association between the political richness of the home environment and later political activity becomes even more dramatic when we consider the volume of activity rather than simply the proportion of respondents who undertook some activity other than voting. The vote is unique among political acts in that there is mandated equality in political input: we each get only one. But for other kinds of activity, those who have the will and the wherewithal can multiply their political input. Using dollars and hours as the metrics, we found that the 28 percent of respondents in the lowest category of home political environment produce only 10 percent of total hours given to politics and 5 percent of the total dollars contributed to political campaigns and causes. In contrast, the 22 percent of respondents in the top category of home political environment produce 40 percent of total hours and 55 percent of the total dollars.

The second part of Figure 5.2 demonstrates the intergenerational transmission of education. The higher the educational attainment of their parents, the more likely it is that respondents are high school graduates.[11] Eighty percent of those whose parents were in the top quartile in education, compared to only 28 percent whose parents were in the lowest quartile in education, finished high school. Data not given on the figure show that those whose parents were in the top quartile in educational attainment are five times more likely to have graduated from college than those whose parents were in the lowest quartile on education. Not only do well-educated parents have well-educated children, they create homes that are politically stimulating.

Parental and Respondent Activity

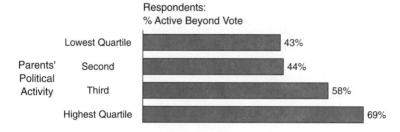

Parental and Respondent Education

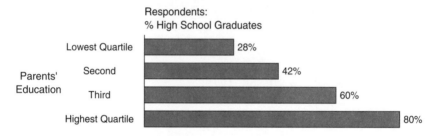

Parental Education and Respondents' Exposure to Politics

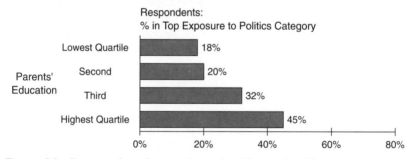

FIGURE 5.2. Correspondence between Parental and Respondent Characteristics

The last part of Figure 5.2 presents data about parents' education and respondents' reports about the political environment at home when they were adolescents: whether their mothers and fathers were politically active and whether there was political discussion at home. Forty-five percent of the respondents whose parents were in the highest quartile on education, compared to only 18 percent of respondents whose parents were in the lowest quartile on education, grew up in the most politically stimulating homes.

Figure 5.2 thus provides tantalizing clues about the nature of the connection between parental characteristics and the political activity of offspring. However, it is essential to model how the parental legacy maps onto a process of accumulation of participatory factors.

FAMILY BACKGROUND AND THE FACTORS THAT FOSTER PARTICIPATION

Earlier we asserted that individuals are more likely to take part politically if they command the necessary resources, in particular money and civic skills; if they are in networks from which they can be recruited to politics; and if they are psychologically engaged with politics by virtue of being politically interested, informed, and efficacious. We would expect that education would be key to acquiring the first two sets of participatory factors but that political stimulation at home would play only a limited role when it comes to resources and recruitment. In contrast, with respect to psychological involvement with politics, both education and home environment should be important.

Table 5.1 presents the results of several regression analyses that examine the effect of education and reported stimulation at home on the socioeconomic status of offspring and their accumulation of resources and recruitment opportunities.[12] For each of these participatory factors whose origins in the family we seek to understand, we first present the effect of parental education and then a regression that also includes the two family-based characteristics: respondent's education, and exposure to political stimulation in the home while growing up.[13] The specific dependent variables include:[14]

A. *Job level.* The five-point job-level scale measures the amount of formal education and on-the-job training the respondent thinks are necessary to handle a job like the one he or she holds. Job level affects the individual's earnings, his

TABLE 5.1. The Consequences of Parental Education, Respondent's Education, and Politics at Home for Political Resources (Ordinary Least Squares Regressions,[a] Coefficients, and Statistical Significance)

Effect on	Step 1	Step 2
A. Job level		
Parents' education	.42**	−.01
Politics at home		.00
Respondent's education		.77**
B. Family income		
Parents' education	.12**	.05**
Politics at home		.02*
Respondent's education		.13**
C. Civic skills		
Parents' education	.29**	.06*
Politics at home		.05*
Respondent's education		.38**
D. Political recruitment		
Parents' education	.08**	−.02
Politics at home		.03
Respondent's education		.17**

Source: Citizen Participation Study—Main Survey.
[a]Race, ethnicity, gender, and age are included in each of the equations.
*p < .05, **p < .01.

or her opportunities to develop civic skills, and the likelihood that he or she will be located in recruitment networks.

B. *Family income*. Income is an important political resource, especially when it comes to making political contributions.

C. *Civic skills*. The measure of civic skills is an enumeration of the number of communication and organizational skills the individual exercises on the job, in nonpolitical organizations, and in church.

D. *Political recruitment*. The recruitment measure counts the number of requests for political activity received on the job, in nonpolitical organizations, and in church.

As shown in the first-step regressions, parental education is related to each of these participatory factors, in particular to the respondent's job level and civic skills. More important from our perspective are results of the regressions when the respondent's education and the measure of political stimulation at home are added in Step 2. The respondent's education plays a major role in the acquisition of all four of these participatory factors. In contrast, with both parents' and respondent's education taken into account, political stimulation at home plays, at most, a statistically significant but weak role in the acquisition of these factors. In addition, it is interesting to note that the effect of parental education diminishes—in two cases to the point of statistical insignificance—when the respondent's education is added to the equation, indicating that parental education works indirectly through the child's education.

Table 5.2, which presents a comparable analysis for several measures of political motivation that can stimulate political activity, offers a contrast. Both respondent's education and political stimulation at home are significantly related to each of the measures of psychological involvement in politics: political interest, political efficacy, and political information. It is interesting to compare the patterns for political interest, which would seem to be a clear measure of motivation not dependent on resources, and political efficacy, which would seem, in part, to be a reflection of the availability of resources. In fact, for political interest, education and stimulation are equally influential, but education is a better predictor of political efficacy than is stimulation at home. As expected, education is also the most potent predictor when it comes to political information, but political stimulation at home, which presumably functions to focus attention on politics, has a positive effect as well. When we decompose the overall measure of political information, shown in Table 5.2C, into two components, we note that political stimulation at home is less strongly associated with civics information—that is, textbook knowledge of constitutional principles and government institutions and processes—shown in Table 5.2D than with knowledge of the names of elected political figures, shown in Table 5.2E. The former represents knowledge cultivated in school, while the latter is presumably acquired by paying attention to politics. Thus, this pattern is also consistent with the distinction we make between the impact of education and the impact of political stimulation.

In sum, the data in Tables 5.1 and 5.2 tell a coherent story and reinforce the notion that there is more than one path from parental socioeconomic status to political activity. Education is crucial for the stockpiling of all participatory factors. In contrast, exposure to a rich political environment at home enhances the

TABLE 5.2. The Consequences of Parents' Education, Respondent's Education, and Politics at Home for Political Engagement (Ordinary Least Squares Regressions,[a] Coefficients and Statistical Significance)

Effect on	Step 1	Step 2
A. Political interest		
Parents' education	.36**	.01**
Politics at home		.27**
Respondent's education		.28**
B. Political efficacy		
Parents' education	.26**	.08*
Politics at home		.13**
Respondent's education		.25**
C. Political information (composite measure)		
Parents' education	.29**	.10**
Politics at home		.09**
Respondent's education		.19**
D. Political information (civics information)		
Parents' education	.28**	.05
Politics at home		.05*
Respondent's education		.37**
E. Political information (information about names)		
Parents' education	.42**	.17**
Politics at home		.13**
Respondent's education		.38**

Source: Citizen Participation Study—Main Survey.
[a]Race, ethnicity, gender, and age are included in each of the equations.
*$p < .05$, **$p < .01$.

reservoir of participatory factors that are connected to politics but not to socioeconomic position.

FROM PARTICIPATORY FACTORS TO POLITICAL ACTIVITY

Having established alternative paths connecting parental education to participatory factors, we can now extend the analysis to consider the full set of links between parental education and political activity. In Table 5.3, we consider the paths to two kinds of political activity that depend on political resources: the measure of overall political activity introduced earlier and a measure of the amount of the respondent's political contributions.[15] This analysis consists of the four steps originally depicted in Figure 5.1. The first two steps include regressions analogous to those in Tables 5.1 and 5.2: first, a reduced model including the effect of parental education, then a slightly more expanded model to which the respondent's education and political stimulation at home have been added. The third step adds measures of two resources, family income and civic skills, and a measure of political recruitment. The final step is the full model including a measure of psychological engagement with politics, a summary scale that includes political interest, efficacy, and information.

TABLE 5.3. Predicting Resource-Based Political Activity (Ordinary Least Squares Regressions,[a] Coefficients, and Statistical Significance)

	Step 1	Step 2	Step 3	Step 4
A. PREDICTING OVERALL POLITICAL ACTIVITY				
Parents' education	.38**	.10**	.08**	.05
Politics at home		.14**	.12**	.05*
Respondent's education		.41**	.24**	.14**
Family income			.29**	.23**
Civic skills			.20**	.14**
Recruitment			.30**	.23**
Political engagement				.48**
B. PREDICTING POLITICAL CONTRIBUTIONS (DOLLARS GIVEN TO POLITICS)				
Parents' education	168**	39	5	−3
Politics at home		59**	50**	48*
Respondent's education		198**	74**	66**
Family income			533**	550**
Civic skills			51*	49*
Recruitment			52*	34
Political engagement				69**

Source: Citizen Participation Study—Main Survey.
[a]Race, ethnicity, gender, and age are included in each of the equations.
*$p < .05$, **$p < .01$.

Let us summarize the results briefly. Not unexpectedly, as more variables are added to the analysis, the coefficient on parents' education diminishes progressively until, once all the participatory factors have been included, it becomes insignificant for both overall participation and the size of financial donations. Correspondingly, the coefficients on respondent's education and political stimulation at home also decrease. Still, across the entire table, no matter what other variables are included in the analysis, respondent's education and exposure to politics at home are significantly related to both overall political activity and political contributions. However, in each case, education is a more powerful predictor than is political stimulation at home.[16]

The patterns by which the coefficients change as more variables are added to the analysis bear closer scrutiny. When measures of participatory resources and recruitment are added in Step 3, the coefficient for respondent's education is diminished substantially, while the effect of stimulation falls only marginally. This result does not indicate that education is unimportant. On the contrary, it shows that respondent's education works through political resources and recruitment, while the effect of stimulation is not mediated by these intervening variables. When a measure of motivation is included in the analysis in Step 4, the coefficients on both education and stimulation are both reduced, indicating that part of their effect on activity is through their impact on psychological orientations to politics. The last point to note is the significant role played by the measures of resources and recruitment at the last stage, especially in predicting contributions. At Step 2, respondent's education is almost three times as potent as stimulation as a predictor of contributions. When the intervening effects of the other participatory factors are taken into account—in particular, the effect of family income—the impact of the respondent's education is reduced to a third of its original size. The interpretation is clear: education leads to higher income which, in turn, leads to higher contributions. The impact of exposure to politics at home, in contrast, is direct and does not depend on the intervening effect of family income. Education provides the resources; stimulation adds the relevant political concern.

To recapitulate, education influences participation in a variety of ways including through its impact on all three sets of participatory factors: resources, recruitment, and motivation. Growing up in a rich political environment—which operates most clearly through its impact on motivation—has less powerful consequences for adult political activity than does education.

EDUCATION, HOME POLITICS, AND LESS ACTIVE FORMS OF POLITICAL INVOLVEMENT

We can highlight the contrasting roles of education and political stimulation at home by comparing the paths to the resource-based political activity reported in Table 5.3 with the paths to less active forms of political involvement: frequency of political discussion; exposure to political news—reading newspapers, watching television news broadcasts, and watching other public affairs programming on television; and strength of partisan attachment.[17] We would expect that these modes of political involvement would be less dependent on resources and recruitment and, therefore, that respondent's education would not so dominate stimulation as an explanatory factor. The relevant regressions, which use the four-step mode of analysis introduced earlier, are contained in Table 5.4. The overall pattern in the data is quite different from what we saw for overall political participation and political contributions. The measures of participatory resources are less potent as predictors of these forms of involvement, and once the scale measuring psychological engagement with politics has been incorporated, most of them are reduced to statistical insignificance.

The relative strength of the effects of respondent's education and the home political environment is also quite different from what we saw in Table 5.3. In all three of the full four-step models that include the summary measure of psychological engagement with politics, having grown up in a politically stimulating home is more powerful than education as a predictor. In fact, while stimulation at home retains its statistical significance in the full models for all three variables, the coefficient on respondent's education is insignificant for frequency of political discussion and strength of partisanship and barely significant for exposure to news in the media. The pattern for strength of partisan affiliation is particularly striking. Partisanship is sometimes construed as a way for citizens to cut information costs in making vote choices: that is, knowing a candidate's party affiliation reduces the need for detailed information when voting. If this conceptualization is correct, then education should be less powerful than political stimulation at home in predicting strength of party affiliation. In fact, even in Step 2, respondent's education is barely significant while stimulation at home is a much more powerful predictor.

TABLE 5.4. Predicting Non-Resource-Based Political Involvement (Ordinary Least Squares Regressions,[a] Coefficients, and Statistical Significance)

	Step 1	Step 2	Step 3	Step 4
A. PREDICTING POLITICAL DISCUSSION				
Parents' education	.27**	.08**	.07*	.02
Politics at home		.24**	.22**	.12**
Respondent's education		.19**	.10**	−.03
Family income			.18**	−.10*
Civic skills			.10**	.01
Recruitment			.16**	.06*
Political engagement				.67**
B. PREDICTING EXPOSURE TO NEWS				
Parents' education	.17**	.02**	.01	−.03
Politics at home		.14**	.14**	.07**
Respondent's education		.18**	.13**	.06*
Family income			.13**	.07
Civic skills			.02	−.03
Recruitment			.13**	.06*
Political engagement				.46**
C. PREDICTING PARTISAN AFFILIATION				
Parents' education	.13**	.03**	.03	.00
Politics at home		.18**	.17**	.11**
Respondent's education		.07*	.03	.00
Family income			.11	.09
Civic skills			.04	.01
Recruitment			.10*	.06
Political engagement				.21**

Source: Citizen Participation Study—Main Survey.
[a]Race, ethnicity, gender, and age are included in each of the equations.
*$p < .05$, **$p < .01$.

These data reinforce the interpretation that the legacy of parental social class operates in at least two ways, one of which is much more explicitly political than the other. Parents' SES is associated both with the extent to which the home environment is politically stimulating and, especially, with the educational attainment of their offspring. Both factors have consequences for adult political life. Educational attainment is an especially powerful predictor of overall political participation and making political contributions, but it takes a back seat to the effects of political stimulation at home when it comes to forms of political involvement— for example, taking part in political discussions—that are less active and less resource-dependent.

CHOOSING THE POLITICAL

Given the importance of the role of education in the accumulation of participatory resources and the importance of coming of age in a politically rich environment in orienting an individual to politics, these two influences could work

TABLE 5.5. Focusing Activity: Predicting the Proportion of Voluntary Contributions Going to Politics (Among Those Contributing; Ordinary Least Squares Regressions,[a] Coefficients, and Statistical Significance)

	Step 1	Step 2	Step 3	Step 4
Parents' education	.14**	.01	−.02	−.03
Politics at home		.12**	.14**	.11**
Respondent's education		.18**	.14**	.13**
Family income			.25**	.24**
Civic skills			.00	−.01
Recruitment			.00	.01**
Political engagement				.08**

Source: Citizen Participation Study—Main Survey.
[a]Race, ethnicity, gender, and age are included in each of the equations.
*$p < .05$, **$p < .01$.

together—with education providing the wherewithal for voluntary participation, whether political or nonpolitical, and political stimulation at home channeling that participation into politics rather than some other sphere of activity. We can consider this conjecture in relation to the most resource-dependent form of voluntary activity, making financial contributions. Table 5.3 made clear that the single strongest factor in predicting the amount of political contributions is family income, and Table 5.1 demonstrated that education is much more strongly related to family income than is political stimulation at home. Table 5.5, in which we consider the decision to direct financial contributions to political causes rather than to nonpolitical ones or to religious institutions, allows us to assess the influence of education and political stimulation at home in respondents' choice of politics over other forms of voluntary activity. The dependent variable is the proportion of the respondent's total voluntary contributions—to charity, religious institutions, and politics—that is directed to politics. Education has a substantial role, as does family income. The effect of politics at home is more direct and, once other variables are included in the analysis, is of the same magnitude as the effect of education. Thus, even for an activity (making financial contributions) that is substantially constrained by the need for resources and is, therefore, heavily dependent on socioeconomic status, growing up in a politically stimulating home can play a role in channeling those resources to politics rather than to some other cause.[18]

BREAKING THE CYCLE OF POLITICAL INEQUALITY

This analysis makes clear that political inequality is passed on from generation to generation. Both because they are more likely to grow up in a politically engaged home and, especially, because they are more likely to become well educated, those who hail from socially advantaged families are more likely to be politically active than those who do not. This intergenerational transmission of inequality implies that democratic politics in America is not a level playing field. The disparities in political participation that are carried from one generation to the next involve not just individuals but also politically relevant groups: most obviously, those defined by social class but also groups defined along other dimensions, such as race and ethnicity.

In other democracies, where there are strong labor unions or electorally competitive labor or social democratic parties, the links between social class and political participation are weaker than they are in the United States.[19] In the American context, the traditional answer to breaking the cycle of political inequality that is rooted in class differences has been mobilization through social movements. Although the power of labor unions has become attenuated in recent decades, the past half-century has witnessed a variety of other kinds of social movements in America. Some of these—for example, the environmental movement—are firmly anchored in the middle class. Others—such as the pro-life movement—focus on social issues rather than the needs of the economically disadvantaged.

There was, of course, one movement that mobilized a socioeconomically disadvantaged group, the civil rights movement. We were curious to learn whether African Americans who were adolescents at the time of the civil rights movement were more likely to report having grown up in a politically rich home environment than would be expected on the basis of their parents' socioeconomic status and, if so, whether they showed corresponding gains in political participation during adulthood.[20] Figure 5.3 divides respondents into four cohort groupings and shows—for Anglo whites, African Americans, and Latinos—the likelihood of having experienced a politically stimulating home environment at age sixteen. With one exception, in each of the age cohorts Anglo whites are the most likely of the three groups to report political stimulation at home. That exception is the generation that came of age during the civil rights era, for which African Americans

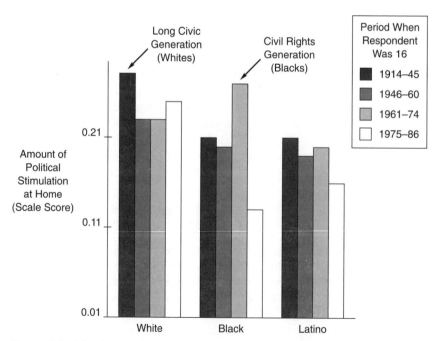

Figure 5.3. Stimulation at Home by Generation and Race/Ethnicity

were the most likely to report a politically engaged home. It is interesting to consider the oldest cohort—most of whom came of age during the Depression or World War II—a group whose high level of civic engagement was noted by Robert Putnam (2000), who labeled them "the long civic generation."[21] Anglo whites and Latinos in this cohort were more likely than their younger counterparts to report a politically stimulating home. In contrast, among African Americans, the members of the civil rights generation were not only more likely than African Americans in other cohorts but also more likely than Anglo whites or Latinos of their generation to report a politically stimulating home.[22]

We conclude this discussion by asking whether the blacks who came of age during the civil rights era translate the political stimulation they experienced at home into political activity. Table 5.6 contains an OLS regression predicting political activity.[23] Along with measures of education and income, it contains a dummy variable for being a black adolescent during the civil rights era. Table 5.6 confirms that being a black teenager during the civil rights era is related significantly to political activity.[24]

The data make clear that the pattern of perpetuation of political inequalities across generations can be modified by politics itself. Significant political events are brought home to create a stimulating political environment, which leads to increased political activity later in life. However, as we saw in Figure 5.3, the spike in political stimulation at home that occurred during the civil rights movement was temporary. Blacks in the post–civil rights generation were less likely than either their Anglo-white or their Latino age-mates to report having grown up in a politically stimulating home. Nevertheless, in the case of the civil rights movement, there is a more lasting legacy that speaks fundamentally to the second path from parents' SES to adult political participation. Over the past several decades, the education gap between African Americans and Anglo whites has narrowed considerably. In 1960, 43 percent of whites, but only 20 percent of blacks, had finished high school. By 1995, the figures were 83 percent for whites and 74 percent for blacks (U.S. Bureau of the Census 1996, 159). While it would be an oversimplification to ascribe the expanded educational opportunities for African Americans solely to the impact of the civil rights movement and the policy changes it spawned, it is clear that the diminution of the racial disparity in education that occurred in the wake of the civil rights movement will have long-term consequences for group differences in political participation.

TABLE 5.6. Predicting Political Activity: Do Blacks in the Civil Rights Generation Participate at Higher Rates? (Ordinary Least Squares Regressions,[a] Coefficients, and Statistical Significance)

Member of the Civil Rights generation	.11**
Member of the Civil Rights generation × Black	.19*
Respondent's education	.42**
Family income	.00**

Source: Citizen Participation Study—Screener Survey.
[a]Gender and age are included in the equation.
$*p < .05, **p < .01.$

Summary

It is well known that, in spite of the promise of equality of opportunity implied by the ideology of the American dream, parents often pass social class advantage (or disadvantage) along to their offspring. The transmission of political advantage has received considerably less attention. In this chapter, we have considered not only whether politically active parents have politically active children, but how that outcome is produced. What we found is not simply analogous to, but intertwined with, the process by which socioeconomic advantage is handed down from one generation to the next. Although in both cases the ability of parents to reproduce their advantage is imperfect, current inequalities with respect to both socioeconomic status and political participation have their roots, at least in part, in the patterns of past. Where the processes are connected, however, is that the key to the intergenerational transmission of political activity is parental SES, in particular, parents' education.

There are at least two mechanisms by which well-educated parents produce politically active children. The first is consistent with the learning model in the political-socialization literature. Well-educated parents are likely to take part in politics themselves and to create homes in which there is political discussion. Those who come of age in such a politically rich environment are likely to absorb explicit and implicit lessons and, as adults, to have psychological orientations to politics— to be more politically interested, informed, and efficacious—that predispose them to take part. Growing up in a politically stimulating home is an especially powerful predictor of less active forms of political involvement—for example, engaging in political discussion or identifying strongly with one of the parties—that do not require substantial resources.

A second path from parental socioeconomic status to political activity has been explored less fully by students of political socialization. Well-educated parents are likely to have well-educated children, a relationship that is stronger than the relationship between parental education and the political environment at home. Educational attainment is, in fact, the single most potent predictor of an adult's political activity. Not only does education have a direct impact on political activity, but it enhances the stockpile of factors that facilitate participation. The well educated are likely to be well endowed with participatory resources: to command both a high family income and civic skills, to be located in networks through which activists are recruited, and to be motivated to take part.

We noted in concluding that one way to break the cycle of self-perpetuating political inequality is through politics itself. In a brief example, we discussed how the legacy of the civil rights movement had the potential to narrow the gap in political participation between African Americans and Anglo whites. In a striking analogy to the processes by which parents' SES is linked to political activity, the impact is felt both through political stimulation at home and through education. Blacks who came of age during the civil rights movement are more likely than older and younger blacks—and more likely than Anglo whites or Latinos of the same age—to report having grown up in a politically stimulating home, an experience that had a lasting impact on their interest in politics and their propensity to be politically active. In addition, public policy can have an impact on participatory inequalities. The narrowing of the education gap between African Americans and Anglo whites that ensued in the aftermath of the civil rights movement has unambiguous consequences for disparities in participation between the groups. Thus, our dual lessons: family matters, but so does politics.

APPENDIX A

For our analysis, the data we really need are longitudinal, in which the same respondents are assessed directly starting in their early years and continuing at intervals until they are mature adults and either active or inactive in politics. Instead, our data come from a single point in time. In one sense, however, they might represent longitudinal data. We ask respondents to report about earlier times, and we relate those memories to their reports of current activity. If memory were perfect, such data would be longitudinal, but of course memory is often unreliable. Among our major retrospective measures, we believe that respondents' memories of parents' education ought to be fairly accurate. Memories of political stimulation, however, could be less precise and more easily colored by current circumstances. Politically involved respondents might remember more politics in the family of origin than was the case.

While one must be cautious, we have evidence to suggest that memories of parental education and of political stimulation are relatively undistorted. Data in Tables 5A.1 and 5A.2 support our belief that there is little backward distortion of memory in the light of current circumstances. Table 5A.1 shows the respondents' reports of their own education and political activity within several categories. As one can see, our respondents vary in their educations and current involvement in politics. The variations we show in respondents' education are by race, ethnicity, and gender. The variations in political involvement are by respondents' race and ethnicity, education, and gender. As one can see, minorities, people with less education, and women are less active in politics. Further, minorities and women have somewhat less education.

Table 5A.2 shows respondents' reports about parental education and home stimulation at the time they were adolescents. The remembered circumstances for the several racial/ethnic and educational groups show lower political stimulation for the less advantaged categories. And for race/ethnicity, the reports of parental education show lower levels among

TABLE 5A.1. Respondents' Current Education and Political Involvement

MEAN EDUCATIONAL LEVEL BY GENDER, RACE, AND ETHNICITY			
By race and ethnicity		By gender	
Whites	.41	Men	.42
Blacks	.34	Women	.38
Latinos	.29		

MEAN POLITICAL ACTIVITY BY GENDER, RACE, ETHNICITY, AND EDUCATION					
By race and ethnicity		By education		By gender	
Whites	.41	Some high school	.13	Men	.42
Blacks	.34	High school graduate	.25	Women	.38
Latinos	.29	Some college	.34		
		College graduate	.44		

Source: Citizen Participation Study—Main Survey.
Note: Educational level and political activity are measured on scales that range from 0 to 1.

TABLE 5A.2. Reports of Parental Education and Home Political Stimulation by Respondents' Race, Ethnicity, Education, and Gender

REPORTED MEAN EDUCATION OF PARENTS					
By respondents' race and ethnicity		By respondents' education		By respondents' gender	
Whites	.24	Some high school	.10	Men	.23
Blacks	.18	High school graduate	.18	Women	.22
Latinos	.13	Some college	.24		
		College graduate	.34		

REPORTED MEAN POLITICAL STIMULATION BY PARENTS					
By respondents' race and ethnicity		By respondents' education		By respondents' gender	
Whites	.25	Some high school	.19	Men	.24
Blacks	.23	High school graduate	.20	Women	.24
Latinos	.18	Some college	.27		
		College graduate	.30		

Source: Citizen Participation Study—Main Survey.
Note: Education and political stimulation are measured on scales that range from 0 to 1.

the disadvantaged groups. This is consistent with a causal connection between earlier and current patterns (since minorities and less educated respondents are likely to have been raised in families with less education and less political involvement) but could also be consistent with memories distorted by current circumstances. For our purposes, the contrast with the gender data is crucial. The women in our sample are somewhat less educated than men and somewhat less active, but they are born randomly into families of varying education and political involvement. If memories are accurate, they should report levels of parental education or political stimulation that are similar to what men report. If memories are distorted by current circumstances, they should report lower levels of parental education and stimulation. As one can see in Table 5A.2, the former situation holds.

APPENDIX B: DATA AND MEASURES

Data

We use data from the Citizen Participation Study, which was conducted in 1990. For wording of all questions and for additional information about the survey, its oversamples of Latinos and African Americans, its oversamples of those who are active in politics, and the characteristics that allow it to be treated as a national random sample, see Verba, Schlozman, and Brady (1995, Appendixes A and B).

Measures

Activity: Throughout the chapter we measure political activity by an eight-point summary scale that includes the following political acts: voting; working in a campaign; contributing to a campaign; contacting an official; taking part in a protest, march, or demonstration; being affiliated with an organization that takes stands in politics; being active in the local community; and serving as a volunteer on a local board.

The scale has a Cronbach's alpha of 0.60. The individual items in the scale are weakly correlated: the average correlation between the items is .17. Thus, while the realized distribution does not appear to be perfectly normally distributed, the realized distribution and the pattern of correlations reassure us that an ordinary least squares regression is the appropriate technique to use. This technique is, of course, especially useful because of its robustness. Small changes in data and specification do not yield different results, as they might with less robust methods. For a sense of the consequences of these small correlations for the distribution of the data, we used three variables that were more strongly correlated than others in the scale: informal local activity, organizational involvement, and campaign contributions. We calculated what percentage of our respondents would have engaged in two or more of these three acts had the acts been completely independent of one another. If they had been independent, 25 percent of the sample would have engaged in two or more of the three acts. In our data, with the small correlations between acts, 26 percent of our sample participated in two or more of these acts. These are not, then, especially rare or especially correlated events; therefore, a Poisson or negative binomial specification would be inappropriate here.

Other Forms of Involvement: The scale measuring political discussion includes the frequency with which local and national politics are discussed as well as a measure of how much the respondent reports enjoying political discussion.

The scale measuring media exposure to news includes frequency of reading newspapers, watching news on television, and watching televised public-affairs programs.

We measure partisan affiliation in terms of the strength of partisanship without regard to direction. Thus, a strong Republican and a strong Democrat have the same score, and the direction of partisanship is lost.

The proportion of voluntary contributions to political causes is the percentage of the respondent's total contributions to charity, religious institutions, political campaigns, and political causes that goes to the latter two.

Explanatory Variables: In order to facilitate comparisons across different independent variables that were originally measured in different metrics having different ranges, in Table 5.1 and other multivariate analyses we have transformed the independent variables to have a range from 0 to 1.

Politics at Home: We measure exposure to politics at home as the sum of the respondent's mother's political activity, the respondent's father's political activity, and the level of political discussion at home when the respondent was sixteen years old (all as reported by the respondent).

Parents' Education: We measure parents' education as the average of the respondent's report of mother's education and father's education. There are missing data on parents' education and on the variables that compose politics at home. We worked extensively with these measures to ensure that substituting the average value for the missing values does not change the results in any way. This is the appropriate place to fill these missing data. In addition, one might think that we should use the highest educated parent's education as our measure of parents' education. We think not. First, the results using both measures are identical. Second, standard measurement theory suggests that two measures deal with measurement error better than one, and so we rely on the average here.

For our comparisons to be informative, we need to take account of the fact that older parental generations have, on average, lower levels of education than younger ones do. To address that complication, throughout our analysis we use an age-adjusted measure of parental education that calculates the respondent's parents' education relative to the average educational level at the time. Thus, the variable measuring parents' education reflects both mother's and father's education and the educational distribution in the parental age cohort.

Civic Skills: We measured civic skills by asking whether, in the past six months, the respondent wrote a letter, went to a meeting where he or she took part in decision making, planned or chaired a meeting, or gave a presentation or speech in one or more adult institutions: the workplace, religious institutions, and nonpolitical organizations. We asked these questions separately for each institution. The variable we use is the sum of the number of skills practiced in all three institutions.

Institutional Recruitment: Similarly, our measure of requests for political activity is about requests originating in each of these three nonpolitical institutions. We asked whether, in the last five years, the respondent was asked by the organization, by the religious institution, and in the workplace to vote a certain way in an election for public office or take some other action on a local or national political issue—sign a petition, write a letter, go to a meeting, attend a protest or march, or get in touch with a public official. The measure of recruitment sums these requests across these three institutions.

Age: As controls we have included two variables measuring age: the respondent's age in decades and whether the respondent is older than 65, to account for the curvilinear relationship of age to participation.

PART II

FRIENDS, WORKMATES, NEIGHBORS, AND POLITICAL CONTEXTS

The Effects of Weak Ties on Electoral Choices and Political Participation

6 Changing Class Locations and Partisanship in Germany

What accounts for the well-established association between social class and partisanship in European democracies? Consider three well known answers:

- "Interest theory": People usually support the party that represents their interests, which are linked in turn to their positions in the structure of social classes. (See, for example, Bendix and Lipset 1967, 12.)
- "Interaction theory": People usually support the party that is preferred by those with whom they interact. These interactions are conditioned by jobs, residences, and families, all of which are influenced by social class (Lazarsfeld et al. 1948, and the sources noted in the Preface and Chapter 1 in this volume).
- "Identification theory": People learn partisanship from their parents, with whom they usually also share the same position in the class structure (Campbell et al. 1960).

Each theory posits a correlation between social class and political preference, and so finding a synchronic association is not an adequate test of their relative power. In this chapter I propose a longitudinal approach. I assess the effect of a "social structural event"—a change of a social characteristic of a specific person, such as change in class position, job, or marital status—on partisanship.

How might these relationships be depicted? Figure 6.1 (from Allison 1994) displays some possible outcomes of a social structural event. Line A shows a person who has a particular party preference and who changes immediately after the event happens. In Line B, a person continuously changes her preference in one direction, and the event leads her to make an additional quick step in that direction. Lines C and D display immediate effects as well; the event leads to a development that changes over time. Lines E and F show cases where the event starts gradual processes. The three theories of the relationship between social class and partisanship imply three different hypotheses depicted by these lines about the effects of social structural events.

Hypotheses

Interest theory maintains that people in different social classes use different strategies to reach their goals. As partisanship structures vote choice, it responds to calculations of class interest. Consider a scheme of social class composed of employers, the self-employed, the service class, and the working class. Because members of the working class reach their goals through collective action, they should be more receptive to socialist or interventionist parties than other classes. Employers or the self employed, on the other hand, are interested in conditions favorable to private enterprise and individual success. Hence, they should be particularly

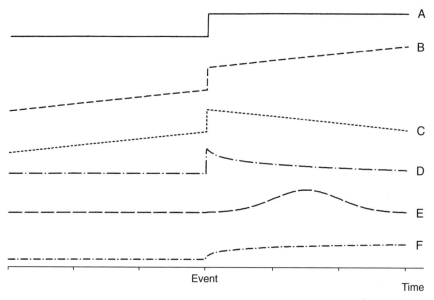

FIGURE 6.1. Possible Effects of Social Structural Events on Party Preference

receptive to individualistic and free-enterprise policies (see, for example, Heath and Savage 1995; Heath et al. 1985; Müller 1998). Analysts differ over the expected partisanship of those in the service class (see, for example, Brooks and Manza 1997; De Graaf, Dirk, and Steijn 1996; Dunleavy 1979; Goldthorpe 1982; Heath and Savage 1995; Hout et al. 1995; Kriesi 1989; McAdams 1987; Müller 1998; Savage 1991). All agree that at any particular time, partisanship derives from a person's current class position. In other words, there is no difference between the person who has always belonged to the working class and someone who used to be self-employed and recently joined the working class. This theory hypothesizes that a shift, for example, from being self-employed to joining the working class will immediately change voting behavior from conservative to liberal. Thus, Hypothesis 1: A person who changes from one class position to another should stop supporting the party of the origin class and start supporting the party of the destination class.

Interest theory poses strong assumptions about political knowledge. People must know which strategies will help them reach their goals, and they must know which political party will help them pursue their strategies. Variations in political information affect the rate by which persons learn about political parties and, therefore, their ability to match their class interest and partisanship (see Zuckerman, Fitzgerald, and Dasović in this volume). Therefore, Hypothesis 2: The higher the political interest, the stronger are the expected effects on partisanship of changes in class position.

As interaction theory implies, conversations with friends, colleagues, neighbors, or relatives also provide political information; and as individuals use these sources, their partners influence them (see Huckfeldt, Johnson, and Sprague; Johnson and Huckfeldt; Stoker and Jennings; Zuckerman; and Zuckerman, Fitzgerald and

Dasović in this volume). Hence, Hypothesis 3: If two partners *ego* and *alter*, with different political preferences, meet, the former will change to agree with the latter. Further, there is reason to expect that variations in the level of political interest help to specify this relationship. Hypothesis 4: The higher is ego's political interest, the weaker is the effect of the new interaction partner.

As noted in Chapter 1, the Michigan school implies that partisanship is a relatively stable psychological attachment to a political party. Even if change occasionally occurs, people almost always return to the original partisan home (Campbell et al. 1960; Converse 1969, 1976). Therefore, partisanship is relatively immune to the effects of a social structural event. Hypothesis 5: People do not change their political decisions after a social structural event. A modified interpretation expects partisanship to respond slowly to current political experiences (Fiorina 1981; Franklin 1984; Franklin and Jackson 1983; Jackson 1975; Markus 1979, 1983). Thus, Hypothesis 6: Social structural events have gradual effects on partisanship.

Data and Methods

Examination of the hypotheses stated in the previous section requires data with specific characteristics: a longitudinal set with information on social structural events and indicators of partisan preference before and after the events. Panel surveys, such as the German Socioeconomic Panel (GSOEP), are ideal.[1] Begun in 1984, GSOEP is a wide-ranging, representative, longitudinal study of private households in Germany. All members of participating households age sixteen and above are interviewed annually on topics like household composition, occupational history, current employment, earnings, political opinions, and so on (SOEP-Group 2001).[2] The following analyses are based on all waves of the GSOEP between 1984 and 2000 in an unbalanced panel design,[3] omitting respondents from the former German Democratic Republic (GDR).[4]

The Model

The statistical model used in the analysis is a fixed-effects panel logit model. In order to understand the general purpose of fixed-effects models, it is useful to consider the possible sources of variation in panel data. By way of example, Table 6.1 shows two artificial data sets with three respondents and the variable X measured at time points T1, T2, and T3. The table on the left shows data with between-person variation; here the values of X differ between the respondents. The table on the right shows data having within-person variation. In this case, the values of X are equal for each respondent, but change over time for each.

TABLE 6.1. Illustration of Sources of Variation in Panel Data

Between-person variation				Within-person variation			
i	$X_{t=1}$	$X_{t=2}$	$X_{t=3}$	i	$X_{t=1}$	$X_{t=2}$	$X_{t=3}$
1	4	4	4	1	4	5	9
2	5	5	5	2	4	5	9
3	9	9	9	3	4	5	9

Regression models for panel data differ in how to incorporate the two sources of variation. Fixed-effects models only use the variation within the respondents (Balestra 1992). For a dichotomous dependent variable, the fixed-effects model can be estimated by using conditional logistic regression, which is the probability that person i has a success at time t, conditional on the number of successes of this person (Chamberlain 1980).

There is some discussion about the relative merits of different panel data models (Allison 1994; Burr and Nesselroade 1990; Liker, Augustyniak, and Duncan 1985; Rodgers 1989). The main reason to apply a fixed-effects model here is that the question about effects of social structural events is at its heart a question about effects within a person. Moreover, the model parameters of the fixed-effects model cannot be biased due to the omission of time-invariant variables. A disadvantage of the model is that only those respondents who have at least one change in party preference, within the specified time frame, can be included in the analysis.

In order to estimate the effects of social structural events, the independent variables of the model are coded as proposed by Allison (1994). In order to investigate the immediate effects, an event indicator is added to the model. This measure is set to 1 if the event has already occurred and 0 if it has not. Investigation of gradual effects is done with an event indicator that equals the logarithm of the number of time-points since the event occurred.

In order to illustrate the coding of the event indicators, Table 6.2 displays some typical examples: Respondent 1 changes status from self-employed to working class somewhere between 1984 and 1985. The variable "Indicator 1" is generated, which is 1 in 1985 and each of the following years. Note also that there is a second social structural event between 1986 and 1987, but this event does not change "Indicator 1." Hence, the effect of changing from self-employed to worker is regarded as permanent. In order to incorporate the second social structural event, there is a second variable ("Indicator 2"), which again is 1 after the event occurs and 0 otherwise. More generally, there is an event indicator for each type of social structural event that occurs.

TABLE 6.2. The Coding of Event Indicators

Time (year)	Class	Indicator 1	Indicator 2	Indicator 3 (gradual)
		RESPONDENT 1		
84	Self-employed	—	—	—
85	Worker	1	0	$1 + \ln 1$
86	Worker	1	0	$1 + \ln 2$
87	Service	1	1	$1 + \ln 3$
88	Service	1	1	$1 + \ln 4$
		RESPONDENT 2		
84	Self-employed	—	—	—
85	Worker	1	0	$1 + \ln 1$
86	Self-employed	1	1	$1 + \ln 2$
87	Worker	2	1	$1 + \ln 3 + 1 + \ln 1$
88	Worker	2	1	$1 + \ln 4 + 1 + \ln 2$
89	Worker	2	1	$1 + \ln 5 + 1 + \ln 3$

Respondent 2 of Table 6.2 has two social structural events of the same type. This represents a status change from self-employed to working class between 1984 and 1985, and then again between 1986 and 1987. Moreover it is always possible that a specific event occurred before the observation period of the study. Therefore, I have combined each social structural event of the same type into one variable by simply adding them together. This assumes that social structural events have the same effect whenever they occur.

After these general decisions have been made, the generation of event indicators for gradual effects (see line F in Figure 6.1) is straightforward. I use 1 + the logarithm of time-points after the event and 0 before the event. The variable "Indicator 3" in Table 6.2 shows an example for the event of a status change from self-employment to working class. Note that all event indicators are missing at the first time-point for each respondent. In addition, remember that the fixed-effects logit model can only incorporate respondents with at least one change in the dependent variables. Taken together, each respondent included in the analysis has at least three observations.

The Dependent Variable

In order to test the hypotheses stated above, an indicator for partisanship is needed. GSOEP provides the following question: "Many people in Germany lean toward one party in the long term, even if they occasionally vote for another party. Do you lean toward a particular party?" Respondents who answer positively are then given a card naming the parties and asked which party they favor. This analysis focuses on three responses: support for the Social Democratic Party (SPD), support for the Christian Democratic Union/Christian Social Union (CDU/CSU), and no party preference (Kohler 2002, 169–89; and also see Zuckerman, Fitzgerald, and Dasović, in this volume). Because many persons vary their choices over time between one of the major parties and supporting no party, the design of the dependent variable needs to be clarified. Two possibilities come to mind: a measure in which 1 = SPD and 0 = CDU/CSU, or 1 = CDU/CSU and 0 = SPD, with the omission of all observations without a partisan choice; or one in which 1 = SPD and 0 indicates the choice of the CDU/CSU or no party, or 1 = CDU/CSU and 0 = SPD or no party. Because the analysis of the impact of social structural events on partisanship requires many data points and because most of the movement is between one of the parties and no partisan preference, this analysis pursues the second option. Consider the case of a changeover from worker to self-employed. Here there should be a negative effect on the dependent variable SPD versus any other choice, and a positive impact on the dependent variable CDU/CSU versus any other choice. In both cases, the effect will not be very strong because many respondents shift between naming a major party and proclaiming support for no party. Taken alone, neither model answers the question about the effects of social structural events. In combination, they begin to shed light on the relationship between social structural events and partisanship.

THE INDEPENDENT VARIABLES

Interest theory is best tested by examining the effects of changes between positions in the class structure. I focus on four such events, or movements: between employers and self-employed; within the category of administrative services; between workers and salaried persons in the social services; and between experts and any of the other categories. The operationalization of these class positions is based on the class scheme of Erikson and Goldthorpe (1992), known as EG. Each individual was assigned to the class position of the person with the highest income in the household (Erikson 1984; Goldthorpe 1983). Following Müller (1998), the two service classes of the EG class scheme were pooled together and split along certain occupations into the subgroups "administrative services," "experts," and "social services." Then the positions of the class scheme were combined into the four groups. The event "change between class positions" happens if a respondent at time t has a different class position than at t_{-1}.

The analysis tests interaction theory by measuring the variable "meeting a new interaction partner with a different partisan preference." Although GSOEP does not contain data on complete social networks, it provides a useful proxy: the partisanship of household members (see Zuckerman, Fitzgerald, and Dasović in this volume). Here, the social structural event is "moving in with a new partner who does not share the same partisanship." Interpretation of the proxy variable must respect that the new partner usually is not a new interaction partner. Before moving in together, people have usually interacted for some time. Therefore, it is quite possible that the effect of meeting the new interaction partner has already appeared, and in such a case the proxy variable would underestimate the effect of the theoretical construct.

As Stoker and Jennings; Levine; and Zuckerman, Fitzgerald, and Dasović (this volume) recognize, the analysis faces a potential problem of endogeneity. In this case, the respondent's partisanship may influence the choice of spouse or domestic partner. Note, however, if this were the case, the event indicator would be zero because both interaction partners would have the same partisan choice. As a result, the coefficient of the event indicator would be biased downward. On the other hand, the event indicator is not influenced if the new partner changes his mind after moving in with the respondent (possibly due to the influence of the respondent). There is only endogeneity before, but not after, the event in question. As a result, it biases the coefficients upward only if the respondent forces the partner to adopt a partisan choice different from her own before they move in together—and to change to that partisan choice after he has moved in with the interaction partner—an unlikely sequence.

Several other variables complete the models. There is a measure of political interest, which varies along a four-point scale (see the description in Zuckerman, Fitzgerald, and Dasović in this volume). As mentioned earlier, fixed-effects models need not include time-invariant variables, such as gender or age cohort. They should include variables, like age or political circumstances, which do depend on time. The analysis includes, therefore, a dummy variable for each year. It also controls for a potential association between aging and moving to the political right (here to the CDU/CSU). To control for possible effects of such events, indicators for the following are included in the model: completing primary education, earning a university degree, finishing vocational training, starting the first job, marrying for the first time, birth of the first child, and birth of the second or other child.

Results

The method applied in the following analysis imposes certain restrictions on the data. As already noted, I use West German respondents who are interviewed at least three times; 10,209 respondents meet this condition. Among them, I examine only those who have at least one change on the dependent variable. Therefore, the subsample used in the estimation depends on the definition of the dependent variable, and so I begin by describing the data in the different estimation subsamples. I then present the results of the statistical models. I start with an examination of the hypotheses from interest theory, where the statistical model expects immediate and permanent effects of social structural events. Then I extend the model in two ways: by including interaction terms of the social structural events with political interest and by the inclusion of parameters for new partners, examining the hypothesis derived from the interaction theory. Afterward, I recalculate the models by imposing gradual effects for the social structural events. Each of the models includes all event indicators presented in Table 6.3 and dummy variables for each year of observation. In presenting the results, I restrict myself to the effects of a change between working class and salaried persons in the social services on one hand, and self-employed/employers on the other hand. I also present the effects of moving in with a new partner.

The Estimation Sample

The SPD model includes 3,883 respondents, those persons who change at least once between support for that party and preference for the CDU/CSU or no party. The CDU/CSU model examines 3,017 respondents. On average, each respondent is interviewed twelve times, though most were interviewed in each of the sixteen years.

Table 6.3 shows the frequencies of the social structural events used in the statistical models, displaying the absolute and relative frequency of respondents who have undergone the specific event at least once. The numbers are presented for both model types, as well as for all those in the GSOEP sample who were interviewed at least three times during the years of the survey. As is evident, relatively few persons are characterized by a social structural event, especially as that relates to class positions. As a consequence, the standard errors of the coefficients in the models are high.

More important, however, is the comparison between the proportions in the entire database and those of the estimation samples. Differences between them stem from the exclusion of respondents who do not change their partisanship. We can use the differences in frequencies between the entire database and the estimation sample for a cursory analysis of the hypotheses. If social structural events enhance the probability of a change in party preference, the proportion of social structural events should be higher in both estimation samples than in the entire database.

An easy way to compare the events summarized in Table 6.3 is displayed in Figure 6.2. The proportion of each event in the full database is connected by a straight line to the proportion of the same event in the SPD model, or to that in the CDU/CSU model. If the hypotheses are sustained, we would expect ascending lines, and, in fact, most of the lines rise. The exceptions are primarily due to the indicators for typical events in the life course.

TABLE 6.3. Frequencies of Respondents with Socio-structural Events by Estimation Sample

	Absolute frequency			Relative frequency		
Event	GSOEP	SPD	CDU/CSU	GSOEP	SPD	CDU/CSU
Changeover to self-employed/ employer from ...						
Admin. services	245	65	113	.02	.02	.04
Experts/others	283	95	123	.03	.02	.04
Workers/soc. services	345	134	131	.03	.03	.04
Changeover to admin. services from ...						
Self-employed/employer	256	73	121	.03	.02	.04
Experts/others	1,089	424	405	.11	.11	.13
Workers/soc. services	376	164	121	.04	.04	.04
Changeover to experts/others from ...						
Self-employed/employer	228	88	95	.02	.02	.03
Admin. services	919	344	357	.09	.09	.12
Workers/soc. services	1,847	830	556	.18	.21	.18
Changeover to worker/social services from ...						
Self-employed/employer	286	109	97	.03	.03	.03
Admin. services	366	155	120	.04	.04	.04
Workers/soc. services	1,701	740	505	.17	.19	.17
Typical events in life course						
Finish school	1,414	532	359	.14	.14	.12
Finish university	423	191	133	.04	.05	.04
Finish voc. training	1,628	648	493	.16	.17	.16
Start first job	810	240	187	.08	.06	.06
Marry first time	1,508	678	441	.15	.17	.15
Birth first child	2,394	911	664	.23	.23	.22
Birth other children	2,120	832	598	.21	.21	.20
New partner with other partisan choice than respondent						
SPD partner	424	209	111	.04	.05	.04
CDU/CSU partner	335	95	142	.03	.02	.05
Total	10,209	3,883	3,017	1.0	1.0	1.0

First, I present the results of a model that poses immediate and permanent effects of social structural events, testing Hypothesis 1 and interest theory. Table 6.4 displays some summary statistics for the SPD and the CDU/CSU model. The goodness of fit of both models can be examined from the McFadden Pseudo R^2 (p^2_{MF}), the Bayesian Information Criterion (BIC), and the Likelihood-Ratio Chi-Square (XL).[5] For technical reasons, the goodness-of-fit statistics are calculated from a model without weights, whereas the model parameters reported below are calculated using weights.[6]

As mentioned earlier, one would not expect the overall fit of the models to be high, and, indeed, the Pseudo R^2 of both models is quite low. The coefficients are

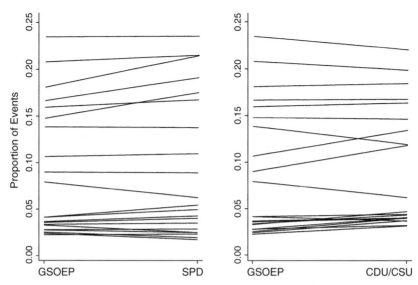

FIGURE 6.2. Proportion of Persons with Social Structural Events in the GSOEP versus Estimation Samples

much lower than one would expect for an equivalent model using cross-sectional data.[7] This may be taken as an indicator that changed class positions do not have the same "within person" effect as that between different persons. On the other hand, the negative values of the BIC show that there is "strong evidence" (Raftery 1995) for preferring both models over a model without any independent variables. The same conclusion is drawn from the Likelihood-Ratio Chi-Square in the last row of Table 6.4. Therefore, one may conclude that a change in class position has a limited impact in terms of changing partisanship.[8]

Consider now the relationship between changing class positions—between the working class and salaried persons in the social services on one side and the self-employed and employers on the other side—and partisanship. Those coefficients are presented in Figure 6.3. Here, the upper panel shows the results of the SPD model, and the lower panel shows the results of the CDU/CSU model. The left side of each panel shows the effects of the change from employees in the working class or social services to self-employed/employers, and the right panel shows the effects of the shift in the other direction. Each quadrant of the figure adapts the general idea represented in Figure 6.1. The horizontal axis of each graph rep-

TABLE 6.4. Measures of Fit for Models with Immediate and Permanent Effects

	Model type	
	SPD	CDU/CSU
R^2MF	.018	.019
BIC	−388	−247
XL (*df*)	645 (31)	496 (31)

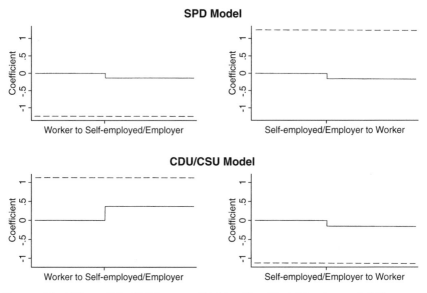

FIGURE 6.3. Effects of the Shift between Working Class/Social Services and Self-employed/Employer (Complete Information)

resents time, with the time-point of the event located in the middle. The vertical axis represents the coefficient of the fixed-effects panel logit model. The solid line shows the effect of the event. The step in the line indicates how much the dependent variable differs before and after the event. The dotted line in each graph shows the effect of the class position between respondents. This line can be regarded as a rough estimate of the size of the fixed effects assuming the interest theory is true.[9]

The figure shows that movement between these two sets of class positions has a very small effect on partisan choice. After a shift to self-employed/employer status, former members of the working classes are slightly more likely to support the CDU/CSU than before, but the relationship is by no means as strong as one would expect if their choices were guided solely by interest theory. The effect of a shift into the working class or salaried persons in the social services category in the SPD model is even in the wrong direction. In sum, these results deny the implications of interest theory for the relationship between social class and partisanship.

Now consider hypotheses that expect stronger effects of social structural events for politically interested people. The extension of the model leads to a model with fifty-five parameters. The results of the first model are shown in the first column of Table 6.5 and those of the new model appear in the second column.

The fit of the models indicated by the McFadden Pseudo R^2 has increased from .02 to about .05 or .04 respectively. However, the value is still low. The BIC measure is much lower than before, strong evidence that the model with incomplete information should be preferred over the model with complete information. The likelihood ratio chi-square values are not directly comparable because the models are not nested in a strict sense, [10] but a comparison implies that the second model is a significant improvement over the first.

TABLE 6.5. Measures of Fit for Models of Incomplete Information

	Model type			
	SPD		CDU/CSU	
	(1)	(2)	(1)	(2)
R^2MF	.018	.052	.019	.044
BIC	−388	−1,350	−247	−708
XL (*df*)	645 (31)	1,804 (55)	496 (31)	1,149 (55)

Consider now the coefficients of the model. The effects of a status shift between working class/social services and self-employed/employer are displayed in Figure 6.4. The graphs of the figure are set up as before, except that this time the effects are drawn for people with different levels of political interest. The solid line represents the effect of the social structural events for those with the lowest political interest and the dashed line represents the respondents with the highest political interest.

From Hypothesis 2 we expect that the line of the politically interested respondents will be closer to the "expected effect," indicated by the dotted line. In fact, this expectation is only partially confirmed. As it stands, persons with high political interest change toward the party of their new social structural position; however, they do not give up their original partisan choice, as expected. One might argue that this pattern stems from those respondents expressing no partisan choice before the social structural event. Hence it might be easier for them to adopt the partisan choice of their new social structural position. On the other hand, one

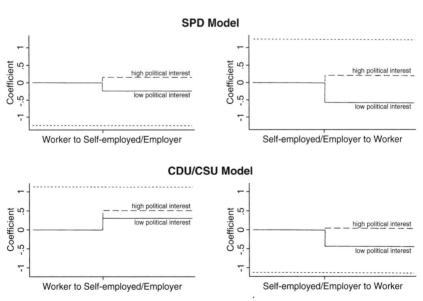

FIGURE 6.4. Effects of the Shift between Working Class/Social Services and Self-employed/Employer (Incomplete Information)

should not be especially pleased with the results. The coefficients for the SPD model are not nearly as high as the class effect between respondents. Hence, even for the politically interested respondents, it is not possible to explain the class differences in political behavior with interest theory.

Before allowing for gradual effects, I show the impact of changing interaction partners. Two different events are observed: moving in with a partner who leans toward the SPD, and moving in with one who leans toward the CDU/CSU. The results of the former are displayed in the upper panel and of the latter in the lower panel of Figure 6.5. Note that there is no reference line from the between-respondent model in the figure. The construct "new partner" can hardly be defined in a comparable way in a cross-sectional model. Theoretically, it is expected that a new Social Democratic partner will pull the respondent toward the SPD, and a new Christian Democrat/Social partner should pull the respondent toward that party. The effects should be stronger among respondents with low political interest.

The empirical results partly confirm these expectations. As anticipated, new partners draw the respondents away from their prior political preference. New partners who are SPD adherents also pull the respondents to that party, but that occurs when the partner displays high levels of political interest. New partners favoring the CDU/CSU do not pull the respondents to that party. New partners seem to push respondents away from their old party but not toward the new party. Even as this model improves the analysis, it suggests the need to add gradual effects of social structural events.

In order to examine Hypothesis 6, I recalculated the models by using the gradual-event indicators instead of event indicators with immediate and permanent effects. I also included the interaction terms between events and political interest from the last model. In addition, the analysis controls for the tendency of persons

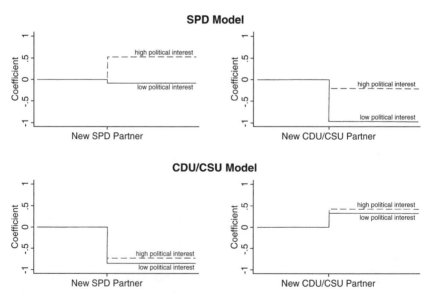

FIGURE 6.5. Effects of Moving In with a Partner with a Party Identification Other Than One's Own

TABLE 6.6. Measures of Fit for Models with Gradual Effects

	Model type			
	SPD		CDU/CSU	
	(2)	(3)	(2)	(3)
R^2MF	.052	.054	.044	.047
BIC	−1,350	−1,409	−708	−760
XL (*df*)	1,804 (55)	1,872 (56)	1,149 (55)	1,208 (56)

who are interested in politics to move away from no partisan support toward one of the parties. As the gradual-event indicators include the time after an event, the effect of changing to a party at any point in time has to be controlled. I do this by including an interaction term of political interest with the logarithm of the number of observations at every point in time.

Table 6.6 shows the goodness-of-fit statistics of the model with gradual effects in comparison to the model under the assumption of incomplete information. The statistics of the gradual-effects model are in columns (3) and the statistics of the incomplete-information model are reproduced in columns (2).

The statistics in Table 6.6 indicate at least some improvement of the model. Although the Pseudo R^2 remains almost constant, BIC drops about 60 points, strong evidence to prefer the model with gradual effects over the model without them. Moreover, the likelihood ratio chi-squares increase considerably, although a formal test of the improvement is not possible because the models are not nested.

The effects of a shift in status between the working class/social services and self-employed/employer categories are displayed in Figure 6.6. The four graphs

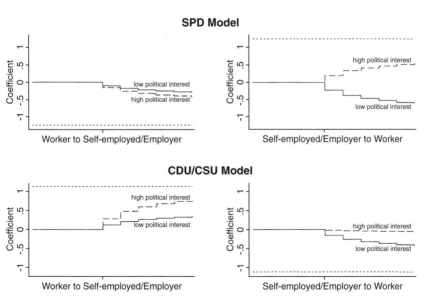

FIGURE 6.6. Effects of the Shift between Working Class/Social Services and Self-employed/Employer (Gradual Effects, Incomplete Information)

are set up as before. Again, the solid line without symbols represents the effect of the event for those with the lowest political interest and the line with plot symbols represents the respondents with the highest political interest. To indicate the gradual effects, the coefficients are multiplied by ln (the number of time points after the event).

As one can see in Figure 6.6, the model with gradual effects comes closest to the theoretical expectations: former members of the working classes/social services group with high political interest transfer their support for the SPD to its major rival sometime after they join the self-employed/employers group. Conversely, former members of the self-employed/employers group give up their identification with the CDU/CSU and move to the SPD after moving to the working class. In the CDU/CSU model, on the other hand, this is true only for the change from the working class/social services category to the self-employed/employer group. Adding high political interest and an expectation of gradual effects permits interest theory to account for the relationship between social class and partisanship. Persons with low levels of political interest stand apart from this process.

Figure 6.7 shows the gradual effects of moving in with a new partner who supports a different political party. The left half of the figure shows the effect of a new SPD partner and the right portion displays the effect of a new CDU/CSU partner. People with low and high political interest are indicated as before.

From Hypothesis 4, we expect less politically interested respondents to be pulled in the direction of their new partners' preferences. In the model without gradual effects this was only partially true. Now, the empirical findings are much more compelling. Each portion of the figure shows that less politically interested people tend to move to the party of their partner, and they do so at a rate that is higher than among persons with high levels of political interest.

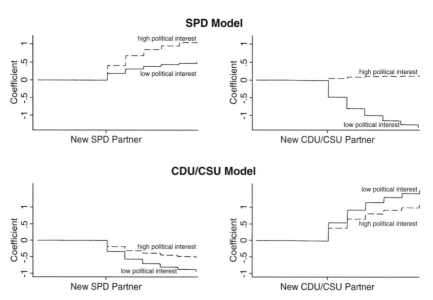

FIGURE 6.7. Effects of Moving In with a Partner with a Party Identification Different from One's Own (Gradual Effects)

Summary

This analysis has modeled alternative understandings of the effects of social structural events on party support. The first step of the analysis was made under the assumption of perfect information of the respondents. In this situation, the effect on a person of a change between classes should be the same as the difference between persons of different class positions. The empirical findings did not fit this expectation. By themselves, changes in objective social class do not imply partisan change. The second portion of the analysis highlights two critical variables. High political interest and joining together with a partner who supports a different party leads to change in partisanship. Finally, the analysis shows that the social structural events have gradual effects on changes in party support.

What do these results mean for explanations of the relationship between social class and partisanship? Interest theory requires high political interest and stable class positions to account for the relationship. Persons with low levels of political interest are not influenced by their interests. In the long run, they tend to share the political preferences of their partners. Politically interested people are more attuned to their class interests. Therefore, as long as social contacts are confined to the same social class, there will be a persistent relationship between social class and partisanship for all persons, those with low as well as high levels of political interest.

7   Choosing Alone?

The Social Network Basis of Modern Political Choice

THE SHIFT AWAY from the social logic of politics noted by Alan Zuckerman in Chapter 1 has not only served to reinforce the perception that social location is a secondary, less important determinant of political choice but also led some to conclude that modern citizens have become largely independent of groups and social influence. For example, Dalton and Wattenberg (1993, 212–13), in their review of the voting literature, argue that the balance of research regarding voting behavior suggests that modern citizens are increasingly employing a more individualized approach to decision making, one that leads them to rely only marginally on others in this process.

Although few would agree that this asocial model of political choice accurately represents reality for most Americans, it is striking how little empirical evidence exists to challenge it. The purpose of this chapter is to take a closer look at the network basis of modern political choice in order to assess the extent to which modern citizens conform to the individualized model.

I seek to determine, first, whether social networks exert an impact on choice that is both immediate and powerful, even after controlling for key attitudinal variables. As noted, few political scientists argue that modern citizens make decisions entirely without the help of social contacts. Nevertheless, it is important to demonstrate not only the existence of network effects but also their relative strength.

I also look to see whether social influence operates beyond the boundaries of close relationships such as family members and close friends to involve more casual acquaintances. Information that is communicated through such acquaintances has two important characteristics: It is more likely to be both contradictory and current than information received through intimate contacts (Granovetter 1973; Huckfeldt and Sprague 1995; Huckfeldt et al. 1995; also see Kotler-Berkowitz and Lin, in this volume). As a consequence, evidence that social influence occurs outside cohesive social groups would indicate that social interaction consists of more than a simple exchange of opinions between like-minded citizens. Instead, it would suggest that citizens engage in the sort of the discussions long considered necessary to the democratic process—those in which they are exposed to novel and contradictory points of view (Berelson 1952, 324).

I find that that even after controlling for powerful individual-level attitudinal variables, social network members exert a direct, powerful, and consistent influence on key political decisions, including candidate choice, partisan affiliation, and key issue opinions. In addition, the analyses confirm that social influence is not restricted to networks of family members or close friends; a significant amount of persuasion occurs outside of such intimate relationships. These results not only present a strong empirical challenge to the individualized model of citizen choice but also suggest the existence of a modern citizenry capable of engaging in informal deliberation and debate.

A RETURN TO THE NETWORK BASIS OF CHOICE

In a series of articles, Zuckerman and his colleagues argue that instead of assuming that membership in demographic categories ties people together in ongoing political relationships, it may be useful to employ a less confining view of the way members of society are linked (Zuckerman 1982; Zuckerman et al. 1994). They suggest that citizens in mass democracies may best be viewed as connected by networks of social interaction. Membership in an objective social category, such as social class, is a relatively weak electoral cue by itself. It can only function as an important cue and influence behavior if it is reinforced by social interactions. Thus, in order to understand fully the link between social location and politics, they argue that it is most useful to study citizens' particular social circles.

Although this argument has been made relatively recently, the general notion that social networks may be an important determinant of political choice is not, of course, a novel proposition. Researchers at Columbia University (Berelson et al. 1954; Katz and Lazarsfeld 1955; Lazarsfeld et al. 1944; McPhee 1963) argued nearly fifty years ago that individual political choice is fundamentally dependent on informal interactions with others in the immediate social environment. As Zuckerman notes in Chapter 1, even the authors of *The American Voter* argued that conversations with family and friends play an important and direct role in shaping individual political choice.

In spite of these early efforts, the network basis of political choice has received relatively little empirical attention. Early studies, particularly those conducted by the researchers at Columbia University, were not designed to be network studies and, as a result, do not present much explicit evidence concerning the role of social networks in political life (Eulau 1980, 225–26). More recent attempts at such analyses provide better information concerning the nature of social networks but are not able to investigate directly the impact of networks on political choice (e.g., Mondak 1995; Weatherford 1982; Zuckerman et al. 1994). These sorts of studies obtain information concerning respondents' networks from the respondents themselves, precluding true network analysis of influence.

Thus far, the only studies that have directly investigated the impact of social networks on political choice have employed Huckfeldt and Sprague's unique 1984 South Bend Study data set. Although much progress has been made using this data, the bulk of the analyses have focused on the nature and substance of network interaction among citizens (Huckfeldt and Sprague 1995). Research on the influence of networks on decision making has been more limited, confined chiefly to Huckfeldt and Sprague's (1991, 1995) work exploring network influence on candidate choice among South Bend voters in the 1984 presidential election (also see Kenny 1993b, 1994, 1998).

The purpose of this chapter is to extend and enhance the current state of our knowledge concerning networks and their impact on political choice by conducting an analysis of their role in three recent presidential election years: 1984, 1992, and 1996. Specifically, I examine the extent to which social influence occurs beyond the bounds of the closest social circles, both inside and outside citizens' families. The analyses are broader than previous network studies, focusing on the role that networks play in a wide variety of key political choices, including candidate choice, partisanship, and issue preference.

The chapter is divided into two main sections. In the first, I seek to determine what role social networks play in shaping modern candidate choice. Do they exert a significant and direct impact, even after controlling for key variables like partisanship and issue position? In the second section, I consider whether social influence regarding partisanship and issue preferences is restricted to intimate friends and acquaintances or whether more casual social contacts exert a significant impact as well.

THE NETWORK BASIS OF MODERN CANDIDATE CHOICE

Data and Methods

Obtaining an estimate of the effects produced by political discussion is a challenging proposition. This is because in order to estimate the influence that one citizen has on another, it is necessary to disentangle the reciprocal nature of social interaction. In a political discussion, social influence can flow in two directions. In the present case, it is not only likely that the candidate preferences of the members of the respondent's network (i.e., discussants) have an impact on the respondent's preference but also likely that the respondent's preference influences that of the discussants. Thus, simply showing a strong correlation between the political preferences of respondents and their discussants does not isolate the unique effects that are due to the discussion partners. In order to estimate these effects, it is first necessary to obtain data with particular characteristics. Most importantly, the data must contain information about main respondents' discussion partners that are obtained from the discussants themselves. Fortunately, such data are available in the American portion of the 1992 Cross National Election Study. In the months immediately following the 1992 presidential election, a nationally representative sample of 1,318 respondents were asked to identify up to four people with whom they discuss important matters and one person with whom they discuss political matters.[1]

As Appendix Table 7A.1 shows, many respondents were willing to identify such discussants, suggesting that modern citizens are far from socially inactive. Indeed, a total of 3,747 discussants were identified by respondents. Approximately 80 percent of the respondents identified at least one "important matters" discussant, 30 percent named at least four "important matters" discussants, and almost 60 percent of the respondents named a political discussant. Of these 3,747 discussants, 1,112 were subsequently interviewed directly.[2]

On the basis of the interviews completed by the main respondents and their discussants, a data matrix of relationships between them can be constructed. Each observation in the data matrix represents a relationship that includes self-report information from both the main respondent and the discussant, as well as the main respondent's perception of various discussant characteristics. Because main respondents could name up to five discussants, they can be included in more than one relationship and thus appear in more than one observation within the data matrix.

The next step in obtaining a valid estimate of the influence that discussants have on main respondents is to construct a measure of discussant candidate preference that is purged of the reciprocal influence of the main respondent. The broad strategy for doing so is fairly simple. All that needs to be done is to construct a discussant candidate-preference instrument using variables that strongly predict discussant candidate preference and only weakly predict main respondent preference.

Previous work as well as intuition suggest that discussant partisanship and demographic characteristics should be much stronger predictors of discussant choice than main respondent choice. The logit analysis in Table 7.1 supports this expectation. Discussant partisanship, education, and age each exert a much stronger impact on discussant preference for Clinton than main respondent preference for Clinton, even after controlling for several main respondent attitudinal and social group variables.[3]

The second step is to identify the final model. Main respondent choice is the dependent variable. In addition to the discussant instrument, several attitudinal and group variables are included as explanatory variables because they have been shown to exert a strong impact on candidate choice in the 1992 election: partisanship, opinion about abortion, opinion on the state of the economy, income,

TABLE 7.1. Logit Estimates of Discussant Clinton Choice and Main Respondent Clinton Choice as a Function of Various Discussant and Main Respondent Characteristics, 1992

Variables	Discussant Clinton choice	Main respondent Clinton choice
Constant	−5.23	−5.34
Discussant		
Partisanship	1.73 (13.30)**	.39 (3.55)**
Education	.09 (2.25)*	.04 (1.00)
Age	.015 (1.50)*	−.01 (1.00)
Main respondent		
Partisanship	.18 (1.50)	1.10 (9.17)**
Abortion	.55 (2.03)*	.69 (2.56)**
National economy	.41 (2.16)*	1.21 (5.50)**
Income	.03 (.38)	−.08 (1.00)
South	−.16 (.64)	−.33 (1.38)
Union	.01 (.04)	.65 (2.60)**
Age	.01 (1.00)	.01 (1.00)*
Class	.15 (.63)	−.65 (2.60)**
Protestant	−.04 (.17)	−.33 (1.43)
Education	.05 (1.00)	.05 (1.25)
N	723	708
Log likelihood	−301.63	−310.08

Source: 1992 Cross National Election Study.

Note: Coding and question wording for variables are given in the Appendix, Table 7A.4. *T* values are in parentheses. Analysis done with all nonmarried discussion pairs.

*$p \le .05$, two-tailed; **$p \le .01$, two-tailed.

region, union membership, age, social class, religion, and education (Abramowitz 1995; Alvarez and Nagler 1995; Dalton and Wattenberg 1993; Leighley and Nagler 1992; Stanley and Niemi 1991; Wolfinger and Rosenstone 1980).[4]

Once the variables to be included in the analyses are identified, the final three steps are to estimate the discussant instrument, place it in the final model, and estimate its impact on main respondent choice. There are several ways to do this. The discussant instrument and the impact of the instrument on main respondent candidate choice can be estimated using either a two-stage probit or logit procedure, as long as the standard errors are corrected either by the construction of covariance matrices (Greene 1995, 664; Maddala 1983, 246–47) or through a bootstrapping procedure (Mooney 1996; Mooney and Duval 1993). Alternatively, a modified two-stage logit procedure can be employed, one that does not require the use of such corrective measures (Huckfeldt and Sprague 1991, 1995).[5] I employ each of these strategies here.

First, I use two-stage probit, correcting the standard errors using covariance matrices.[6] Second, I employ a two-stage logit procedure, this time correcting the standard errors using a bootstrapping approach.[7] Finally, I use Huckfeldt and Sprague's (1991, 1995) modification of the two-stage logit procedure.[8]

Findings: The Impact of Network Influence on Clinton and Bush Choice

The chief statistic of interest in the models is the coefficient for discussant candidate choice. If the modern citizen is, in fact, strongly dependent on others to make choices, the coefficient should be both statistically and substantively significant, even after controlling for important attitudinal and social-group variables. The findings support this expectation.

As Table 7.2 demonstrates, the candidate preference of nonmarried discussants exerts a strong and consistent impact on main respondents' Clinton choice. Indeed, in each of the three models, the coefficient for discussant candidate choice is statistically significant at the .01 level.

The effect of discussant preference on candidate choice is also substantively significant. For example, as Model 3 suggests, a shift in discussant preference from no active support of Bill Clinton to casting a vote for Bill Clinton results in a change of 4.45 in the odds of the main respondent voting for Clinton, holding all other variables constant. Or, equivalently, mobilization on the part of the discussant to support Clinton increases the odds of the main respondent voting for Clinton by 345 percent![9]

An examination of expected probabilities further highlights the importance of social networks. Indeed, main respondents whose discussion partners do not vote for Clinton have only a .07 chance of supporting Clinton whereas respondents whose discussants do support Clinton have a .25 probability of casting a vote for Clinton.

Clearly, these results differ sharply from the citizen depicted as a socially isolated decision maker. As discussed, demonstrating that citizens are influenced by nonmarried associates, people through whom current and contradictory information is likely to be transmitted, strongly suggests that citizen choice is a function of true social deliberation. This conclusion is reinforced when the analyses presented in Table 7.2 are duplicated using a sample of discussants who are even less

TABLE 7.2. Estimates of Main Respondent Clinton Choice as a Function of Discussant Clinton Choice for All Nonmarried Discussion Pairs, 1992

Variables	Model 1: Two-stage probit	Model 2: Two-stage logit (bootstrap)	Model 3: Two-stage logit (Huckfeldt and Sprague)
Constant	−2.87	−4.39	−6.02
Discussant Clinton choice	.25 (12.50)**	.22 (3.14)** *1.25*	1.50 (3.41)** *4.45*
Partisanship	.64 (16.00)**	1.07 (8.23)** *2.92*	1.13 (8.69)** *3.09*
Abortion	.32 (.65)	.61 (1.97)* *1.84*	.64 (2.13)* *1.90*
National economy	.69 (8.63)**	1.14 (3.93)** *3.13*	1.21 (5.04)** *3.36*
Income	−.01 (.33)	−.06 (.67) *.94*	−.08 (.89) *.92*
South	−.12 (.46)	−.31 (1.24) *.73*	−.36 (1.33) *.70*
Union	.34 (.28)	.46 (1.59) *1.58*	.53 (1.96)* *1.70*
Age	.07 (1.40)	.01 (1.00) *1.01*	.01 (1.00) *1.01*
Class	−.41 (.79)	−.66 (2.13)** *.52*	−.65 (2.41)* *.52*
Protestant	−.27 (1.80)	−.36 (1.29) *.70*	−.30 (1.15) *.74*
Education	.33 (1.14)	.03 (.60) *1.03*	.08 (1.60)* *1.09*
N	535	610	591
Log likelihood	−222.11	−263.93	−255.40

Source: 1992 Cross National Election Study.

Note: Coding and question wording for variables are given in the Appendix, Table 7A.4. T values are in parentheses. In the two-stage logit models, factor change in odds coefficients are in italics, and unaltered logit coefficients are in standard type.

*$p \leq .05$, two-tailed; **$p \leq .01$, two-tailed.

intimately connected to the main respondent and, thus, more likely to transmit discrepant views: nonrelative discussants (Granovetter 1973; Huckfeldt and Sprague 1995; Huckfeldt et al. 1995). As Table 7.3 demonstrates, networks made up of such discussants also exert a strong influence on support for Clinton.[10]

The findings presented in Tables 7.2 and 7.3 are especially impressive when one considers that they persist in spite of control variables like partisanship, abortion opinion, perceptions of the national economy, and income, variables shown to be among the most important predictors of candidate choice in 1992 (Abramowitz 1995; Alvarez and Nagler 1995). The fact that networks exert a strong effect after controlling for these variables also lends validity to the assumption that the effect of discussants on main respondents is the result of social influence. Indeed, by taking account of social attributes and political predispositions, I reduce the likeli-

TABLE 7.3. Estimates of Main Respondent Clinton Choice as a
Function of Discussant Clinton Choice for All Nonmarried,
Nonrelative Discussion Pairs, 1992

Variables	Nonmarried, nonrelative discussion pairs
Constant	−4.99
Discussant Clinton choice	1.26 (2.03)*
	3.53
Partisanship	1.09 (5.45)**
	2.98
Abortion	.84 (1.79)
	2.30
National economy	1.10 (3.79)**
	3.01
Income	−.21 (1.75)
	.81
South	−.50 (1.35)
	.61
Union	.05 (.14)
	1.05
Age	−.01 (1.00)
	1.00
Class	−.74 (1.80)
	.48
Protestant	−.48 (1.37)
	.62
Education	.12 (1.71)
	1.13
N	286
Log likelihood	−124.89

Source: 1992 Cross National Election Study.
Note: Coding and question wording for variables are given in the Appendix, Table 7A.4. T values are in parentheses. Factor change in odds coefficients are in italics, and unaltered logit coefficients are in standard type. The model was estimated using Huckfeldt and Sprague's (1991, 1995) modified two-stage logit procedure.
*$p \leq .05$, two-tailed; **$p \leq .01$, two-tailed.

hood that the appearance of shared preferences between discussion partners is actually a spurious byproduct of shared predispositions (Huckfeldt and Sprague 1991, 30).

Thus far, analyses have focused solely on the impact of discussants' preference for Clinton on main respondents' Clinton preference. It is also worth examining the role that networks have in shaping preference for the other major party candidate in 1992. Table 7.4 demonstrates that support for George Bush is also subject to strong influence from social network members. Indeed, in models containing nonmarried discussants as well as nonrelative discussion pairs, the coefficient for discussant candidate choice is statistically significant at the .05 level. As with the Democratic Party candidate, support for Bush is subject to strong network effects, effects that endure after controlling for key attitudinal variables.[11]

TABLE 7.4. Estimates of Main Respondent Bush Choice as a Function of Discussant Bush Choice, 1992

Variables	Nonmarried discussion pairs	Nonmarried, nonrelative discussion pairs
Constant	−1.43	−3.03
Discussant Bush choice	1.67 (3.71)**	1.21 (1.81)*
Partisanship	−1.58 (8.78)**	−1.62 (6.23)**
Abortion	−1.66 (5.53)**	−2.26 (4.43)**
National economy	−1.00 (5.00)**	−1.12 (3.50)**
Income	.29 (2.90)**	.47 (2.76)**
South	−.16 (.50)	.08 (.16)
Union	−.38 (1.15)	−.05 (1.00)
Age	.04 (4.00)**	.04 (2.00)**
Class	.47 (1.47)	.82 (1.46)
Protestant	.40 (1.33)	.25 (.52)
Education	.02 (.33)	.11 (1.10)
N	591	286
Log likelihood	−184.73	−77.42

Source: 1992 Cross National Election Study

Note: Coding and question wording for variables are given in the Appendix, Table 7A.4. T values are in parentheses, and unaltered logit coefficients are in standard type. The models were estimated using Huckfeldt and Sprague's (1991, 1995) modified two-stage logit procedure.

$*p \leq .05$, two-tailed; $**p \leq .01$, two-tailed.

THE ROLE OF INTIMACY IN THE SOCIAL INFLUENCE OF POLITICS

Thus far, I have shown that social networks exert a direct, strong, and consistent impact on candidate choice. Although I have shown that citizens are subject to personal influence by nonrelative discussion partners, it is still possible that, even among nonrelatives, influence is largely confined to intimates, such as close friends. The purpose of this section is to determine whether influence occurs beyond the confines of close friendships.

Many studies have assumed that the most important social communication of political information takes place between people who are intimately connected to each other (Berelson et al. 1954; Campbell et al. 1960; Katz and Lazarsfeld 1955; Kenny 1993b, 1994, 1998; Lazarsfeld et al. 1944). Intimates are thought to be powerful agents of political influence because they are trusted, frequently encountered, and believed to be knowledgeable about politics. The notion is that citizens are more likely to trust opinions and information obtained from others whom they hold in high esteem, both as friends and as knowledgeable informants (Huckfeldt et al. 1995, 1027).

Although this model has been applied to social communication and influence inside families (e.g., Jennings and Niemi 1974, 1981), almost all of the studies concerning social influence in politics have used it to explain the nature of influence among unrelated individuals. Indeed, beginning with the Columbia sociologists, scholars have argued that social influence concerning political matters is enhanced among intimate associates, such as close friends (Berelson et al. 1954; Campbell et al. 1960; Kenny 1993b, 1994; Lazarsfeld et al. 1944). Berelson and his colleagues, for example, only collected information on an individual's three closest friends and three closest co-workers because "with the family, they make up the primary social groups whose members mold each other's political opinions as well as other behavior" (1954, 93–94).

Although there is evidence to support this view (e.g., Berelson et al. 1954; Katz and Lazarsfeld 1955; Lazarsfeld et al. 1944),[12] two more recent empirical findings call it into question. First, and most directly, Huckfeldt and Sprague (1991, 1995) found strong evidence to suggest that social influence is *not* enhanced among close friends. They discovered that close friends actually have a weaker effect on vote choice than less intimate contacts, such as more distant friends or regular contacts (Huckfeldt and Sprague 1991, 147). Second, Huckfeldt and his colleagues found that citizens frequently engage in political discussions with others who are less than intimate associates (Huckfeldt and Sprague 1991, 1995; Huckfeldt et al. 1995). Of course, contact is not synonymous with influence; citizens may, for a variety of reasons, simply not be affected by the opinions of their discussion partners. Nevertheless, because communication is a precondition for influence, its frequent occurrence among nonintimates raises the possibility that important influence may also pass through such relationships.

Clearly, there is reason to be uncertain about whether social influence is enhanced among intimate associates. A clearer understanding of the role of intimacy, therefore, calls for a more comprehensive examination of nonrelative intimate relationships and their role in political influence.

The Nature of Intimate Relationships

The first step in determining the role of intimacy in social influence is to take a careful look at the nature of intimate relationships. Researchers have identified many characteristics that can be expected to enhance social influence (Cacioppo and Petty 1979; DeBono and Harnish 1988; McGuire 1985; Milburn 1991). Because of space constraints, here I consider only those that can be readily measured using survey data and that have been shown to facilitate social influence in a political context.

I concentrate on four characteristics, each of which can be assessed using large opinion surveys and each of which has been shown to encourage social influence concerning political matters: correct perception, frequent political discussion, absence of political disagreement, and perceived political competence (Huckfeldt and Sprague 1991; Kenny 1993b, 1994; Jennings and Niemi 1981; Tedin 1974). To determine whether nonmarital relationships characterized by intimacy (i.e., close friendships) are more likely to possess these characteristics than less intimate relationships (i.e., friendships, regular contacts), I employ four bivariate regression models.

The explanatory variable in the models is a measure of whether the discussant is viewed as a close friend, friend, or regular contact by the main respondent.[13] The dependent variables are measures of the four characteristics just discussed: accuracy of perception,[14] frequency of political discussion, frequency of political disagreement, and perceived level of political expertise. If intimacy among nonrelatives facilitates influence, I would expect to find that close friends are far more likely to possess the characteristics that encourage social influence than "just friends" or regular contacts. This expectation, however, is not supported by the data.

Part A of Table 7.5 demonstrates that being a close friend, as opposed to just a friend or a regular contact, does not significantly increase the likelihood of possessing any of the characteristics found previously to facilitate social influence. Indeed, none of the coefficients is statistically significant (even at the .1 level, one-tailed), indicating that close friends are not more likely to be perceived accurately, not interacted with more frequently, not agreed with more frequently, and not perceived as being more knowledgeable than less intimate contacts. In fact, two of the coefficients imply that, compared to friends and regular contacts, close friends are *less* frequently interacted with and *less* likely to be viewed as politically knowledgeable. Clearly, intimate relationships among nonrelatives do not possess the characteristics commonly expected to facilitate social influence.[15]

How can these results be explained? Two partial, and admittedly post hoc, explanations come to mind. First, it is possible that many citizens choose their close friends on some basis other than politics and, consequently, rarely have reason to discuss or learn about their friends' political views. Second, in the United States, where there is a great deal of geographic mobility, the friends that citizens consider to be close may not be seen or even spoken to for long periods of time, thus making it easy to lose touch of their political views.

Although these findings taken by themselves are telling, it is also useful to view them in comparison with an analysis of spousal relationships. Researchers have found that social influence is profoundly magnified among married pairs (Huckfeldt and Sprague 1991; Jennings and Stoker in this volume; Kenny 1994;

TABLE 7.5. Characteristics of Discussants Named as Close Friends and Spouses

Dependent variable	Coefficient of close friend	T value	N
A. NONRELATIVE DISCUSSANTS			
Accuracy of perception	.02	.09	448
Political discussion frequency	−.03	.33	516
Political disagreement frequency	.03	.38	489
Extent of political knowledge	−.04	.80	515

Dependent variable	Coefficient of spouse	T value	N
B. ALL DISCUSSANTS			
Accuracy of perception	1.08	3.72**	806
Political discussion frequency	.17	3.40**	921
Political disagreement frequency	−.02	.29	884
Extent of political knowledge	.09	1.80*	918

Source: 1984 South Bend Study.

Note: Coding and question wording for variables are given in the Appendix, Table 7A.5. The "accuracy of perception" models were estimated using logistic regression, and the other models were estimated using Ordinary Least Squares.

$*p \leq .10$, two-tailed; $**p \leq .05$, two-tailed.

Zuckerman, Fitzgerald, and Dasović in this volume). If so, I would expect to find that, unlike close friendships, spousal relationships display at least some of the characteristics expected to amplify social influence. Part B of Table 7.5 supports this expectation. Spouses are much more likely to be accurately perceived, interacted with, and viewed as politically knowledgeable than are other discussants.

In sum, the results call into question the assumptions underlying the notion that intimate relationships outside the family are important for social influence. Indeed, intimate relationships outside the family (unlike spousal relationships) do not possess the characteristics widely considered to be important for social influence. With this evidence in mind, I turn to a more direct examination of the impact of intimacy on social influence.

The Impact of Intimacy on Social Influence

The goal of this section is to investigate directly the impact of intimacy on the social communication of several political choices: partisanship and opinion concerning abortion, women's rights, school prayer, government aid for minorities, and economic trade barriers. By conducting comparable analyses for each political decision, I can answer two key questions. First, and most fundamentally, does intimacy enhance social influence? Second, does the role of intimacy vary systematically according to the attitude or behavior under consideration? In particular, does the tendency to look to intimate friends vary according to the personal and emotional nature of the choice?

The first step in estimating the impact of discussant opinion on main respondent opinion is to obtain variables that can be used to construct a discussant instrument. Appendix Table 7A.6 contains a list of the variables used to predict the discussant instrument in each of the models. The second step is to identify the final models. In each model, the dependent variable is the main respondent's reported behavior or attitude (e.g., partisanship, opinion about abortion). In addition to the discussant choice instrument, the explanatory variables include several standard predictors of each dependent variable,[16] a dummy variable that is set to 1 if the discussion partners are "close friends" and 0 if the discussion partners are "just friends" or "regular contacts" ("intimacy"), and an interaction term designed to determine whether discussion partners who are close friends have a significantly greater impact on the political opinions of the main respondents than discussion partners who are just friends or regular contacts ("discussant instrument × intimacy").

It is important to note that the intimacy interaction term had to be estimated with some care because one of the variables involved in the interaction, discussant opinion, is an endogenous variable. Although it is straightforward to include nonlinear functions of exogenous or predetermined observed variables in simultaneous equation models (Bollen 1989, 128–29), the treatment of nonlinear functions that involve endogenous variables in such models requires the use of special procedures (Achen 1986, 46). The development of such procedures is still in its infancy (Bollen 1995, 223), but techniques have been proposed to cope with interaction terms that include endogenous variables (e.g., Busemeyer and Jones 1983; Kenny and Judd 1984). More recently, Bollen (1995) suggested a procedure that, unlike most techniques, is both relatively easy to implement and produces consistent estimates with a known asymptotic distribution.

The basic approach is to treat the interaction between the endogenous variable ("discussant instrument") and the exogenous variable ("intimacy") as another instrument that needs to be estimated before it can be included in the final model. Thus, all that needs to be done is to find variables that uniquely and strongly predict the interaction term and only weakly predict main respondent choice. In the present case, a number of such variables can be constructed for each model by interacting the "intimacy" variable with each of the discussant variables used to predict the discussant instrument (see Appendix Table 7A.6) (Bollen 1995).

Once the variables to be included in the analyses are identified, the final three steps are to estimate the discussant instrument and the intimacy interaction term, place them in the final model, and estimate their impact on the main respondent's opinion. I use a simple two-stage, least-squares model to estimate both the discussant instrument and its effect on main respondent opinion for each model.

Two different data sets are used in the analyses. The 1984 South Bend Study and the 1996 Political Network Study are both used to estimate the partisanship and abortion opinion models, and the 1996 Political Network Study is used to estimate models for the four other issue opinions: women's rights, school prayer, government aid for minorities, and economic trade barriers.[17]

Because the primary purpose of this section is to determine whether intimate relationships among nonrelatives enhance social influence, the chief coefficient of interest in each model is the intimacy interaction term. If, as some researchers suggest (e.g., Berelson et al. 1954; Kenny 1993b, 1994; Lazarsfeld et al. 1944), there is a tendency for intimate relationships significantly to enhance social influence, the coefficient of the interaction term should be statistically significant, with close friends exerting a larger influence on main respondent opinion than just friends or regular contacts. These expectations, however, are not supported by the data.

As Tables 7.6 through 7.9 demonstrate, for each decision, the preferences of discussants who are close friends do not exert a significantly greater impact on main respondent opinion than the preferences of discussants who are less intimately tied to the main respondent.[18] Indeed, the coefficient for the intimacy interaction variable is not statistically significant (at the .05 level) in any of the models, indicating that close friends do not exert an impact on main respondent opinion that is much different from friends or regular contacts. Clearly, there is strong empirical evidence to suggest that, for a wide variety of political decisions, close friendships do not significantly magnify the impact of social influence, a result that strongly contradicts the conventional wisdom regarding intimacy and its role in social influence.[19]

The results also indicate that the impact of intimacy does not, as some have proposed (Katz and Lazarsfeld 1955; Kenny 1993b), appear to vary according to the decision at hand. That is, intimacy seems to be of little consequence to any of the decisions. It is important to make two other points about these findings.

First, the rather weak discussant effects shown in many of the models in Tables 7.6 through 7.9 should not be taken as evidence that political decisions are impervious to the influence of nonrelatives. Quite the opposite. As Table 7.10 demonstrates, when all nonrelative discussant pairs are considered, there is often a significant discussant impact on main respondent opinion.

TABLE 7.6. Main Respondent Partisanship by Interaction between Discussant
Partisanship and Intimacy

	Partisanship (1984)		Partisanship (1996)	
	Beta	T value	Beta	T value
Constant	4.12	4.29	1.53	2.00
Discussant instrument × intimacy	−.15	−.92	.11	1.21
Discussant instrument	.41	3.11**	.05	.61
Intimacy	.64	.95	−.45	−1.27
Age	−.01	−2.85**	.01	.34
Education	−.16	−3.53**	−.01	−.07
Income	−.10	−1.49	−.17	−2.76**
Ideology	.49	7.78**	.75	17.33**
Sex	.01	.04	−.01	−.06
Race	1.61	2.63**	.98	2.97**
N	350		414	
Standard error of regression	1.77		1.60	

Sources: 1984 South Bend Study and 1996 Political Network Study.
Note: Coding and question wording for variables are given in the Appendix, Tables 7A.6 and 7A.7. For
each of the models, relatives are excluded.
*p ≤ .05, two-tailed; **p ≤ .01, two-tailed.

TABLE 7.7. Main Respondent Abortion Opinion by Interaction between Discussant
Abortion Opinion and Intimacy

	Opinion on abortion (1984)		Opinion on abortion (1996)	
	Beta	T value	Beta	T value
Constant	−1.68	−1.53	.44	.64
Discussant instrument × intimacy	.11	.38	−.03	−.20
Discussant instrument	.06	.39	.26	2.72**
Intimacy	−.66	−.83	.23	.58
Age	.03	3.67**	.01	2.12*
Education	.21	3.86**	−.06	−1.71
Income	−.06	−.87	.13	2.67**
Ideology	.10	1.38	.21	6.11**
Catholic	−.10	−.41	−.53	−3.47**
Church attendance	.49	6.16**	.45	9.22**
N	240		414	
Standard error of regression	1.75		1.31	

Sources: 1984 South Bend Study and 1996 Political Network Study.
Note: Coding and question wording for variables are given in the Appendix, Tables 7A.6 and 7A.7. For
each of the models, relatives are excluded.
*p ≤ .05, two-tailed; **p ≤ .01, two-tailed.

TABLE 7.8. Main Respondent Issue Opinion by Interaction between Discussant Issue Opinion and Intimacy

	Equal rights for women		Prayer in schools	
	Beta	T value	Beta	T value
Constant	2.71	2.93	5.71	6.20
Discussant instrument × intimacy	−.23	.40	−.39	−1.80
Discussant instrument	.28	1.38	.25	1.29
Intimacy	.98	.85	1.21	1.78
Partisanship	.06	2.82**	—	—
Race	.16	.88	—	—
Sex	−.07	−.76	—	—
Age	.00	1.09	.01	.60
Income	−.05	−1.36	−.09	−1.74
Church attendance	.07	2.17*	−.16	−3.21**
Ideology	—	—	−.25	−6.94**
Jewish	—	—	−1.01	−2.37*
Protestant	—	—	−.02	−.14
Education	—	—	−.11	−3.13**
N	512		414	
Standard error of regression	1.03		1.32	

Sources: 1996 Political Network Study.
Note: Coding and question wording for variables are given in the Appendix, Tables 7A.6 and 7A.7. For each of the models, relatives are excluded.
*$p \leq .05$, two-tailed; **$p \leq .01$, two-tailed.

TABLE 7.9. Main Respondent Issue Opinion by Interaction between Discussant Issue Opinion and Intimacy

	Government aid for minorities		Protecting economy with trade barriers	
	Beta	T value	Beta	T value
Constant	1.26	2.53	4.37	5.03
Discussant instrument × intimacy	.20	1.19	.07	.21
Discussant instrument	.16	1.15	.08	.34
Intimacy	−.46	−.97	−.16	−.20
Partisanship	.07	2.32*	—	—
Race	1.00	4.19**	.22	.85*
Sex	.02	.22	.26	2.05
Age	—	—	−.01	−1.58
Income	.06	1.42	—	—
Ideology	.08	2.04*	−.07	−2.33*
Education	.01	.38	−.08	−2.75**
N	385		437	
Standard error of regression	.98		1.18	

Sources: 1996 Political Network Study.
Note: Coding and question wording for variables are given in the Appendix, Tables 7A.6 and 7A.7. For each of the models, relatives are excluded.
*$p \leq .05$, two-tailed; **$p \leq .01$, two-tailed.

TABLE 7.10. Main Respondent Partisanship and Issue Opinions by Discussant
Partisanship and Discussant Issue Opinions

Dependent variable	Coefficient of discussant opinion		
	Beta	T value	N
Partisanship (1984)	.34	3.84***	352
Partisanship (1992)	.12	2.35**	412
Abortion (1984)	.14	1.63*	242
Abortion (1992)	.27	4.05***	412
Women	.23	1.55*	508
Prayer	.01	.11	412
Minority	.30	2.73***	383
Trade	.12	.65	435

Sources: 1984 South Bend Study and 1996 Political Network Study.
Note: Analysis was done only using nonrelative discussants. The full models, not presented here,
include the explanatory variables as described in the Appendix, Table 7A.7, except for the interaction term
("discussant instrument × intimacy") and the "intimacy" variable. The magnitude and direction of the control variables change very little from those presented in Tables 7.6 through 7.9.
*$p \leq .10$, two-tailed; **$p \leq .05$, two-tailed; ***$p \leq .01$, two-tailed.

Second, it is important to reemphasize that the results presented here apply only
to intimate relationships outside the family. As other studies have demonstrated
(e.g., Huckfeldt and Sprague 1991; Kenny 1993b, 1994), social influence is magnified among married pairs. The findings here imply only that it is unwise to
assume that intimacy inside the family has the same implications for social influence as intimacy outside the family.

These findings raise an important question: If intimacy does not influence political choice, what does? Although a complete answer cannot be provided here, it
is interesting to explore one of the major possibilities: frequency of interaction.
In previous studies, scholars have argued that the ability of a nonrelative discussant to influence others might be dependent on immediacy and regularity of contact (Huckfeldt and Sprague 1991, 147). Indeed, learning theory suggests that
reinforcement is particularly powerful when it is immediate, recurring, and sustained through time (Sprague 1982). Contrary to this expectation, however, I find
that there is little evidence to suggest that increased regular contact significantly
boosts social influence.

Consistent with Huckfeldt and Sprague's (1991, 1995) analysis of vote choice
in the 1984 presidential election in South Bend, Table 7.11 demonstrates that
the preferences of discussants who are interacted with more frequently do not
tend to exert a significantly greater impact on main respondent opinion than
the preferences of discussants who are interacted with less frequently.[20] Indeed,
in nearly all the models, the coefficient of the interaction between frequency
of political discussion and discussant opinion is not statistically significant,[21]
indicating that frequency of contact does not affect influence among nonrelative discussion partners. Clearly, therefore, more extensive analyses are necessary to determine which factors enhance or inhibit the impact of nonrelative
network members on choice.

TABLE 7.11. Main Respondent Opinion by Interaction between Discussant Opinion and Frequency of Interaction

Dependent variable	Coefficient of discussant opinion $\times$ frequency of interaction		
	Beta	T value	N
Partisanship (1984)	.02	.18	349
Partisanship (1992)	.15	2.54*	412
Abortion (1984)	.02	.07	239
Abortion (1992)	−.06	.07	412
Women	−.06	−.43	508
Prayer	−.07	−.53	412
Minority	−.09	−.73	383
Trade	.65	1.51	435

Sources: 1984 South Bend Study and 1996 Political Network Study.
Note: Analysis was done only using nonrelative discussants. The full models, not presented here, include the explanatory variables as described in the Appendix, Table 7A.7, except for the interaction term ("discussant instrument $\times$ intimacy") and the "intimacy" variable. The magnitude and direction of the control variables change very little from those presented in Tables 7.6 through 7.9.
*$p \leq .05$, two-tailed.

DISCUSSION

The conception of the electorate that emerges from much of the empirical research in political science is an extreme one. One gets the impression that the modern citizen relies heavily on his or her own beliefs and attitudes, and only marginally on the advice of others, when making political choices. Of course, few would agree that this "social vacuum" model of political choice accurately represents reality for most Americans. The question this chapter has attempted to answer, therefore, is to what extent modern voters do conform to the model of the socially isolated citizen.

By shifting the focus away from the demographic groups typically studied in political science and toward social networks, I demonstrate that even after controlling for powerful individual-level attitudinal variables, social network members exert a direct, powerful, and consistent impact on the choices of modern citizens. These findings provide evidence using a national sample focused on a recent election year to support the notion that individual choice is fundamentally dependent on informal interactions with others, a claim originally made decades ago but only sparingly tested since.

In addition, the evidence suggests that social influence is not restricted to networks of family members or close friends; a significant amount of persuasion occurs outside such intimate relationships. Indeed, I discovered that nonmarried discussants as well as nonrelative discussants exert a powerful impact on political choice. What is more, intimate relationships outside the family do not appear to possess the characteristics that have been widely found to facilitate social influence, and, for six important political decisions, there is scant evidence to suggest that intimacy actually enhances social influence.

In sum, there is very little evidence to suggest that citizens in the post–New Deal era have abandoned social cues in favor of a more individualized and inwardly oriented style of choice. Modern choice is strongly tied to extended networks of social interaction. Although citizens may, as Putnam (2000) argued, be increasingly likely to "bowl alone," there is scant evidence to suggest that they "choose alone." This conclusion has potentially important implications for how we understand and study modern political choice.

As discussed, the broad tendency in political science is either to ignore the sociological basis of citizen choice or to treat social location as a secondary, less important determinant of political choice. This has allowed scholars to question the ability of citizens to fulfill one of the most fundamental requirements of a successful democracy: to engage in social deliberation as part of the political decision-making process. I propose that the evidence presented here provides good reason to be more optimistic about the chances for such deliberation.

Scholars concerned with democratic theory frequently agree that a crucial component of the democratic process is citizens who consult with other citizens. This process, however, must be more than a simple exchange of opinions between like-minded citizens. A citizen truly engaged in democratic deliberation must engage in real debate, where opinions are not only expressed but also challenged and sometimes altered (Berelson 1952, 322–24). The evidence presented here suggests that a fair amount of such interaction takes place in modern American society. Indeed, the evidence shows that modern individual citizen choice is likely to be influenced and altered by discussions with network members who are likely to carry information that is both novel and often contradictory. Thus, consistent with modern democratic theory, there appears to be a tendency for modern citizens to engage in social deliberation on the way to making final political choices.

The sort of deliberation that takes place among the electorate affords us some insights into the nature of public opinion. The analyses demonstrate that social influence is not restricted to strong ties (those between close friends and family). Instead, citizens are just as likely to be influenced by weaker ties among casual acquaintances. Since information that is communicated through weak ties typically travels further than signals received through strong ties (Granovetter 1973), public opinion appears to be more than the aggregation of opinions held among individuals and their cohesive subgroups. Instead, public opinion can also be characterized as an amalgamation of the views of many different individuals and subgroups in the population.

APPENDIX

TABLE 7A.1. Number of Discussants Named by Main Respondents

	Important matters discussants				Political discussant	Total discussants
	1	2	3	4		
Number named	1,066	885	614	395	787	3,747
Percentage of respondents naming discussant	80.9	67.1	46.6	30.0	59.7	

Source: 1992 Cross National Election Study.
Note: N = 1,318.

TABLE 7A.2. Logit Estimates of Main Respondent Willingness to Give Discussant Last Name and Phone Number as a Function of Main Respondent Political Interest, Political Participation, Partisan/Ideological Extremism, and Demographic Group Identity

Variables	Logit coefficient
Constant	$-.59$
Interest	.31 (.12)**
Turnout	.14 (.20)**
Extreme partisanship	.09 (.03)**
Extreme ideology	$-.01$ (.05)
Education	.01 (.03)
Income	.00 (.05)
Female	.28 (.14)**
Class	$-.14$ (.16)
Black	.05 (.26)
Catholic	$-.29$ (.17)
Church attendance	$-.08$ (.05)
Age	$-.01$ (.01)**
N	914
Log likelihood	-613.51

Source: 1992 Cross National Election Study.
Note: Standard errors are in parentheses. For coding of education, income, age, and class variables, see Table 7A.4. For all other variables, see Table 7A.3.
**$p \leq .05$, two-tailed.

TABLE 7A.3. Coding and Question Wording for Variables in Table 7A.2

Dependent variable
   Call: 0 = main respondent did not provide contact information for any discussants; 1 = main respondent did provide contact information for at least one discussant

Explanatory variables
   Interest: 1 = not much interested in the recent political campaigns; 2 = somewhat interested; 3 = very much interested
   Turnout: 0 = did not vote in election; 1 = voted in election
   Extreme partisanship: 0 = weakly lean toward one of the parties to 6 = strongly lean toward one of the parties
   Extreme ideology: 1 = ideologically neutral to 5 = ideologically committed (either conservative or liberal)
   Female: 0 = male; 1 = female
   Black: 0 = white; 1 = black
   Catholic: 0 = not a Catholic; 1 = Catholic
   Church attendance: 1 = attends every week to 4 = never attends church

Note: For coding of education, income, age, and class variables, see Table 7A.4.

TABLE 7A.4. Coding and Question Wording for Variables in Tables 7.1–7.4

TABLES 7.1–7.3

For main respondent

Clinton choice: 0 = vote for Bush, Perot, or no vote; 1 = vote for Clinton
Partisanship: −1 = Republican; 0 = independent; 1 = Democrat
Abortion: 0 = government should restrict abortions; 1 = women should be able to choose
National economy: 1 = gotten better; 2 = about the same; 3 = gotten worse
Income: 1 = less than $25,000 to 6 = more than $75,000
South: 0 = nonsouth; 1 = south
Union: 0 = not a union member; 1 = union member
Age: age in years
Class: 0 = not working class; 1 = working class
Protestant: 0 = not Protestant; 1 = Protestant
Education: education in years

For discussant

Clinton choice: 0 = vote for Bush, Perot, or no vote; 1 = vote for Clinton
Partisanship: −1 = Republican; 0 = independent; 1 = Democrat
Age: age in years
Education: education in years

TABLE 7.4

Bush choice: 0 = vote for Clinton, Perot, or no vote; 1 = vote for Bush (for both main respondent and discussant)

TABLE 7A.5. Coding and Question Wording of Variables for Table 7.5

Close: "Would you say [discussant] is a close friend, a friend, or just someone that you regularly come into contact with?" (1 = close friend; 0 = friend, regular contact)
Spouse: "Is [discussant] a member of your family? If so, how is [discussant] related to you?" (0 = other relatives, not related; 1 = spouse)
Accuracy of perception: (0 = does not accurately name the vote choice of the discussant in the 1984 presidential election; 1 = accurately names vote choice)
Political discussion frequency: "When you talk with [discussant], how often do you discuss politics?" (1 = never; 2 = only once in a while; 3 = fairly often; 4 = most times)
Political disagreement frequency: "When you discuss politics with [discussant], how often do you disagree?" (1 = often; 2 = sometimes; 3 = rarely; 4 = never)
Extent of political knowledge: "How much do you think that [discussant] knows about politics?" (1 = not much at all; 2 = an average amount; 3 = a great deal)

TABLE 7A.6. Variables Used to Construct Discussant Instruments in Tables 7.6–7.9

	Discussant instruments					
	P	A	W	Pr	M	T
dPartisanship	—	—	x	—	x	—
dRace	x	—	x	—	x	x
dSex	x	—	x	—	x	x
dAge	x	x	x	x	—	x
dIncome	x	x	x	x	x	—
dChurch attendance	—	x	x	x	—	—
dIdeology	x	x	—	x	x	x
dJewish	—	—	—	x	—	—
dProtestant	—	—	—	x	—	—
dCatholic	—	x	—	—	—	—
dEducation	x	x	—	x	x	x

Note: P = partisanship, A = abortion, W = women, Pr = prayer, M = minority, T = trade. All variables beginning with "d" are discussant variables. Coding and question wording of discussant variables are the same as for the corresponding main respondent variables (see Table 7A.3).

TABLE 7A.7. Coding and Question Wording of Variables for Tables 7.6–7.11

Dependent variables
    Partisanship: 1 = strong Republican to 7 = strong Democrat
    Abortion opinion (1984):[a]   0 = strong pro-life to 6 = strong pro-choice
    Abortion opinion (1992):   1 = strongly oppose abortion to 5 = strongly favor abortion
    Women: 1 = strongly oppose equal rights for women to 5 = strongly favor
    Prayer: 1 = strongly oppose organized prayer in public schools to 5 = strongly favor
    Minority: 1 = strongly oppose government aid for blacks and other minorities to 5 = strongly favor
    Trade: 1 = strongly oppose protecting the economy with trade barriers to 5 = strongly favor

Explanatory variables
    Intimacy: 0 = friend/regular contact; 1 = close friend
    Discussant instrument
    Discussant instrument × intimacy
    Education: years of education
    Income: 1 = under $5,000 household income to 8 = $50,000 and over
    Age: age in years
    Race: 0 = white; 1 = black
    Sex: 0 = male; 1 = female
    Ideology: 1 = strong conservative to 7 = strong liberal
    Church attendance: 1 = every week to 5 = never
    Catholic: 0 = otherwise; 1 = Catholic
    Partisanship: 1 = strong Republican to 7 = strong Democrat
    Protestant: 0 = otherwise; 1 = Protestant
    Jewish: 0 = otherwise; 1 = Jewish

[a]This measure was constructed using responses to a set of six questions designed to measure preferences on the abortion issue. The questions ask whether abortion should be legal in a variety of situations. I combined the responses of these questions into a scale by summing the number of circumstances in which a respondent would allow an abortion to take place. Thus, the scale ranges from 0 (disapproves of abortion under all circumstances: strong pro-life) to 6 (approves of abortion under all circumstances: strong pro-choice).

LAURENCE KOTLER-BERKOWITZ

8   Friends and Politics

Linking Diverse Friendship Networks to Political Participation

VERY FEW PEOPLE are social isolates who receive information only from impersonal sources such as the media. For almost all of us, the people with whom we interact—family, friends, neighbors, work colleagues, and co-religionists—are important sources of information on topics ranging from essential concerns such as jobs, housing, and healthcare to the more pleasurable topics of entertainment and vacations. One important principle about our social interactions posits that the more people we know and the more different they are both from us and from each other, the more varied is the information we receive from them, and the greater are the social opportunities and benefits made available to us.

The sociological literature offers numerous examples of this proposition. Granovetter (1973) first established the theoretical importance of "weak ties" (1973) and showed their benefits in job seeking and community organizing. Burt's "network range" (1983), Stoloff, Glanville, and Bienenstock's "network composition" (1999) and Erickson's "network variety" (2003) support Granovetter's initial insight in a variety of other areas, including corporate management, women's labor force participation, and mental and physical health. Though Granovetter, Burt, Stoloff and her colleagues, and Erickson employ different conceptual terms and definitions, together they point to a crucial aspect of social networks. Relative to social connections with people similar to oneself, ties to a diverse set of people—or to a set of people located across a diverse set of social groups—facilitate greater access to varied and nonredundant types of information that in turn enhance opportunities for undertaking social action, engaging in social activities, and reaping social and personal benefits.

Applied to politics, the same principle links political and other forms of activity in an expanding theoretical web that reinforces the explanatory power of social networks in a variety of social contexts. Social networks that are more diverse, especially relative to one's total network size and one's own social characteristics, produce higher levels of political participation.[1] Political activity results from the participatory influence of social ties, which works through three factors: information, recruitment, and mobilization; and it is further heightened by the nonredundancy of the same factors that is inherent in diverse social connections. Diverse networks also have an effect on political participation because much of politics is structured around the claims of social groups defined by traits such as race, ethnicity, class, religion, and sexual orientation. In turn, many opportunities for political participation are also structured around these social groups, as political entrepreneurs and community leaders use a group's social contexts to mobilize mass-level participation (Rosenstone and Hansen 1993; Verba, Schlozman, and

Brady 1995), press the group's claims on the political system, and seek allies in their efforts.

This analysis examines the positive relationship between diverse social networks and political activity through the specific prism of friendships and the role they play in fostering nonelectoral participation. Friendships are a key component of social networks, generating a series of direct, frequent, voluntary, and purposeful interactions (Huckfeldt and Sprague 1993, 290). More generally, friends provide social and emotional support, companionship and confidentiality, advice and assistance, information and news. As such, friendships have tremendous potential for influencing the daily decisions that people must make, the preferences they adopt, and the activities in which they partake. Indeed, friends can be as influential as family members and sometimes more so.

The influence of friendships extends to politics as well. Friends variably affect each other's political preferences (Levine in this volume) by reinforcing or challenging current views on parties, politicians, and policy issues. Friends may be equally important for political participation. They expose us to political information, recruitment, and mobilization in the forms of requests to sign a petition, attend a rally, or join in the work of a political group. These invitations come more frequently from friends than from those with whom we are more distantly connected or from strangers (Verba, Schlozman, and Brady 1995, chapter 5).[2] Relatively few friendships form and revolve primarily around political choices and political activity, but many friendships incorporate dimensions of politics related either to preferences or participation. Indeed, this claim about the relative primacy of friendships over politics derives from the general principle that the choice of social contexts and the social networks embedded in them result primarily from nonpolitical factors and considerations, with political consequences being largely if not fully derivative (Huckfeldt and Sprague 1993).

Building on (1) the sociological principle connecting diverse social connections to expanded social opportunities and benefits, (2) the structuring of politics around social status groups, and (3) the claim that friendships in and of themselves are important mechanisms for drawing people into political activity, one can develop a series of increasingly precise hypotheses about the connection between friendship diversity and political activity.

Hypothesis 1: *Diverse friendships, defined as friendships across multiple group boundaries, are positively related to higher levels of political participation.* Diverse friendships tie the participatory effects of friendships to broader opportunities for political participation. Diverse friendships multiply the general effects of friendships by providing nonredundant opportunities for and recruitment into political participation in different and unconnected social groups. As such, diverse friendships across social groups are especially likely to provide greater opportunities for, knowledge about, and recruitment into political participation than friendships that are confined to a more limited number of social groups. Friendships with community leaders are particularly likely to strengthen the general participatory effects of diverse friendship networks. Because community leaders are often directly tied to the political arena, they frequently have an interest in recruiting and mobilizing others to political participation.[3]

Hypothesis 2: *The greater the diversity of friendships relative to friendship network size, the higher will be the level of political participation.* An important correlate of friendship diversity is the size of one's network of friends. The more friends a person has, the more likely she is to have a socially diverse set of friends. In contrast, those with smaller friendship networks tend to have friends within a more limited set of social groups. As a result, the positive effect of a socially diverse set of friends on political participation may be due in part to friendship network size. Hypothesis 2 specifies more precisely the independent effect of friendship diversity on political participation, controlling for the size of friendship networks.

Hypothesis 3: *The greater the diversity of friendships relative to one's own social characteristics, the higher will be the level of political participation.* All else being equal, one's own membership in a social group—be it ethnic, religious, racial, or class—will increase the likelihood of knowing about political issues relevant to the group and opportunities to engage in politics regarding those issues; and as a result the participatory boost from having friends in the same social group will be reduced. In contrast, greater participatory benefits will result from having a diverse set of friends in other social groups: that is, in ethnic, racial, religious, and class groups different from one's own.

Hypothesis 4: *The greater the diversity of friendships relative to friendship network size and relative to one's own social characteristics, the higher will be the level of political participation.* This hypothesis logically joins Hypotheses 2 and 3 into a single hypothesis that expresses the effect of friendship diversity on political participation in a more precise way than either does separately.

ALTERNATIVE EXPLANATIONS OF POLITICAL PARTICIPATION

In contrast to the social network hypotheses, the literature on political participation identifies five alternative explanations for why people engage in politics. These five focus on socioeconomic resources, participation in nonpolitical organizations, social group membership, psychological engagement with politics, and social stability.

The empirical correlation between socioeconomic resources and political participation is well established (Nie, Junn, and Stehlik-Barry 1996; Verba and Nie 1972; Verba, Schlozman, and Brady 1995; Verba, Schlozman, and Burns, in this volume; Wolfinger and Rosenstone 1980).[4] Various theoretical linkages have been suggested to explain the empirical association.[5] High levels of education provide the cognitive and analytic skills people need to understand politics and to navigate the political arena. Additionally, education socializes people to civic values of participation, stimulates their interest in politics, and makes them more aware of opportunities to protect their interests. Advanced education is also typically associated with higher-status occupations and, more importantly, the higher incomes that facilitate and subsidize participation.

Participation in nonpolitical organizations affords a second explanation for political activity (Knoke 1990a; Leighley 1996; Rosenstone and Hansen 1993; Verba and Nie 1972; Verba, Schlozman, and Brady 1995; Verba, Schlozman, et al. 1993). Here, too, various theoretical linkages have been posited to explain how nonpolitical participation leads to political activity. Nonpolitical activity helps develop communication and organizational skills that can be applied to politics. In addition, nonpolitical organizations create institutional and social contexts and networks that expose members to political mobilization and recruitment. Nonpolitical organizations may provide political cues, such as encouragement to vote or to contact elected officials, that stimulate political engagement. From a different perspective, organizational activity may advance political participation by stimulating members' concerns about protecting a group's interests through political activity (Uhlaner 1995). Church membership is an important example of these theoretical linkages: participation in religious congregations helps develop communication and organizational skills (Verba, Schlozman, et al. 1993) while religious contexts provide social settings to educate members about politics and mobilize them for political activity (Wald 1997).

Participation in nonpolitical organizations is particularly important to those with fewer socioeconomic resources because it offers a compensating mechanism for becoming politically involved (Verba, Nie, and Kim 1978). Involvement in nonpolitical organizations helps to close the gap in political activity that reduced socioeconomic resources open. In that sense, then, nonpolitical organizations are a rival factor to socioeconomic resources not only for political scientists and sociologists trying to explain political activity but also for political entrepreneurs who seek to mobilize into politics persons with fewer economic resources.[6]

A third stream in the literature on political participation focuses on differences between social groups defined by race, ethnicity, gender, and religion. Numerous studies have shown that African Americans and Latinos are less likely to participate in politics than are whites, and that women are less likely to participate than men (Burns, Schlozman, and Verba 2001; Leighley and Vedlitz 1999; Verba, Schlozman, and Brady 1995; Verba, Schlozman, et al. 1993). As Verba and his colleagues have noted (Verba, Burns, and Schlozman 2002; Verba, Schlozman, et al. 1993), much and in some cases all of the participatory differences between racial, ethnic, and gender groups can be explained by differences in group socioeconomic status, but this observation does not mean that ethnicity, race, and gender are unimportant. To the contrary, that groups display such wide variation in socioeconomic status reflects the extent to which class and other bases of social stratification are tied together and jointly produce important political consequences.

In addition to race, ethnicity, and gender, religion may be a factor in political participation. Religion as a set of beliefs and in its institutional forms promotes political participation (Wald 1997). Differences in how religious traditions interpret the political implications of their beliefs and their institutional responses to social and political events may produce differential rates of political participation among their members (Fowler and Hertzke 1995; Lipset and Raab 1995; Wald 1997; Wuthnow 1983).

A fourth explanation of participation is psychological engagement in politics (Leighley and Vedlitz 1999; Rosenstone and Hansen 1993; Verba, Schlozman, and Brady 1995). Some people find politics more interesting and satisfying than others do, and, as with most subjects, psychological engagement increases the likelihood of participation. Those who are more psychologically engaged in politics also tend to be more politically informed, and information reduces costs of participation. Psychological engagement is a theoretically proximate explanation of political activity, and, as such, it will provide a difficult test for more theoretically distant determinants of participation, especially friendship diversity.

Lastly, a fifth alternative explanation of political participation is social stability (Jennings 1979; Leighley 1995; Leighley and Vedlitz 1999). The literature on political participation has not focused extensively on social stability—long-term residence in a community or stable employment, for example—as a major factor in political engagement.[7] Nonetheless, one may plausibly argue that, in comparison to persons in more transient phases of life, socially stable people may have, and be particularly aware of, social and economic interests that promote political participation.

INTERACTION EFFECTS

Now that the theoretical logic linking friendship diversity to political participation has been presented along with established explanations of political engagement, a potentially important source of variation can be considered. Specifically, the effects of friendship diversity may vary by social groups or by other individual-level characteristics that shape political activity. Lower rates of political participation characterize those with fewer socioeconomic resources; those who are not involved in nonpolitical organizations; some groups defined by race, ethnicity, gender, or religion; people with less political interest and knowledge; and the socially transient. How might friendship diversity interact with these relationships? Two competing hypotheses are added to the hypotheses already posited above:

Hypothesis 5: *The effects of diverse friendships on political participation will be stronger among those who, all else being equal, participate in politics at lower levels than among those who participate at higher levels.* In this hypothesis, network effects become stronger as other characteristics weaken in their ability to shape political behavior (Beck, Dalton, et al. 2002; Zaller 1992). Specifically, friendship diversity counteracts the dampening effects of reduced socioeconomic resources, lack of organizational participation, membership in selected social groups, low levels of psychological engagement with politics, and social transience.

Hypothesis 6: *The effects of diverse friendships on political participation will be weaker among those who participate in politics at lower levels than among those who participate at higher levels.* In this supposition, those who already participate in politics at higher levels are more likely to take advantage of the opportunities for further participation that friendship diversity provides. Those who participate less often are less likely to accept the additional opportunities for participation that diverse friendships make available, thereby reinforcing their relative estrangement from the political arena.

DATA AND MEASURES

Data for the analysis come from the Social Capital Benchmark Study 2000. The data file contains two samples from the United States, a nationally representative sample of 3,003 respondents and a collection of forty-one community samples from across the country with over 26,000 respondents. This analysis utilizes the U.S. national sample. After employing sample weights and accounting for missing data, the effective national sample size is 2,351, though it varies slightly in the multivariate analyses due to changes in explanatory variables.[8]

The dependent variable used in the analysis is a count measure of nonelectoral political participation. The components of the measure include the following five categories of activity in the twelve months prior to participants' being interviewed: attending a political meeting or rally; participating in a demonstration, boycott, or march; signing a petition; participating in a political group; and belonging to any group that took local action for reform. Each of the components is a dichotomous variable; these were summed to produce a measure running from 0 to 5 to indicate how many of the specific activities respondents undertook.[9] The final three categories were then collapsed into a single category to avoid small response category sizes; thus, the final measure of nonelectoral participation runs from 0 to 3. Table 8.1 displays the variable's distribution, which shows that over half of all respondents did not take part in any nonelectoral activity, slightly more than one-quarter took part in one activity, 11 percent undertook two activities, and just over 10 percent participated in three or more activities.[10]

The major explanatory variables of interest are a series of five variables needed to test Hypotheses 1–4. The measures are: (1) friendship diversity by itself; (2) friendship network size; (3) friendship diversity standardized over friendship network size; (4) friendship diversity purged of respondents' own characteristics; and (5) friendship diversity both purged of respondents' own characteristics and standardized over friendship network size.

1. *Friendship diversity by itself* is an interval scale produced by summing eleven dichotomous indicators of different types of people that respondents identify as their personal friends.[11] Four indicators measure the diversity of respondents' ethnic networks and include whether they have a friend who is white, African American, Hispanic, or Asian. Four other indicators measure the diversity of class networks, including whether respondents have a friend who owns a vacation home, owns a business, is a manual worker, or has been on welfare. Three additional indicators are whether respondents have a friend of a different religion or, for those with no religion, whether they have a friend who is "very religious"; whether they have a friend who is gay or lesbian; and whether they have a friend who is a community leader.[12]

2. *Friendship network size* is a scale indicating the total number of close friends respondents report having, with response category 1 equaling no close friends[13]

TABLE 8.1. Distribution of Nonelectoral Political Activities

Number of activities	Weighted N	Percentage
0	1,227	52.2
1	627	26.7
2	256	10.9
3 or more	242	10.3
Total	2,351	100.0

and response category 5 equaling ten or more close friends. Social networks of course are composed of more than friends, but a measure of the size of friendship networks is particularly apt for standardizing measures of the diversity of friendship networks.

3. *Friendship diversity standardized over friendship network size* was constructed by dividing friendship diversity by network size; the measure ranges from 0 to 10. The higher a respondent's score on the scale, the more diverse her friendship network is relative to the total number of close friends she has. For two reasons, a person could report a greater number of friends with particular characteristics than their total number of close friends. First, questions on specific characteristics referred only to "friends" rather than the more restrictive "close friends" used to measure network size, so that some friends may be included in the diversity scale who were excluded from the count of close friends. Additionally, some friends, even close friends, may have been counted twice with regard to diversity of characteristics. For example, a single friend could have both a different ethnicity and religion from a respondent, while only counting as one close friend.

4. *Friendship diversity purged of respondents' own characteristics* modifies the original friendship diversity scale by removing friends who match respondents' own characteristics. Doing this reduces the range of the interval scale by three, so that the minimum score is still 0 but the maximum score is now 8 (rather than 11).

To remove respondents' own ethnic-racial attributes, white respondents received no points on the scale for claiming a white friend, African American respondents received no points for having an African American friend, and so on for Hispanic and Asian respondents and their friends.

To account for class characteristics, respondents were first categorized into the working and middle classes. Respondents who belong to a labor union but not a professional group, or who have less than a high school education, were classified as working class. Respondents who participate in a professional, trade, farm, or business association and not in a labor union, or who have a college degree, were designated as middle class. Respondents remaining unclassified were categorized according to household income. Those with income less than $50,000 a year were classified as working class and those with income of $50,000 or more were placed in the middle class. Working class respondents then received one point for having a friend who owns a vacation home and one point for having a friend who owns a business. Middle class respondents received points for having a friend who is a manual worker and a friend who has been on welfare.

The measure of religious diversity remains unchanged because the original question already excludes the respondents' own characteristics, asking respondents whether they have a friend of a different religion from theirs or, among respondents with no religious identification, if they have a friend who is very religious.

The two remaining components of the scale—a friendship with someone who is gay or lesbian, and a friendship with a community leader—also remain the same. These unchanged indicators constitute a minor drawback: they could not be purged of the respondents' characteristics because respondents were not asked about their own sexual orientation or whether they consider themselves a community leader. In the case of gay and lesbian friends, this is somewhat mitigated by the fact that gay men and lesbians constitute a social minority, so that for many people having a friend who is gay or lesbian would represent a diverse tie. In sum, nine of the eleven components of the friendship diversity scale explicitly remove the respondents' own social characteristics, providing a very reasonable measure of friendship diversity relative to respondents' own attributes.

5. The final measure, *friendship diversity both purged of respondents' own characteristics and standardized over friendship network size,* was constructed by dividing the interval scale of friendship diversity purged of respondents' attributes by the number of close friends respondents report having. The resulting scale ranges from 0 to 8, with higher scores indicating a more diverse friendship circle relative to both the respondents' own characteristics and total number of close friends.

Measures of the alternative factors that have been used to explain political participation are employed as explanatory controls in multivariate analyses. The controls include education and income; the number of nonpolitical organizations in which respondents participate; a series of dummy variables that reference three ethnic-racial groups (African Americans, Hispanics, and Asians), five religious traditions (Catholics, evangelical Protestants, other Christians, other religions, and secular), and females;[14] political interest and political knowledge; years living in current community; currently married; currently working; and age. The Appendix provides further details on variable construction and coding.[15]

FINDINGS

The empirical analysis consists of a series of multinomial logistic (MNL) regression models designed to test the hypotheses detailed above. Tables 8.2.1 through 8.2.4 present four sets of MNL regression models that test Hypotheses 1–4, respectively. The dependent variable is the four-point measure (0–3) of political participation. The reference category is always zero acts of political participation, with the set of models in each table predicting one, two, and three or more acts of participation against no acts. The explanatory variables, consisting of the four measures of friendship diversity and the control variables, are listed in the leftmost column. The increasingly precise measures of friendship diversity are entered successively into the respective sets of MNL models, while all control variables are entered in each set of models.

The regression models provide consistent and strong support for the hypotheses. In Table 8.2.1, the set of models testing Hypothesis 1 shows that friendship diversity by itself is positively related to one, two, and three or more acts of political participation and is statistically significant in each case at the .000 level. The greater the diversity of friends a person has, the more likely he is to engage in political activities, and the less likely he is to engage in no political acts, even after controlling for the independent effects of other theoretically important variables.

Table 8.2.1. Multinomial Logistic Regression Analyses: Political Participation Regressed on Friendship Diversity by Itself and Control Variables (Hypothesis 1)

Explanatory variables	Model predicting		
	One political act: Coeff. (SE)	Two political acts: Coeff. (SE)	Three or more political acts: Coeff. (SE)
Friendship diversity by itself	.11 (.02)***	.13 (.03)***	.27 (.04)***
Education	.08 (.03)**	.17 (.05)***	.19 (.05)***
Household income	.17 (.04)***	.10 (.06) *	.03 (.07)
Participation in nonpolitical groups	.20 (.03)***	.40 (.04)***	.73 (.06)***
African American	−.44 (.18)**	−.38 (.26)	−.82 (.31)**
Hispanic	−.27 (.21)	.25 (.28)	−.34 (.36)
Asian	.24 (.36)	−.24 (.54)	−.36 (.60)
Catholic	−.10 (.17)	−.09 (.24)	.29 (.29)
Evangelical Protestant	−.06 (.16)	.04 (.23)	.42 (.28)
Other Christian	−.01 (.30)	1.07 (.37)**	1.06 (.48)**
Other religion	−.03 (.32)	.52 (.40)	1.30 (.42)**
Secular	−.04 (.21)	.25 (.30)	1.17 (.34)**
Female	.02 (.11)	.11 (.16)	.02 (.18)
Political interest	.33 (.08)***	.96 (.11)***	1.50 (.14)***
Political knowledge	.35 (.12)**	.31 (.17)*	.48 (.20)**
Years living in community	.10 (.04)**	.09 (.06)	.03 (.07)
Currently married	−.17 (.12)	−.17 (.17)	−.18 (.20)
Currently working	.20 (.13)	−.01 (.18)	.48 (.22)**
Age	−.01 (.00)	−.02 (.01)**	−.04 (.01)***
(Constant)	−2.84 (.34)***	−4.82 (.48)***	−7.67 (.60)***

Note: Pseudo R^2 = .36. Weighted N = 2,351.
*.05 < p < .10, **.00 < p < .05, ***p = .000.

In the models testing Hypothesis 2 (Table 8.2.2), friendship diversity standardized over friendship network size is entered as an explanatory variable. Recall that the purpose of standardizing over friendship network size is to control for the effect of friendship network size on friendship diversity; indeed, the two variables are correlated at .28 (p = .000). In these models, friendship diversity remains positively related to each level of political participation against no participation, and the coefficients remain statistically significant at either the .05 or .000 level.

What happens when friendship diversity is modified in a different way, by purging it of respondents' own characteristics and thus isolating the effects on political participation of friends with characteristics that respondents do not share? The models testing Hypothesis 3 in Table 8.2.3 address this question. Again, the coefficients for friendship diversity are strongly significant statistically (p = .000 in all models), showing that increases in friendship diversity are associated with a greater likelihood of engaging in one, two, and three or more political acts rather than zero acts.

In Table 8.2.4, the series of models testing Hypothesis 4 utilizes the measure of friendship diversity that is both purged of respondents' characteristics and standardized over friendship network size. Even purged of respondents' characteristics, friendship diversity is significantly correlated with friendship network

TABLE 8.2.2. Multinomial Logistic Regression Analyses: Political Participation Regressed on Friendship Diversity Standardized over Friendship Network Size and Control Variables (Hypothesis 2)

	Model predicting		
Explanatory variables	One political act: Coeff. (SE)	Two political acts: Coeff. (SE)	Three or more political acts: Coeff. (SE)
Friendship diversity standardized over friendship network size	.15 (.05)**	.15 (.07)**	.29 (.08)***
Education	.08 (.03)**	.17 (.05)***	.20 (.05)***
Household income	.19 (.04)***	.12 (.06)**	.07 (.07)
Participation in nonpolitical groups	.22 (.03)***	.43 (.04)***	.79 (.05)***
African American	−.54 (.18)**	−.48 (.26)*	−1.01 (.31)**
Hispanic	−.34 (.21)*	.17 (.28)	−.50 (.37)
Asian	.15 (.36)	−.35 (.54)	−.54 (.59)
Catholic	−.09 (.17)	−.08 (.24)	.27 (.29)
Evangelical Protestant	−.03 (.16)	.07 (.23)	.46 (.28)*
Other Christian	.03 (.30)	1.12 (.36)**	1.19 (.48)**
Other religion	−.01 (.32)	.56 (.40)	1.40 (.41)**
Secular	−.04 (.21)	.25 (.30)	1.08 (.33)**
Female	.02 (.11)	.12 (.16)	.05 (.18)
Political interest	.34 (.08)***	.98 (.11)***	1.53 (.14)***
Political knowledge	.35 (.12)**	.29 (.17)*	.47 (.20)**
Years living in community	.10 (.04)**	.09 (.06)	.02 (.07)
Currently married	−.18 (.12)	−.18 (.17)	−.21 (.20)
Currently working	.21 (.12)*	.01 (.18)	.56 (.22)**
Age	−.01 (.00)	−.02 (.01)**	−.04 (.01)***
(Constant)	−2.54 (.33)***	−4.46 (.47)***	−6.79 (.57)***

Note: Pseudo R^2 = .35. Weighted N = 2,348
*.05 < p < .10, **.00 < p < .05, ***p = .000.

size (r = .26, p = .000), so that standardizing over network size again controls for the positive effect of network size on diversity. Once again, the regression coefficients for friendship diversity are statistically significant in the multivariate models at the .05 level or below. As friendship diversity increases—even purged of respondents' characteristics and standardized over the size of respondents' friendship networks, and even after controlling for other important variables that have long explained political participation—so too does the likelihood of engaging in one or multiple political acts.

Just how much do variations in friendship diversity affect political participation? In MNL regressions, the coefficients reflect how changes in explanatory variables affect each nonreference category in the dependent variable against the reference category. However, probabilities can be calculated for each discrete category of the dependent variable relative to all other categories simultaneously, not just the reference category, as values of the explanatory variables vary.[16]

Table 8.3 presents changes in the probability of engaging in 0, 1, 2, and 3 or more political acts as the values of explanatory variables change from low to high, or as dummy variables are changed from the reference category to the dummy cat-

Table 8.2.3. Multinomial Logistic Regression Analyses: Political Participation Regressed on Friendship Diversity Purged of Respondents' Own Characteristics and Control Variables (Hypothesis 3)

	Model predicting		
Explanatory variables	One political act: Coeff. (SE)	Two political acts: Coeff. (SE)	Three or more political acts: Coeff. (SE)
Friendship diversity purged of respondents' own characteristics	.13 (.03)***	.16 (.04)***	.29 (.05)***
Education	.08 (.03)**	.17 (.05)***	.19 (.05)***
Household income	.17 (.04)***	.10 (.06)*	.04 (.07)
Participation in nonpolitical groups	.20 (.03)***	.40 (.04)***	.74 (.05)***
African American	−.47 (.18)**	−.41 (.26)	−.86 (.31)**
Hispanic	−.29 (.21)	.22 (.28)	−.41 (.36)
Asian	.19 (.36)	−.29 (.54)	−.42 (.59)
Catholic	−.10 (.17)	−.10 (.24)	.25 (.29)
Evangelical Protestant	−.05 (.16)	.04 (.23)	.41 (.28)*
Other Christian	.00 (.30)	1.08 (.37)**	1.08 (.48)**
Other religion	−.05 (.32)	.49 (.40)	1.26 (.42)**
Secular	−.05 (.21)	.24 (.30)	1.11 (.33)**
Female	.02 (.11)	.11 (.16)	.01 (.18)
Political interest	.33 (.08)***	.96 (.11)***	1.50 (.14)***
Political knowledge	.36 (.12)**	.31 (.17)*	.47 (.20)**
Years living in community	.10 (.04)**	.10 (.06)	.04 (.07)
Currently married	−.17 (.12)	−.16 (.17)	−.16 (.20)
Currently working	.20 (.13)	−.01 (.18)	.50 (.22)**
Age	−.01 (.00)	−.02 (.01)**	−.04 (.01)***
(Constant)	−2.69 (.33)***	−4.68 (.47)***	−7.19 (.58)***

Note: Pseudo R^2 = .36. Weighted N = 2,351.
*.05 < p < .10, **.00 < p < .05, ***p = .000.

egory. Probability changes are calculated for the statistically significant variables in Table 8.2.4, which includes the most precise measure of friendship diversity. When calculating the probability changes for any one particular variable, the values of other variables are held constant at means, or for dummy variables at the reference category.[17]

Looking at the probability changes highlights the effect of friendship diversity on political participation. Across the entire diversity scale, the probability of engaging in zero political acts drops by 41 percentage points, the single steepest decline of any explanatory variable. At the lowest level of friendship diversity, the probability of not participating in any political acts is 58 percent; at the highest level of friendship diversity, the probability of not engaging in any political act is just 17 percent. In turn, the probability of participating in one political act increases by 27 percentage points (36 percent to 63 percent), in two political acts by 6 percentage points (5 percent to 11 percent), and in three or more political acts by 8 percentage points (1 percent to 9 percent).

Participation in nonpolitical groups rivals the effect of friendship diversity on reducing the likelihood of remaining at zero acts of participation, with an overall

TABLE 8.2.4. Multinomial Logistic Regression Analyses: Political Participation Regressed on Friendship Diversity Purged of Respondents' Own Characteristics and Standardized over Friendship Network Size and Control Variables (Hypothesis 4)

	Model predicting		
Explanatory variables	One political act: Coeff. (SE)	Two political acts: Coeff. (SE)	Three or more political acts: Coeff. (SE)
Friendship diversity purged of respondents' own characteristics and standardized over friendship network size	.23 (.07)**	.24 (.09)**	.40 (.11)***
Education	.07 (.03)**	.16 (.05)***	.20 (.05)***
Household income	.19 (.04)***	.12 (.06)**	.06 (.07)
Participation in nonpolitical groups	.22 (.03)***	.43 (.04)***	.78 (.05)***
African American	−.55 (.18)**	−.50 (.26)*	−1.01 (.31)**
Hispanic	−.35 (.21)*	.16 (.28)	−.51 (.37)
Asian	.13 (.36)	−.37 (.55)	−.56 (.59)
Catholic	−.09 (.17)	−.09 (.24)	.26 (.29)
Evangelical Protestant	−.03 (.16)	.07 (.23)	.45 (.28)
Other Christian	.02 (.30)	1.11 (.36)**	1.18 (.48)**
Other religion	−.02 (.32)	.54 (.40)	1.36 (.41)**
Secular	−.04 (.21)	.24 (.30)	1.07 (.33)**
Female	.02 (.11)	.12 (.16)	.04 (.18)
Political interest	.34 (.08)***	.98 (.11)***	1.53 (.14)***
Political knowledge	.35 (.12)**	.30 (.17)*	.47 (.20)**
Years living in community	.10 (.04)**	.09 (.06)	.03 (.07)
Currently married	−.18 (.12)	−.18 (.17)	−.20 (.20)
Currently working	.20 (.13)	.01 (.18)	.56 (.22)**
Age	−.01 (.00)	−.02 (.01)**	−.03 (.01)***
(Constant)	−2.51 (.33)***	−4.44 (.46)***	−6.70 (.56)***

Note: Pseudo R^2 = .35. Weighted N = 2,349.
*$.05 < p < .10$, **$.00 < p < .05$, ***$p = .000$.

decline of 40 percentage points. Relative to friendship diversity, participation in nonpolitical groups has a somewhat weaker effect on generating a single act of political participation but a stronger effect on producing multiple acts of political participation, with increases of 14, 11, and 16 percentage points for one, two, and three or more acts respectively.

Among the other variables, none comes close to friendship diversity in generating probability changes in political participation. Rising household income and political interest yield declines of more than 20 percentage points in the probability of remaining at zero political acts; rising education generates a reduction of 14 percentage points in the probability of no political activity. Compared to non-Hispanic whites, African Americans are more likely not to engage in any political acts, by 13 percentage points. Changes in the probability between no political participation and any other level are 10 percent or less for the remaining explanatory variables in Table 8.3, and of course such changes are zero for explanatory variables that were not statistically significant in Table 8.2.4.

TABLE 8.3. Change in Probability of Participating in Zero, One, Two, and Three or More Political Acts, for Statistically Significant Explanatory Variables, from Table 8.2.4

Explanatory variables	Number of political acts			
	0	1	2	3 or more
Friendship diversity purged of respondents' own characteristics and standardized over friendship network size				
Education	−.41 (.58 → .17)	.27 (.36 → .63)	.06 (.05 → .11)	.08 (.01 → .09)
Household income	−.14 (.56 → .42)	.07 (.38 → .45)	.04 (.05 → .09)	.02 (.01 → .03)
Participation in nonpolitical groups	−.21 (.60 → .39)	.21 (.32 → .53)	.01 (.06 → .07)	−.01 (.02 → .01)
African American	−.40 (.65 → .25)	.14 (.32 → .46)	.11 (.03 → .14)	.16 (.00 → .16)
Other Christian	.13 (.51 → .64)	−.11 (.41 → .30)	−.01 (.06 → .05)	−.01 (.02 → .01)
Other religion	−.08 (.51 → .43)	−.06 (.41 → .35)	.10 (.06 → .16)	.03 (.02 → .05)
Secular	−.03 (.51 → .48)	−.02 (.41 → .39)	.00 (.06 → .06)	.05 (.02 → .07)
Political interest	−.02 (.51 → .49)	−.01 (.41 → .40)	.00 (.06 → .06)	.03 (.02 → .05)
Political knowledge	−.24 (.61 → .37)	.07 (.36 → .43)	.10 (.03 → .13)	.06 (.01 → .07)
Years living in community	−.09 (.54 → .45)	.08 (.38 → .46)	.01 (.06 → .07)	.00 (.02 → .02)
Currently working	−.09 (.56 → .47)	.10 (.35 → .45)	−.01 (.07 → .06)	.00 (.02 → .02)
Age	−.01 (.51 → .50)	−.01 (.42 → .41)	.00 (.06 → .06)	.01 (.01 → .02)
	.06 (.47 → .53)	.05 (.39 → .44)	−.07 (.10 → .03)	−.05 (.05 → .00)

Note: Entries are percentage change in probability of participating in specified number of political acts, followed in parentheses by actual probabilities of participating, as value of explanatory variable changes from low to high. Weighted $N = 2,349$.

INTERACTION MODELS

The effect of friendship diversity on political participation applies generally to the U.S. population, but does it vary across individual-level characteristics and social groups? Hypotheses 5 and 6 posited two competing claims: groups that engage less often in politics will benefit more (Hypothesis 5) or less (Hypothesis 6) from diverse friendships than those who already have a participatory advantage.

To test these competing hypotheses, the MNL regression model in Table 8.2.4 was re-specified with interaction terms between the most precise measure of friendship diversity—purged of respondents' own characteristics and standardized over network size—and other explanatory variables from Table 8.2.4 that were statistically significant in any of the three models.

Conventional interaction terms were constructed between friendship diversity and dummy control variables. Control measures at the ordinal level or higher were recoded into a series of dummy variables (excluding the necessary reference groups), and interaction terms were constructed between friendship diversity and each of the new dummy measures. (See the Appendix for details on coding of interaction terms.) The interaction terms allow an evaluation of whether the effects of friendship diversity on political participation vary by socioeconomic resources, participation in nonpolitical groups, social groups defined by ethnicity, race, gender, and religion, psychological engagement with politics, and social stability.

Table 8.4 displays the results of the MNL interaction models. There is scattered evidence for each hypothesis. In the model predicting two political acts, the benefit of diverse friendship networks rises for those with incomes between $50,000 and $74,999 compared to those with incomes of $75,000 or more, and for those with low levels of political interest relative to those with high levels of political interest, both of which support Hypothesis 5. In contrast, Hypothesis 6 is supported in four instances. In the model predicting one political act, the effect of friendship diversity is reduced among those with incomes between $30,000 and $49,999 compared to those with incomes of $75,000 or more. In the model predicting two political acts, the benefit of friendship diversity is diminished for those with some college education or an associate or technical degree compared to those with at least a bachelor's degree; for African Americans relative to non-Hispanic whites; and for Catholics and Protestants relative to other Christians.

Overall, however, the models provide little support for either hypothesis. In no case are all the dummy variables of a particular category—for example, education—statistically significant in even one model, let alone significant in a consistent manner relative to the reference category. Similarly, no particular interaction term is significant across even two of the three models, let alone across all three models. Different categories of income are significant in two models, but their effects are contradictory. Furthermore, none of the interaction terms associated with participation in nonpolitical groups, political knowledge, years resident in a community, employment status, or age are ever statistically significant. Scattered evidence for the competing hypotheses notwithstanding, the general picture is one in which the effect of friendship diversity on political participation does not systematically vary by other factors that shape engagement in political activity.

TABLE 8.4. Multinomial Logistic Regression Analyses: Political Participation Regressed on Friendship Diversity Purged of Respondents' Own Characteristics and Standardized over Friendship Network Size, Control Variables, and Interaction Terms (Hypotheses 5 and 6)

Explanatory variables	Model predicting		
	One political act: Coeff. (SE)	Two political acts: Coeff. (SE)	Three or more political acts: Coeff. (SE)
Friendship diversity purged of respondents' own characteristics and standardized over friendship network size	.69 (.36)*	−.01 (.47)	1.07 (.55)*
High school or less education	−.48 (.29)*	−.53 (.44)	−.79 (.50)
Some college, associate, or technical degree	.09 (.29)	.64 (.41)	−1.21 (.50)**
Household income< $30,000	−.58 (.33)*	−.75 (.49)	−.08 (.56)
Household income $30,000–49,999	.12 (.31)	−.83 (.45)*	−.18 (.51)
Household income $50,000–75,000	.24 (.34)	−.89 (.50)*	−.45 (.56)
Involved in 0 nonpolitical groups	−.97 (.31)**	−2.10 (.50)***	−4.68 (1.17)***
Involved in 1–3 nonpolitical groups	−.26 (.27)	−1.07 (.36)**	−1.79 (.40)***
African American	−.26 (.32)	.43 (.47)	−.76 (.60)
Hispanic	−.40 (.36)	.73 (.50)	−.29 (.66)
Other Christian	−.39 (.54)	−.46 (.77)	.98 (.97)
Other religion	.13 (.57)	.50 (.74)	−.18 (.84)
Secular	.38 (.32)	−.27 (.51)	1.39 (.50)**
Not at all or slightly interested in politics	−.57 (.29)*	−2.76 (.47)***	−3.07 (.58)***
Somewhat interested in politics	−.03 (.27)	−.98 (.36)**	−1.45 (.44)**
Knows no U.S. Senator from home state	−.07 (.23)	.04 (.34)	−.04 (.41)
Lived in community 5 years or less	−.45 (.27)	−.32 (.43)	.29 (.51)
Lived in community 6–10 years	−.21 (.33)	−.06 (.49)	.23 (.59)
Lived in community 11–20 years	.27 (.29)	.45 (.42)	.63 (.52)
Not currently working	−.23 (.25)	−.59 (.38)	−.79 (.48)*
Age 18–24	.02 (.44)	.42 (.68)	2.28 (.90)**
Age 25–44	−.05 (.37)	.27 (.57)	1.23 (.82)
Age 45–64	−.11 (.36)	.15 (.55)	.99 (.80)
Interaction terms: Friendship diversity purged of respondents' own characteristics and standardized over friendship network size X			
High school or less education	−.01 (.20)	−.19 (.28)	−.07 (.31)
Some college, associate, or technical degree	.00 (.19)	−.63 (.27)**	.37 (.29)
Household income < $30,000	−.04 (.23)	.22 (.33)	.02 (.35)
Household income $30,000–49,000	−.41 (.22)*	.42 (.30)	−.08 (.31)
Household income $50,000–75,000	−.31 (.24)	.54 (.32)*	.01 (.34)
Involved in 0 nonpolitical groups	−.20 (.22)	−.06 (.35)	−.71 (.97)
Involved in 1–3 nonpolitical groups	−.15 (.17)	.02 (.23)	−.22 (.24)
African American	−.17 (.20)	−.54 (.29)*	.01 (.31)
Hispanic	.08 (.21)	−.31 (.30)	−.05 (.35)
Other Christian	.41 (.39)	1.01 (.47)**	−.05 (.62)

TABLE 8.4. (*Continued*)

	Model predicting		
Explanatory variables	One political act: Coeff. (SE)	Two political acts: Coeff. (SE)	Three or more political acts: Coeff. (SE)
Interaction terms (*continued*)			
Other religion	.04 (.36)	.12 (.46)	.79 (.51)
Secular	−.24 (.23)	.31 (.31)	−.46 (.32)
Not at all or slightly interested in politics	−.03 (.20)	.53 (.28)*	.04 (.34)
Somewhat interested in politics	−.05 (.19)	.14 (.24)	−.04 (.27)
Knows no US. Senator from home state	−.22 (.16)	−.26 (.23)	−.31 (.25)
Lived in community 5 years or less	.10 (.18)	.07 (.28)	−.16 (.31)
Lived in community 6–10 years	−.07 (.23)	.18 (.32)	−.19 (.35)
Lived in community 11–20 years	−.32 (.20)	−.10 (.28)	−.27 (.32)
Not currently working	.01 (.18)	.37 (.24)	.10 (.30)
Age 18–24	.28 (.32)	.35 (.46)	−.20 (.58)
Age 25–44	.06 (.28)	.05 (.39)	−.29 (.52)
Age 45–64	.12 (.28)	.11 (.39)	−.23 (.51)
(Constant)	.20 (.50)	.59 (.69)	−.31 (.88)

Note: Pseudo R^2 = .37. Weighted N = 2,349.
*.05 < p < .10, **.00 < p < .05, ***p = .000.

DISCUSSION

Political participation is a function of the diversity of friends that people have. The empirical analyses support the theoretical claim that social networks made up of a diverse set of friends expose people to various nonredundant opportunities and requests for political participation that inhere in groups defined by ethnicity, class, religion, and sexual orientation and in community leadership circles. In contrast, people whose friendship networks are more circumscribed in their heterogeneity are less likely to be exposed to and recruited into multiple acts of political participation. The empirical findings supporting these theoretical claims endure across the multiple and increasingly precise ways friendship diversity is measured and the relationship between friendship diversity and political participation is specified.

The effects of diverse friendships hold in multivariate models controlling for a series of other variables that influence political participation. Consistent with almost all of the previous research on political participation, the findings here show that education, income, involvement in nonpolitical organizations, and psychological engagement with politics increase the number of political activities people undertake. Other social factors—including selective racial and religious group memberships, years living in a community, employment status, and age—also influence political participation. Notwithstanding these factors, people with more diverse friendship networks engage in more nonelectoral political acts than people with a less diverse set of friends. In fact, transforming logistic regression coefficients to probabilities demonstrates just how important friendship diversity is in shaping political participation. Movement across the friendship diversity scale produces a steeper decline in the likelihood of remaining politically disengaged than movement across any of the other explanatory variables.

Beyond the detailed findings and support for the theoretical claims linking friendships and political participation stand two important conclusions for political science specifically and social theory in general. First, contexts and networks matter specifically and systematically in determining political behavior. It is abundantly clear that people's social settings and interactions influence their political activities and preferences. Atomized individuals are very rare. For most of us, engagement with politics depends in varying degrees on our social environments, our interactions with other people, and, importantly, how different those other people are from us. Second, and more broadly, the relationship between diverse networks and political behavior is part of a larger theoretical net that incorporates various types of social behavior. In politics as in job hunting, community organizing, corporate management, and healthcare (Burt 1983; Erickson 2003; Granovetter 1973; Stoloff, Glanville, and Bienenstock 1999), social networks that incorporate a diverse set of people provide greater access to information, opportunities for social action, and social and personal advantages. Political behavior, like behavior in other fields of human endeavor, responds fundamentally to the composition of our social contexts and networks.

APPENDIX: VARIABLE CODING

Dependent Variable

Political participation: 0 = no political activities, 1 = 1 political activity, 2 = 2 political activities, 3 = 3 or more political activities.

Explanatory Variables

Friendship diversity by itself: interval scale from 0 to 11, in which 0 = no friends identified with any of the 11 specified social characteristics and 11 = friends identified with all 11 of the specified social characteristics. The characteristics were not all mutually exclusive (although some subsets of characteristics were), so that a single friend could be identified as having one or more of the specified characteristics.

Friendship network size: 1 = no close friends, 2 = 1–2 close friends, 3 = 3–5 close friends, 4 = 6–10 close friends, 5 = 10 or more close friends.

Friendship diversity standardized over network size: a scale ranging from 0 to 10 produced by dividing *friendship diversity by itself* by *friendship network size.*

Friendship diversity purged of respondents' own characteristics: a scale ranging from 0 to 8, in which 0 = no friends identified as having one of the 11 specified characteristics different from respondent; 8 = friends identified having eight specified characteristics different from respondent.

Friendship diversity both purged of respondents' own characteristics and standardized over network size: a scale ranging from 0 to 8 produced by dividing *friendship diversity purged of respondents' own characteristics* by *friendship network size.*

Control Variables

Education: 1 = less than high school, 2 = high school diploma or general equivalency degree, 3 = some college, 4 = associate or technical degree, 5 = bachelor's degree, 6 = some graduate school, 7 = graduate or professional degree.

Household income: 0 = $20,000 or less; .51 = less than $30,000 but unspecified; 1 = $20,001–$29,999; 2 = $30,000–49,999; 3 = $50,000–74,999; 4 = $75,000–99,999; 4.1 = more than $30,000 but unspecified; 5 = $100,000 or more. Respondents classified as "less than $30,000 but unspecified" were given a value of .51, the mean value of respondents in response categories 0 and 1; respondents classified as "more than $30,000 unspecified" were given the value of 4.1, the mean value of respondents in response categories 2, 3, 4, and 5.

Participation in nonpolitical organizations: interval scale ranging from 0 to 6, in which 0 = no participation in any of fourteen specified groups or organizations, and 6 = participation in six or more of the fourteen specified groups or organizations. The fourteen groups and organizations include the following: religious group; sports club, league, or outdoor activity; youth organization; parent association or other school-support group; veterans group; neighborhood association; seniors group; charity or social welfare organization; service or fraternal organization; ethnic, nationality, or civil rights organization; literary, art, or music group; hobby, investment, or garden club; self-help group; and other kinds of clubs or organizations.

Ethnic-racial groups: Non-Hispanic whites: reference group in multivariate analysis; *African American:* 0 = not African American, 1 = African American; *Hispanic:* 0 = not Hispanic, 1 = Hispanic; *Asian:* 0 = not Asian, 1 = Asian. Measures are based on the existing data file variable constructed by study investigators from a series of questions asking respondents to identify their ethnicity and race.

Mainline Protestants: reference group in multivariate analyses: Mainline Protestants include those classified as Protestant on a question of religious preference and any of the following categories in a follow-up question on denomination: Episcopalian; Anglican; United Church of Christ; Lutheran—Evangelical Lutheran Church in America or all other; Methodist—United Methodist Church—Evangelical United Brethren; Presbyterian; Reformed Church in America; Reformed—all other references; Disciples of Christ.

Catholic: 0 = not Catholic, 1 = Catholic. Catholics include those classified as "Catholic" on a question of religious preference.

Evangelical Protestant: 0 = not evangelical Protestant, 1 = evangelical Protestant. Evangelical Protestants include those classified as Protestant on a question of religious preference and indicating any of the following categories in a follow-up question on denomination: Baptist—Southern Baptist; Baptist—all other; Seventh Day Adventist/Fundamentalist Adventist/Adventist; Mennonite/Amish/Quaker/Brethren; Christian and Missionary Alliance; Church of the Nazarene; Free Methodist Church; Salvation Army; Wesleyan Church; Independent Fundamentalist Churches of America; Lutheran Church—Missouri Synod or Wisconsin Synod; Methodist—African Methodist Episcopal Church; Pentecostal—Assemblies of God; Pentecostal (not specified); Church of God; Christian Reformed Church or Dutch Reformed; Christian Churches; Churches of Christ; nondenominational Protestant; community church; interdenominational Protestant. Also included are those classified as "other Christian" on a question of religious preference coupled with any of the following in a follow-up question: Born Again Christian; Full Gospel; Charismatic.

Other Christian: 0 = not other Christian, 1 = other Christian. Other Christians include those classified as "another type of Christian" on a question of religious preference.

Other religion: 0 = not other religion, 1 = other religion. Other religions include those classified as Jewish or "some other religion" on a question of religious preference.

Secular: 0 = not secular, 1 = secular. This category includes those classified as having "no religion" on a question of religious preference.

Female: 0 = not female, 1 = female.

Political interest: 0 = not at all or only slightly interested in politics, 1 = somewhat interested in politics, 2 = very interested in politics.

Political knowledge: 0 = does not know name of either U.S. Senator from state of residence, 1 = knows name of at least one U.S. Senator from state of residence.

Years living in community: 1 = less than one year, 2 = one to five years, 3 = six to ten years, 4 = eleven to twenty years, 5 = more than twenty years.

Currently married: 0 = not currently married, 1 = currently married.

Currently working: 0 = currently working, 1 = not currently working.

Age: interval scale from 18 to 89 reporting respondents' age in years.

Interaction Terms

The following control variables were recoded into dummy variables, each of which was then utilized to construct an interaction term with *friendship diversity both purged of respondents' own characteristics and standardized over network size*.

Education: recoded into dummy variables for *high school or less* and *some college, associate or technical degree*, with *bachelor's degree or higher* the reference category.

Income: recoded into dummy variables for *less than $30,000*, *$30,000–49,999*, and *$50,000–74,999* with *$75,000 or more* the reference category.

Participation in nonpolitical organizations: recoded into dummy variables for *no group involvement* and *involvement in one to three groups*, with *involvement in four or more groups* the reference category.

Political interest: recoded into dummy variables for *not at all or only slightly interested in politics* and *somewhat interested in politics*, with *very interested in politics* the reference category.

Years living in community: recoded into dummy variables *five years or less in community*, *six to ten years in community*, *eleven to twenty years in community*, with *more than twenty years in community* the reference category.

Age: recoded into dummy variables for *age 18–24*, *age 25–44*, and *age 45–64*, with *age 65 and older* the reference group.

Interactions terms were also created between friendship diversity both purged of respondents' own characteristics and standardized over network size and each of the following dummy explanatory variables: *African American, Hispanic, other Christian, other religion, secular, political knowledge*, and *currently working*. For political knowledge and currently working, the original reference categories were used in the interaction term in order to examine groups initially disadvantaged in political participation.

9   Networks, Gender, and the Use of State Authority

Evidence from a Study of Arab Immigrants in Detroit

MUCH RECENT RESEARCH on social networks in politics has focused on the role of interlocutors in political decision making. Huckfeldt and Sprague make this point admirably: "Politics is a social activity imbedded within structured patterns of social interaction . . . political information is processed and integrated not by isolated individuals but rather by interdependent individuals who conduct their day-to-day activities in socially structured ways and who send and receive distinctive interpretations of social events in a repetitive process of social interaction" (1987, 1197; see also Preface and Chapter 1, this volume). Yet while this statement defines "politics" expansively, network research has focused mainly on voter behavior and candidate choice (Berelson, Lazarsfeld, and McPhee 1954; Huckfeldt 2001; Huckfeldt and Sprague 1991, 1995; see also Johnston and Pattie and Levine, in this volume). While some scholars have studied the information one gets from discussants (Huckfeldt, Johnson, and Sprague, in this volume; Schneider, Teske, Roch, and Marschall 1997), elections have been the main focus of research on political networks.

Interest in the influence of social networks on candidate choice is understandable, given political science's emphasis on voting and other participatory "acts." Networks, however, may be even more influential in giving people a basic understanding of the political system—in reinforcing, or changing, ideas about what government should or should not, can or cannot do for its citizens. This kind of understanding can lead to stances on issues: for instance, favoring lower taxes or a more generous provision of social services. But it will be most visible in the day-to-day relationship that citizens have with the state: their willingness to use state institutions for support in everyday problems and to exercise their political voice in seeking to change those institutions (Singerman 1995).

Much of the research on citizens' ordinary interactions with government has examined people's personal experience with policy or with government agents (Goodsell 1981; Soss 2000) or individual beliefs about justice (Fine and Weis 1998; Tyler and Huo 2002). The interaction from which citizens learn thus takes place between the state and the individual and not primarily among citizens themselves. Roch, Scholz, and McGraw (2000), a rare exception, found that citizens actively sought out weak-tie discussants to help them anticipate the impact of the 1986 Tax Reform Act on their taxes, and that those discussants, in turn, influenced their willingness to comply (or cheat) on their returns. The authors argue, "These contacts could provide new information, help interpret information gleaned from other sources, or help decide which of the available compliance and noncompliance strategies to follow" (p. 778). Their study suggests that horizontal interaction among citizens, not just the vertical interaction between citizens and the state, is an essential element in forming one's relationship with government.

Why might we expect networks to have a strong influence on citizens' interactions with state institutions? As Roch, Scholz, and McGraw (2000) demonstrate, one reason is the structure of problem solving. When one confronts a problem, it is reasonable to talk about it with friends, neighbors, family members, or acquaintances. One may be looking for information about how to solve the problem; one may be recruiting allies or hoping for assistance; one may simply be looking for sympathy. Problem solving, in other words, has a social dimension, one that is widely recognized in the psychological literature on social support (Cohen, Underwood, and Gottlieb 2000; Cross 2001; Vaux 1988; Warren 1981).

Decisions about whether and how to look to the government for help are social in another way as well. To ask for government help, or to complain about government actions, requires that one's problem be defined as a *public* problem, one involving a public good (or public bad), a right inhering in some officially recognized status, a failure by some government agent to live up to his or her role. But how does one know whether one's problem should be defined as a public problem? Cues from others are one important way to tell whether one has a legitimate claim, and whether government can be trusted to respect that legitimacy.

In short, applying concepts of network influence to questions about citizen interaction with government can yield important insights into how networks shape political opinion, knowledge, and action. In this chapter, I explore the effect of social networks on the willingness of immigrants from the Middle East to involve government in two kinds of problems: fixing a pothole on one's street, and complaining about a police officer's inappropriate behavior. Using qualitative data from answers to open-ended questions about hypothetical situations, I examine the type of action that these immigrants believe they would take and the ways that they justify and explain their choices.

For each of these problems, networks matter in two ways. First, the diversity of one's networks matters: in particular, whether one has "weak ties" to people who are acquaintances as well as "strong ties" to those who are constant companions, friends, or family members (see Kotler-Berkowitz, in this volume). Those with more diverse networks are more likely to know about government solutions to these problems, and therefore more likely to understand their benefits and disadvantages. By contrast, those with only strong ties in their networks are more likely to be isolated and to have interlocutors who are isolated as well (Granovetter 1973, 1974). This should affect both the availability of knowledge about government and the willingness to interact with it.

Second, the composition of one's networks matters. That is, the background of the members of one's network should influence the role one thinks government should play, and the identification that one feels with it. In particular, I argue that gendered patterns of interaction lead to different networks for men and women, even when those networks are equally diverse (or equally homogenous). That is, an isolated man is differently isolated than an isolated woman, and these differences carry over into their willingness to use state authority. In general, women in this sample have more models of ethnic and neighborhood action than men, whether their networks are narrow or broad. However, the isolation that women with narrow networks experience also leads them to be more fearful of interacting with government, while men with narrow networks tend to identify with the authority of the state.

DATA AND METHODS

One of the challenges in exploring the influence of networks on political beliefs is that beliefs almost certainly develop over time and with experience. It is necessary to bound the research question in some way, both to maximize the possibility of distinguishing network effects from other kinds of influences, and to prevent the over-attribution of influence to present interlocutors rather than previous experiences. Thus, as described earlier, the literature on network influence in candidate choice has examined specific elections and the discussion preceding them, while other work on networks has focused on citizens' need to learn about new legislation or policy initiatives.

In this chapter, I adopt a different strategy. I use a study of immigrants, a category of people whose experience with American institutions is telescoped into their adult lives and whose networks generally include others who are learning about those institutions. I then ascertain their willingness to use state institutions by describing a set of hypothetical circumstances and asking how the respondent would deal with them. While this approach does not allow me to generalize to actual decisions, it reveals how the respondent reasons—the knowledge she draws upon and the inferences she takes from that knowledge. It also allows me to isolate the process of reasoning from the idiosyncratic qualities of any particular decision: the randomness of the people involved, or the emotional tension aroused by the problems. One should understand these results, therefore, not as predicting how immigrants might solve the specific problems presented to them. Instead, the results illuminate how respondents *think about* the interaction between public and private solutions more generally (see also Hochschild 1981).

Between April 1998 and January 2000, a colleague and I conducted in-depth interviews with fifty-three Arab immigrants, a sample nearly evenly divided between females and males, living in the Detroit metropolitan area, an area which has the highest concentration of Arabs in the United States.[1] All had emigrated as teenagers or adults and had been in the United States for between five and fifty years. They occupied a variety of economic circumstances, ranging from women on welfare to storekeepers to small businessmen to wealthy suburban families; and they lived in a variety of neighborhoods, from majority-Arab streets in an Arab enclave to upscale suburbs. Twenty-five percent were Christians, primarily Orthodox or Catholic; another 70 percent were Muslim, from various Sunni or Shi'a groupings; and the remainder were Druze. They claimed seven nationalities of origin—Palestinian, Syrian, Lebanese, Iraqi, Jordanian, Algerian, and Egyptian—and ten sending areas, including all of the above as well as Morocco, Saudi Arabia, and Canada. Sixty-seven percent were U.S. citizens; all but two of the rest had permanent residency status.

The respondents were recruited through a radio advertisement, personal networks in mosques and churches, and referrals from various acquaintances. Other respondents were approached in the waiting room of a social service agency catering primarily to Arab Americans, or in Arab-owned restaurants and stores. The resulting sample is not statistically representative of the Arab community in Detroit or in the United States. Rather, we deliberately attempted to maximize the diversity of our respondents, with the intention of learning about the immigrant experience both within and outside of ethnic enclaves and ethnic-primary social circles.

All the interviews were tape-recorded, transcribed, and then analyzed using NUD*IST, a qualitative software package. This package allows for coding of the attributes of the respondent along with the language, examples, and themes he or she used. All text coded for a particular theme could then be compared, reorganized, and examined for parallels to text with other meanings. Thus, for this project, I used two sets of hypothetical questions to look for what I call "political engagement": the willingness to use state institutions for support in everyday problems and to exercise political voice in seeking to change those institutions.

First, to understand whether the immigrants felt empowered to take action on a conventional, low-controversy municipal problem, respondents were asked what, if anything, they would do about potholes in their neighborhood. If respondents did not say that they would contact the city, they were asked explicitly whether they would; they were also asked whether they felt the city would be responsive. Next, to understand whether they felt empowered to complain about government misconduct, respondents were asked what advice they would give an Arab friend who was harassed by police while being issued a speeding ticket. They were then asked whether they would ever recommend complaining to the police department or letting the incident go, and how they would advise a friend who faced a similar situation in their country of origin.

Respondents were not asked about actual experience with any of these issues. In part, this was because some of these questions imply guilt or wrongdoing, either by the respondents or by their families and friends. In part, it was because respondents who were afraid of contacting the state might be afraid that the questions could get them into trouble. In answering, however, respondents often voluntarily referenced personal experiences, or the experiences of people they knew, to bolster their answers. They also described similar personal experiences when asked about political activity and beliefs, discrimination, and social activities. Thus, in addition to data from the hypothetical questions and from an extensive profile of each respondent's networks, I incorporate relevant information from other questions in the interview as well.

The analysis in the following pages proceeds in two steps for each section. First, I define the concepts and construct a table showing the percentages of people who fall into each category of analysis. These tables use simple percentages and are not meant to prove points. Instead, they offer guidance as to which differences in the data merit closer textual examination. Generally, I consider differences of 20 percent enough to suggest a closer look. I report the chi-square and its statistical significance for each table. However, given the small N in the study, the goal is not to approximate statistical significance but to structure a primarily qualitative examination of themes in the interviews. That qualitative examination comes second and consists of quotations and interpretations of their significance.

Strong Ties, Weak Ties, and Potholes

American immigration policy gives the kinship network pride of place: the Immigration Act of 1990 reserves 480,000 visas, or 71 percent of the 675,000 permanent residence spaces available annually, for immigrants sponsored by a parent, child, spouse, or sibling. Undocumented immigration depends heavily on family networks as well. Both types of migration are facilitated by the example, the funds, and the encouragement of siblings, parents, or extended family members who are already in the United States (Chavez 1992; Hondagneu-Sotelo 1994). Thus it is the rare immigrant who does not enter the country with at least a few ties to kin, and the process of settling into a new country strengthens those ties. Immigrants depend upon relatives for information about jobs, housing, and schools; and spending time with relatives decreases the sense of isolation and disorientation that new arrivals often feel (Foner 1997; Pozetta 1991). The same needs also lead immigrants to join village clubs, to create "fictive kin" relationships with people who emigrated from the same area, and to cluster in neighborhoods where others from the same town or same social background live (Shryock 2000).

The importance of kinship networks and the benefits of immigrant clustering mean that most immigrants have a well-developed network of "strong ties." These are relationships between people with similar social backgrounds, strengthened by frequent contact or by contact in a variety of different environments. Two Iraqi immigrants who live in the same neighborhood and work in the same automobile factory, who are both Shi'a and whose children go to the same school, are likely to be connected by a strong tie. Immigrants may also have strong ties to people who are not in their ethnic group: two doctors in the same practice, one Lebanese and one third-generation Italian, may socialize together and send their children to the same Catholic school. But the factors that promote immigrant clustering facilitate the development of strong-tie relationships among immigrants of the same ethnic or regional background.

It is not, therefore, the presence or absence of strong ties that most distinguishes immigrants from each other. Rather, it is whether immigrants' networks are composed primarily of strong-tie relationships, or whether they have weak ties in their network as well. Immigrants develop weak ties in workplaces that promote interaction with a variety of people, in organizations whose membership includes casual acquaintances as well as close friends, and through participation in settings where most people around them are from different backgrounds. Note here that while people are usually on terms of intimacy with their strong-tie acquaintances, the opposite is not true: having a weak tie does not imply a lack of friendship or fellow feeling. But because weak ties are not reinforced with multiple contacts across multiple contexts, weak ties are generally a function of one's surroundings, and the types of information and experiences exchanged are more likely to be public rather than intensely personal (Granovetter 1973; Kotler-Berkowitz, in this volume).

I classified twenty-two of the immigrants in this study as having narrow networks composed primarily of strong ties, and thirty-one as having diverse networks including both strong and weak ties. In order to delineate their networks, we asked respondents a battery of questions about their workplace, organizational participation, volunteer activity, and neighborhood; these questions are listed in the chapter Appendix. In addition, I looked through the answers to other questions for stories about the level and type of interaction immigrants had with others. It was quite common, for instance, for a respondent to answer a question about coming to the United States with a discussion of how her interactions had changed since she arrived. Immigrants whose workplaces were diverse and who told me about extended interactions with co-workers or customers; who were members of organizations that brought them into contact with people they did not already know; or who were active in a variety of jobs, volunteer positions, or both, were coded as having diverse networks, or weak as well as strong ties. Immigrants who spoke primarily of interactions with friends and family, who had only limited or sporadic contact with co-workers or customers, or who eschewed organizational participation were coded as having narrow networks, or primarily strong ties.

I expected that the immigrants with diverse networks would be more likely to know of government resources and more willing to call on them for assistance. The questions were calibrated so that the barriers to asking for government intervention increased with each scenario. Thus the first scenario was the easiest, one which our respondents would likely have encountered. We asked, "Imagine that a street in your neighborhood is full of potholes. What would you do? Would you do anything?"

Nadia is a good example of someone who thought the question was obvious. A young professional woman, she laughed when we asked her about potholes. "Call the city, and say, What's up with the potholes? How much of my taxes do you get? Can you fix this street?" Simple on the surface, her answer epitomizes a direct and immediate model of connection between local residents and their government, in which the right to be heard resides not in the power of one's affiliations but in the individual herself. In this model, potholes are the quintessential city problem, the kind of public matter that cities were created to handle. If the city could not be held accountable for this, what could it be held accountable for?

Table 9.1 shows that over 75 percent of all immigrants, no matter the nature of their networks, agreed with Nadia. Those with broad networks are more likely to complain, although the chi-square for Table 9.1 falls just outside of the 10 percent confidence level. Most illuminating, however, are the responses of those who did not know what to do about the potholes. Unaware or misinformed about where responsibility for potholes was located, they answered like Faruq: "I would try to fix it. If they're small potholes I would do it. And in our neighborhood we have

TABLE 9.1. Proportion of Respondents Willing to Complain about Potholes, by Network Type

	Narrow networks	Diverse networks	Total
Willing and aware of how to complain	64%	84%	75%
	($n = 14$)	($n = 26$)	($n = 40$)
Unwilling or unaware of how to complain	36%	16%	25%
	($n = 8$)	($n = 5$)	($n = 13$)
Total	($n = 22$)	($n = 31$)	($n = 53$)

$\chi^2 = 2.84$, $0.10 < p < 0.25$, $df = 1$.

about four or five houses where we all cooperate with each other. We all clean for each other the snow and try to help with the grass."

Faruq's good-natured willingness to take potholes into his own hands and his analogy to neighborhood tasks show that a solution as obvious as calling the city is in fact not obvious at all. The 36 percent of those with narrow networks who shared Faruq's ignorance also replicated his effort to find the right comparison. Some knew what to do if a private entity owned the roadway (say, a condominium driveway or a mosque parking lot), but they were stuck in the case of a public street. Others wondered if potholes were, like Michigan sidewalks, the responsibility of the householder on that stretch of road. The same was true for the 16 percent in diverse networks who did not know what to do: There was an effort to find an appropriate analogy, as with David, who first said that he would hang a sign, then suggested calling his congressman, and finally thought about informing local government. The effort to use past experience to construct an answer shows why networks might be important: Those who have extensive contacts are likely to have more analogies at hand, and more knowledge about which might be the right one to rely upon.

Networks, however, do more than provide knowledge about government responsibilities. They also carry messages about whether individuals can and should hold government accountable for those responsibilities. The latter might not follow the first. In a country where the relationship between political leaders and citizens is mediated through family connections, the appropriate response might be to ask an uncle to contact his son-in-law, who might work in the right department. In a country where leaders may behave well or badly, but citizens have little influence either way, expressing an opinion would make no sense. And in a country where immigrants feel like sojourners, fearful of the government or present only on sufferance, complaining about the roads could seem both unwise and ungrateful.

All of the respondents with narrow networks who knew they could call the city, but said that they would not, expressed views of this sort. Zahid felt that his complaint would not be heard: "It's not my business. I will not call the city. . . . They might think that this guy is coming from a foreign country and coming to impose his opinion." Fadwa felt she did not need to bother because the government would take care of the problem on its own. "I would do nothing about it. There is nothing to do because the government is good here. Without us telling them, they will come and do it. They are slow, but they will do a good job." Amina, least inhibited, nevertheless sees government moving forward on its own. "I have no time to complain for the street! But this happened; they're fixing the street. I didn't complain; they have plans for the area and they're fixing it, for everyone."

The 64 percent of respondents in narrow networks who would complain about potholes show that broad or narrow networks do not, in and of themselves, cause a lack of efficacy. But the quotes just cited suggest that when those in narrow networks avoid protest, they do so because they have little influence over the benevolence, or hostility, of government. By contrast, nearly all of those with broad networks said they could complain about potholes; they just wouldn't bother. As Tariq, a medical student, said, "That I would ignore. I mean, what else can you do? If I had more time, yeah, I'd call the city council or I'd send a letter, or I'd send an e-mail, or something like that. But I think that I would ignore. Because that affects society in general. Things I wouldn't ignore are things that affect me personally." This is not the statement of someone who believes that he cannot influence government. Instead, this is someone who is saving his activism for more important issues.

The citizen's relationship with government becomes particularly important when we turn to the next topic, police harassment. Here network diversity also affects people's willingness to complain about the police. But what is most intriguing is that the composition of one's diverse ties, and not just their variety, affects the conditions under which complaints are considered legitimate.

SUPPORTING OR CHALLENGING THE AUTHORITY OF THE POLICE

The second hypothetical scenario raised the stakes by pitting two different concerns against each other: what people owe to the law, and what the law's enforcers owe to the people. We asked, "Imagine that an Arab friend told you that he had been stopped by the police for speeding, and he was speeding. But when they were giving him the ticket, they harassed him; they were rude and insulting. Your friend is really upset and he asks you for advice. What would you advise him to do?" The wording makes clear that the police went out of their way to be insulting, and while it does not indicate that the harassment was racial, many of the respondents clearly assumed it was. This raises issues of both abuse of power and of discrimination, topics that touch directly upon the respondent's sense of authorization. At the same time, the question emphasizes that the friend was guilty of breaking a law. The driver's guilt and the police officers' behavior are, logically, two different issues. But together they force respondents to pit their sense of entitlement against their fear: should one complain, even if one is at fault? Might one fear retaliation because of one's guilt?

The data clearly supported the hypothesis that those with more diverse networks were also more willing to lodge a complaint. Ninety-one percent of those with diverse networks said they would recommend complaining about the police officers' behavior, compared to only 46 percent of those with narrow networks. Twenty-nine percent of those with narrow networks would counsel their friend against complaining, compared to only 9 percent of those with broad networks. The hypothesis that these differences were independent of network diversity can be rejected with $p < 0.001$.[2] But even more interesting was an issue that emerged in the process of coding. As Table 9.2 shows, while 15 percent of the respondents did express fear of lodging a complaint, and 45 percent felt that complaining was the only way to protect the speeder's rights, the remaining 40 percent were animated by a different concern. For them, the important issue was not whether to complain. Rather, it was the speeder's guilt—and thus, the sense that any intercession with the friend should focus on the importance of upholding the law and not on picayune complaints about the law's enforcers.

Many of those in this group, when pressed, were willing to agree that true victims of harassment had a right to complain. However, because they believed in the fairness of the legal system and considered themselves law abiding, those in this group perceived harassment as unlikely. Faris, a longtime resident who presented

TABLE 9.2. Respondents' Answers to Speeding Question, by Gender and Network Type

	Narrow networks (n = 23)		Diverse networks (n = 32)		
	Men	Women	Men	Women	Total (n = 55)
Speeder's rights	10% (n = 1)	31% (n = 4)	47% (n = 13)	76% (n = 7)	45% (n = 25) 22% of all in narrow networks (n = 5); 63% of all in diverse networks (n = 20)
Police authority	80% (n = 8)	31% (n = 4)	53% (n = 8)	12% (n = 2)	40% (n = 22) 52% of all in narrow networks (n = 12); 31% of all in diverse networks (n = 10)
Fear police	10% (n = 1)	38% (n = 5)	0% (n = 0)	12% (n = 2)	15% (n = 8)[a] 26% of all in narrow networks (n = 6); 6% of all in diverse networks (n = 2)

[a]Includes two people who also identified with speeder's rights.
$\chi^2 = 21.59$, $0.001 < p < 0.005$, $df = 6$.

himself as an elder in the community, explained, "You don't have to go to that hypothetical. I did have some people, they come and they ask me, and I always provide [ask] them, first of all, Why would they [the police] have to be prejudiced against you? I've got to make sure that it was true, because the Arab friend . . . if the police asked him for his license, to him that's being prejudiced. So you have to understand what happened first. You don't prejudge. And especially if he [the Arab] don't speak good English, he consider everything prejudiced and harassment. And when you go ask the officer or the police, you know it's laughable matter."

By contrast, those who considered the speeder's rights paramount saw harassment as an evil with widespread implications, and thus the offensive police officers as the real threat to law and order. Linda, a social worker, advised the driver to "[e]xpress his complaint to the police, to a judge, wherever he has an opportunity. . . . Nobody expresses his opinion, nothing will change. . . . We're paying taxes, and we're doing the best we can. I think you deserve right treatment, and it's the police department's responsibility to ensure that their staff handles themselves properly." Najwa, a teacher, took up the same theme: A person who has been harassed has an obligation to complain. "Ignorance is the worst enemy of anybody. So when you voice you say that hurts me, that was wrong for the person to do, they will be more careful next time. It won't happen to another person. You are protecting the other people. Our forefather when they wrote the amendment to the constitution, they said freedom of speech. This is the freedom of speech. You voice your point of view. It's hurtful to be prejudice."

Network diversity is clearly part of the explanation for this difference. Fifty-two percent of those with narrow networks prioritized police authority, while only 31 percent of those with broad networks did so. Similarly, 62 percent of those with broad networks prioritized the speeder's rights, compared to 22 percent of those with narrow networks. The greater access to information available to those with diverse ties may be part of the explanation, particularly because many of those with broad networks have participated in advocacy on behalf of Arabs and Muslims. That is, one of the reasons that people with weak ties have information about harassment is that their ties were formed in groups that work against it. One might even wonder if the causal arrow goes in the opposite direction: Perhaps those who consider harassment a problem look for advocacy groups to join, acquiring diverse ties as a result.

But while participation in advocacy groups might account for the correlation between those with diverse ties and stronger concerns about speeder's rights, one would not expect participation to explain the respect for police authority, also high among men with diverse networks. In fact, men and women have noticeably different answers to this question, even when controlling for the type of network. A second look at Table 9.2 reveals that men are more likely than women to express a concern for upholding the authority of the police. And women present a paradox: They are more likely than men to want to take action against harassment but also more likely to fear pursuing a complaint.

These responses suggest that men and women might differ not so much in the quantity or strength of their ties but in the composition of their networks. This turns out to be true. Among the immigrants in this sample, women with narrow networks typically stayed at home to raise their children. Even when they were employed, they worked for family or family friends or ran in-home businesses like daycare. Their friends were primarily women like themselves. Their work and their social lives took place largely outside the ambit of government and its agents. Thus when they express fear of complaining to the police, it is rooted in a generalized fear based on distance and unfamiliarity rather than in specific instances of unjust treatment or personal danger. Fadwa, the housewife quoted earlier as saying that the government, being good, would take care of potholes on its own, here transformed her unwillingness to interact with government into self-protection. "It's the police. What are you going to do with the police? No, don't complain. Just stay away from evil, just don't have to complain." Mary, another housewife, agreed: "I get upset too. But it's not right, you know. I think forget about this." The interviewer asked, "Would you suggest that he complain?" "No," she said. "Why?" the interviewer asked. Her reply: "I don't want to go through this."

This reluctance to get involved persisted even when the respondent believed that complaints were possible. When Ikhlas was asked what she might do, she immediately said, "Here in America, there is a law. Even if there is a government and you are right, you can complain. Even if he is a police, you can complain and sue him." But then she told a story about being threatened by an immigration official at the Canadian border. Her daughter, who was in the car with her, took offense and challenged the immigration official's rudeness.

> [My daughter] told her, "You should talk to me in a better way. If you don't know how to talk to me, let me talk to somebody else." I got scared. . . . Maybe they could

have arrested us; well, not arrest us . . . what could they do? Nothing, but they would ask us questions. And question-answer things, I am afraid of them. My daughter said, "Why are you scared? There is nothing to be scared of. If you are in the right, you should not stay quiet."

By contrast, men with narrow networks were not distanced from government or fearful of authority in the same ways. Although they also cultivated few ties to others, their work—as employees or owners of restaurants, repair shops, stores, or small factories—of necessity brought them into more contact with government regulation and law enforcement. Their efforts to achieve and maintain economic security, primarily through small-business ownership, were dependent upon order, respectability, and law-abiding behavior. This explains why 80 percent of the men with narrow networks identified not with the speeder but with the police. Abdul-Arif, a retired doctor, illustrated this when he said, "If he has the right, I will tell him to go complain. If not, I will tell him you got what you deserve. . . . But in most cases the police are right and not wrong." Like Abdul-Arif, people in this group generally do not believe that harassment would occur. Salem, a restaurant worker and refugee from Iraq, asserted, "The police do not harass in America. They just give you a little paper with your ticket and that's it. They don't do these things here." It also explains why 53 percent of men with diverse networks identified with police authority rather than the victim of harassment. Men with diverse networks have more contacts than their counterparts in narrow networks, but they often have similar occupational profiles and thus a similar appreciation for social order and government control.[3]

But if this explains why men—especially but not exclusively men with narrow networks—identified with the police, why did women, especially women with diverse networks, defend the speeder's rights? As Table 9.2 shows, 76 percent of the women in diverse networks, and 31 percent of the women in narrow networks, made the condemnation of harassment their priority. The answer lies in the different nature of the networks that women in this sample created as they, like men, worked to establish themselves in American society. As these women moved away from the more isolating roles of child rearing and family- and home-based business, they did not enter the small business or entrepreneurial sectors. Rather, they usually took on professional work on a paid or volunteer basis, and much of that work was focused upon ethnic or religious community activities. Thus educated working women and housewives alike spoke of teaching in Muslim parochial schools, working in community service organizations, taking part-time employment as realtors while devoting their free time to organizing cultural activities, and the like (Lin, Jamal, and Stewart 2000). As mentioned above, one activity they participated in was advocacy, through groups such as the American Arab Anti-Discrimination Committee (ADC) or the Council on American-Islamic Relations (CAIR), with its obvious connection to combating harassment. But even other types of community work, such as involvement in the Syrian Club or the Lebanese Club, reinforce one's ethnic identity; moreover, simply being around co-ethnics increases one's chance of hearing about incidents of discrimination.

Being part of a social group is not, however, the only explanation for condemning police harassment. Twenty percent of those who would complain about harassment were in narrow networks. Four of the five individuals in this group were women; none had more than a high school education; none attended a mosque regularly, much less community activities. They did not seem like people who would be eager to challenge a police officer who treated them badly. And yet they were also part of a network that had taught them to act politically. Three of the four women lived in neighborhoods where collective action had taken place: Their neighbors asked them to help protest a homeless shelter in the neighborhood, sign petitions for environmental causes, or join a neighborhood watch group. The other two people in this group, a couple, were impelled to protest a personal experience of police harassment. While they did not learn to do so from talking to others, their own accounts of their experience make it possible that their strong-tie acquaintances might learn to protest from them.[4] Put another way, it is possible to "learn" activism from narrow networks as well as broad ones, even though the chances of doing so are obviously reduced. The variety of one's ties increases the probability of acquiring information and experience that lead to engagement with state authority. But the composition of one's ties within a network can sometimes substitute for variety.

Conclusion

This chapter has argued that the composition of social networks in a sample of Arab immigrants helps to explain the variation in their knowledge of and willingness to use government solutions to everyday problems, or to protest unjust treatment by government agents. The patterns and textual passages displayed here link fears, expectations, and images of government together in an inescapably social process. The immigrants not only position themselves as members of a polity—whether on its margins or in its center—they also reinforce for each other what they believe, or challenge each other's objections.

The relatively simple exploration of networks here obviously lends itself to greater elaboration. Within these examples, for instance, it is clear that class background—particularly as it is expressed through education and occupation—will influence the kinds of networks one creates (see Kohler in this volume). It is also clear that beliefs, while they can be created by networks, also influence their creation. For instance, take the decisions of educated women to cluster in occupations that serve the needs of the ethnic or religious community, or to structure their paid work so that they have time for community activities. In previous work my colleagues and I have argued that this is an adaptation of gendered beliefs assigning women to the care and nurturance of the extended family (Lin, Jamal, and Stewart 2000), but the pattern is also reinforced by sisters and sisters-in-law, friends, or co-workers who invite women to chair a committee, organize a party, or volunteer in the school's lunchroom. Similarly, some occupations will promote network interactions with non-Arabs and non-immigrants, while others will not. Distinguishing the causal impact of networks, net of the influences that cause certain networks to exist, is therefore likely to be as challenging as it is rewarding.

It is also possible, however, that the real contribution of studies of network influence will lie less in isolating the independent causal effect that networks have, and more in clarifying why causal factors, such as class, race, gender, or philosophical predisposition, have the impact they do. These causal factors are often studied primarily at the individual level. As the early studies of social context in politics argued, however, an understanding of networks helps us to understand how individual responses can be reinforced within groups or persist as outliers. It can also suggest when groups might function as aggregates rather than as mere collections of individuals (Lazarsfeld, Berelson, and Gaudet 1968). The result can be to understand causal mechanisms as well as causal relationships (Lin 1998) and in doing so, to place the study of individual political behavior in a new light.

APPENDIX: NETWORK QUESTIONS

The questions reproduced below were used in interviews with the study respondents to establish the composition and diversity of their social network. Material from these questions was also supplemented with information drawn from other parts of each respondent's interview.

- Usually I just start by asking you to tell me a little about yourself. What do you do? Are you married, and do you have children? Where are you from, and when did you come to the U.S.? Are you Muslim or Christian? Are you a permanent resident, or a citizen? When did that happen?
- What factors made it easier for you to adjust to the U.S.? What made it difficult?
- Now I'd like to ask you about the work you do, and the activities that you participate in here. You said that you [*mention occupation*]. Where do you work? Are any of the people you work with Arab? Do you belong to a union?
- I'm going to read a list of activities. Tell me if you attend any of the following activities consistently? At all? [*If yes:*] How did you get involved in that? Why?
    Professional or business associations? Mosque/church? Religious groups/activities? Parent-teacher organization? Neighborhood association? Arab community events? Volunteer work? Hobbies/clubs, including Arab social clubs? Political activities, either around homeland issues or U.S. issues?
- Do you know of any [other] organizations that work on Arab-American or Middle East issues? What's your opinion of them?
- How did you learn about these groups? Do you ever give them money?

Ron J. Johnston and Charles J. Pattie

10   Putting Voters in Their Places

Local Context and Voting in England and Wales, 1997

MOST ANALYSES OF voting behavior in the United Kingdom treat the electorate as so many atomized individuals whose decisions are made apart from any social context. With few exceptions, for example, there is no treatment of the household context within which most people are continuously socialized (but see Zuckerman, Fitzgerald, and Dasović, in this volume). And although there has been more attention to neighborhood and regional contexts, much written about these has been contested, and there is no consensus that people are influenced by such contexts. Indeed, Dunleavy (1979) challenged the notion of neighborhood effects on both procedural and theoretical grounds, and McAllister and Studlar (1992) criticized studies of regional variations in voting during the 1980s on the grounds that the models tested were under-specified. In better-specified models, they claimed, geographical-spatial differences become insignificant.

In the view of some, circumstantial evidence strongly suggests that local contexts (at a variety of scales) influence voter attitudes and behavior, and that many individual characteristics associated with such behavior are themselves locally stimulated, if not created (see M. Johnson et al. 2002; Marsh 2002). Most models treat independent variables such as social class as universal characteristics, however—as meaning the same thing to all people in all places, whatever their backgrounds and local situations. Social class is not a pre-given characteristic, however. Rather, its meaning is learned in context—in the home, neighborhood, school, workplace, and so on. Class positions are interpreted according to how we learn about them and from whom, and many of the sources live in or close to our homes.

There is a probable issue of simultaneity involved in local contexts at some scales, as some people may choose where to live (though not their parents!) on the basis of their perception of neighborhood characteristics and quality. In such cases, neighborhood effect will not influence their attitudes and behavior; rather, neighborhoods are selected that are consonant with those perceptions. Behavior precedes residential choice rather than vice versa. Cross-sectional analyses here cannot separate out the relative importance of the two processes. If the expected pattern emerges, however, it is for later studies to evaluate why.

One component of local effects, therefore, consists of home and neighborhood and the people we interact with both regularly and frequently. Such neighborhood effects are just one of the ways in which local contexts can influence voter behavior. Books and Prysby (1991) identified four such mechanisms: individuals' observation of local conditions; their contacts with neighbors and others in local social networks; exposure to information flows through local media; and contact with the mobilization and campaigning strategies of political parties and other interested actors. All four suggest that how we think politically, and how we vote, can be influenced by our local context, by the material circumstances that we observe there, and by the people, organizations, and institutions we interact with.

To evaluate these arguments it is necessary to identify the processes at work, which is more feasible for some than others. For example, if we hypothesize that people are influenced through their interpersonal contacts, then studies of the flow of information through social networks—such as those by Huckfeldt and his collaborators (e.g., Huckfeldt and Sprague 1995; Huckfeldt, Johnson, and Sprague, in this volume)—may provide strong evidence of links between contacts, information flows, and voting decisions. For some of the other processes, however, uncovering direct links is more difficult—as with those that affect people's voting decisions are influenced by their observations of local material circumstances, such as local levels of unemployment. When determining which party or candidate to support, some voters may make an immediate decision based on habitual behavior patterns ("I always vote Labour"; "The Conservatives are the party for people like us"). Others may be subject to a range of influences, and no one cause may outweigh the others. Even if one does predominate, it may be difficult to discover it—assuming that the voter is aware of it her- or himself! In such cases, strong circumstantial evidence, set in a clear theoretical framework, may be the best we can get.

Whatever the difficulties of identifying the reasons why people vote as they do, circumstantial evidence can set the context for more detailed investigations. Such evidence is usually found in the aggregate rather than at the individual level. It may introduce problems of both underspecified models and ecological fallacies, but it can provide compelling arguments that local contexts do matter, that people are not just members of universally defined categories, such as social classes, but are also socialized and politically mobilized in particular geographical-spatial milieus with their own characteristics and influences on how members behave: that is, people act differently according to the type of place they live in.

That approach is adopted here with regard to voting at the 1997 general election in England and Wales, for which specially constructed information on local contexts was added to the data produced by the British Election Study (BES) post-election survey.[1] The goal is to establish whether there were spatial variations in voting behavior that were apparently unconnected to individual voters' characteristics but were related to the type of neighborhood in which they lived. In this context, we are referring to geographical space, not social space, which is the focus of other chapters in this book. (See particularly the chapter by Huckfeldt, Johnson, and Sprague; also Baybeck and Huckfeldt 2002a, and Kotler-Berkowitz in this volume. Gimpel and Lay's chapter in this volume looks at local contextual effects for one population subset.) The analyses reported here place survey respondents in their local neighborhood context. This may be the same as their social space—that is, their social networks are contiguous with their immediate neighborhoods. Our argument, however, is that people may be influenced not only by people who live locally but also by other characteristics of their local milieu, such as the state of the local economy.

The Miller-Shanks "Funnel of Causation" Model and Local Context

Despite the considerable British literature on voting over the last forty years, little work developed a locally focused, structured model of the stages in the decision-making process. The pioneering early work by Butler and Stokes (1969, 1974) was set in the context of the Michigan model (see Chapter 1). Rose and McAllister's "lifetime learning model" similarly drew directly on a central concept in the Michigan work: "on election day, a voter is at the exit point of a 'funnel of causality' that concentrates a lifetime of learning in the act of voting" (Rose and McAllister 1990, 35, citing Campbell et al. 1960, 24).

The model adopted here is also based on the Michigan paradigm, as reformulated by Miller and Shanks (1996; we refer to it as the MS model). Their *funnel of causation*—although never represented diagrammatically—has the voting decision comprising a series of six stages, from the most distant in time (at the funnel's mouth) to that most proximate to the election. As electors move through the stages, their choices become more constrained.

The first stage incorporates *sociological models of voting*. Electoral choice is a function of voters' individual characteristics, indexed by such variables as parents' class and political preferences, plus respondents' class, education, housing tenure, and union membership. The first two represent the home environment where initial political socialization occurred. There young people learn about their family's and their own position in society (about class, for example), as well as about their parents' and other kin's worldviews and political orientations. This provides the foundation for the development of a personal notion of self, one's position in society, and how political action can promote or change this.

In "classic" sociological models, the variables identified in stages 1–2 of the MS model lead directly to vote choice. Once political identities are established, many people habitually vote in the same way—what classic American studies termed the "normal vote." Some do not, however, either because they have no stable identification with any one party or because contemporary events cause them to deviate from their "normal" voting pattern (as enunciated in Key's 1955 classic theory of critical elections). In Great Britain, for example, opinion pollsters suggest that approximately 30 percent of the electorate form the Conservative party's core support, while another 30 percent are Labour's core electorate and 20 percent are linked to the Liberal Democrats, plus the Scottish and Welsh nationalist parties, leaving a further 20 percent who might be open to persuasion at any one election. (The data are from Worcester and Mortimore 2001, 3.) For the committed 80 percent, the main issue is not which party they support, therefore, but whether they turn out and express that support at the ballot box. A main task for the parties is to identify and then to mobilize their core supporters.

The sociological model has increasingly been found wanting, however. Some dismiss it entirely; others show that its main variables lack the quantitative predictive ability of previous electoral epochs. (See the debates on class and voting in Evans 1999.) Voters are increasingly open to alternative claims, and their identification with individual parties has weakened—a process termed partisan dealignment (Särlvik and Crewe 1983). Their decisions are largely influenced by evaluations of current conditions (dominantly but not solely economic; Johnston and Pattie 2001a), by the perceived performance of the parties and candidates in government, plus their assessments of the policy directions offered by rivals. Such behavior is the subject of *responsive voter* models, which occupy stages 3–6 of the MS model.

In responding to the various salient issues at an election, electors make their choices close to the point of the funnel: whether to vote or abstain (an increasingly important decision, given recent turnout decline in many countries) and whom to vote for. Those choices reflect a complex interplay of two major sets of processes: political socialization, the processes by which the principles underlying behavior are learned; and political mobilization, the processes of vote-seeking by interested parties.

Bringing the Geography In

Although we use the MS model as a framework, three basic criticisms stimulate suggestions for its expansion. First, it presents a linear decision-making sequence (as does Rose and McAllister's 1990 version), but not all voters go through all the stages at every election; some may be skipped and some potential influences ignored. Furthermore, there will be feedback loops. Political socialization is continuous, even if slower and less effective as people age. Older people are more set in their ways and also less likely to change their basic socioeconomic characteristics, such as housing tenure and educational achievements. Additionally, pre-election political mobilization efforts, when voters may evaluate the current situation, could lead to reassessments of political attitudes and even ideology.

Secondly, the model largely ignores some key players, notably political parties and others seeking power. It assumes a responsible electorate making informed choices. But where do electors get relevant information, especially in the responsive-voter stages? Many rely on sources most immediately affected by their potential choices—the political parties and their candidates. Much rational choice–inspired research (deriving from Downs 1957) shows that acquiring information takes time and is costly, with benefits often incommensurate with those costs. Thus many voters depend on freely provided, readily accessible information distributed by those with money to spend on campaigning and canvassing—including vested interests who try to influence their decisions, such as media organizations.

Finally, the MS model suggests that geography, or local context, influences all stages of the sequence, along with the later processes of translating votes into seats. This does not imply, however, in Agnew's (1990) terms, that geography is either an epiphenomenal or a residual influence—either a superficial representation of a deeper set of influences (geography as merely a surrogate) or a trivial influence, to be taken into account when all others have been considered. Critics of electoral geography have attacked it on both grounds (see McAllister and Studlar 1992). The response underpinning this chapter is that geography is a "real" influence at all stages of the MS model and of its feedback loops.

People initially learn about politics and political parties in their homes and other local milieus. The resulting personal political ideologies may remain fixed throughout the rest of their lives, although they will almost certainly be at least challenged at some periods. For most, however, ideologies will shift as personal and household characteristics are transformed in tandem with changing national and local contexts. New circumstances and sources of information will be brought to bear, and many of these will relate to contemporary concerns. Just as home background provides a context within which political attitudes are structured and restructured during the life trajectory, so those attitudes provide the framework within which contemporary events and concerns are evaluated.

Furthermore, many contemporary events, even if they are framed as national issues, may be evaluated in a local context. Retrospective evaluations of economic conditions, for example, may take into account not only the national situation but also the regional and the local (Johnston et al. 2000b; Johnston and Pattie 2002). Similarly, evaluations of the state of public services may be based on local experiences. For example, the National Health Service may be performing well on national indicators but failing in one's home area (Johnston and Pattie 2001a).[2]

Local milieus are important at every stage of the sociological and responsive-voter models within the funnel of causation, therefore, putting national issues and concerns into contexts within which voters can readily access information and make judgments about universal arguments. How can we evaluate such claims? The remainder of this chapter charts and illustrates a methodology for "putting voters in their places" in tests of the MS model.

DEFINING LOCAL CONTEXT

In the ideal situation, tests of local contextual influences would use measures of the nature of voters' local milieus specifically designed for the hypotheses being evaluated. More realistically, however, those milieus will be defined on general criteria using available data that can be applied to a range of situations.

At the core of many arguments regarding local contextual influences—especially as they apply to the sociological models—is the claim that people are influenced by the social composition of their local neighborhood, which can be defined using census or similar variables relating to individual and household characteristics. One problem for researchers proposing to test this argument in Britain has been the lack of relevant data at meaningful spatial scales. Most analyses have used data at the constituency scale; these average some 70,000 electors in England (close to 100,000 residents in total). Much finer-scale data are needed to identify the characteristics of local neighborhoods within which many people conduct much of their daily lives.

Such data were developed in a project linked to the 1997 British Election Study (BES).[3] For each of the 2,731 respondents to this study in England and Wales, we created a series of bespoke neighborhoods around their homes, containing the nearest 500, 1,000, 2,500, 5,000 and 10,000 residents to those locations. (For details on the procedure, see MacAllister et al. 2001; for a similar approach, see Buck 2001.) The building blocks were the enumeration districts used in the 1991 census (with an average population of about 500), for which a wide range of socio-demographic data were available. This allowed us to characterize each respondent's local milieu at a variety of scales. Earlier analyses of the relationships between these individualized milieus and voting behavior provided strong circumstantial evidence directly related to the neighborhood effect model (Johnston et al. 2000a; MacAllister et al. 2001). They also suggested that in certain circumstances the implied processes operate at a variety of scales. For the present analyses, however, we have used data for one scale only—that of the 1,000 persons nearest to each respondent's home. Other studies (Johnston et al. 2001a) have shown very similar patterns at a range of bespoke neighborhood scales. Focusing on just one such scale in the center of the range encapsulates the basic patterns.

Neighborhood characterizations were generated by principal-components analyses of ten census variables, shown in Table 10.1. Three main components were identified, accounting together for some 78 percent of the total variation. The first categorizes neighborhoods on an *economic deprivation* continuum. At one extreme (shown by the positive loadings) are areas with high levels of unemployment, of car-less households, and of single-parent families; at the other (the negative loadings) are those dominated by owner-occupiers and two-car households. Smaller loadings show that the more advantaged areas tend to have above-average percentages of adults with higher education qualifications, while the less advantaged areas have above-average percentages of people suffering long-term illnesses.

The predominant loadings on the second component indicate that it characterizes areas according to their employment structure. At one end of the continuum are those with large percentages of people employed in manufacturing industry; at the other are areas where service industries predominate. Finally, the third component characterizes areas according to their age structure, with those at one end of the continuum having relatively high percentages of pensioners and people with long-term illnesses.

Each of these three components represents a different aspect of an area's socio-demographic characteristics, and each may be relevant as an influence on people's political attitudes and behavior. To test whether this was so, the scores on each of the components are used as independent variables—representing local milieus— in the test of the MS funnel-of-causation model that follows.

TABLE 10.1. Varimax-rotated Component Loadings for Local Bespoke Neighborhood Data

Variable (%)	I	II	III
Households no car	0.93	−0.20	0.18
Males in workforce unemployed	0.88	−0.20	0.03
Households owning/buying home	−0.86	0.11	−0.11
Households 2 or more cars	−0.80	0.33	−0.20
Households single parent	0.82	0.02	0.01
Population pensioners	0.06	0.00	0.97
Persons long-term ill	0.42	−0.24	0.83
Male workforce in manufacturing	0.00	−0.82	−0.12
Male workforce in finance sector	−0.15	0.77	−0.14
Adult population higher educated	−0.37	0.66	−0.19
Eigenvalue (%)	49.2	15.3	13.3

Local Context and the Sociological Model

To test the MS model with local context added, we use independent variables selected from the 1997 BES post-election study. Six represent the model's household background and personal/household characteristic components, based on what other studies have found to be significant (as in Franklin 1985). More could have been included—Kotler-Berkowitz (2001) has identified significant differences in party support between religious groups, for example—but those used here were considered sufficient for current purposes. They are commonly deployed in other studies of British voting behavior. They are:

Home background
1. Father's social class[4]
   (Salariat, Routine non-manual, Petty bourgeoisie, Manual foremen, Working class, Not applicable)
2. Party father voted for
   (Conservative, Labour, Liberal, Other, Did not vote, Don't know)

Personal and household characteristics
3. Own social class
   (Salariat, Routine non-manual, Petty bourgeoisie, Manual foremen, Working class, NA)
4. Household's housing tenure
   (Owner-occupied, Social housing, Privately rented, Other)
5. Currently member of a trade union
   (Yes, No)
6. Highest educational qualification
   (Degree, Other, None)
7. Household income
   (Less than £12,000, £12,000–25,999, £26,000–40,999, £41,000 or more)
8. Age group
   (Under 25, 25–44, 45–64, 65 and over)

Respondents' votes in these categories are given in Table 10.2. This shows the expected differences between the two main parties (recalling that the Conservative Party got its smallest vote share for more than a century in the 1997 General Election). Those from working-class homes whose father voted Labour were more likely to vote Labour than Conservative, for example, as were those who were currently members of the working-class, lived in social housing, belonged to a trade union, had no educational qualifications, and had low household incomes. Despite claims regarding the disappearance of a class divide from British politics, it was still clearly there. In addition, older people were more likely to vote Conservative.

Introducing Subjective Class

Models of the voting decision based in social psychology argue that there is no direct path between sociological characteristics and the vote. Rather, the decision-making process is mediated by the respondent's personal ideology and its links to partisan orientations. In much American work, this mediating position is represented

TABLE 10.2. Party Voted for in the 1997 General Election by Home Background and Personal/Household Characteristics (Percentage of All Respondents)

	Conservative	Labour	Liberal Democrat	Did not vote
HOME BACKGROUND				
Father's social class				
Salariat	28.4	28.4	17.1	20.6
Routine non-manual	34.3	30.4	30.4	16.7
Petty bourgeoisie	28.4	28.4	17.3	20.7
Manual foremen	21.9	39.9	10.7	23.0
Working class	18.3	45.3	11.4	20.8
Other	21.3	34.7	13.9	24.8
Party father voted for				
Conservative	40.2	20.7	16.6	18.2
Labour	13.9	52.1	10.6	19.6
Liberal	27.1	27.1	25.6	10.9
Other	16.7	25.0	20.8	16.7
Did not vote	15.9	22.7	13.6	43.2
Don't know	20.4	32.3	12.4	30.0
PERSONAL AND HOUSEHOLD CHARACTERISTICS				
Own social class				
Salariat	29.2	32.3	18.2	15.0
Routine non-manual	26.4	34.7	12.8	21.7
Petty bourgeoisie	33.8	26.3	12.9	21.3
Manual foremen	15.3	41.8	14.1	24.9
Working class	13.6	46.5	10.0	25.1
Other	24.3	28.8	9.9	35.1
Household's housing tenure				
Owner-occupied	28.1	34.8	15.2	16.8
Social housing	7.6	51.3	6.2	30.0
Privately rented	16.7	31.8	13.5	35.0
Other	20.0	26.7	26.7	26.7
Trade union member				
Yes	15.0	45.5	15.7	17.8
No	25.4	34.7	13.0	22.3
Highest educational qualification				
Degree	19.9	36.4	21.2	17.5
Other	25.2	33.4	14.1	22.4
None	21.1	43.0	10.6	21.0
Household income group				
Less than £12,000	16.8	43.1	10.2	25.0
£12,000–25,999	23.0	36.9	16.1	19.6
£26,000–40,999	29.2	32.5	14.2	18.9
£41,000 or over	36.9	24.4	15.2	20.7
Age group				
Under 25	16.0	29.2	12.8	40.6
25–44	17.8	37.1	13.5	27.6
45–64	27.8	39.8	13.8	14.2
65 and over	30.2	35.9	13.6	13.7
Self-assessed class				
Middle	35.7	25.3	16.6	18.0
Working	15.3	44.7	11.8	23.4
None	25.0	29.8	11.9	25.0
Actual result (England and Wales)	23.5	31.7	12.6	32.2

by the party with which people identify and the strength of that identification. This variable has much less purchase in Great Britain, however, where the pressures to identify with a party are generally weaker. More importantly, attempts to measure party identification, especially in immediate post-election surveys, find considerable contamination between declared identification and vote: People tend to identify with the party they have just voted for, and are thus quite unstable over time in their degree (if not direction) of party identification (Johnston and Pattie 1997b, 1999). Hence, although the data are available, party identification is not deployed here.

An alternative measure of personal political ideology can be obtained from people's assessment of their class position. Issues of class still resonate strongly through British society, and most people are prepared to identify with either the middle or the working class. In the 1997 BES, all but 3 percent were prepared to identify with one of the two: 38 percent identified with the middle class and 59 percent with the working class. The bottom portion of Table 10.2 shows that the self-assessed working class was much more likely to vote Labour than Conservative, whereas a plurality of the self-assessed middle class preferred the Conservatives, a stronger association than for any of the other measures of current socio-demographic status. (Only those whose father voted Conservative had a stronger pro-Conservative disposition in 1997.) The class cleavage as indexed by "objective" measures may have declined, but in subjective terms it remains very apparent.

Subjective and objective class positions are likely to be related. Model I in Table 10.3 reports a logistic regression that estimates whether or not a respondent identified her- or himself as working class using the eight sets of dummy variables introduced above. (Respondents were categorized as 1 if they identified with the working class and 0 otherwise.) Model I correctly classifies 74 percent of all respondents on this binary division (those unable or unwilling to identify with a class were excluded), and almost 87 percent of those self-assessed as working class.

According to our arguments regarding local context, the development of people's personal political ideologies, and hence their self-assessed class positions, should reflect not only their personal situations and home backgrounds but also their neighborhood milieu. People from working-class backgrounds living in middle-class areas, for example, may be less likely to identify with the working class than those living in working-class areas. In the latter case, their self-ascription would be confirmed by those in their local networks; in the former case, it could be diminished. Model II in Table 10.3 reports a re-run of the logistic regression, incorporating the three component score measures of neighborhood context as continuous variables. Although the overall predictive success increases only marginally over Model I, two of the three additional variables are highly significant (at the 0.05 level or better), providing strong circumstantial evidence that neighborhood context and self-assessed class are linked. The significant positive relationship with the first component shows that the more deprived the local neighborhood, ceteris paribus, the greater the probability of a resident identifying with the working class. The significant negative relationship with the second indicates that the more a neighborhood's occupational structure focused on manufacturing industry, the more likely a respondent living there was to identify as a member of the working class. Perhaps not surprisingly, there was no link between self-assessed class and neighborhood age structure.

TABLE 10.3. Logistic Regressions of Self-Assessed Class by Home Background, Personal/Household Characteristics, and Neighborhood Context

	Model I	Model II
Constant	0.01	0.12
Father's social class (comparator: Salariat)		
Routine non-manual	0.31	0.30
Petty bourgeoisie	0.21	0.20
Manual foremen	0.70***	0.64***
Working class	0.79***	0.76***
Other	0.33*	0.27
Party father voted for (comparator: Conservative)		
Labour	0.78***	0.75***
Liberal	0.10	0.12
Other	0.99*	1.06**
Did not vote	0.26	0.52
Don't know	0.65***	0.61***
Own social class (comparator: Salariat)		
Routine non-manual	0.37**	0.33**
Petty bourgeoisie	0.44**	0.43**
Manual foremen	0.88***	0.81***
Working class	0.83***	0.70***
Other	−0.06	−0.01
Household's housing tenure (comparator: Owner-occupied)		
Social housing	0.28*	0.14
Privately rented	−0.01	−0.04
Other	0.17	0.29
Union membership (comparator: Yes)		
No	−0.29**	−0.26*
Highest education qualification (comparator: Degree)		
Other	1.20***	1.22***
None	1.36***	1.41***
Household income group (comparator: Less than £12,000)		
£12,000–25,999	−0.13	−0.07
£26,000–40,99	−0.62***	−0.52***
£41,000 or more	−1.34***	−1.17***
Age group (comparator: Under 25)		
25–44	0.23	0.27
45–64	−0.04	0.11
65 or over	−0.48**	−0.40*
Neighborhood context		
Economic deprivation	0.14**	
Economic structure	−0.17***	
Age structure	0.04	
N	2,285	2,228
Percent correctly classified		
All	74.0	74.0
Dependent variable	86.9	86.5
Nagelkerke R^2	0.30	0.31

*$0.1 < p < .05$, **$.05 < p < .001$, ***$p < .001$.

Although the description of a pattern cannot indicate the process by which it was generated, where the pattern is entirely consistent with a process-based hypothesis it provides strong circumstantial evidence sustaining the underlying argument. Hypotheses of neighborhood effects rarely identify their likely strength, however; hence the importance of evaluating the differences between neighborhoods. To do that, we estimated the probabilities of members of two archetypal groups assessing their status as working class. The groups are:

The middle class group: Individuals whose fathers were in the salariat and voted Conservative, and who themselves are in the salariat, live in owner-occupied homes, are not members of a trade union, have a degree, have household incomes in excess of £41k, and are aged 25–44.

The working class group: Individuals whose fathers were in the working class and voted Labour, and who themselves are in the working class, live in social housing, are members of a trade union, have no educational qualifications, have household incomes less than £12k, and are aged 25–44.

For each, the relevant coefficients in Table 10.3 were used to estimate the probabilities of members being in the self-assessed working class across the neighborhood type continua ranging from the least (a component score of −2.0 on the first component) to the most deprived (a component score of +2.0), and also ranging from neighborhoods whose economic structure was predominantly service industry (a component score of +2.0 on the second component) to those dominated by manufacturing (a component score of −2.0).[5]

Figure 10.1 plots those estimates, clearly indicating a substantial difference in the proportion identifying with the working class across neighborhood types among the middle-class group. Thus on the deprivation component (Figure 10.1A),

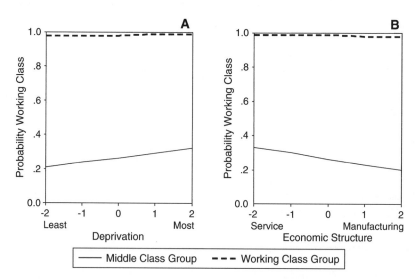

FIGURE 10.1. The Probability of Archetypal Middle and Working Class Individuals Identifying with the Working Class, (A) by Neighborhood Deprivation and (B) by Neighborhood Economic Structure

whereas the probability of a middle class individual identifying with the working class was 0.21 in the least deprived areas, it was over 50 percent higher (at 0.32) in the most deprived. On the other hand, the archetypal working class individual was almost certain to identify with the working class, whatever the neighborhood. The same was the case with the working class group in neighborhoods categorized according to their economic structure (Figure 10.1B). Whereas members of the middle class group living in areas dominated by service sector employees were 0.33 likely to identify with the working class, however, the probability was only 0.20 for those living in areas where manufacturing employment predominated. Members of the working class (as defined by occupation) were almost certain to identify with that class wherever they lived, therefore, but members of the middle class varied in their identification with the working class. Those living in more deprived areas were more likely to see themselves as working class than were those living where manufacturing dominated.

ESTIMATING VOTING PATTERNS

How successful were these variables at predicting voting at the 1997 election? In particular, were neighborhood characteristics related to vote when individual characteristics were held constant? Table 10.4 reports four logistic regression equations, two each for the Conservative and Labour parties. In the first of each (Model I), the home background, personal/household characteristics, and self-assessed class variables are included. In the second (Model II), the three neighborhood characteristic scores are added.

The first model (I) for the Conservatives shows, as expected, that people in blue-collar occupations and rented housing (whether in the public or private sector) were less likely to vote Conservative than those in the salariat and in owner-occupied housing, as were those whose fathers voted for any other party than the Conservatives. Better-off and older voters were more likely to vote Conservative, whereas the self-assessed working class was much less likely to do so than those who said that they occupied a middle-class social position. (The exponent for the regression coefficient of –0.94 indicates only a 0.4 probability that a self-assessed member of the working class would vote Conservative compared to a self-assessed middle-class member.) Finally, the coefficients for educational qualifications show that those with either sub-degree qualifications or none were more likely to vote Conservative than were those having degrees.[6]

Model II adds the three neighborhood characteristic variables. Only two of the significant variables in Model I become insignificant in Model II (the difference between those under 25 and those aged 25–44 in their propensity to vote Conservative, and also that between owner-occupiers and those in privately rented housing). The majority of the significant coefficients not only have the same sign but also the same magnitude. Only those for housing tenure change somewhat, suggesting some collinearity between individual and neighborhood characteristics plus the spatial concentration of different tenure groups in separate neighborhood types.[7] Only one of the three additional variables representing neighborhood characteristics is statistically significant: the more economically deprived an area, holding individual characteristics constant, the smaller the probability of a Conserva-

TABLE 10.4. Logistic Regressions of Party Voted for at the 1997 General Election by Home Background, Personal/Household Characteristics, Self-Assessed Class, and Neighborhood Context

	Conservative		Labour	
	Model I	Model II	Model I	Model II
Constant	−2.13***	−2.17***	−1.16***	−1.17***
Father's social class (comparator: Salariat)				
Routine non-manual	0.27	0.31	−0.09	−0.03
Petty bourgeoisie	0.11	0.17	−0.09	−0.08
Manual foremen	0.09	0.10	0.06	−0.03
Working class	0.29*	0.33*	0.05	0.00
Other	0.07	0.13	−0.06	−0.11
Party father voted for (comparator: Conservative)				
Labour	−1.22***	−1.20***	1.09***	1.07***
Liberal	−0.78***	−0.83***	0.36	0.40*
Other	−0.55	−0.61	−0.25	−0.25
Did not vote	−1.04**	−0.88*	0.18	−0.05
Don't know	−0.71***	−0.63***	0.33**	0.26*
Own social class (comparator: Salariat)				
Routine non-manual	−0.10	−0.15	−0.10	−0.05
Petty bourgeoisie	0.25	0.31	−0.51**	−0.54***
Manual foremen	−0.53*	−0.50*	0.13	0.11
Working class	−0.40**	−0.36**	0.18	0.16
Other	−0.18	−0.24	−0.48	−0.53
Household's housing tenure (comparator: Owner-occupied)				
Social housing	−1.18***	−0.90***	0.21	0.08
Privately rented	−0.35*	−0.26	−0.23	−0.29
Other	−1.34	−1.55	−0.56	−0.52
Union membership (comparator: Yes)				
No	0.55***	0.44***	−0.35***	−0.34***
Highest education qualification (comparator: Degree)				
Other	1.11***	1.15***	−0.67***	−0.66***
None	1.21***	1.32***	−0.56***	−0.57***
Household income group (comparator: Less than £12,000)				
£12,000–25,999	0.48***	0.40**	−0.26**	−0.21*
£26,000–40,999	0.81***	0.71***	−0.38**	−0.29*
£41,000 or more	0.99***	0.80***	−0.67***	−0.53**
Age group (comparator: Under 25)				
25–44	0.45***	0.37	0.18	0.18
45–64	1.05***	0.88***	0.16	0.21
65 or over	1.48***	1.29***	−0.12	−0.02
Self-assessed class (comparator: Middle)				
Working	−0.91***	−0.92***	0.63***	0.61***
None	−0.38	−0.41	0.16	0.10

TABLE 10.4. (*Continued*)

| | Conservative | | Labour | |
	Model I	Model II	Model I	Model II
Neighborhood context				
Economic deprivation		−0.43***		0.15***
Economic structure		0.04		−0.09*
Age structure		0.08		−0.07
N	2,347	2,287	2,347	2,287
Percent correctly classified				
All	79.6	80.1	67.5	67.6
(Con-Lab only)	(77.3)	(78.2)	(77.3)	(78.2)
Dependent variable	29.4	31.0	44.3	44.0
(Con-Lab only)	(63.4)	(64.4)	(85.6)	(86.5)
Nagelkerke R^2	0.26	0.28	0.16	0.41
(Con-Lab only)	(0.39)	(0.41)	(0.39)	(0.37)
(N for Con-Lab only)	(1,417)	(1,385)	(1,417)	(1,455)

*$0.1 < p < .05$, **$.05 < p < .001$, ***$p < .001$.

tive vote. People living in deprived areas are less likely to vote Conservative, therefore, whatever their own situation on the variables included in the model, presumably because of strongly anti-Conservative attitudes in the area and individual responses to the material and other forms of deprivation around them. (Recall that the Conservatives had been in government for the previous eighteen years, and many living in deprived areas may have blamed the Conservatives for their local situation or had greater hopes that Labour would remedy it.)

The relationship with neighborhood economic deprivation can be used to produce estimates of how particular types of people voted in different situations. The two groups that we contrasted in Figure 10.1 are used again, with a further characteristic added to each: For the middle class group, we add those who identified with that class; for the working class group, those who identified with it. Figure 10.2A shows the estimated probabilities of voting Conservative by the two classes, according to the level of neighborhood deprivation. Again, the greatest variation is for the middle class group, with a threefold difference in the probability. Archetypal members of the middle class who identify with that class had a probability of 0.57 of voting Conservative in the least deprived neighborhoods, but only 0.19 in the most deprived. For members of the working class who identified with it, the probability of a Conservative vote was very small, and ranged from 0.06 to 0.01 across the spectrum of neighborhood deprivation.

Turning to the models of Labour voting (which are not just a mirror image of those for the Conservatives), we find that only 55 percent of the respondents voted for one of those two parties (Table 10.2). Model I is substantially less successful than that for the Conservatives. Only some 40 percent of Labour voters were successfully predicted, with the Wald coefficients (not reproduced here) showing that how the respondents' fathers voted was the most significant influence, followed by self-assessed social class: People from Labour backgrounds who identified with the working class were more likely to vote Labour. At an election where it

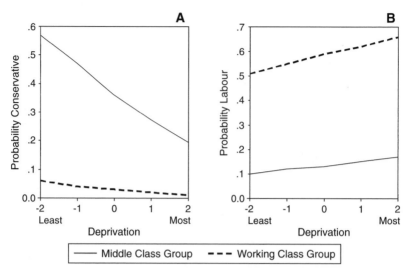

FIGURE 10.2. The Probability of Archetypal Middle and Working Class Individuals (A) Voting Conservative and (B) Voting Labour, by Neighborhood Deprivation

staged a massive recovery in its fortunes after four successive defeats (two by very large margins by British standards), Labour drew votes from widely across the social spectrum, although less so among the better- than the poorer-off.

Adding the neighborhood characteristic variables increased the model's predictive power only slightly, although one of them was highly significant. The more deprived the area, the greater the probability of a Labour vote, whatever the individual's characteristics—a mirror image of the Conservative pattern. In addition, the greater the proportion of the local workforce in manufacturing, the greater the probability of a Labour vote, suggestive of strong Labour solidarity in such areas.[8]

Figure 10.2B shows very similar trends for the two archetypal groups in their estimated probability of voting Labour across the range of neighborhood deprivation scores. For members of the middle class group who identified themselves as middle class, the probability of a Labour vote ranged from 0.10 to 0.17; for members of the working class who identified with it, the range—from 0.51 to 0.66—was larger in absolute but not relative terms.

One initially disappointing feature of these models is their relatively poor fit. Although all four are very good at predicting non-Conservative and non-Labour voting respectively, neither is very successful at predicting support for the particular party—around 25 percent only for the Conservatives and 40 percent for Labour. This is largely because those two parties only accounted for the votes of about 55 percent of the respondents, with the remainder either voting for minor parties or abstaining. If the regressions are re-run excluding all respondents who voted neither Conservative nor Labour, then their predictive power increases very substantially, as shown by the classification and goodness-of-fit statistics at the bottom of Table 10.4. The regression coefficients change very little in direction, size, and significance (hence they are not reported here, but see below); but the percentages of Conservative and Labour voters successfully predicted are approximately doubled, as are the Nagelkerke pseudo R^2 values. The models are very good at distinguishing Conservative from Labour supporters, but much less so at distinguishing them from either abstainers or those who voted for the Liberal Democrats and minor parties.

THE RESPONSIVE VOTER: ECONOMIC VOTING AND PLACE

The theory of responsive voting is based on the general argument that voters reward governments that deliver what the electorate wants by supporting their re-election, but that they vote against governments that fail to deliver. "Delivery" could range across a wide number of policy areas, but most work in the U.K. has focused on economic voting (e.g., Sanders 1996, 2000; Sanders et al., 2001): governments that deliver economic prosperity tend to be re-elected, whereas those that do not are defeated (Lewis-Beck and Stegmaier 2000).[9]

Analyses of economic voting have almost all concentrated on two scales only—the national economic situation (national sociometric voting) and the individual voter (or household: egocentric voting). Those who consider that the national economy has improved prior to an election are more likely to vote for the governing party than those who think it has worsened. Those whose personal or household situations have improved are similarly more likely to vote for the government's return to office than those whose situations have deteriorated. In addition, however, we have identified a third scale—the local sociometric. The economic situation in some parts of the country may differ significantly from that elsewhere, and people may not vote according to their evaluation of how things are changing nationally but rather on what the perceived local situation has been (Johnston and Pattie 2001b; Pattie and Johnston 1995).

Most studies of retrospective economic voting regress party choice against voters' evaluations at the various scales. But not all voters may credit the government with an improving situation or blame it for a deteriorating one; other factors may be considered more relevant. Those who credit or blame the government for an observed situation should be most likely to vote for or against it accordingly. Those who blame other factors are less likely to have their voting decision influenced by the economic changes. After all, if government isn't responsible, why should it influence your behavior (Johnston and Pattie 2002)? This thesis is illustrated in Table 10.5, which shows the pattern of voting on the three scales according to evaluation of recent changes and attribution of credit or blame. Since the Conservative Party was in power over the period preceding the 1997 election, its prospects should have been most influenced by retrospective economic voting behavior. With regard to the general standard of living, for example (national sociometric voting), there was a tenfold difference in propensity to vote Conservative between those who thought things had got better over the previous year and credited government policy with that improvement and those who thought things had become worse because of government policy. The other four categories—those who thought things had either improved or worsened for other reasons, and those who thought the situation had remained largely constant, for whatever reason—showed much less variation in their propensity to vote for the incumbent government. Exactly the same pattern occurs

TABLE 10.5. Party Voted For in the 1997 General Election, by National Sociometric, Egocentric, and Local Sociometric Evaluations and Attribution of Credit/Blame

	Conservative	Labour	Liberal Democrat	Did not vote
General standard of living				
Better—government	50.9	16.2	11.0	18.6
Better—other	25.5	31.0	19.6	21.0
Same—government	26.2	36.4	14.9	18.8
Same—other	20.9	30.9	17.4	24.8
Worse—government	5.0	56.7	12.1	21.4
Worse—other	16.8	32.6	13.7	28.4
Respondent's standard of living				
Better—government	57.3	21.6	4.2	16.0
Better—other	25.1	28.3	17.1	25.8
Same—government	25.3	39.7	11.7	17.4
Same—other	24.8	33.4	18.5	18.5
Worse—government	5.5	57.3	12.3	19.6
Worse—other	21.2	33.9	11.3	28.3
Local area economy				
Better—government	42.8	24.4	11.1	14.8
Better—other	20.6	33.7	15.7	23.7
Same—government	26.7	38.6	13.1	18.6
Same—other	26.4	30.5	16.5	20.4
Worse—government	9.3	55.6	11.3	18.4
Worse—other	29.0	31.0	14.5	20.0

for responses to both the egocentric economic question and the local sociometric: A government seen to deliver prosperity at whatever scale was rewarded, whereas one that presided over perceived relative decline was not.

ACCOUNTING FOR SOCIOMETRIC AND EGOCENTRIC EVALUATIONS

These economic evaluations may be strongly linked to individuals' class and other positions, in which case they are unlikely to add substantially to the predictive value of voting models. On the other hand, those links may be weak. To test which was so, we regressed variables derived from the economic evaluations against the independent variables used in the earlier models (Table 10.3). There were two regressions at each scale: for those who thought things had got better because of government policy (coded 1; all others coded 0 in Table 10.6), and those who thought things had deteriorated because of government policy (coded 1; all others coded 0 in Table 10.6).

Only one set of variables stands out as significantly related to these economic evaluations: household income. In general, those with higher incomes were more likely to think things had improved because of government policy and less likely to think government policy had caused deterioration. (The rich believed they were being rewarded by the Conservative government.) In addition, trade union members were more likely to think government policies were making situations worse, as were those whose fathers voted Labour and those who identified with the working class. But the models provided poor fits to the data, with no pseudo R^2 value exceeding 0.15 and very low percentages correctly predicted. In general, economic evaluations were independent of respondents' personal positions in society and also of the sort of neighborhood they lived in. The exception to the last conclusion, as anticipated, is provided by voters' perceptions of their local area's economic performance. This is related to the actual economic circumstances in the area, and in predictable ways. Those living in an area dominated by service industries were more likely to think that their local economy was improving than were those in areas dominated by manufacturing. Similarly, those living in areas of lower economic status and in those dominated by manufacturing were most likely to think their area's condition was deteriorating: Respondents' economic perceptions reflected the "objective" situation in their local neighborhoods.

Party Campaigning

One final set of influences comes closest to the choice variables in the funnel of causation: the parties' local campaigns. It is increasingly recognized among British political analysts that the more intensively a party campaigns in an area, the better its performance there. This comes about not because its activities in the short campaign period (usually four to six weeks) win over large numbers of new supporters but rather because it is better able to identify and then ensure that its own committed supporters turn out and vote on election day.

Constituency campaigns in the U.K. complement the national campaigns aimed at converting those who might otherwise vote for another party or abstain, as well as convincing committed supporters to vote. The prime focus of the constituency campaign is the canvass, which contacts prospective voters at home, either in person or (to a lesser extent) by telephone, in order to identify those likely to vote for the party. Then, where it is considered desirable (and especially for marginal seats), the campaign follows up by (1) sending voters materials (leaflets, targeted letters, videos, and the like) designed to bolster their support and convince them of the need to vote; (2) arranging, if required, for them to have a postal or proxy ballot; and (3) on polling day, identifying those who have not yet voted so that they can be encouraged to cast their ballot. (On the entire process, see Denver and Hands 1997.)

Estimates reported earlier suggest that about 30 percent of the electorate is strongly committed to each of the two main parties, but not all of them will bother to vote unless encouraged to. Thus the more intensive a party's campaign aimed at identifying and mobilizing its core support (plus that of any waverers), the better its performance should be—holding constant its opponents' campaign intensity. In other studies, we have indexed campaign intensity by the reported amount each party spent on its local campaign (Johnston 1987; Johnston and Pattie 1997a; Pattie, Johnston, and Fieldhouse 1995). There is a legal maximum that can be spent in each, and so we represent the amount actually spent as a percentage of that figure. The more a party spends, the better its performance should be and the poorer its opponents'.

TABLE 10.6. Logistic Regressions of National Sociometric, Egocentric and Local Sociometric Evaluations, by Home Background, Personal/Household Characteristics, Self-Assessed Class and Neighborhood Context

	National		Personal		Local	
	B	W	B	W	B	W
Constant	−1.33***	−1.38***	−2.39***	−2.40***	−3.15***	−1.86***
Father's social class (comparator: Salariat)						
Routine non-manual	0.11	−0.21	0.65*	−1.14**	−0.05	−0.35
Petty bourgeoisie	0.01	−0.18	−0.13	−0.30	0.04	0.28
Manual foremen	0.21	−0.19	−0.12	−0.18	0.04	0.01
Working class	0.10	−0.12	0.21	−0.14	−0.32	0.14
Other	0.29	−0.20	0.33	−0.56**	−0.50*	0.05
Party father voted for (comparator: Conservative)						
Labour	−0.36**	0.55***	−0.10	0.36**	−0.53***	0.56***
Liberal	−0.39	−0.10	−0.15	0.14	−0.79*	0.04
Other	−0.61	0.21	0.84	0.35	0.39	0.42
Did not vote	0.09	0.48	−0.32	0.36	−0.78	0.60
Don't know	−0.44***	0.15	−0.19	0.19	−0.31	−0.12
Own social class (comparator: Salariat)						
Routine non-manual	−0.18	0.05	−0.04	0.28	0.29	−0.27
Petty bourgeoisie	−0.20	−0.12	−0.21	0.19	0.23	−0.64***
Manual foremen	−0.45*	0.25	0.25	0.64***	0.32	−0.17
Working class	−0.35**	0.18	0.14	0.25	0.29	−0.26
Other	0.02	−0.52	−0.09	−0.20	0.62	−0.99
Household's housing tenure (comparator: Owner-occupied)						
Social housing	−0.23	0.37**	−0.49	0.31*	0.03	−0.11
Privately rented	−0.04	0.25*	−0.05	0.27	−0.01	−0.03
Other	0.69	−0.15	1.20	−0.79	−3.82	0.52
Union membership (comparator: Yes)						
No	0.31**	−0.44***	0.31	−0.44***	−0.13	−0.37***
Highest education qualification (comparator: Degree)						
Other	0.46**	−0.05	1.03***	0.20	0.21	−0.30
None	0.40*	−0.12	1.17***	0.16	0.12	−0.06
Household income group (comparator: Less than £12,000)						
£12,000–25,999	0.33**	−0.42***	0.43*	−0.65***	0.31	−0.46***
£26,000–40,999	0.74***	−0.65***	1.08***	−1.28***	0.34	−0.84***
£41,000 or more	0.93***	−0.69***	0.80**	−1.69***	0.61**	−0.62**

TABLE 10.6. (*Continued*)

	National		Personal		Local	
	B	W	B	W	B	W
Age group (comparator: Under 25)						
25–44	0.29	0.24	0.22	0.20	0.25	−0.19
45–64	0.40	0.26	0.11	0.29	0.40	0.11
65 or over	0.88***	−0.24	0.44	0.16	0.45	−0.41
Self-assessed class (comparator: Middle)						
Working	−0.74***	0.50***	−0.63***	0.51***	−0.44***	0.43***
None	−0.24	−0.83	−0.39	−0.17	−0.42	0.05
Neighborhood context						
Economic deprivation	−0.14*	0.05	−0.15	0.09	0.12	0.13**
Economic structure	−0.00	−0.02	0.07	0.03	0.28***	−0.19***
Age structure	−0.08	0.05	−0.13	0.09	−0.05	0.06
N	2,287	2,287	2,287	2,287	2,287	2,287
Percent correctly classified						
All	99.1	92.5	92.3	80.8	90.2	78.4
Dependent variable	3.7	19.4	0.0	3.2	0.0	4.6
Nagelkerke R^2	0.12	0.11	0.07	0.15	0.07	0.12

Note: B = situation better because of government policy; W = situation worse because of government policy

*0.1 $< p <$ .05, **.05 $< p <$ .001, ***$p <$ .001.

THE FINAL MODEL

Our final model adds the variables for retrospective economic voting and party campaign spending to those included in the earlier versions (Table 10.4). Three versions are reported in Table 10.7. Model I for each party contrasts those who voted for it (coded 1) against all other respondents (coded 0). Model II for the Conservatives does the same, but only for those who voted either Conservative or Labour (the latter are coded 0); a similar model for Labour voting would be its mirror image, so no Model II is reported for Labour in Table 10.7.

In Model I, the importance of the additional variables—retrospective economic voting and party campaign intensity—is readily appreciated. Using variables reflecting home background, personal and household characteristics, self-assessed class, and neighborhood context (Model II in Table 10.4), we were able to predict only 31 percent of those who voted Conservative and 44 percent of those who voted Labour. Inclusion of the additional variables increases those percentages to 47 and 54 respectively. The basic patterns identified by the regression coefficients in Table 10.4 remain—not surprisingly, given the findings in Table 10.6, which show that economic evaluations were largely orthogonal to the individual-characteristic variables. In addition the new variables are strongly related to voter choice patterns. Compared to those who thought that the economic situation had improved because

Table 10.7. Logistic Regressions of Party Voted for in the 1997 General Election by Home Background, Personal/Household Characteristics, Self-Assessed Class, Neighborhood Context, Economic Voting, and Party Spending

	Conservative		Labour: Model I
	Model I	Model II	
Constant	−3.05***	−1.68**	−1.52***
Father's social class (comparator: Salariat)			
Routine non-manual	0.04	−0.32	0.04
Petty bourgeoisie	0.01	−0.15	−0.03
Manual foremen	−0.02	−0.20	0.11
Working class	0.18	0.21	0.01
Other	−0.09	−0.22	−0.12
Party father voted for (comparator: Conservative)			
Labour	−1.11***	−1.49***	0.97***
Liberal	−0.88***	−1.02***	0.40
Other	−0.78	−0.61	−0.29
Did not vote	−0.86*	−0.76	−0.15
Don't know	−0.70***	−0.75***	0.24
Own social class (comparator: Salariat)			
Routine non-manual	−0.18	−0.02	−0.05
Petty bourgeoisie	0.29	0.79**	−0.59***
Manual foremen	−0.59*	−0.19	0.01
Working class	−0.31	−0.30	0.05
Other	0.05	−0.29	−0.48
Household's housing tenure (comparator: Owner-occupied)			
Social housing	−1.00***	−0.95***	0.13
Privately rented	−0.29	−0.14	−0.22
Other	−2.05	−1.17	−0.19
Union membership (comparator: Yes)			
No	0.33*	0.42**	−0.19
Highest education qualification (comparator: Degree)			
Other	1.21***	1.42***	−0.73***
None	1.44***	1.40***	−0.59***
Household income group (comparator: Less than £12,000)			
£12,000–25,999	0.28	0.40*	−0.12
£26,000–40,999	0.28	0.35	0.06
£41,000 or more	0.49*	0.49	−0.30
Age group (comparator: Under 25)			
25–44	0.31	0.08	0.27
45–64	0.99***	0.75*	0.23
65 or over	1.14***	1.19***	0.16

TABLE 10.7. (*Continued*)

| | Conservative | | Labour: |
	Model I	Model II	Model I
Self-assessed class (comparator: Middle)			
Working	−0.73***	−0.85***	0.45***
None	−0.41	−0.71	0.29
General standard of living (comparator: Better-government)			
Better—other	−0.60***	−0.62**	0.44**
Same—government	−0.64***	−1.07***	0.74***
Same—other	−1.07***	−1.35***	0.88***
Worse—government	−2.15***	−2.65***	1.38***
Worse—other	−1.35***	−1.40***	0.73**
Don't know	−0.65**	−0.76**	0.69***
Personal standard of living (comparator: Better-government)			
Better—other	−0.99***	−0.60*	0.08
Same—government	−0.81***	−0.71**	0.39
Same—other	−0.88***	−0.68**	0.17
Worse—government	−1.74***	−1.67***	0.50**
Worse—other	−0.82***	−0.52	−0.12
Don't know	−0.86*	−0.54	0.45
Local area economy (comparator: Better-government)			
Better—other	−0.77***	−0.81**	0.32
Same—government	−0.26	−0.52*	0.25
Same—other	−0.37	−0.44	0.16
Worse—government	−0.84***	−0.91***	0.38*
Worse—other	−0.39	−0.37	0.09
Don't know	−0.39	−0.40	−0.06
Neighborhood context			
Economic deprivation	−0.23**	−0.26**	0.42***
Economic structure	0.06	0.05	−0.09*
Age structure	0.09	0.03	0.02
Party spending			
Conservative	0.013***	0.014***	−0.004*
Labour	−0.004	−0.010**	0.012***
Liberal Democrat	−0.005**	0.002	−0.005**
N	2,107	1,311	2,163
Percent correctly classified			
All	82.4	82.3	71.8
Dependent variable	46.7	73.8	53.7
Nagelkerke R^2	0.43	0.58	0.28

*$0.1 < p < .05$, **$.05 < p < .001$, ***$p < .001$.

of government policy, those who thought it had deteriorated for the same reasons were much less likely to vote Conservative at each scale, and much more likely to vote Labour. The extent of this difference is shown by the exponents associated with those significant coefficients. Compared to somebody who thought the national economic situation had improved because of government policy, the probability of a respondent who thought it had deteriorated because of such policies voting Conservative was only 0.12, whereas the chances of his or her voting Labour was 3.99 times greater. Regarding the respondents' household situations, the comparable odds ratios were 0.18 and 1.65 respectively; and for the local sociometric evaluation they were 0.43 and 1.47.

Party campaign intensity was significant too. According to the Conservative model, the more the party spent, the greater the likelihood of a respondent voting for it. The exponent associated with the significant regression coefficient indicates that the probability of a Conservative vote increased by 0.013 with every one percentage point increase in the party's local campaign expenditure. And the more that the Liberal Democrats spent, the smaller the probability of a Conservative vote. Labour spending had no influence on whether a respondent voted Conservative according to the model of Conservative voting. In the model of Labour voting, however, there is both a strong and a positive coefficient for Labour spending—the more it spent in a voter's constituency, the more probable that the respondent voted Labour. There are also significant negative coefficients for spending by the other two parties: The more they spent, the smaller the likelihood of a Labour vote.

Finally we return to the relationships with local context, which remain both significant and substantial relative to what is reported in Table 10.4. For the Conservatives, holding constant the wide range of other variables included in the final model, the more deprived the area the smaller the probability of a respondent voting Conservative.

Turning to Labour voting, not only are the coefficients for two of the context variables statistically significant but in addition one—that for local area economic deprivation—is substantially larger than the comparable figure reported in Table 10.4. The more deprived the area, the greater the probability of a Labour vote, whatever the respondents' personal and household characteristics and economic evaluations. In addition, the more manufacturing workers in an area, the greater the probability of a Labour vote, suggesting greater party solidarity in its areas of traditional strength.

The last model—Model II for the Conservatives in Table 10.7—contrasts those who voted Conservative or Labour only, omitting those who voted Liberal Democrat, the small numbers who voted for another party (Plaid Cymru and the Referendum Party: 11 and 49 of the 2,731 respondents respectively), plus those who either abstained or refused to disclose their vote (23 percent of the sample). This model successfully predicts 73.8 percent of the Conservative supporters and 82.3 percent of all voters' choices, which means it successfully predicts 87.4 percent of Labour's voters. The model is extremely successful, therefore, when applied just to the two main parties, for whom the sociological model is most relevant.

Once again, the geography of the voting decision remains both significant and substantial. With regard to party campaigning, the more that each party spent, the better its performance and the poorer its opponents'. Local context remains a sig-

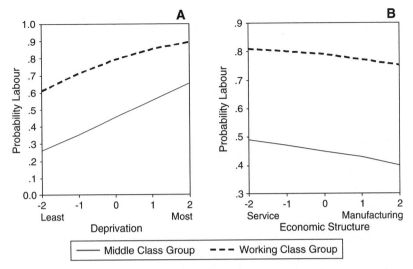

FIGURE 10.3. The Probability of Archetypal Middle and Working Class Individuals Voting Labour, (A) by Neighborhood Deprivation and (B) by Neighborhood Economic Structure, Holding Constant Economic Evaluations and Party Campaign Spending

nificant influence: The more deprived the area, the smaller the likelihood of a Conservative vote and therefore the greater the probability that a respondent, whatever her or his personal characteristics and economic evaluations, will vote Labour.

What is the size of the neighborhood effect, when all other variables have been held constant? The graphs in Figure 10.3 illustrate the differences using the two archetypal middle class and working class groups identified earlier, with four further factors held constant: (1) the general standard of living stayed the same because of government policy; (2) the respondent's personal standard of living stayed the same because of government policy; (3) the economy of the respondent's local area stayed the same because of government policy; and (4) each party spent 50 percent of the allowed maximum. Figure 10.3A plots the estimated probabilities of voting Labour according to neighborhood deprivation. Again, the two trends are largely parallel, with the probability of a Labour vote increasing by about 0.30 between the least and the most deprived areas. Figure 10.3B plots the probabilities by neighborhood economic structure, and again there is a greater probability of a Labour vote in the predominantly manufacturing than in the predominantly service-sector neighborhoods—although the differences are much less than in the case of the deprivation measure.

CONCLUSION: CONTEXT MATTERS

The prime purpose of this analysis of voting in the 1997 general election in England and Wales has been to conduct a rigorous (if circumstantial) test of the hypothesis that local context matters in voter choice. People are influenced, it is argued, not only by appeals to them as members of a socioeconomic class or some other vested interest group, nor just by their evaluations of government policy, but also by their local context—by the people who live there and their political opinions, by its material circumstances, and by the intensity of local party mobilization campaigns. This argument has been confirmed.

The analysis, using bespoke neighborhoods constructed individually for every respondent to an electoral survey, shows that people vary in their social and economic attitudes (such as their self-assessed class and their perceptions of the economic situation) as well as their voting decisions, not only according to their individual characteristics but also according to those of their local milieu. The differences between milieus are substantial. Holding constant individual characteristics, for example, the probability of an individual voting Labour at the 1997 general election in England varied by 0.3 between the most and the least deprived areas.

Aggregate analyses cannot identify the processes by which the local context becomes influential. This calls for other types of study, which may or may not be feasible. In some circumstances, for example, it may not be possible to decompose a voter's decision-making process in order to identify the determinants of behavior. In such situations, we have to be content with inferences drawn from rigorous ecological studies. And from this one the conclusion is clear: context does matter. Where (at least some) people live is linked to how they vote.

JAMES G. GIMPEL AND J. CELESTE LAY

11   Party Identification, Local Partisan Contexts, and the Acquisition of Participatory Attitudes

PUBLIC OPINION RESEARCH has consistently found major differences in political socialization outcomes across racial and ethnic groups, suggesting that the political information circulating within ethnically distinct communities varies in both quantity and content. Here our focus is not on racial minorities but political ones. We investigate whether party identification and partisan context influence a variety of outcomes associated with the political socialization process. Racial minority status is not the only minority status that matters to the formation of attitudes that enable participation and crystallize public opinion. Political minorities are also worth investigation, particularly given that local settings across the nation present variable distributions of partisan leaning and policy preference (Beck, Dalton, Greene, and Huckfeldt 2002; Huckfeldt and Sprague 1995; Levine in this volume).

In many big cities, Republicans are a tiny minority, accounting for less than 10 percent of registered voters in many neighborhoods. In rural and small-town areas, the reverse is sometimes true, with Democrats being at a severe disadvantage. Party registration is usually more even in suburbs and smaller cities, socializing residents in an environment of heterogeneous preferences. According to insights drawn from social psychology, growing up in one of these locations cannot have the same implications for political learning as growing up in another. In one-sided settings, minority views wind up being squelched because minorities have few politically compatible neighbors, encounter greater dissonance, and resist discussions of politics (Huckfeldt 1986; Huckfeldt and Sprague 1995, 155). Minorities generally keep quiet, so the theory goes, because people have a sensitive "social skin" that makes them fear isolation and adopt conforming attitudes to avoid it (Noelle-Neumann 1993). The supply of political information within a particular jurisdiction, then, is determined by the political orientation of majority groups (Berelson, Lazarsfeld, and McPhee 1954; Huckfeldt 1986; Huckfeldt and Sprague 1990; Huckfeldt and Sprague 1995, 155; Huckfeldt, Plutzer, and Sprague 1993). By supplying only certain types of information and reinforcement, local populations in one-party dominant areas remain politically homogeneous for long periods. In politically diverse locales, however, citizens confront a highly varied supply of information, there is far less informational coercion, and political views maintain a corresponding heterogeneity.

To be sure, individuals reside in multilayered political systems and can be thought of as possessing several political contexts, each geographically broader than the previous one. At the level of highest geographic density is the friendship network, often measured by asking survey respondents to name their discussion partners. The next most dense context is the neighborhood, usually measured by census tract and precinct political characteristics (but see Johnston and Pattie for a focus on the "bespoke neighborhood," in this volume). The next most proximate level would be the local macro-environment, measured at the community or perhaps the county level (MacKuen and Brown 1987). Individuals are also members of state and national political communities, and may evaluate their political majority or minority status against these larger communities as well (Anderson and Paskeviciute, in this volume).

Because local social interactions are judged to be important vehicles for information transmission, we are most concerned about measuring diversity in the neighborhood or community, a level that likely encompasses the friendship network but is not as broad as the state or nation. We acknowledge, though, that all of our subjects were nested within a broader geographic setting that harbors a substantial bias in party registration and a long history of electing Democrats to statewide office. Given that the respondents to our survey belong to multiple contexts in which they may gauge their majority or minority status, we should be cautious about generalization from research in focused geographic locations.

Political Heterogeneity: Mobilizer or Demobilizer?

In research reported in this volume and elsewhere, several intriguing studies suggest that political heterogeneity in one's network of associates may demobilize rather than stimulate greater participation (Mutz 2002a, 2002b). Those who have diverse discussion networks mostly avoid political conversations in order to minimize conflict, but over time their exposure to diverse viewpoints diminishes the kind of partisan intensity that stimulates participation. In this sense, heterogeneous friendship networks foster political tolerance but strip away much of the participatory impulse. We should pause to ask if our suggestion that local political diversity stimulates political participation is in contradiction to these fascinating findings on the political heterogeneity of discussion networks. We do not believe that there is a contradiction because political diversity in a neighborhood (our measure) may not be highly related to the nature of individual friendship networks that are not necessarily confined to a local domain (Anderson and Paskeviciute, and Huckfeldt, Johnson, and Sprague, in this volume). The two contexts are not the same. A politically heterogeneous macro-environment stimulates participation because it increases information flow and mobilization efforts by attracting the attention of candidates and parties, not because it necessarily alters the quality of an individual's discussion network.

Political heterogeneity is not the only aspect of the local environment that matters to political socialization. Even in areas that lack competitive politics, high voter turnout generated through other means can provide adolescents with clear and consistent examples of good citizenship. High turnout is associated with more frequent discussions of politics, suggesting that a much richer political information exchange takes place where people vote regularly compared to areas where participation is taken less seriously. Since we do find locales where high participation is rooted in civic-minded attitudes rather than ideological heterogeneity and political competition (Campbell 2002), we must evaluate the effects of local turnout even when it exists independently of partisan diversity.

How Do Contexts Matter?

It is not obvious that political contexts matter at all to political behavior. While a growing body of literature now points to the important influence of local political environments on opinion formation, several researchers have expressed doubt about the extent to which social and political contexts matter. Some have argued that the effects of context are small, adding very little to our understanding of individual political choice (King 1996). Others have suggested that geographic variations in political behavior amount to nothing more than differences in population characteristics such as race, class, or occupation (Gimpel and Schuknecht 2003, chapter 1; Kelley and McAllister 1985). Once we account for the political, social, and economic traits of those we survey, neighborhood or community effects cannot be demonstrated to exist. People in the same neighborhood vote similarly not because they socialize with each other but because they share a common characteristic, such as high income, that influenced their search for a neighborhood.

Prominent theories of opinion formation mostly ignore the role of local context. In his landmark book, *The Nature and Origins of Mass Opinion* (1992), John Zaller suggests that most political information is disseminated through media elites to the masses in either two-sided or one-sided message flows. Two-sided flows are characterized by elite disputation, while one-sided flows reflect elite consensus. Zaller's theory suggests that messages flow from elites to masses pretty much unfiltered and unaltered by local political context. An information flow downward (or outward) from national media sources will penetrate all settings to a similar degree, affecting politically aware voters in much the same way. But the public has sources of information apart from national political elites. People rely upon their friends and neighbors for information, and place value on the opinions of spouses, co-workers, and community leaders (Huckfeldt and Sprague 1995; Huckfeldt, Johnson, and Sprague, in this volume; Mutz 1998, 2002a; Mutz and Mondak 1997; Zuckerman, Fitzgerald, and Dasović, in this volume; Zuckerman, Kotler-Berkowitz, and Swaine 1998). The distribution of political opinion may show two distinct sides nationally, but one side locally. To the extent that voters are more responsive to the local climate of opinion than to unfiltered national media sources, context counts. One important study has shown that *local* perceptions of media bias in news stories are more influential on political behavior than *actual* news content (Beck, Dalton, Greene, and Huckfeldt 2002).

The way in which a news story is received and processed by a local population will vary directly with salient population characteristics. In a community where there is broad consensus about the value of farm subsidies, debates about government involvement in farming seem distant and irrelevant. Immigration may be an intensely controversial issue in California, but in many towns in the Midwest it is still possible for natives to live out their lives without meeting *any* immigrants. The vitriolic immigration debate is alien to them, and they do not fully understand why some people feel so intensely about it. This does not make them uninformed about politics and issues; it simply means that their understanding of the issue is conditioned by the intensity of their interest in it—an intensity that is defined locally.

With respect to the political socialization of the young, the case for local contextual effects operating to influence opinion is even stronger than it is for opinion formation among the adult population. For adolescents and small children, even more than for adults, sources of information have their origin in the local community. Depending upon where they live, young people may have only the vaguest sense that there are multiple sides on such controversial issues as welfare reform, civil rights enforcement, and immigration. Because national news stories are filtered through local agents of information and socialization, we expect the interaction of contextual and individual-level variables to exhibit a dramatic impact on broad classes of socialization outcomes that directly influence later political participation.

It is certainly possible that once we control for the party loyalties of individuals in the community, the effects of neighborhood context will be washed away. If the party composition of neighborhoods signals nothing more than the number of survey respondents at each location who identified themselves as Republicans, Independents, and Democrats, then we can expect no significant effects of partisan environments on political socialization—at least once an individual's party identification is taken into account. But if partisan environments are more than just a collection of individuals with party identities, and also tell something about the way in which these individuals communicate and learn about politics, then something may be added by partisan context that is missed by studies that neglect the social logic of the socialization process (and see Johnston and Pattie, in this volume).

Party Identification, Partisan Contexts, and Political Socialization Indicators

In developing the link between party identification, local partisan contexts, and political socialization, we focus on four indicators of political socialization that have been discussed widely in previous literature: frequency of political discussion, political knowledge, internal political efficacy, and external political efficacy (Delli Carpini and Keeter 1996; Gimpel, Lay, and Schuknecht 2003; Jennings 1996; Jennings and Niemi 1974, 1981; Niemi and Junn 1998; Niemi and Sobieszek 1977). These four key indicators by no means exhaust the attitudinal outcomes that interest students of political socialization, but they are of special interest to us because they speak to the factors that directly enable political participation among adults.

The acquisition and expression of partisanship is an important step toward good political socialization for a variety of reasons. Studies of adults have established that partisans follow political news coverage more closely than Independents or nonpartisans, and are much more likely to vote and take the other duties of citizenship seriously (Green, Palmquist, and Schickler 2002; Zaller 1992). The propensity either to adopt or to avoid a partisan stance has major implications for all of the socialization outcomes we measure. For example, much of the existing research predicts that adolescents who label themselves as Republicans or Democrats engage in more frequent discussions of politics than those who do not. Nevertheless, partisan environments can temper the extent of discussion because adolescents are highly sensitive to peer pressure and are generally anxious to conform.

While locales exhibiting greater political diversity undoubtedly produce an information bonanza that stimulates political discussion, social pressures may act to suppress discussion in areas that are politically lopsided. The young partisans we find in environments where their party is a decisive minority are less likely to speak up about politics than those who belong to the majority or who find themselves in more heterogeneous settings.

An extensive body of political science research has established that competition between political parties influences turnout, heightening the sense that one's vote counts (Key 1949; Rosenstone and Hansen 1993). The psychological linkage between political competitiveness and voter participation is through internal efficacy: If voters believe their vote counts, they feel capable of influencing the election outcome. Related to the competitiveness of the system is the voter's sense that he or she is represented at some level of government by officeholders who are like-minded—or that, with some reasonable effort, one could be represented by such a person. In 1988 the simple prospect that Jesse Jackson could become the Democratic Party's presidential nominee led to record levels of black mobilization (Tate 1991). In related work, there is evidence that blacks living in cities that have elected African Americans to prominent political offices feel more efficacious and are more attentive to politics than those living in areas where blacks are not among the visible officeholders (Bobo and Gilliam 1990). Minority political incorporation, then, is instrumental to the feeling that minorities can trust the system and count on it to be responsive to them. Empowerment leads to higher efficacy (Bobo and Gilliam 1990, 387).

The generalization that the political efficacy of minority group members is contingent upon electing at least some representatives of that group to public office may generalize to other political (not necessarily racial) minorities. There is a similar effect for gender, for example. Women are more likely to talk to others about politics and feel more politically efficacious during election campaigns in which women are on the ballot (Hansen 1997). Given that federal systems permit substantial autonomy among local units of government in the conduct of elections, it is not difficult to imagine that one could be a local political minority while being a member of a national political majority. If one's local minority status is acute, it could erode one's expectations about local government responsiveness. And if local political offices are the most familiar and tangible governmental institutions, this doubt could translate into a fatalistic sense that one's voice does not count and participation does not matter. One might expect that Democrats in areas of long-standing Republican dominance would exhibit lower efficacy than their Republican-identifying counterparts, and vice versa. Citizens functioning under conditions where their policy interests are consistently defeated will feel less efficacious than citizens whose interests dominate (Iyengar 1980; Weissberg 1975). One point of our hypothesis testing will be to examine party dominance measured at the local level for its effects on internal and external efficacy.

To test our hypotheses, we adopt a couple of strategies. First, we take a structural equations approach, depicted in Figure 11.1, where individual party identification is understood as a function of community-level political variables (turnout levels, local partisan bias, and partisan diversity). In this framework, the political context is thought to have both a direct and an indirect impact on political social-

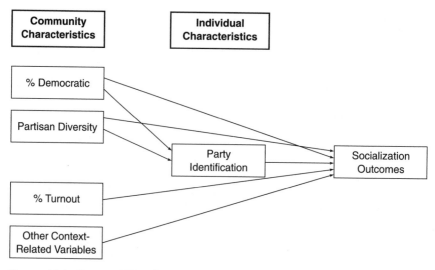

FIGURE 11.1. Structural Equation Model of the Relationship between Community Context, Individual Partisan Identification, and Political Socialization Outcomes

ization, with effects largely, but not entirely, mediated through the acquisition of individual partisan identity.

The second model we examine looks at the direct effects of individual partisanship, combined with interactions from a hierarchical linear model that capture the effect of local political majority and minority status. Generally, we hypothesize that partisans living in environments where their party is a local minority will be socialized differently from those in which their party is a strong local majority. The advantage of estimating such a model is that it does not assume that an individual's partisanship has constant, fixed effects across all local political environments. While the two parties may be roughly even in their support on the national stage, the hierarchical linear model allows us to evaluate whether the experience of the local balance of partisanship matters most to adolescent socialization since that is the distribution of opinion adolescents experience daily.

DATA DESCRIPTION

Toward the end of testing for causal influences across communities, the setting for the study is twenty-nine distinct school sites, in twenty-nine different communities, within and outside of the Baltimore, Maryland, and Washington, D.C., metropolitan areas (see Figure 11.2). The academic community has long needed research on neighborhood and community influences on political socialization. Many previous studies have been unable to capture enough variation across neighborhoods and communities to test for the presence of such causal factors. Research carried out in one, two, or a few schools of necessity treats community characteristics as a constant, missing whatever causal impact they may have. Other studies have simply failed to record neighborhood and community-level information that could be used to investigate the effects of these variables on attitudes and

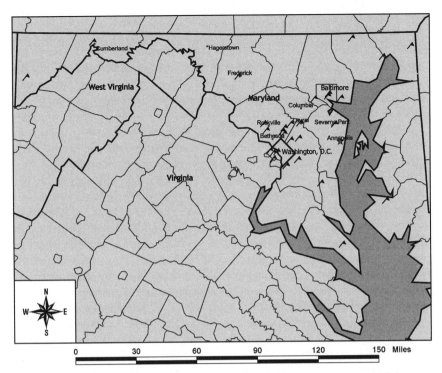

FIGURE 11.2. Map Showing Locations of Participating Schools in the Metro Civic Values Study

behavior. Still other studies have gathered limited contextual information, but not at a sufficiently fine level of granularity to be of much explanatory value.

The study area's high schools generally track students into two or three groups: "honors" and "standard" tracks were most common, with the standard track being less oriented toward college preparation. Often more than half of a school's students were in the honors-level courses, with more than one-third aiming at Advanced Placement (AP) college credit. In forming our research samples, we would typically choose students from no more than two honors-level courses at each school, with at least half of each school's subjects coming from the standard academic tracks or levels. We generally sought to survey between 70 and 150 students at each school, depending largely upon the school's size. Public high schools in our study area range in size from a low of about 600 students to a high of nearly 3,000.

How well did we represent each school's population with the nonrandom selection of students we surveyed at each location? More information about the sample can be obtained directly from the authors and in related work (Gimpel, Lay, and Schuknecht 2003). While we did not have the luxury of a strict random draw from school enrollment lists, the resulting sample did achieve substantial representativeness in terms of race and ethnic group. Aggregating the individual samples from all school sites, our study includes responses from 748 African American students (24 percent of the total population), 263 Asian students (8.6 percent), 215 Latinos (7 percent), 203 biracial or mixed-race students (6.6 percent), and 1,546 Caucasian students (50.5 percent). Census data, and reports from the states' Departments of Education, suggest that these percentages reflect the area's population and its public school population. In 1999–2000, about 54 percent of Maryland's student population was Caucasian, 4 percent Hispanic, 4 percent Asian, and 37 percent African American. In suburban Arlington County, Virginia, where we included four high schools, the same figures were: 40 percent white, 33 percent Hispanic, 15 percent black, and 11 percent Asian–Pacific Islander. Data on biracial or mixed-race students were unavailable from education authorities.

Our tabulations also show that our sample includes 402 students who are foreign-born (13.1 percent) and another 373 who are the children of at least one foreign-born parent (12.2 percent). Realizing that the large population of government employees living in the Washington, D.C., suburbs might inflate students' perceptions of government's role and value, we were careful to include questions about parental employment and government employment on the survey questionnaire (Conway, Stevens, and Smith 1975). In the data analysis we introduce statistical controls for government employment to control for any effects it might have on political efficacy, knowledge, and other socialization-related responses. Sample weights have been calculated to adjust the sample and the data analysis to reflect total student enrollment by school district. In the end, we are confident that we have obtained an accurate representation of the students in the study area even though the practical constraints of working with fourteen separate school systems and twenty-nine school administrations did not permit a strictly random sampling procedure (see Gimpel, Lay, and Schuknecht 2003).[1]

Since our study theorizes that communities make a difference to the way people receive and process information, and that the broader social and political environment in which students reside may have an impact independent of media, family, and peers, we should provide some account of the characteristics of the communities in which our survey was conducted. What do we mean by "community"? In this case, we define community as the population living in the geographic area served by the school. School authorities term these jurisdictions "catchment" areas. Contextual variables included in our data analysis are measured in one of two ways: by the school's zip-code demographics provided by the U.S. Census capturing median family income, education levels, and racial composition, and by precinct-level data aggregated to school catchment areas for the political-context measures capturing political participation levels, partisan bias, and political party heterogeneity.

The Dependent Variables

Two of our dependent variables are formulated as principal components factor scores from sets of survey items, then rescaled to range between 0 and 100 in order to ease interpretation in regression analysis. The details for the factor analyses are reported in this chapter's Appendix, but basically there are two dependent variables formulated within the factor analytic framework: internal political efficacy and external political efficacy. The factor analyses and factor loadings for each question from which these latent variables were constructed are reported in the chapter Appendix. In addition, two other variables from specific survey items are treated as dependent variables in our analysis: the amount of political discussion youth reported with family and friends in the preceding week (in number of days) and the students' scores on the seven-item, factual-knowledge test, expressed as the percentage of correct answers.

Assessing the Influence of Party Identification and Partisan Context

If one of the fundamental means for learning about politics is through political discussion, then it is clear that our Republican-identifying youth have a narrow advantage over Democrats and Independents, and all three of the major identities maintain a significant lead over those who refused to identify at all. Specifically, we find that Republican-identifying youth engaged in 11 percent more discussion in the previous week than nonidentifiers, Independents about 10.5 percent more, and Democrats about 9 percent more (see Table 11.1). Evaluating our respondents according to the extent of their political discussion on a standard grading scale, we found both partisans and Independents would rank about one letter grade higher than nonidentifiers. Party identification and interest in political discussion do go hand in hand. The major gap is between the identifiers and nonidentifiers, not between partisans and Independents.

Notably, direct effects of partisan context exist independent of individual party identification, with discussion dropping about 1 percent with every ten-point increase in local Democratic dominance. Conversely, Republican-dominant areas are typically characterized by greater discussion, probably because the GOP-dominant areas are full of well-informed and politically active adults. Moreover, the areas of Republican strength are not as lopsided as the areas of Democratic strength, so there may be greater party and campaign mobilization in the heavily GOP neighborhoods than in the most lopsided Democratic ones. Still, we find that partisan diversity depresses the frequency of political discussion, although the effect is not strong: a one-point reduction for every ten-point increase in political diversity. Even though competitive political settings place a high premium on political information, and the absence of a single dominant view allows disagreement to thrive, we do not find that discussions with family and friends are surging in the highly diverse locations once we control for other variables, including individual partisanship.

Clearly the level of turnout in the neighborhood counts as a major socializing force. We find that high-turnout locales dramatically increase the amount of political information exchanged through discussion, moving it up by a considerable 8 percent for every ten-point increase in local participation levels. While there is no question, then, that individual party identification has a direct impact on the level of discussion, contextual political factors also remain important to this aspect of the socialization process. Furthermore, it is highly unlikely that the causal influence runs in the other direction—from frequency of discussion to high-turnout neighborhoods—since we are not addressing adult political discussions here but instead the discussions of youth, the vast majority of whom are ineligible to vote.

Partisan and Independent identifiers benefit from the extensive political discussion they engage in with family and friends, and they also exhibit much higher levels of political knowledge than nonidentifiers (see Table 11.1). Knowledge test scores were highest among Democrats, with Republicans ranking second, and Independents third. The difference between Republican and Independent identifiers was a considerable 4.7 points, or about half a letter grade measured on a standard high school grading scale. Democratic identifiers ranked nearly an entire letter grade ahead of non-party identifiers.

Notably, contextual effects on political knowledge acquisition remain strong even after controlling for individual partisanship. Homogeneous Democratic political contexts did not further knowledge-building processes, inasmuch as a 10 percent increase in Democratic bias yielded a .73-point drop in the knowledge test score. Of course, what that means is that one-party Republican jurisdictions were more productive of knowledge than the most lopsided Democratic ones. By far the most influential neighborhood effect on knowledge is for turnout, where a 10 percent increase in political participation is associated with a seven-point surge in the knowledge test scores of the youth in our survey. The best climate for stimulating the acquisition of political knowledge among the young is one in which there are ample adult role models of political engagement, even if there is not a great deal of partisan diversity.

Neighborhood participation levels exercise a strong and independent impact on internal efficacy too, although its positive impact on external efficacy is modest. Republicans and Democrats rank 7–8 percent higher than nonpartisans in their level of internal efficacy. For convenience, one could think of this as nearly one letter grade higher. It is clear that the big difference in internal efficacy is not between partisans and Independents but between Independents and those who reported not knowing their party identification. From a political socialization standpoint, our findings show that calling oneself an Independent is not at all similar to having no party identification at all—at least among adolescents.

Finally, the influence of political context on both internal and external efficacy was robust, particularly for our neighborhood participation indicator. Low-turnout jurisdictions are productive of cynicism about one's voice and influence (internal efficacy), and negative evaluations of government performance and responsiveness (external efficacy). In these politically lifeless environments, adults rarely put the system to the test, and have largely given up hope about government ever serving them. Consequently adolescents almost never hear positive appraisals of government or political leadership. They rarely see excitement and optimism accompanying an election campaign. To compound the problem, these youth are often in settings where their schools and social studies classes are in no position to compensate for the inadequate political socialization they are receiving at home.

But why do our results show that it is Republican-leaning locations that exhibit lower internal and external efficacy? This finding is likely the result of the fact that the GOP areas in most of our study are nested within a broader Democratic context at the state level. The Republican-identifying citizens in Maryland had very little chance of electing visible statewide officeholders from their political party. Before the stunning 2002 general election, Republicans had not won the Maryland governorship in thirty-four years, twice as long as any of our teen-aged

TABLE 11.1. Structural Equations Estimation of Direct Effects of Political Context and Party Identification on Political Socialization, Controlling for Indirect Effects of Political Context and Direct Effects of Other Community Characteristics

Explanatory variable	Frequency of political discussion	Ǝ	Level of political knowledge	Ǝ	Internal political efficacy	Ǝ	External political efficacy	Ǝ
Democratic respondent	9.144** (1.012)	.16	8.096** (.774)	.18	7.535** (.595)	.22	.854 (.582)	.03
Republican respondent	10.983** (1.272)	.15	5.055** (.973)	.09	7.358** (.748)	.17	1.356* (.732)	.03
Independent respondent	10.583** (1.692)	.11	3.399** (1.295)	.04	6.722** (.995)	.11	-1.369 (.973)	-.02
Percentage Democratic	-.108** (.035)	-.06	-.073** (.026)	-.05	.049** (.020)	.04	.037* (.020)	.04
Local party diversity	-.084* (.044)	-.03	-.043 (.034)	-.02	-.046* (.026)	-.03	-.067** (.026)	-.05
Percentage turnout	.787** (.078)	.17	.710** (.060)	.19	.195** (.046)	.07	.088* (.045)	.03
R^2	.123		.192		.134		.086	
N	2,938		2,919		2,936		2,933	

Source: Metro Civic Values Study.

Note: Structural equations estimation: Cell entries are regression coefficients for direct effects only with standard errors in parentheses. Standardized regression coefficients are listed under Ǝ. Control variables with parameters for direct effects not shown in this model are: percentage black; percentage Asian; percentage Hispanic; population density; median income; percentage with four years college. See model in Figure 4.1 for complete specification.

*p < .10, **p ≤ .05.

respondents had lived! A Republican had not served in a U.S. Senate seat from Maryland since 1985, about the time many of our respondents were born. The internal efficacy of youth living in GOP neighborhoods is low because neither they nor their mostly Republican-leaning parents saw that their interests were regularly voiced in visible political venues, and their external efficacy is low because they doubt that the state government serves them well. They are not unlike the racial minorities described by the black-empowerment literature (Bobo and Gilliam 1990; Tate 1991). The fact that they are part of a local or neighborhood majority may not outweigh their sense of minority status in the broader geopolitical context in which they are situated. This explanation speaks to the fact that individuals find themselves anchored in multiple political contexts, exhibiting varying distributions of partisanship and opinion, and that the most local context is not the only important one when it comes to assessing government's responsiveness and one's voice in it.

Judging from the results shown in Table 11.1, if one could choose where to live in order to produce politically knowledgeable, efficacious children, destined for good citizenship, the best choices are jurisdictions exhibiting high voter turnout. The worst place to bring up good citizens is in cities and towns with low levels of adult political activism, communities where youth never encounter political discussions, learn little about politics, and conclude that they have no voice. Local partisan heterogeneity does not appear to be a *direct* force driving adolescent socialization—at least once we control for individual party identification and turnout levels, which are both strong correlates of neighborhood political diversity. Our findings suggest that local partisan diversity is beneficial to socialization and participation indirectly, through the acquisition of individual partisanship. Partisan diversity may also promote socialization if it occurs at multiple levels of an individual's political context: in local affairs *and* state government, since state government officeholders are frequently more visible than local ones. We also conclude that it is best to raise one's child around adolescents and adults who identify with one of the two major parties. Growing up around partisans will greatly assist the inexperienced to match their emerging self-conceptions to the social groups that are associated with the major parties. Making this match between self-conception and party identity greatly facilitates later participation by simplifying the tasks of candidate evaluation and political judgment (Green, Palmquist, and Schickler 2002).

Party Identification in Interaction with Partisan Context

Table 11.2 presents results from a two-level hierarchical linear model where we assess the effects of the respondents' party identification in neighborhood contexts of variable turnout, partisan diversity, and political party bias. These results indicate whether individual partisanship has different effects on measures of knowledge, discussion, and efficacy that are contingent upon the community context of respondents. Three interactions we report gauge the effect of being a Democrat in a heavily Democratic context, a Republican in a Republican context, and an Independent in a Democratic context. (We could just as easily have chosen to test for the effects of being an Independent in a Republican context—the choice is mostly arbitrary.) We also examine the interaction of party identification and turnout, and party identification and local partisan diversity. We add a control for the effect of family socioeconomic status in this model, to eliminate the possibility that the effects we observed for neighborhood turnout in Table 11.1 were simply a function of living in an affluent household.

Briefly, our expectation was that in each case the condition of living in an environment in which one's own party was dominant locally would create dispositions opposite to those we would observe among partisans who were distinct political minorities. In other words, if Republicans were generally prone to frequent political discussions when they found themselves among like-minded partisans, or in politically mixed environments, Republicans in lopsided Democratic contexts would be more inclined to avoid such discussions—primarily because they would have fewer compatible discussion partners. At the very least, we expected the youth who found themselves to be political minorities would show ambivalent quantities and intensities on the various socialization outcomes, compared with fellow partisans residing in more compatible political settings.

The results displayed in Table 11.2 confirm some of these expectations, especially for Republicans, the minority party throughout much of the study area. Our results closely mirror those of Finifter (1974), who discovered that political minorities (Republicans and Independents) working in a factory were more sensitive to their local contexts than those identifying with Democrats, the majority party. Given the general Democratic orientation of the study area, local party diversity is especially stimulating to Republican-identifying youth while having little impact on Democrats. For example, Republican-identifying youth engage in more frequent political discussion than any other group, consistent with the results from Table 11.1, but Republicans in politically lopsided contexts engage in considerably less discussion than those in more heterogeneous environments. Republicans in politically lopsided contexts also exhibit less political knowledge (see Figure 11.3), and a lower level of internal efficacy, than the GOP youth in the most politically diverse areas we studied.

Because the vast majority of the one-sided neighborhoods in our study area are strongly Democratic, not Republican, we can infer that Republicans living in them are less politically efficacious, less interested in discussion, and less knowledgeable—the result of being around hostile partisans in a broader context that does not favor the election of their candidates. Our results for Republicans are consistent with the idea that political minorities are discouraged by their status, avoid discussions of politics, and have less incentive to seek greater knowledge (Huckfeldt and Sprague 1995). These political minorities wind up thinking and acting very much like outnumbered racial minorities, uncertain of the value of their voice and despairing of the prospect of electing one of their own (Bobo and Gilliam 1990). Most notably, our results hold up controlling for family socioeconomic status, indicating that even youth from well-off Republican homes are subject to these effects of their minority or majority position. Even people whom we otherwise consider resource rich are vulnerable to the political context in which they live (Verba, Schlozman, and Burns, in this volume).

TABLE 11.2. Two-Level Model of the Influence of Partisanship and Political Context on Political Socialization Outcomes, Controlling for Family Socioeconomic Status

Fixed effects	Explanatory variable	Frequency of political discussion	Level of political knowledge	Internal political efficacy	External political efficacy
Location means (β_0)	Intercept	.35	61.64**	41.16**	12.01
		(17.99)	(22.72)	(13.51)	(13.02)
	Percentage turnout	.51**	.21*	.06	.09
		(.16)	(.11)	(.11)	(.09)
	Party diversity	−.22*	−.07	−.06	.12
		(.13)	(.18)	(.09)	(.08)
	Percentage Democratic	−.06	−.16	.02	.17**
		(.08)	(.14)	(.07)	(.07)
Democratic identifiers (β_1)	Intercept	.68	−8.93	−6.34	−.54
		(17.98)	(20.42)	(16.34)	(9.97)
	Percentage turnout	.06	.20**	.10	.11
		(.14)	(.08)	(.13)	(.08)
	Party diversity	.08	.03	.10	−.004
		(.17)	(.14)	(.13)	(.06)
	Percentage Democratic	−.08	−.01	−.05	−.10**
		(.10)	(.13)	(.09)	(.05)
Republican identifiers (β_2)	Intercept	3.51	−37.21**	−25.54**	−11.88*
		(13.81)	(10.58)	(11.68)	(6.61)
	Percentage turnout	−.37*	.27**	.15	.12
		(.22)	(.12)	(.17)	(.09)
	Party diversity	.37**	.31**	.27*	.06
		(.20)	(.15)	(.14)	(.07)
	Percentage Republican	.003	−.10	−.03	−.01
		(.14)	(.12)	(.10)	(.04)

TABLE 11.2. (Continued)

Fixed effects	Explanatory variable	Frequency of political discussion	Level of political knowledge	Internal political efficacy	External political efficacy
Independent identifiers (Ξ_3)	Intercept	-98.92** (34.89)	7.49 (44.19)	-37.05** (16.05)	17.08 (13.39)
	Percentage turnout	.32 (.26)	.17 (.23)	.20* (.11)	-.04 (.11)
	Party diversity	.73** (.26)	-.11 (.30)	.27** (.12)	-.07 (.08)
	Percentage Democratic	.39** (.14)	-.11 (.26)	.10 (.08)	-.15** (.04)
Socioeconomic status (Ξ_4)	Intercept	.24** (.07)	.29** (.05)	.16** (.03)	.04* (.02)
N of level 1 respondents		2,785	2,781	2,712	2,709

Random effects	Frequency of political discussion		Level of political knowledge		Internal political efficacy		External political efficacy	
	Variance	Signif.	Variance	Signif.	Variance	Signif.	Variance	Signif.
Intercept	16.33	.001	29.28	.001	7.26	.002	1.87	.500
Democratic identifiers	10.28	.004	.62	.211	6.59	.001	.34	.324
Republican identifiers	25.86	.008	9.34	.500	8.51	.001	1.39	.500
Independent identifiers	23.91	.016	21.85	.001	4.12	.123	.41	.500
Socioeconomic status	.05	.000	.02	.003	.004	.285	.001	.500
Level 1 R	665.69		378.40		234.72		228.56	

Note: Hierarchical linear model, slopes and intercepts estimation: Cell entries are regression coefficients (standard errors). Significance is for the chi-square test on the variance components. Results for reliability estimates do not appear in the table, but are available from the authors upon request.

*p < .10, **p < .05.

We do not find strong neighborhood effects acting on our Democratic youth from the results in Table 11.2. Their participation-enabling attitudes appear to be largely independent of contextual political forces, except that Democratic-identifying youth do show greater internal efficacy in locations exhibiting higher turnout.

Independent-identifying youth appear to benefit from living in politically heterogeneous areas in much the same way that Republican youth do. The regularity of political discussion and the strength of internal efficacy increase significantly in places where the parties are closely matched in major elections. At the same time, Independent identifiers show lower levels of discussion and internal efficacy in locations of GOP dominance. It may be that Republicans exert more social pressure on Independents in the areas where they are dominant than Democrats do in the locations where they are dominant. The areas of Democratic dominance are substantially more one-sided than the locations where Republicans are the majority. Alternatively, the Independents may feel especially vulnerable to Republican pressures because Independents tend to resemble less informed or weak Democrats throughout most of the study area.

From this set of findings, we underscore the previous conclusion that high-turnout neighborhoods remain influential in interaction with party identification, increasing the internal efficacy of Democratic and Independent identifiers, and elevating the political knowledge of Republicans (see Table 11.2). The example provided by highly participatory adults in one's community produces a highly positive socialization experience.

The legitimate question arises as to what extent these results have external validity. Would we find similar results outside the Mid-Atlantic region, and specifically outside the Baltimore-Washington metropolitan area? Some of these findings

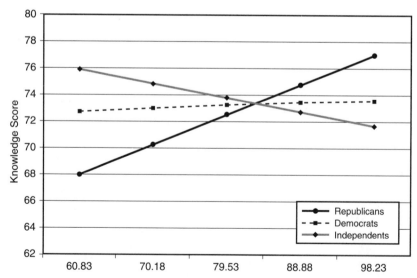

FIGURE 11.3. Political Knowledge Increases among Republican-identifying Youth in Areas of Partisan Diversity, but Remains Unchanged among Democratic Youth and Drops among Independent Identifiers

are undoubtedly an artifact of the study's setting in a predominantly Democratic state (Maryland) and a predominantly Democratic region of a second state (Arlington, Virginia), and they may not generalize to other places in the nation. We have observed that Republican identifiers in this one-party setting are easily discouraged and inefficacious, knowing that they rarely win statewide offices and are lucky to control a handful of state legislative seats. Party registration in Maryland exhibited a solid 2–1 Democratic edge throughout the final decade of the twentieth century and the early years of the twenty-first. We suspect that Republican youth are more vulnerable to feelings of political inferiority and inefficacy in this area than they would be in more evenly divided states such as Ohio, Colorado, or Pennsylvania.

Still, the local context can mitigate these feelings of despair. In the few places where the GOP is competitive locally, we found that the air of defeatism is much thinner and youthful Republican identifiers were more confident that they had a voice. Local party diversity is not as productive of political interest and efficacy for Democratic identifiers because Democrats are the majority party across most locales and certainly statewide. For majority parties, greater partisan diversity can only mean the dismal prospect of losing some elections. Future research would do well to explore the socialization experiences of Democratic youth in majority-Republican settings, perhaps in states such as Kansas, Utah, or Idaho, where one might find politically mixed locales a boon to the efficacy and knowledge of Democratic youth. One implication of the specific geography of our study is that the kind of strong neighborhood effects that we observe for Republicans might well be true of Democratic youth in states where all prominent officeholders are Republicans and have been for decades. Clearly a study replicating this research in a different part of the country would add to our understanding of socialization patterns of majority and minority partisans and the influence of overlapping state and local partisan contexts.

Conclusions

The good news is that partisanship is alive and well among the adolescents we surveyed at the beginning of the new millennium. This is a positive finding because the acquisition of partisanship is an important step in the process of becoming a responsible, participatory citizen. Identifying with one of the two major parties is strongly associated with enhanced political discussion, greater political knowledge, and higher internal efficacy.

Neighborhood effects remain important to the political socialization of adolescents, well after individual partisan identification is taken into account. It is not just one's own partisanship that matters to one's future citizenship; the partisanship of others does too. Probably the main conclusion we draw from our findings is that the more acute one's political-minority status, the worse these socialization outcomes will be. Being part of a perpetual minority is demoralizing, and the accompanying despair and feelings of inferiority undermine the sense of efficacy that promotes participation. Minority status perpetuates itself over time by discouraging the participation of minor-party partisans in the construction of more effective campaign and party-building efforts. The Republican-identifying youth from predominantly one-party Democratic regions were greatly encouraged when they lived in locales where there was some modicum of partisan diversity.

That individuals are members of overlapping political contexts is also important to our understanding of these results (Mackuen and Brown 1987). Citizens functioning under conditions where their policy interests are consistently defeated or shouted down understandably feel less efficacious than citizens whose interests dominate (Weissberg 1975; Iyengar 1980). Given that federal systems permit substantial autonomy among local units of government in the conduct of elections, it is not difficult to imagine that one could belong to a local political minority while being a member of a statewide or national political majority. But if one is consistently shouted down in a broader political context, such as the state level, one might find a local context to be especially stimulating, and even comforting. This is exactly what we found: Political minorities (Republicans and Independents) were more sensitive to local contexts than adherents of the majority party (Finifter 1974). Given the general Democratic orientation of the study area, strong local party diversity is especially stimulating to Republican- and Independent-identifying youth but has little significant impact on Democrats. What this means is that Democratic youth appear to exhibit fairly uniform levels of political knowledge, efficacy, and discussion participation, regardless of the partisan heterogeneity of their home community. Again, our suggestion is that local contextual forces may play less of a role for Democratic youth since they know they are a majority in the broader contextual setting of the study area, where the Democratic Party has a history of winning most major statewide offices. Local contexts make a much larger difference for those who are in the broader minority than those who are more safely in the majority, a conclusion that Finifter (1974) reached after studying the social interactions of Republican and Democratic workers in a factory dominated by Democrats.

The best place to raise politically efficacious and knowledgeable children is in an environment where partisanship thrives, participation is high, and where elections for major offices are regularly contested across multiple geographic contexts, local and statewide. Nothing is worse for the development of good citizenship than living in a low-turnout environment with low levels of political information where youth develop ample reasons not to believe in the responsiveness of government. Given what we have learned here and in previous research about the environments that produce high turnout and strong party identity among adults, we take from our findings the conclusion that neither extreme minority nor supermajority status for one's party makes for an optimal climate for political socialization.

APPENDIX

TABLE 11A.1. Principal Components Factor Scores for Dependent Variables from the Regression Analysis Presented in Tables 11.1 and 11.2

Survey items	Factor loading
INTERNAL EFFICACY	
Other people understand better	0.73
I have a good understanding	−0.70
I'm as well informed as others	−0.72
Government is too complicated	0.72
Eigenvalue	2.05
Variance explained by factor	51.2%
Number of additional factors extracted with eigenvalues > 1	0
EXTERNAL EFFICACY	
People in government waste money	0.30
Problem is no equal voice	0.40
Public officials don't care	0.48
Public officials don't listen	0.45
I have no say in government	0.39
Eigenvalue	2.17
Variance explained by factor	36.8%
Number of additional factors extracted with eigenvalues >1	0

Note: All of the survey item responses are on a 5-point Likert scale running from 1 (strongly agree) to 5 (strongly disagree).

TABLE 11A.2. Multiple Choice Political Knowledge Questions

	Percentage correct
Where can you find the Bill of Rights?	74.2
How often are presidential elections held?	89.2
The system of government where power is divided between two levels of government is called ...	61.0
Who is the current Chief Justice of the U.S. Supreme Court?	62.8
How many Senators does each state have in the U.S. Senate?	61.8
The member who is elected to preside over the U.S. House of Representatives is called ...	75.6
Who is the current Vice President of the United States?	94.0

Note: Students were given four choices in response to each question.

CHRISTOPHER J. ANDERSON AND AIDA PASKEVICIUTE

12 Macro-Politics and Micro-Behavior

Mainstream Politics and the Frequency of Political Discussion in Contemporary Democracies

Too much agreement kills a chat.
—Eldridge Cleaver

POLITICAL PHILOSOPHERS AND democratic theorists since Aristotle have considered political discussion—or at least its ideal version, democratic deliberation—an essential, albeit potentially conflictual element of the democratic process (Bohman 1996; Elster 1998; Fishkin 1991; Macedo 1999). Discussions about politics, it is argued, allow citizens to express their preferences, debate contentious issues, and even transform individual preferences to achieve a collective decision of superior quality. (For a discussion of these issues, see Knight and Johnson 1994.) Recent empirical studies suggest that at least some of these claims have merit (Conover, Searing, and Crewe 2002). For example, discussing politics generally improves citizens' knowledge of public affairs (Bennett, Flickinger, and Rhine 2000), enhances political tolerance (Mutz 2002a), increases political sophistication among participants in face-to-face discussions (Gastil and Dillard 1999), and significantly elevates opinion quality (Wyatt, Katz, and Kim 2000). In contrast, relatively infrequent political discussion can breed a culture of conformity and intolerance, especially if discussion partners lack diversity (Gibson 1992; see also Gimpel and Lay, in this volume).

Political discussion is a critical element in the formation of individuals' political attitudes and behavior (Jennings and Niemi 1981), and it has been found to be an indicator of increased political sophistication and attentiveness (Inglehart 1977). Researchers have also been interested in political discussion because it constitutes a prime source of information about political affairs (Huckfeldt and Sprague 1995; Huckfeldt, Johnson, and Sprague, in this volume) and because it constitutes a crucial mechanism of political mobilization, in particular during election campaigns (Lazarsfeld, Berelson, and Gaudet 1944; Leighley 1990, 1995). Thus, given the central role that political conversations play in the life of a democracy, it is surprising that the determinants of political discussion have been the focus of investigation much less often than other acts of political participation (see, e.g., Leighley 1995). And while a rich literature has examined various aspects of political discussion, few (if any) researchers have systematically examined the determinants of political discussion from a comparative perspective.[1] Moreover, while a number of studies have examined the role of opinion diversity at the micro-level (for a discussion, see Zuckerman and Kotler-Berkowitz 1998), few have considered the impact of the national political community on people's willingness to engage in political discussions.

To help close these gaps, we investigate the determinants of the frequency of political discussion in fifteen contemporary democracies. We argue that an explanation of political discussion that is valid across countries requires consideration of both individual-level variables and a country's macro-political climate. Moreover, and relatedly, we examine the impact of citizens' attitudes relative to the distribution of opinions among others in the country. Our analyses show that political heterogeneity at the macro level and an individual's position relative to mainstream opinion in society systematically affect the likelihood of their getting involved in political discussions. Specifically, we find that being outside the political mainstream and living in a country marked by heterogeneity of political preferences significantly increases the frequency of political discussion in contemporary democracies. Below we discuss extant research on both the individual-level and contextual determinants of political discussion. Consequently, we derive a series of hypotheses and develop an estimation model that is tested with data from fifteen contemporary democracies. A concluding section discusses the findings and points out areas for future research.

THE MACRO-POLITICAL CLIMATE AND POLITICAL DISCUSSION

Typically, talking about politics is considered both an individual and a social activity that shapes political behavior, but that can also be viewed as a political act itself (Huckfeldt 1986; Gamson 1992). And while a rich body of research focuses on how individual-level variables as well as the immediate (micro-) political environment affects citizens' propensity to engage in political discussion (e.g., Huckfeldt and Sprague 1995), few studies have considered how the macro-political context affects people's frequency of political discussion (but see Noelle-Neumann 1993).[2] This relative inattention to the impact of the wider political community is perhaps not surprising given that most studies of political discussion have been conducted in single-country settings where the macro-political context can be held constant.

The use of a single-country design has two important drawbacks, however: For one, it is difficult to establish whether the individual-level factors that drive political discussion in one country also play a role in others. It is easy to imagine that such factors may have dissimilar effects on individuals exposed to different political, social, and cultural contexts where political discussion may have a different meaning as a form of political participation and social interaction. Furthermore, single-country studies cannot consider whether and how differences in countries' political environments influence political discussion. Given that political discussion is both an individual and a social political act, the specific question we seek to answer, then, is how an individual's placement in the macro-political space, measured at the level of countries, may affect the frequency of his or her engagement in political discussions.

THEORIZING ABOUT THE EFFECTS OF MACRO-POLITICS ON POLITICAL DISCUSSION: THE ROLE OF MAINSTREAM OPINION

Because of differences in opportunities for discussion, preferences for avoiding unpleasant social interactions, and pressures to conform, people outside the mainstream might be expected to discuss politics less frequently than those in it (Conover, Searing, and Crewe 2002; MacKuen 1990, 64).[3] However, a contrasting perspective suggests that individuals in the mainstream may discuss politics less frequently because they are content with the status quo and have fewer incentives to express their views. This expectation is based on the idea that extremists, or hard-core opinion holders, may be more committed to their views and more willing to share them. They are, by definition, not in the mainstream and therefore unlikely to be content with the status quo.[4] Moreover, people may locate themselves in the political mainstream because they are not much involved in politics; instead, they simply accept the dominant position without giving it much consideration. As a result, the very lack of interest in political affairs that leads to the acceptance of the mainstream position in society may also be responsible for individuals' low engagement in political discussions.

While these arguments provide competing ways to think about how attitude distribution may affect citizens' propensity to engage in political discussion, they are silent about what it means to be in the mainstream. Here we propose two explicit ways to conceptualize the political mainstream and locate citizens in it. First, citizens find themselves either in the political majority or minority with respect to support for incumbent political authorities. Second, we can measure the distance of an individual's opinion from a country median.[5] Both conceptualizations of the political mainstream lead us to propose that those outside the mainstream are more likely to engage in political discussions.

POLITICAL MAJORITY-MINORITY ALLEGIANCE AND POLITICAL DISCUSSION

Democratic politics frequently are viewed through the lens of majority and minority status because those in the majority determine the authoritative allocation of values (Easton 1953) or "who gets what, when, and how" (Lasswell 1953). As a result, whether an individual is part of the political majority or minority frequently has been found to affect political attitudes. It is not clear, however, whether and how support for the political majority should affect the frequency of political discussion. Extrapolating from studies that have documented the positive effects of being in the political majority on political attitudes and behavior (Anderson and Guillory 1997; Anderson and LoTempio 2002; Anderson and Tverdova 2001; Bowler and Donovan 2000), we expect those identifying with a governing party to view the national political arena as a friendlier place and, as a result, be more willing to express and discuss their views.

However, supporters of the opposition have a greater incentive to make their views known because of the potential to bring about political change. Because political institutions are the result of distributional conflicts in society, the expression of collective bargains over socially acceptable wins and losses, they will change when the balance of these wins and losses shifts (Knight 1992). At any given moment, the maintenance of political systems is more likely to be challenged by those in the minority than those in the majority. Thus, members of today's political minority are the "instigators of political change" (Riker 1983, 64), and supporters of the incumbent government have the greatest incentive to avoid change. Thus, political discussion may be an important way to help bring about change or mobilize for it. Following this logic, we would expect a positive relationship between being in the political minority and the frequency of political discussion. Hence:

> *Hypothesis 1:* Supporters of the political opposition (the political minority) will engage in political discussions more frequently than supporters of the incumbent government (the political majority).

THE MEDIAN VOTER AND POLITICAL DISCUSSION

Another way we can locate people politically is with the help of the median voter. A country's political discourse and its underlying political space are commonly defined by a simplifying notion of ideology that facilitates political communication and competition. Ideology is usefully expressed in terms of a left-right continuum, which is commonly considered a summary of voters' positions across a range of policies (e.g., see Klingemann 1979). Left-right placement is a useful indicator of people's location in a country's political space because it measures political orientations at a very general level and in commonly understood and widely accepted terms (Klingemann 1979; Fuchs and Klingemann 1989). As importantly, the left-right scale is crucial to understanding how voters choose among parties, how parties compete for voters, and how policy positions are packaged in party platforms (Gabel and Huber 2000; Huber 1989). Simply put, then, the left-right dimension measures the nature of competition in a political system as well as where an individual locates herself within that space: in the political mainstream, close to the median opinion, or at the extreme as her political convictions diverge further from those of others in the country.[6]

Assuming that being close to the median voter connotes holding a mainstream opinion, we can translate the arguments made above to voters who are located differently in the left-right political space. That is, theories of social conformity and opportunity, which are designed to operate on the micro-level, would suggest that individuals further removed from the median voter would be less likely to engage in political discussions. At the same time, we argue that the effects of the macro-environment on discussion behavior can be linked via a utility-based perspective that focuses on incentives to change the (macro-level) status quo and people's needs to express their views to bring about this change. According to this view, we would expect those at the extreme ends of the distribution to report *more* frequent political discussions. Hence:

> *Hypothesis 2:* As individuals locate themselves further toward the extreme ends of the political spectrum, they will engage in political discussions more frequently than individuals who are close to the median voter.

MACRO-LEVEL EXPLANATIONS: POLITICAL HETEROGENEITY AND THE SIZE OF GOVERNING MAJORITIES

As the above discussion indicates, each conversation about politics takes place in a political environment that is structured in particular ways.[7] And as we argue above, the most fundamental characteristic of this context is the makeup of the national political landscape in terms of majority-minority power relations and the left-right dimensions of political contestation. Information about where an individual stands relative to the median voter or governing authorities furnishes important, but not the only, pieces of information about the shape of the macropolity. In particular, it does not allow us to make statements about how differences across countries affect the frequency of political discussion. Therefore, it is important to examine the overall distribution of political preferences in a society and the aggregate level of government support to fully understand what drives political discussions in various countries. Because most political discussions take place in the generally nonthreatening company of family, friends, neighbors, and work-mates with whom individuals establish long standing relationships (Bennett, Flickinger, and Rhine 2000; MacKuen 1990, 83; Zuckerman, Kotler-Berkowitz, and Swaine 1998), it is reasonable to expect that heterogeneity of political opinions would lead to more frequent political conversations. In addition, opinion diversity means that a political conversation is more likely to provide discussants with valuable new information (Huckfeldt, Johnson, and Sprague, in this volume). This, in turn, may well motivate more interaction and discussion (Huckfeldt and Sprague 1995, 54; MacKuen 1990, 71). And because politics occupies only a small part of people's daily lives, it is relatively easy for people to ignore differences in political beliefs or to discover them after a relationship has already become established (Mutz 2002a).

More generally, heterogeneous settings may stimulate political conversations if there is "a tradition of moderation" (MacKuen 1990, 85)—that is, if the country's political culture does not stigmatize disagreement and creates a sufficiently friendly environment for crosscutting interactions. Thus, such environments may increase the levels of "expressivity" for an entire community (MacKuen 1990, 73),[8] although probably more so in established rather than emerging democracies. In transforming political systems, social and political divisions have a potential to produce frequent, highly charged but insulated political discussions that might prevent cross-fertilization of public dialogue (MacKuen 1990, 86). In contrast, long periods of stability in established democracies suggest that people generally agree about their country's political goals, and that major controversies exist only with regard to the means of achieving those goals. Since conversations are easier when opposing sides disagree about how to achieve consensual goals rather than about the goals themselves (MacKuen 1990, 85), we posit that political heterogeneity in our sample of established democracies should lead to higher frequency of political discussion. Hence:

Hypothesis 3: Individuals in countries with more heterogeneity in citizen political preferences will discuss politics more frequently than individuals in countries with less diversity.

DATA AND MEASURES

Research that investigates the impact of variation in national contexts in addition to individual differences requires a cross-national research design. The data analyzed here include both individual-level and aggregate-level information. Our individual-level data come from the World Values Surveys (WVS) in 1990 as part of the 1990–93 waves. Countries that provided the most important survey items and had a sufficient number of cases for multivariate analysis included Austria, Belgium, Canada, Denmark, France, Germany, Great Britain, Ireland, Italy, the Netherlands, Norway, Portugal, Spain, Sweden, and the United States.[9] Thus, we were able to employ surveys from a diverse set of contemporary democracies with widely varying political cultures, structures, and histories.

Dependent Variable

The dependent variable investigated in this study is the frequency of political discussion. Specifically, respondents were asked, "When you get together with your friends, would you say you discuss political matters frequently, occasionally, or never?" The values of this variable range from 1 to 3, with 3 indicating frequent discussion and 1 indicating the respondent never discussed politics. This measure focuses on people's political discussions with friends and is not designed to capture all conversations a respondent could conceivably have regarding politics. Beside conversations with strangers, this measure might also omit political conversations among members of the same household (see, e.g., Zuckerman, Kotler-Berkowitz, and Swaine 1998). However, we feel that this does not necessarily compromise the variable's validity as a measure of the general concept of democratic deliberation—first, because even private conversations among friends or family members meet the minimum standards of democratic deliberation and, second, because discussions among friends and family members are likely to share important characteristics.

Political theorists conceptualize democratic deliberation as contested political discussions that take place in public spaces, relate to matters of public concern, are addressed to unrestricted audiences, and are open to all citizens (Conover, Searing, and Crewe 2002). These elements are deemed necessary to ensure a truly democratic discussion where all interested citizens of diverse viewpoints may encounter each other and voice their opinions. In our view, political discussion among friends, especially in mature democracies, meets these criteria.

Conover et al. (2002) provide evidence that conversations among family members and friends share important characteristics. Specifically, using survey and qualitative data from the United States and Britain, the authors report that private political conversations are no less deliberative—based on reason, open to all, and contentious—than public discussions. Moreover, political conversations among friends and family serve a valuable rehearsal or socialization function. They provide opportunities to develop and practice arguments in a supportive and relatively safe private environment (Ibid.), particularly for the kinds of opinions that individuals are more careful about voicing in public contexts. Thus, we do not think that the qualifier "friends" handicaps our investigation systematically.

Figure 12.1 shows the distribution of responses to the question across the fifteen countries included in this study. As the figure indicates, slightly over 50 percent say they discuss politics occasionally, about 15 percent say they do so frequently, and nearly one-third say they never discuss politics. The graph also shows that political discussions are most common in Norway (88.5%) and Germany (84.2%), followed by Sweden, Denmark, Canada, and the Netherlands (75–80%). In contrast, we find political discussions are least common in Portugal (49.2%), while over 50 but below 60 percent of citizens in countries such as Spain, Belgium, Ireland, and Italy reporting that they discuss politics at least on occasion. Moreover, the absolute frequency of political discussions also varies within countries: While about a third of respondents in Austria, France, and Britain indicate that they never discuss politics, almost 20 percent of Austrians say that they discuss politics frequently. In contrast, only 12 to 14 percent report frequent discussion in France and Britain. This considerable cross-country and within-country variation in the frequency of political discussion warrants further investigation.[10]

Measuring Mainstream Opinion at the Individual Level

Recall that our primary goal is to test the relationship between mainstream opinion and the frequency of political discussion at the level of both individuals and countries. To estimate an individual's location in the political space with regard to political majority-minority support and distance from the median voter, we need information about an individual's political preferences and how these compare with those of their compatriots. The individual-level variables measuring political preferences, as well as a variety of control variables described below, are based on items from the World Values Survey.

Political Majority and Minority Status

The political majority and minority status variable was created by asking which political party the individual would vote for if a national election were held. After

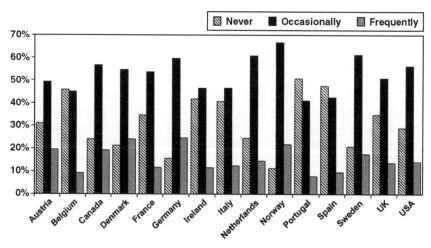

FIGURE 12.1. Frequency of Political Discussion in Fifteen Democracies

determining which political parties constituted the government in each country under study, we combined the information about the person's vote intention with the information about the party currently in power. If the respondent expressed a preference for that party, she or he was coded as being in the majority.

Distance from the Median Voter

Understanding how individual citizens' distance from the median voter (in our conception, the political mainstream) affects their propensity to engage in political discussion requires a way to summarize people's political preferences. We rely on the widely used ten-point, left-right, self-placement scale (Klingemann 1979; Fuchs and Klingemann 1989). Respondents who did not place themselves, did not respond, or responded "don't know" were excluded from the analysis. We then calculated the median voter's position for each country and subsequently measured the absolute distance of each respondent from that median. Visual inspection of left-right distributions in each country showed them to be single-peaked with very little skewness, and additional analyses of kurtosis and skewness suggested that all distributions are close to normal. The median voter located herself at a 5 in eleven countries in our study and at a 6 in the remaining four countries. Thus, individual voters' distance from the median measure ranged between 0 (when respondents were at country median position) and 5.

Control Variables

We also sought to control for a variety of factors that have been found to predict political discussion in previous analyses, such as social capital in the form of organizational membership (in church groups, professional organizations, political parties, and unions) and interpersonal trust, as well as left-right self-placement[11] and a standard set of demographic variables (see van Deth 1991; Topf 1995). Coding procedures and descriptive statistics for all variables are listed in the Appendix.

COUNTRY-LEVEL ANALYSIS

Our analysis proceeds in two steps: First, we examine the impact of individual-level variables on the frequency of political discussion for each of the fifteen countries in our sample. Second, by combining the data for all countries, we analyze the joint effects of individuals' status relative to the political mainstream, macro-level heterogeneity, and the country's percentage of government support in the last election on political discussion frequency.

Table 12.1 shows the ordered logit estimation results of the individual-level model for each country. Supporting the government was a significant determinant of political discussion in only three of the fifteen countries (20 percent of our cases): Austria, Belgium, and Spain. However, in all three cases, the coefficient was negative, suggesting that opposition supporters were consistently more likely to engage in political discussions than supporters of the incumbent government. This finding favors the view that being outside the mainstream enhances the frequency of political discussion. The result also shows that larger distance from the median increases the frequency of political discussion in all countries examined in our study, although it fails to achieve conventional levels of statistical signifi-

TABLE 12.1. Ordered Logit Models of the Effects of Position in the Political Mainstream on the Frequency of Political Discussion in Fifteen Democracies

Independent variable	Austria	Belgium	Canada	Denmark	France
Government support	−.537***	−.373***	−.023	−.042	−.030
	(.229)	(.146)	(.167)	(.211)	(.236)
Distance from median	.136*	.091*	.203***	.237***	.260***
	(.081)	(.053)	(.061)	(.071)	(.081)
Left-right self-placement	−.024	−.021	−.027	−.077	−.065
	(.061)	(.032)	(.046)	(.053)	(.057)
Gender	.156	.205	.117	.472**	.448**
	(.209)	(.135)	(.136)	(.160)	(.210)
Age	.099**	.100***	.075**	.068**	.073*
	(.035)	(.025)	(.026)	(.028)	(.039)
Age^2	−.001**	−.001***	−.001	−.001**	−.001
	(.001)	(.001)	(.001)	(.001)	(.001)
Income	.119**	.037	.035	−.065*	.074*
	(.043)	(.028)	(.030)	(.034)	(.041)
Education	−.064	.161***	.182***	.171***	.106**
	(.043)	(.032)	(.035)	(.033)	(.045)
Organizational membership	.107	.430***	.173***	.373***	.305**
	(.088)	(.067)	(.053)	(.092)	(.104)
Size of town	.082	−.040	−.057	.033	.007
	(.055)	(.040)	(.035)	(.036)	(.041)
Interpersonal trust	.062	.137	.244*	.268*	.385
	(.212)	(.140)	(.144)	(.163)	(.239)
μ^1	1.000	6.526***	4.874***	4.712***	4.672***
	(1.203)	(.883)	(.885)	(.975)	(1.286)
μ^2	3.574**	9.252***	7.983***	7.624***	7.842***
	(1.219)	(.916)	(.918)	(1.009)	(1.335)
χ^2	36.87***	144.25***	118.85***	109.58***	67.67***
% correctly predicted	51.16	56.88	60.09	57.89	57.92
Pseudo R^2	.090	.152	.124	.150	.154
N	389	872	897	672	404

Independent variable	Germany	Ireland	Italy	Netherlands	Norway
Government support	−.053	.112	.043	−.187	.070
	(.140)	(.160)	(.161)	(.178)	(.209)
Distance from median	.317***	.158**	.141**	.086	.280***
	(.054)	(.067)	(.052)	(.075)	(.075)
Left-right self-placement	−.120**	.039	.108***	−.050	−.096*
	(.043)	(.045)	(.033)	(.047)	(.053)
Gender	.729***	.636***	1.013***	.265	.350*
	(.122)	(.155)	(.147)	(.174)	(.181)
Age	.025	.069**	.002	.128***	.047
	(.020)	(.026)	(.025)	(.032)	(.039)
Age^2	−.001	−.001**	.001	−.001***	−.001
	(.001)	(.001)	(.001)	(.001)	(.001)
Income	.044*	.107**	.139**	.014	−.012
	(.025)	(.038)	(.055)	(.033)	(.035)
Education	.132***	.137***	.038	.074**	.169***
	(.028)	(.039)	(.029)	(.037)	(.048)

(continued)

TABLE 12.1. (*Continued*)

Independent variable	Germany	Ireland	Italy	Netherlands	Norway
Organizational	.293***	.340***	.502***	.223***	.312***
membership	(.059)	(.091)	(.076)	(.074)	(.073)
Size of town	.017	.038	.026	−.024	.088**
	(.028)	(.026)	(.033)	(.054)	(.042)
Interpersonal trust	.242**	.122	.517***	.397**	.301
	(.121)	(.156)	(.146)	(.180)	(.210)
μ^1	2.523***	6.877***	3.156***	3.570***	3.605**
	(.718)	(1.033)	(.748)	(1.161)	(1.228)
μ^2	5.784***	9.552***	5.828***	7.057***	7.735***
	(.735)	(1.072)	(.772)	(1.197)	(1.274)
χ^2	180.84***	94.43***	175.10***	51.76***	73.60***
% correctly predicted	60.78	56.87	52.46	67.15	67.54
Pseudo R^2	.137	.131	.199	.079	.113
N	1,224	670	791	627	613

Independent variable	Portugal	Spain	Sweden	United Kingdom	United States
Government support	.189	−.523***	−.421	−.167	.046
	(.206)	(.115)	(.289)	(.167)	(.126)
Distance from median	.065	.115***	.313***	.123**	−.001
	(.059)	(.038)	(.096)	(.053)	(.050)
Left-right self-	−.094**	−.087***	−.106*	.054	.023
placement	(.042)	(.025)	(.062)	(.043)	(.040)
Gender	.842***	.537***	.143	.249*	.270**
	(.169)	(.101)	(.213)	(.139)	(.120)
Age	.041	.083***	−.022	.084***	.023
	(.028)	(.018)	(.046)	(.023)	(.021)
Age^2	−.001	−.001***	.001	−.001***	−.001
	(.001)	(.001)	(.001)	(.001)	(.001)
Income	.098**	.078**	−.011	.053*	.059*
	(.038)	(.027)	(.031)	(.029)	(.035)
Education	.176***	.096***	.150**	.124***	.115***
	(.030)	(.019)	(.070)	(.038)	(.031)
Organizational	.371***	.428***	.191**	.288***	.171***
membership	(.095)	(.077)	(.090)	(.073)	(.045)
Size of town	.031	.044**	.095*	.035	.049*
	(.039)	(.022)	(.053)	(.031)	(.027)
Interpersonal trust	.505**	.160	.251	−.071	.089
	(.200)	(.104)	(.241)	(.141)	(.124)
μ^1	5.671***	5.018***	2.715*	5.319***	3.600***
	(.949)	(.604)	(1.578)	(.850)	(.765)
μ^2	8.486***	7.708***	5.900***	8.103***	6.491***
	(.996)	(.627)	(1.610)	(.883)	(.787)
χ^2	132.93***	259.35***	42.15***	88.59***	74.13***
% correctly predicted	59.83	56.33	60.73	56.37	59.62
Pseudo R^2	.199	.153	.104	.100	.064
N	600	1,564	382	839	1,117

Note: Estimates are ordered logit estimates. Standard errors appear in parentheses.
*$p < .05$, **$p < .01$, ***$p < .001$.

cance in the Netherlands, Portugal, and the United States. Taken together, then, individual-level results for each country suggest that (1) those outside the mainstream are consistently more likely to engage in political discussions, and that (2) ideological distance from the median voter has a more frequent effect than support for opposition parties.

To examine the robustness of the results—specifically, whether the effect of the distance from the median was not a measurement artifact—we conducted several additional analyses with alternative indicators that are not reported in tabular form here. We estimated models with individuals' distance from the mean opinion, as well as the frequency in the population with which a respondent's left-right placement was shared. The results all tell a similar story: being further from the middle of the distribution (which also coincided with having fewer people in the population to share one's left-right position) was strongly associated with higher levels of political discussion. Thus, the results we report above are extremely robust.

While not all of the control variables consistently turn out to be significant, many do. Moreover, they paint a picture of political discussion that is characterized by inequalities along important demographic dimensions similar to those found in earlier research (Conover, Searing, and Crewe 2002). For example, education appears to be among the best predictors of political discussion. Specifically, respondents with higher levels of education are more likely to engage in political discussions in thirteen of the fifteen countries.[12] Moreover, in many countries, there appears to be a curvilinear relationship between age and political-discussion frequency such that the very old and the very young are less likely to discuss politics than the middle aged. Finally, men are significantly more likely to engage in political discussion than women in ten of the fifteen countries in our sample.

Indicators of social capital—organizational membership and interpersonal trust—also matter systematically in explaining political discussion frequency. Individuals who are more trusting and more involved in social and political organizations talk about politics more frequently in most countries in our study. Naturally, it would be useful to have additional information about respondents' friendship groups, including, but not limited to, measures of how much the friends like each other or how much time they spend together, in order to see how the quality of social ties affects the frequency of political discussion. While we do not have this information and cannot make any claims regarding these effects, we speculate that such factors may be at least as important as the variables we employ in our analyses (such as organizational membership or education).

CROSS-NATIONAL ANALYSIS: DATA AND MEASURES

As a second step in the analysis, we move beyond the individual countries and seek to replace country names with proper variables. Specifically, in addition to distance from the median as an individual-level variable, we examine the effect of macro-level variables in the form of government support and political heterogeneity on political discussion frequency by combining the data for all countries. Before we present the results of these analyses, however, we first explain our measure of the distribution of government support and left-right preferences in a country.[13]

Measuring Government Support at the Country Level

Our measure of government support was the percentage of each country's population that voted for the incumbent political party or parties in the national election immediately prior to the survey conducted as part of the World Values Survey.

Measuring Ideology and Political Dispersion at the Country Level

Measuring each country's left-right political landscape at the macro-level is slightly more complicated because of issues of validity and cross-national comparability. We rely on data from the Comparative Manifestos Project (CMP), which allow for direct cross-national comparisons and thus are more reliable and valid than expert-based or survey-based measures (McDonald and Kim 2002). The CMP data are based on manifestos (platforms) issued by political parties at the time of each election. The data set employs a total of fifty-six common policy categories to construct a common left-right dimension (see Bowler 1990; Budge, Robertson, and Hearl 1987; Warwick 1992).[14] We employ the CMP data collected for the election immediately prior to the survey we use.

To construct a measure of a country's left-right distribution, we needed to weight each party's left-right CMP measure by the party's size in the electorate. Moreover, because we are not interested in the country's mean, but rather its dispersion around that mean, we used the standard deviation as the simplest measure to calculate dispersion or heterogeneity in a country.[15] Thus, we scored each party according to its left-right position using the CMP data in the last election prior to the survey we use. Next, we calculated the weighted mean and standard deviation of the party left-right positions in a country, where the weights are the percentage of votes received by a party.[16] The result is the mean and dispersion of a country's ideological position as indicated by the left-right positions voters associate with when they cast votes.[17]

These measures of political ideology and dispersion, or heterogeneity, along the left-right dimension can be seen as the electoral representation of cleavages that serve to organize the politics of the country as a whole. Comparative political research tends to treat cleavages as nation-specific phenomena that give rise to party systems (Lipset and Rokkan 1967), and that produce different electoral and institutional arrangements (Lijphart 1984). Thus, it is sensible for our analysis of political discussion to measure dispersion at the level of the nation. In a very real way, ours is a measure of how politically divided or divergent these societies are. And although traditional social cleavages—here measured by left-right self-placement—have been weakening across Western democracies, they still structure much of Europe's political life and have important and predictable consequences for political participation, in particular for individuals' attitudes and voting behavior. These political identities still bind individuals to political parties and structure the formal and informal organization of a country's political life.[18]

Country-Level Control Variables

Our system-level control variables include a national election campaign, a measure of government involvement in the economy, the effective number of electoral parties, and the degree of religious heterogeneity. We expect that the occurrence of an electoral campaign, greater government involvement in the economy (see van Deth 1991), a larger number of political parties, and greater religious homogeneity lead to higher levels of political discussion. Again, coding procedures and descriptive statistics for these variables are listed in the Appendix.

Cross-National Analysis and Results

Our pooled cross-national research design requires combining information at the level of respondents (micro-level) and countries (macro-level). This means that our data have a multi-level structure where one unit of analysis (voters) is nested within the other (countries) (Bryk and Raudenbush 1992). This type of data structure can generate a number of statistical problems, such as nonconstant variance and clustering, leading to the underestimation of standard errors—particularly at the macro-level—and, thus, a higher probability of Type I errors (see also Zorn 2001). We therefore relied on statistical techniques developed specifically for modeling multilevel data structures (Steenbergen and Jones 2002).[19]

One problem for inference in multilevel data structures is that if intercepts vary across countries, the estimates may be biased. Specifically, we may be overestimating the effect of a country's political makeup on discussion behavior, as the macro-level coefficients could be capturing both the true effects of heterogeneity as well as other country-specific effects not accounted for in our estimation model.[20] A secondary concern is that if individual-level variables have unequal slopes across nations, our pooled estimator may be biased for each country. A third concern relates to the robustness of our inferences based on potentially inefficient standard errors resulting from clustering (see Zorn 2001). Thus, multilevel modeling techniques allow for the estimation of varying intercepts and slopes, produce asymptotically efficient standard errors, and provide for a direct estimation of variance components at each level of the model.

Below we show the coefficients of interest (constants and independent variables), as well as the variance components at each level of our data (individual and country-level). These estimations allow us to establish (1) whether political differences within a population (or lack thereof) are significant determinants of the frequency of political discussion once we allow the intercepts to vary across countries and obtain better estimates of standard errors; (2) whether our macro-variables explain a substantial proportion of the country-level variance in order for us to be able to claim that we have minimized a potential omitted variable bias; and (3) whether the effects of distance from the political mainstream are similar across countries.

Analysis of Variance

First, we estimated an ANOVA model that decomposes the variance in the dependent variable.

$$\text{Discussion}_{ij} = \gamma_{00} + \delta_{0j} + \epsilon_{ij}$$

In this model, γ_{00} is the grand mean of discussion; δ_{0j} contains the sources of cross-national variation, which cause countries to deviate from this mean; and ϵ_{ij} contains sources of inter-individual variation. If both variance components are

TABLE 12.2. Multi-level Estimate of the Frequency of Political Discussion: ANOVA

Parameter	Estimate: Frequency of political discussion
Fixed effects	
Constant	1.832***
	(.040)
Variance components	
Country-level	.026**
	(.009)
Individual-level	.419***
	(.004)
−2 log likelihood	51,052.70

Note: Entries are maximum likelihood (IGLS) estimates. Standard errors appear in parentheses.
*$p < 0.05$, **$p < 0.01$, ***$p < .001$.

statistically significant, both levels of analysis are important for understanding political discussion (see Steenbergen and Jones 2002).

Table 12.2 shows that both variance components are statistically significant and that country-level variance is proportionally much smaller than individual-level variance: Individual-level variance constitutes 94.26 percent of the total variance in the frequency of political discussion.[21] Given that the data are measured at the individual level, this is not surprising (Steenbergen and Jones 2002, 231). At the same time, there is significant variation in the frequency of political discussion with regard to both levels of analysis. Thus, we now turn to the question of whether the model we have specified can account for this variance.

Cross-National Models of Political Discussion

Table 12.3 reports the results of multi-level models that simultaneously estimate the effects of micro- and macro-variables on the frequency of political discussion. We show two random intercept multi-level maximum likelihood IGLS (iterative generalized least squares) models. Most importantly, as the results in Model 1 suggest, people are more likely to discuss politics if they live in a country that has greater dispersion on the left-right ideological dimension than if they live in a country marked by more ideological consensus. The results reported under Model 2, which include a number of macro-level control variables, are virtually identical.

Models 1 and 2 also strongly suggest that the effect for the distance from the median variable found in the earlier country-by-country analyses is stable across countries. Again, we find that greater distance from the median increases the frequency of political discussion. To examine whether this effect is similar across countries, we also estimated the variability of the slope for the distance from the median voter measure. The results (not shown here) demonstrate that, once cross-national differences in heterogeneity and other contextual variation are taken into account, there is virtually no variability in the coefficient across countries. Thus, distance from the median has a very similar effect on political discussion, regardless of the country under study.

We analyzed the data in two additional ways to ensure that nonresponses to our left-right self-placement measure do not skew the representativeness of our country samples and, as a result, affect the validity of the inferences we draw. First, we re-estimated the model with the respondents who failed to answer the left-right self-placement question by placing them at the mean level for the country. The results show only very slight differences between the two sets of results (available from the authors on request). Second, we examined how the over-representation of one country in the pooled analyses affected our results. We found that the only country with a disproportionate share of the overall pool was Spain, with around 1,700 respondents relative to roughly 1,000 respondents in the other countries. The results in our re-analyzed models with a dummy variable for Spain were not significantly different from the results reported above.

The multi-level results also suggest that government supporters discuss politics less frequently than opposition supporters. The governing majority size variable, however, fails to achieve conventional levels of statistical significance. Thus, the results speak very clearly in favor of the notion that political variance breeds political talk, both at the level of individuals (in the form of distance from the median voter and opposition-party support) and at the level of countries (in the form of heterogeneity of left-right political preferences).

Most country-level control variables are also significant. We find that the occurrence of a national electoral campaign and greater government involvement in the economy increase the frequency of discussions across countries. The results also indicate that a greater number of political parties are associated with a lower incidence of political discussions. On its face, this result produces an apparent contradiction, given the finding that political heterogeneity breeds discussion. Post hoc, we speculate that countries marked by a larger number of political parties may also be more politically divided into subcommunities—a typical example may be the pillarized nature of Dutch politics—which may lead to less discussion.[22] Religious homogeneity, finally, is not significantly related to political discussion. In the end, controlling for these macro-variables does not change the major finding reported here—namely, that individuals in countries with higher levels of political dispersion report a significantly higher incidence of political discussion than citizens in countries that are more politically homogeneous.[23]

Supplementary Analyses

To validate the robustness of our results, we conducted a series of supplementary analyses. Specifically, we sought to determine whether our results are driven by the nature of the dependent variable we employed in our study. Recall that the political discussion measure asks respondents about the frequency of political conversations with friends. This measure might not capture a large portion of the political conversations that occur among members of the same household (Zuckerman, Kotler-Berkowitz, and Swaine 1998) or among strangers. Recall also that Jennings and Stoker (in this volume) demonstrate that marriage has a homogenizing effect on spouses' political attitudes through a long-term process of mutual accommodation and compromise to maintain marital harmony that usually privileges the views of husbands over those of wives.

Although we do not have a direct way to account for the frequency and nature of political conversations among spouses, we can test whether our results for individuals who are married or living with partners would differ from those for other

TABLE 12.3. Multilevel Models of the Frequency of Political Discussion in Fifteen Democracies

Independent variable	Model 1: Random intercept model	Model 2: Random intercept model
Fixed effects		
Constant	−.164	−.229
	(.170)	(.172)
Government support	−.044***	−.044***
	(.012)	(.012)
Distance from median	.047***	.047***
	(.004)	(.004)
Governing party electoral support (%)	−.044	.001
	(.012)	(.002)
Political heterogeneity	.015**	.014***
	(.005)	(.004)
Left-right self-placement	−.013***	−.013***
	(.003)	(.003)
Gender	.135***	.135***
	(.011)	(.011)
Age	.017***	.017***
	(.002)	(.002)
Age^2	.000	.000
	(.000)	(.000)
Income	.015***	.016***
	(.002)	(.002)
Education	.038***	.038***
	(.002)	(.002)
Organizational membership	.085***	.086***
	(.005)	(.005)
Size of town	.009**	.009**
	(.003)	(.003)
Interpersonal trust	.071***	.071***
	(.012)	(.012)
Campaign	—	.131**
		(.052)
Government share of GDP	—	.009**
		(.004)
Religious homogeneity	—	−.006
		(.110)
Effective no. of parties	—	−.047**
		(.017)
Variance components		
Country-level	.009**	.004**
	(.003)	(.002)
Individual-level	.371***	.371***
	(.005)	(.005)
N	11,661	11,661
−2 log likelihood	21,580.51	21,570.97

Note: Estimates are maximum likelihood estimates (IGLS). Standard errors appear in parentheses.
*$p < .05$, **$p < .01$, ***$p < .001$.

individuals, in order to establish if the frequency of political discussion among household intimates is driven by different factors than for the rest of the population. However, the results of these analyses (not shown) do not support this expectation: Our main explanatory variables remain substantively and statistically significant, pointing to the importance of political heterogeneity and being outside the mainstream for stimulating political conversation.

Recall also that the dependent variable quantifies political discussion in three levels: frequently, occasionally, and never. It is plausible that the meaning of these categories varies systematically across countries, such that the word "frequently" in Country A may have a different meaning in Country B. To examine whether our results are due to such differences, we collapsed the three-category dependent variable into two different dichotomous measures. First, we created a dummy variable of political discussion by combining the "frequently" and "occasionally" categories, with "never" as the remaining category. Next, we combined the "occasionally" and "never" categories (coded 0), with "frequently" constituting the remainder category. Re-estimating the pooled models using these different dependent variables, however, did not produce any changes in our substantive results, suggesting that the original answer categories have similar meanings in different countries.

DISCUSSION AND CONCLUSION

This study was designed to examine the impact of the macro-political climate on the frequency of political discussion in contemporary democracies. While the theoretical literature typically views disagreement and discussion as essential elements of a well-functioning democracy, the empirical research conflicts on the issue of whether political dissension and heterogeneity foster or stifle political discussion. Using data from fifteen western European and North American democracies, we examined the impact of individuals' positions in the political space relative to others and the influence of the macro-political environment on the frequency of political discussion. Contrary to many assumptions in the literature, we found that, at the individual level, increased distance from the median and, to a more limited extent, support for opposition parties lead to a greater frequency of political discussion. We also found that greater country political heterogeneity increases political discussion frequency.

Our research was not designed to determine whether these discussions were of high quality or whether they served to enhance people's civic skills. Moreover, our research could not address what people talk about, or whether respondents typically face sympathetic or hostile others. Similarly, our analysis has little to say about how heterogeneity originates or is sustained. (For an analysis of this question, see Johnson and Huckfeldt, in this volume.) Finally, our conceptualization of political discussion is also one-sided in that we are unable to disentangle whether the nature of the discussions usually involves the rational and considered exchange of ideas among citizens (deliberation) or opinion expression under situations of real or perceived social pressure (Scheufele 1999). Thus, it may well be that citizens who are more ideologically distant from the mainstream or who live in more heterogeneous countries are more likely to create homogeneous and therefore "safe" (micro-) discussion networks, thus enhancing the frequency and intimacy of political discussions. Again, this is an issue further research should be designed to examine.

Finding that the characteristics of the wider political community affect political discussion at all is, on some level, surprising, given that the national political discourse is rather removed from people's lives compared to their immediate social and political environment. This finding raises a couple of questions. First, why do we find any evidence at all that conversations among friends respond so strongly to the macro-political environment? Second, and relatedly, in what sense is the national political community a relevant measure of majority/minority or homogeneous/heterogeneous environments for groups of friends? In answer to the first question, we speculate that in many countries—and particularly in small and unitary states—the country's macro-political environment may actually be the most important (and in some cases the only) level of politics for generating political discussion. Secondly, it is important to bear in mind that the effects we report here are the result of comparisons across the set of countries included in our study. Thus, in terms of simple probabilities, it is likely that any randomly chosen friendship group in a more heterogeneous country will be relatively more heterogeneous than any randomly chosen friendship group in a more homogeneous country. In this way, the macro-environment matters in that the odds of having a friend with the same political views (and thus the odds that the macro-environment reproduces itself at the micro-level) vary sufficiently across countries to produce the results we report.[24]

Furthermore, one of our central findings—that supporters of the country's political opposition are consistently more likely to discuss political matters than are supporters of the political majority—is novel in research on political discussion and the macro-environment. On its face, it may seem to be at odds with the "spiral of silence" theory. We believe, however, that our findings are not incompatible with Noelle-Neumann's argument. For one, Noelle-Neumann (1974) asserts, but does not test, that those who are further away from the mainstream are likely to be "hard-core" opinion holders who are "not prepared to . . . *be silent in the face of public opinion*" (Noelle-Neumann 1974, 48; emphasis added). In a follow-up test of this argument, Glynn and McLeod (1984) found support for the assumption that hard-core opinion holders are not influenced by the prevailing "climate of public opinion" or by the "spiral of silence" in the same way as individuals who belong to the political majority. Thus, our findings seem to reinforce this proposition and slightly modify the "spiral of silence" theory.

Our findings also appear to stand in contrast to the findings by Gimpel and Lay in this volume, namely, that individuals who identify with a political party that is in the minority locally avoid political discussion. Specifically, these authors find that adolescents growing up in one-party-dominant areas are socialized in environments where minority opinions are often squelched and conformity to a single viewpoint is taken for granted. However, Gimpel and Lay's results may not be directly comparable to our findings because their study focuses on the micro-environment of adolescents rather than on a country's macro-politics and the general population. Young people differ from others in that they participate much less in politics, they may not have crystallized political opinions that they are able or willing to defend in public, and, finally, relative to older citizens, teenagers may be much more concerned with approbation from their peers than with standing up for their views. As a consequence, one could expect a much stronger confirmation of the "spiral of silence" theory among adolescents compared to other generational cohorts in the population.

But even if Gimpel and Lay's results do translate to the general population, we would argue that, in terms of aggregate-level effects, our results do not necessarily contradict these findings. Recall our finding that heterogeneous environments generate more political discussions because they provide discussants with valuable new information that motivates citizen interactions. Thus, we conceive of heterogeneity as a condition where opinions can coexist without being suppressed since the odds that no single opinion predominates are greater than in more homogeneous environments. Similarly, Gimpel and Lay suggest that "While locales exhibiting greater political diversity undoubtedly produce an information bonanza that stimulates political discussion, social pressures may act to suppress discussion in areas that are politically lopsided" (p. 213). Moreover, they discover that Democrats are more efficacious in Republican areas than in the neighborhoods where Democrats are in the majority. If political efficacy has the potential to produce more frequent political discussions, Gimpel and Lay's results are in line with the results we report here. In the end, then, our findings are actually quite consistent in that politically competitive environments are conducive to more frequent political discussions because the absence of a single dominant view is favorable to a free flow of information and expression of a plurality of minority opinions. Thus, it is only in very lopsided environments that political discussion is suppressed—and given that none of our country cases exhibits traits of lopsidedness, our results and those of Gimpel and Lay can peacefully coexist.

The results we present here also parallel the analysis by Kotler-Berkowitz in this volume. Similar to our emphasis on the importance of heterogeneous political environments for generating frequent political discussions, he points to the importance of diverse friendship networks in promoting political participation. While Kotler-Berkowitz does not examine the frequency of political discussion, and although his measure of friendship diversity is based on such factors as ethnicity, class status, and religion rather than political preferences, his finding that diverse networks of friends stimulate political participation (especially nonelectoral forms, due to more diverse, "nonredundant" opportunities for participation) is in agreement with our result about the importance of a heterogeneous political environment for producing more political discussion. Similarly, the findings reported by Huckfeldt, Johnson, and Sprague in this volume—in particular that individuals who interact on a regular basis can experience disagreement if their discussion networks transmit divergent political messages—is compatible with our notion that political heterogeneity can be associated with a greater frequency of political discussion.

Our findings indicate that democratic deliberation is stimulated by those outside the political mainstream and, as a result, may well entail some risk of instability. After all, the expression of and exposure to diverse political views may result in acrimony, hostility, or even violence (Mutz 2002a; Scorza 1998). What is more, those who oppose the status quo have the greatest incentive to change it (Riker 1982). Political theory predicts that the legitimacy and stability of political systems is more likely to be challenged by those in the dissenting minority than by those in the majority. Ideological disagreement may thus serve to provoke and mobilize those who are not part of the mainstream.

At the same time, however, we speculate that the articulation of views by those outside the mainstream may well be benign because it contributes to the range of ideas and choices that are available for collective problem solving. Normative theorists and empirical researchers alike have argued that discussion and disagreement are essential components of sound public opinion, and that both are necessary for effective democracy (Price, Cappella, and Nir 2002). Similarly, the expression and reception of dissimilar views are said to benefit the inhabitants of a public sphere by encouraging greater interpersonal deliberation and intra-personal reflection (Habermas 1989), a process that teaches citizens "to see things they had previously overlooked" (Manin, Stein, and Mansbridge 1987, 351) and expands their understanding of others' perspectives (Price, Cappella, and Nir 2002), thereby increasing people's levels of perceived freedom in a polity (Gibson 1992) and producing more legitimate collective decisions (Fearon 1998, 62). Viewed from this perspective, dissent is a necessary ingredient for democracies to function well, while too much harmony could result in inferior democratic outcomes. Thus, if living in a politically heterogeneous country and being distant from the mainstream motivates individuals to get involved in political discussion, this is likely to broaden the set of ideas and choices available to the collective. Given its potential for transmitting information cheaply, frequent talk driven by opposition to the mainstream and heterogeneity of the political space may well enhance the vibrancy and stability of democratic life.[25]

APPENDIX: QUESTION WORDING AND INDEX CONSTRUCTION

Frequency of political discussion. "When you get together with your friends, would you say you discuss political matters frequently, occasionally, or never? Never (1), occasionally (2), frequently (3)."

Organizational membership (in church groups, professional organizations, political parties, and unions). "Now I am going to read off a list of voluntary organizations; for each one, could you tell me whether you are an active member, an inactive member or not a member of that type of organization? Not a member (1), inactive member (2), active member (3)." This was an additive index, with values ranging from 4 (not a member in any group) to 12 (active member in all groups).

Interpersonal trust. "Generally speaking, would you say that most people can be trusted or that you can't be too careful in dealing with people?" Most people can be trusted (1), You have to be very careful (0).

Left-right self-placement. "In political matters, people talk of 'the left' and 'the right.' How would you place your views on this scale, generally speaking? Left (1), Right (10)."

Distance from the median. This was a measure of the respondent's absolute distance from the country median on the left-right self-placement scale.

Political majority-minority status. "If there were a national election tomorrow, for which party on this list would you vote?" If "don't know": "Which party appeals to you most?" If the respondent expressed a preference for the current government, he or she was coded as belonging to the majority (coded 1); all others were coded 0.

Education. "At what age did you or will you complete your full-time education, either at school or at an institution of higher education? Please exclude apprenticeships." The measure is the respondent's age when his or her education had been (or was expected to be) completed.

Gender. Female (0), male (1).

Age. Actual age of respondent.

Income. "Here is a scale of incomes. We would like to know in what group your household is, counting all wages, salaries, pensions and other incomes that come in. Just give the letter of the group your household falls into, before taxes and other deductions." Answers are coded from the lowest income level (1) to the highest (10).

Size of town. This scale ranges from 1 to 8, depending on population. Under 2,000 is coded (1); 500,000 and more is coded (8).

Government support. This measure represents the percentage of votes for the incumbent political party or parties in the national election immediately prior to the survey conducted as part of the World Values Survey.

Religious homogeneity. This eight-category variable classified respondents according to religious preference: "Do you belong to a religious denomination? If Yes: Which one?" Answers were coded as follows: Belong to no religious denomination (0), Roman Catholic (1), mainline or established Protestant church for given country (2), non-established or fundamentalist Protestant churches (3), Jewish (4), Islamic (5), Hindu (6), Buddhist (7), Other (8). Homogeneity within a population is measured using this equation:

$$A_w = \sum_{k=1}^{p} Y_k^2/V$$

where Y_k is the proportion of the population falling into a given category within each of the variables, V is the number of variables, and p is the total number of categories within all of the variables. These indicators of homogeneity represent the proportions of sample characteristics in terms of religion along which a randomly selected pair of individuals will correspond and are interpretable in probabilistic terms. If an infinite number of pairs were selected randomly from a finite population, the average proportion of shared characteristics of these pairs would be A_w. The greater the value of A_w, the more homogenous the population would be with regard to demographic or attitudinal characteristics (Sullivan 1973, 70).

Dispersion of political attitudes. This was measured using Comparative Manifestos Project (CMP) data. These in turn are based on manifestos (i.e., platforms) issued by parties at the time of each election. The data set employs a total of fifty-six common policy categories, including external-relations categories (e.g., anti-imperialism), freedom and democracy categories (e.g., human rights), political system categories (e.g., governmental and administrative efficiency), economic categories (e.g., nationalization), welfare and quality-of-life categories (e.g., environmental protection), fabric-of-society categories (e.g., multiculturalism), and social-group categories (e.g., underprivileged minority groups). For each document the data represent the percentage of all statements comprised by each category. This, in effect, standardizes the data with respect to document length, yielding a measure of party emphasis that is comparable (McDonald and Mendes 2001). We employ the data collected for the election immediately prior to the survey conducted as part of the World Values Survey. Because the CMP data provide a left-right score for each country, we weighted each party's left-right measure by its size in the electorate. We used standard deviation from a country mean to calculate dispersion or heterogeneity. Additional analyses revealed that, because the data are distributed roughly normally, the standard deviation is highly correlated with other indicators that measure the nature of distributions, such as kurtosis and skewness. Thus, we scored each party according to its left-right position using CMP data, where a party's position is measured according to the single-election left-right score in the election preceding the survey we use. Next, we calculated the weighted means and standard deviations of the party left-right positions in a country, where the weights are the percentage of votes received by a party.

National election campaign effect. This variable was coded 1 if the survey was taken within a period of six months before or after a national election (0 otherwise).

Government involvement in the economy. This measure represented the total expenditure of the central government as a percentage of gross domestic product including both current and capital (development) expenditures and excluding lending minus repayments (World Bank 2000).

Effective number of electoral parties. Based on Laakso and Taagepera's (1979) index.

PART III

THE SOCIAL LOGIC OF POLITICS

Looking Ahead

13 Agent-Based Explanations for the Survival of Disagreement in Social Networks

INTRODUCTION

PERSONAL INTERACTIONS BRING people together and offer an opportunity for the exchange of political opinions. Survey research indicates that people who interact frequently disagree with one another and that sometimes persuasion occurs (see Huckfeldt, Johnson, and Sprague, in this volume; Huckfeldt, Johnson, and Sprague 2002, 2004). The observed disagreement levels are something of a thorn in the side of leading theories of political communication. Many theories of political interaction suggest that disagreement will be muted and gradually eliminated within social networks. In this project, we have sought to understand more thoroughly the causes of homogenization and to develop alternative theories that include causal mechanisms that might help to explain how diversity and disagreement can survive over the long run.

Our research methodology is agent-based computer simulation. An agent is a computer representation of a self-contained individual actor, one that provides and receives signals in its environment (for background, see Axelrod 1997b; Johnson 1996, 1999). Simulation offers an opportunity to describe various institutions and behavioral models and explore their implications. Models that are too complicated for analytical treatment, especially ones that introduce heterogeneous agents or complicated, nonlinear interactions, can be explored with agent-based models. Simulation allows one to consider simultaneous processes that occur at different levels of aggregation, contrasting individual, group, and social phenomena. The development of agent-based modeling as a tool for research has coincided with the development of the scientific field known as "complexity," a field that is frequently associated with the Santa Fe Institute.

Two of the leading simulation models that explore social networks and the survival of diversity are Axelrod's (1997) Culture Model (ACM) and the social impact model (SIM), which is based on a theory developed by Bibb Latané (Latané, Nowak, and Liu 1994; Nowak and Lewenstein 1996; Nowak, Szamrej, and Latané 1990). In these models, the opinion holders are thought of as cells arranged evenly on a square grid. Axelrod's model is based on dyadic interactions of cells with their neighbors, while the SIM updates cells according to a sum of influences exerted by all cells (simultaneously).

We have developed computer code for models that replicate and extend both of these classic models.[1] We have extended each of these models by making them more agent-based and less like cellular automata (models in which cells, fixed in place, turn on and off according to mechanical rules). In our agent-based models, individuals are self-contained agents that can move about, gather or offer information, learn from experience, and adapt in an individualistic way.

One of the most interesting issues raised by Axelrod is the possibility that, over the long run, the natural processes of human interaction will homogenize the political culture. The cells are most likely to copy the features of neighbors that are similar to them, and the end result is that most or all cells are surrounded by others that are exactly like them. Under many settings of the parameters, all cells will be completely identical in the end. When diversity is not completely eliminated, the cells are divided into completely homogeneous and totally distinct subgroups, and none of the members of one group interact with the members of any other group.

The SIM addresses many of the same questions. The model's design is quite different because the individual cells do not directly interact with one another. Each cell is "acted upon" (simultaneously) by every other cell according to a distance-based law of influence. The cell changes when the aggregate persuasive impact of an opposing viewpoint exceeds the aggregate supportive impact of cells that hold the current viewpoint. As such, the SIM invokes a sort of "social telepathy" (Erbring and Young 1979) through which agents completely and accurately summarize the entire state of the society at each instant.

While Nowak, Szamrej, and Latané (1990) note that the model outcomes are not completely homogeneous, they are not entirely diverse either. In many runs of the model, the outcome consists of two or three homogeneous clumps of cells. Almost all individuals are surrounded by a belt of others who agree with them. It is not quite right to say that cells interact only with others with whom they share common opinions because the cells do not interact as dyads in this model. But it is fair to say that the immediate environment of most cells—the influential neighbors—are much more likely to be homogeneous than not.

We are concerned about the fact that, in both of these models, the immediate environments of most agents are predicted to be homogeneous. We began the larger project of which this chapter is a part (see Huckfeldt, Johnson, and Sprague 2004) with the empirical research questions driven by the mismatch between the observed levels of disagreement and the theories of political networks. Along the way, some important normative questions have presented themselves. The tendency toward homogenization projected by the theories might lead people who are concerned about preserving diversity to propose radical policy prescriptions. For example, one might argue in favor of segregation, or cultural apartheid, as the only way to preserve diversity on the aggregate social level. We find this prospect to be rather discouraging, and therefore we re-examined the theories of social networks.

In the next section, we describe the original Axelrod model and our software implementation of it. After that, we consider variants of the model that alter its assumptions about the way people select each other for interaction. Observing that the first batch of changes does not solve the problem, we move on to consider variants of the model that focus on persuasion and individual decision making in light of conflicting arguments. In the final part of the analysis, we conclude that diversity can be sustained within informally organized, loosely structured social networks. If political influence is contingent on the social context of interaction, then the homogenizing tendency of interaction is ameliorated. We contend that diversity among people who interact is a sustainable condition.

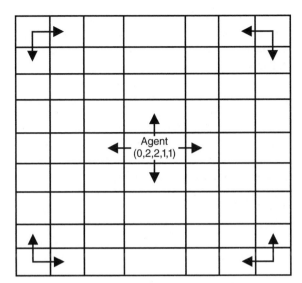

Basic Model

- Grid of agents (villages)
- Feature array for each agent, e.g., (0,2,2,1,1) for a five-feature model
- Interaction within truncated von Neumann neighborhoods

FIGURE 13.1. Axelrod Culture Model

THE CULTURE MODEL

The design of the Axelrod Culture Model is illustrated in Figure 13.1. It consists of a square grid on which agents are distributed, one per cell. Axelrod calls these cells "villages." Each village has a set of discrete-valued features, the values of which are called traits. A feature is to be thought of as an opinion, issue stance, political party allegiance, or any other construct. Suppose there are five features (opinions), F_i, $i = \{0,1,2,3,4\}$, and on each there are three traits (possible positions), $\{0, 1, 2\}$. Each village has a feature array that is assigned randomly (uniformly) at the outset.

Our implementation of the ACM was done in Objective-C with the Swarm Simulation Toolkit (Minar et al. 1996). Swarm began as a research project at the Santa Fe Institute and is now under the stewardship of a nonprofit corporation, the Swarm Development Group. Like Swarm itself, our code for our models is freely available. The most recent edition has been redesigned to facilitate the development of new kinds of agents.

From the standpoint of software design, the model of individual agents has two especially important components. First, there is a "selection process" that puts agents together for a possible interaction. Second, there are "opinion adjustment rules" that determine what happens when an interaction occurs. The remaining design is a fairly standard Swarm model, with the agents implemented as separately instantiated objects that are contained in a collection and their behavior able to be monitored in a number of ways.

In the original Axelrod approach, an agent is randomly selected, then a random neighbor is selected, and the agents interact with probability equal to the similarity of their features. If two villages share two of five features, then they interact with probability 0.40. If they interact, the agent copies one feature on which they differ from the other. Cells that lie on the outside boundaries of the grid have fewer neighbors with whom to interact. We have implemented an option to have the grid "wrap around" to form a torus, and thus eliminate these edges, but have found nothing interesting to report on that component.

Our code explores variations on the ordering of interactions among agents (a general topic known in Swarm as "scheduling"; see Johnson and Lancaster 2000). There are many settings that can be changed when the program is created (compiled) and later when it is run. Axelrod's model repeatedly selects one agent at random and conducts the interaction. Because of anomalies observed in the follow-up study (see Axtell et al. 1996), it is more prudent to employ a Knight's tour approach, in which the agents are randomly sorted at the beginning of each cycle and each is given an opportunity to interact before starting through the list again. The model allows one to select either the one-at-a-time (Axelrod's original) scheduling or the tour through the list. In this report, we present models in which the tour approach is used.

The number of cultural-issue dimensions or topics, called "features" in the culture model, and the number of positions on each topic, called "traits" in his model, can be varied. Axelrod observed that when the number of traits is small, then the system-wide homogenization tendency is the greatest, while raising the number of traits may allow the formation of homogeneous subgroups. When there are many possible traits, the chance that two randomly chosen agents will find something in common is lower, and thus diversity is preserved by prevention of interaction.

Because we seek to develop a general agent-based perspective for social interaction models, we have developed new tools with which to measure diversity. Axelrod's ideas of zone and region do not extend to the general settings that we explore in extensions of the model. We have created "objective" (aggregate level) and "subjective" (agent level) indicators of diversity.

On the objective side, it is possible to tally and summarize the features of the agents. This allows calculation of summary measures, such as the average and variance of each feature. We also calculate a system-wide diversity measure, *entropy*, which is also sometimes called Shannon's information index. That is a normed measure that is equal to 0 if all objects in a set are identical and 1 if every possible type is equally represented in the set (Shannon, 1949; Balch, 2000). If there are F different features (issue dimensions) and there are T different traits (positions) for each feature, then the number of possible issue stances is T^F. If the proportion agents holding a given set of positions is p_j, then the normed total entropy is given by:

$$Total\ Entropy = \frac{\sum_{j=1}^{T^F} p_j * \log_2(p_j)}{\log_2\left(\frac{1}{T^F}\right)}$$

The normed entropy measure depends on both the number of traits and the number of features.

Our subjective measures are built up from the experiences of the individual agents. Each agent keeps a "running tally" of its experiences. First, for each other agent that is encountered, the agent checks to see if the two agree about a randomly chosen feature. The proportion of encounters on which there is a shared feature is kept as a moving average that we call "acquaintance." This represents the individual's belief that it will have something in common with a randomly chosen other. When an interaction occurs, the agents "compare notes" and find out how much they have in common. We use that information to construct the second and third measures. The level of "harmony" is the proportion of opinions that the two agents share. Each agent also keeps track of the proportion of others with whom it is identical. The "harmony" and "identical" indicators reflect information about agents only with whom an interaction occurs, while the "acquaintance" measure is collected for all agents contacted. Please note that these are not accurate summaries of the actual state of the system but rather the experience-based beliefs of the individual agents. Generally, we calculate averages and standard deviations as summary measures.

After a good deal of experimentation with this model, we find considerable support for the original contention that diversity will disappear.[2] While the tendency toward homogeneity is greater for some parameter settings than others, it is powerful in all cases. If the number of traits is small, then interaction is likely to occur (and change of individual opinion is certain). On the other hand, if the number of traits is huge, then two agents are unlikely to interact because they have nothing in common. Diversity is preserved in the aggregate sense, but none of the individual agents interact with others who are different from them, and their perception tends to be that all agents are identical and like themselves.

The summary of one hundred runs of a model in which there are five features and three traits per feature is extremely revealing. The simulation continues until ten passes are made through the list of agents without any changes of opinion. In every single run, the level of entropy at the end was zero, meaning all citizens were identical. The average simulation came to a stop after 441.89 iterations. The average levels of homogeneity experienced by the agents tend up toward 1.0.

When run interactively, the model generates time-plots and color-coded "rasters" to display the state of the grid for each feature. A view of the distribution of opinion in the grid can be seen in the top part of Figure 13.2. The value of a feature at each spot in the grid is represented by a colored square. Values of the feature are color coded, with the dark tones representing the value of zero, and lighter shades used to indicate a progression of values. (In a model with more traits, we use all shades between the extremes.) It is readily apparent that the features are homogenized one at a time. As soon as a single feature is homogenized, we know for certain that all features will be homogenized. This is so because any two agents in the society will have at least one feature in common, so they can interact, and the homogenization will continue. In Figure 13.2a, we show the starting conditions of each of the five features in its own grid. The typical outcome is shown in Figure 13.2b. Each feature has been homogenized because the grid is filled with only one color.

In the bottom panel of Figure 13.2, we present the time plots of some of the diagnostic variables. Note that entropy begins at 0.8, near the maximum, and then it falls to a value of 0. Individual perceptions are roughly in line with that aggregate indicator. The indicators of acquaintance, harmony, and identicality begin with values near 0 and gradually climb toward 1.0.

It is possible to find parameter settings such that the grid is not homogenized, but rather subdivided into groups that do not interact with one another. That never

A. Initial Conditions

B. Final Conditions

C. Time Paths of Summary Variables

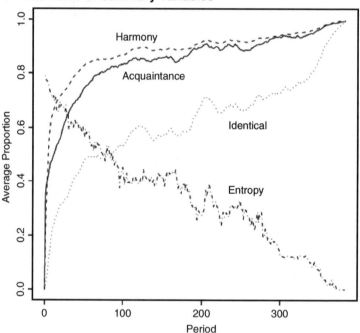

FIGURE 13.2. Axelrod Culture Model Results

happens when there are five features and three traits per feature, but it can happen if the number of traits is increased. Outcomes of that sort are highly unstable, in the sense that any disturbance that allows interaction across the boundaries is likely to displace it. Studies by Shibanai et al. (2001) and Greig (2002) explore extensions of the ACM in which there are ten possible values for each feature. In contrast, we have chosen to focus most of our attention on the difficult case, one in which there is a small number of traits and agents are less likely to be protected from interaction by the fact that they are completely different.

The problem we face, then, is exactly the same one discovered by Robert Abelson thirty-five years ago. His differential equations of social influence led to the prediction that "any compact group of individuals engaged in mutual dyadic inter-actions at constant rates will asymptotically tend toward complete homogeneity of attitude positions" (1964, 152). Later he observed that there is a "virtually inex-orable consensus" (1979, 244), one that he seeks to avoid (with only a qualified amount of success) by exploring various changes in the design of the model. Like Abelson, we have explored a number of variants related to the contacts to which individuals are exposed as well as the way in which people adjust to one another. We have one advantage in this pursuit, however, which is the recent development of agent-based modeling, which allows one to explore the implications of hypothe-ses about truly autonomous agents.

SELECTION VARIATIONS

One argument in favor of the agent-based modeling approach is that it allows experimentation with novel ideas about the way individuals might interact. We can investigate a number of "what if" questions by substituting in new assumptions about the agents and their environment. In this section, we explore changes in the structures that "put agents together." In the process of exploring various designs, we seek to find conditions that preserve political diversity as it is experienced by individual agents.

This section describes several variations on the mechanism that selects agents for interaction. The conclusion will be that, short of erecting behavioral "fire-walls" that completely block interaction among people who differ, the selection component will not preserve diversity.

Multi-agent Villages

When we adopt an agent-based paradigm for extending this model, we can inves-tigate one natural question: What if a village has many individual agents inside it? If the agents are most likely to interact with others inside their village, perhaps self-reinforcing "opinion clusters" will form.[3]

We assign features at random to each village, but then all agents within the vil-lage are identical. The interaction component of the model requires us to intro-duce a new concept, parochialism. Parochialism is the likelihood that an agent will look within its own village when it seeks a partner for interaction. The selection of others with whom to interact proceeds as follows. First, a random draw dictates whether the agent seeks another within the village or from one of the neighbor-ing villages. Agents who seek interaction within their own village choose randomly among the others in their village. The others will choose a neighboring village at random, and then choose at random a candidate for interaction from that village. As in the original ACM, the interaction occurs with probability equal to the sim-ilarity of the two agents. If the level of parochialism is sufficiently high, meaning agents interact with their "own kind" frequently enough, then perhaps the homog-enizing impact of contact with outsiders can be ameliorated.

We have run batches of simulations with multi-agent villages, and we find that, while the homogenization of opinion takes longer, it generally still occurs. Con-trary to our hopes, this model does not lead to the development of self-reinforc-ing clusters. Homogenization occurs even when we set the parochialism parameter at a high level of 0.95, meaning that agents interact with people in their cell almost all of the time. In almost all of the hundred runs of the model, the agent opinions are completely homogenized.

The simulation stops because no agent has changed any culture feature for ten successive time steps. In the multi-agent model, the number of iterations is about twenty times that of the single-agent model, approximately 8,220. The homogenization process takes longer, but the end result is the same. Across one hundred runs, the average total entropy is 0.0004. On most of the runs, entropy is 0.0. However, in four out of a hundred runs, the entropy value is 0.01. In each of those four cases, there is one cell—five out of five hundred agents—that maintains a different position on one issue. In most runs of the model, homogenization overcomes the parochialism effect. In four runs, one cell on the edge of the grid remains distinct on one feature. This simply reflects the "luck of the draw." If the random selection process put them in contact with others from outside the village, diversity would be eliminated.

There is, however, one very interesting property of these multi-agent grid simulations with high parochialism: The individual agents are never aware of the diversity that exists throughout the artificial society. They believe they are in a state of harmony throughout the simulation, but aggregate diversity goes from the maximum to zero during the run of the model. Figure 13.3 presents time paths for indicators from one of the runs with parochialism set at 0.95. Note that, when the simulation begins, the level of entropy is in fact high because opinions are assigned randomly to the cells. However, agents experience little disagreement because

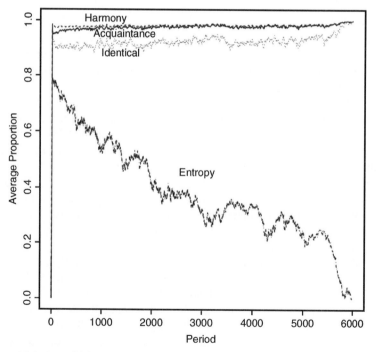

FIGURE 13.3. Parochialism

they frequently interact with other people within their cell, and at the start they are all identical. The measures of acquaintance, harmony, and identicality remain on the high side throughout the simulation. Although the agents do not perceive it, the homogenization process occurs and entropy drops.

Less Selective Agents

One is struck by the fact that these simulations tend to homogenize opinion because people who agree with each other are more likely to interact. The "self-selection" process snowballs to create a situation in which the only people who interact are totally identical, and it appears to be just a matter of randomness whether the result will be one homogeneous society or a few homogeneous subgroups. Suppose that people were open to a broader array of interpersonal contacts? Would it not be possible to forestall the homogenization by raising the interaction rate among people who would not ordinarily interact? It turns out the answer is a decisive "no."

Building on some ideas in the early work of Coleman (1964, chapter 16), we explored a variant of the model that causes interaction to occur more often among people who disagree. As in the original Axelrod model, at each time period, an individual encounters another individual, and an interaction occurs with probability proportional to similarity. If the encounter does produce an interaction, the search for an interaction partner is complete in that period. Alternatively, if the encounter fails to produce an interaction, there is some probability that the interaction will take place anyway. We have called the probability of interaction under these circumstances the Coleman coefficient. If the interaction does not take place, the individual continues to search up to ten times until an interaction partner is located.

To people who expect the increased interaction among people who differ to preserve diversity, the results of this "Coleman model" are surprising. And disappointing. A summary of one hundred runs for three values of the Coleman coefficient is presented in Table 13.1. The homogenization occurs more rapidly than

TABLE 13.1. Restricted Self-Selection: The "Coleman" Model

| | Coleman parameter | | | | | |
| | 0.2 | | 0.5 | | 0.8 | |
	Mean	Std. Dev.	Mean	Std. Dev.	Mean	Std. Dev.
Iterations at end	240.85	79.1	262.92	77.74	272.26	94.58
Variance for each feature						
Feature 0	0	0	0	0	0	0
Feature 1	0	0	0	0	0	0
Feature 2	0	0	0	0	0	0
Feature 3	0	0	0	0	0	0
Feature 4	0	0	0	0	0	0
Total entropy	0	0	0	0	0	0
Average of perceptions						
Acquaintance	0.99	0	0.99	0	0.99	0
Harmony	0.99	0	0.99	0	0.99	0
Identical	0.96	0.02	0.96	0.01	0.96	0.02

Note: Values represent a summary of 100 simulations with 5 features and 3 traits.

it did in the original model. Recall that in the original culture model with one agent per cell (which, implicitly, has the Coleman coefficient equal to 0), the number of iterations averaged 441.89. In all three batches of runs with the Coleman coefficient, the average number of iterations was less than three hundred. Furthermore, as the Coleman coefficient is raised from 0.2 to 0.8, the number of iterations required to homogenize the society gets smaller and smaller. The conclusion, of course, is that the impact of encouraging interactions among dissimilar agents is the accelerated destruction of diversity. Or, viewed more positively, the ACM's component of self-selection serves to *sustain* diversity! People who *avoid* interaction with politically disagreeable encounters are acting to sustain their own beliefs (and, by extension, the beliefs of their neighbors). The attenuation of self-selection does not change the fact that, over the long haul, disagreement disappears. But the preservation of these small clusters tends to delay the process of political homogenization.

Neighborhoods and Workplaces

The extensions of the model presented thus far have stayed within the fundamental constraints imposed by the original model. The agents, or villages, do not move around, and they are never exposed to new contexts or new information. Perhaps redesigning the model so that agents can move among diverse contexts will preserve diversity. We strive to create conditions under which agents can experience political interaction with a more-or-less unpredictable set of others in a variety of contexts. We pursue this strategy with the proviso that we do not want the agents to wander pointlessly seeking political interaction; rather, they wander with a purpose. Agents have "home" neighborhoods where they might interact with family members or neighbors, and they also interact with people in social settings, such as the workplace, church, a labor union meeting, and so forth.

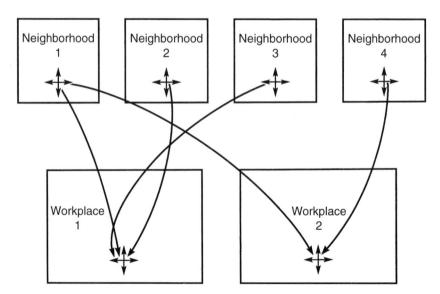

Figure 13.4. Multiple Home Grids and Work Grids

The description of this next step in our modeling exercise requires an explanation of a very significant departure in the design of the simulation model. In Figure 13.4, we present a sketch of the geographical arrangement of the agents and their movement and interaction opportunities. There can be one or more "home grids," which are standard square arrays of agents. There can also be workplaces where agents might go and seek out interactions. In the home grid, there is some regularity to interaction because the identity of the agent with whom one is interacting (if interaction occurs) is relatively more predictable. On the other hand, interactions in the work grids are less predictable. This is so because agents are unevenly "crowded" into the work grids. Agents from any home grid can be assigned to any of the cells in any of the work grids. Some cells in a work grid can have several agents assigned to them, while others might have none. In order to implement this in a meaningful way, it is necessary to redesign the scheduling substructure of the model to allow for movement between the milieus as well as the ability to search for available discussants and interact with them.

We have taken the following approach to scheduling agent actions. This is a discrete event simulation, but up to this point we have thought of a time step as a single pass through the list of agents. Now we take the more explicit approach of thinking of time as the passage of days, each of which is made up of a number of small time steps (say, hours). In the simulations described here, we (arbitrarily) set the number of steps per day to ten, and then we allow the agents to decide when to initiate interactions with neighbors who happen to be in their vicinity at a given instant. Each agent begins the day at home, and stays there, on average, for five time steps. Some agents spend almost no time at home, while others spend all their time at home. When the time comes to move to the work grid, then the agent removes itself from the home neighborhood and inserts itself into its designated work grid. During the time the agent is removed from one grid and "on the way to another," it cannot initiate any interactions and none of the other agents find it available for interaction. At the start of each day, each agent randomly selects a time step during which to seek an interaction. If the chosen time is before movement into the work grid, then the agent seeks interaction at home. The agents are moving about, but they still search for discussants in the von Neumann neighborhood.

The design that allows both movement and flexible interaction patterns diverges conceptually from the standard Axelrod model. The redesign causes several changes in the selection of discussants. First, movement changes opportunities for contact. Agents who move take themselves out of the context of other agents and give themselves opportunities to find new contacts. The workplace offers a relatively unpredictable set of interactions because there can be many agents in each cell. Second, the grids of homes are discrete from one another. Since the residents of different home grids never interact directly with each other at home, each home grid is, at least on the surface, insulated from the homogenizing pressures observed in the other models. Perhaps we will generate neighborhoods in which there is local homogeneity (all people within grid i agree on an issue) but also global diversity (the agents in grid j disagree with the agents in grid i).

The results indicate that homogenization—the adoption of one opinion across all home grids—is likely to occur. We conducted one hundred runs of a model in which there are five 10×10 home grids and three 5×5 work grids. One agent is assigned to each position in each home grid (meaning there are five hundred agents in all), and agents are assigned positions in the work grids in a random way, meaning that some cells in the work grid are empty while others have several occupants. The rules for multi-agent grids described above were used. The parochialism coefficient has been set to 0.5, meaning that an agent who is in a cell with other agents will pick among those agents with equal likelihood one half of the time, and the rest of the time a discussant in one of the four neighbors will be chosen.

Using the standard Axelrod culture model rules for the selection of discussion partners (modified as above for multiple-occupancy grids) and adjustment of opinion, we find that, over the long run, diversity is eradicated. This is true for any geographical setup that follows the home/work grid dichotomy we have described. In all one hundred runs of the model, the familiar homogenization process took place. After an average of 20,286 iterations, all diversity opinion was eliminated.

Identity-based Selection

In the models we have considered thus far, we have found several likely culprits in our search for the explanation of the model's homogenizing tendency. First, agents are likely to have a basis upon which to interact—that is, one or more features in common. Second, the agents interact if they have anything at all in common. If agent A has one out of five features in common with agent B, there is a 20 percent chance they will interact, and A will copy a feature from B. That can happen even if, on the other side of A, there is an agent that agrees with A about everything. Perhaps the shortcoming of this model is that it assumes agents initiate interactions with a randomly drawn individual even though there are more agreeable agents in their immediate vicinity.

We now reconceptualize the selection process in the following way. Rather than giving an agent the opportunity to interact with a randomly chosen neighbor, what if we allow agents to search their neighborhoods for discussants that they expect to be the most agreeable with them? Perhaps doing so will create enough selection bias to create and maintain diversity.

The model is implemented in the following way. Each agent keeps a record about every other agent it has contacted. As the simulation proceeds, the agent searches its neighborhood and draws one possible contact from each neighboring cell. (If the agent's own cell contains other agents, one of them is selected at random.) This creates a list of possible discussants. From this list, the agent then selects the one it expects to have the most in common with it. If several in the list are equally "appealing," then one is selected at random with equal likelihood.

The only substantive complication is that, at the outset, the agents have no accumulation of records upon which to make their decisions. At time 0, there are no acquaintances, and all agents are "strangers." To deal with this, we allow the agents to learn from experience. At the outset, the assumed harmony value for strangers is 0.5. Every time the agent interacts with a stranger, that value is adjusted to reflect experience. The upshot of all of this is that the agents are able to remember the others they have interacted with.

These selective agents can be placed into any of the interaction models, either the original Axelrod grid, the multi-agent grid, or the neighborhood/workplace models. To our surprise, in none of these implementations did we find that heterogeneity was preserved. In Table 13.2, we present two sets of summary statistics for the state of the model when the simulation ends. In Part A of the table, the results for the standard one-grid ACM are shown after the identity-based selection of discussants is introduced. In Part B the results for identity-based selection in a multi-grid model are presented. It is not particularly surprising that the model reaches a steady state in a smaller number of time steps after identity-based selection is introduced. It is not a surprise that the agents believe that, when they interact, they are likely to find others who agree with them about most things. And, furthermore, it is not particularly surprising that agents believe that the probability that they have something in common with a stranger is around 0.6. It is, however, a surprise that the level of entropy is negligible and that the variance of opinion on each feature is 0.

The overall implication of these experiments is that the homogenization of public opinion is a pervasive (irresistible?) tendency when agents adjust their opin-

TABLE 13.2. Identity-based Selection of Discussants

	Mean	Std. Dev.
A. IDENTITY-BASED SELECTION IN THE STANDARD AXELROD MODEL (10 × 10 GRID)		
Iterations at end	282.03	90.88
Variance for each feature		
Feature 0	0	0
Feature 1	0	0
Feature 2	0	0
Feature 3	0	0
Feature 4	0	0
Total entropy	0	0
Average of perceptions		
Acquaintance	0.599	0.010
Harmony	0.99	0.0034
Identical	0.958	0.0166
B. IDENTITY-BASED SELECTION IN THE FIVE-HOME GRID, THREE-WORKPLACE MODEL		
Iterations at end	10,220.6	3,588.51
Variance for each feature		
Feature 0	0	0
Feature 1	0	0
Feature 2	0	0
Feature 3	0	0
Feature 4	0	0
Total entropy	0	0
Average of perceptions		
Acquaintance	0.599	0.005
Harmony	0.999	0.00181
Identical	0.983	0.009

Note: Values represent a summary of 100 simulations with 5 features and 3 traits.

ions according to the logic of Axelrod's original culture model. Tinkering with the structure of the neighborhoods or attempting to condition interaction processes does not generate self-reinforcing social subgroups or diversity of opinion. As a result, we have not yet been able to rebut the nasty implication of this model, which is that in order to preserve diversity on a social level, one must eliminate diversity on an individual level by blocking interactions among people who differ.

OPINION ADJUSTMENT VARIATIONS

The second part of the agent-based model is focused on the way in which individuals respond to new opinions. In the Axelrod model, the agents automatically copy a feature from their neighbor when they interact. This assumption turns out to be the critical one; this one really makes a difference.

Axelrod's model shares certain features with models of population genetics (Gillespie 1998). An agent's culture array, e.g., (1, 1, 2, 1, 0), is scarcely different from a genetic string for an individual, and while interaction in the culture model is not exactly like genetic reproduction, there are certain similarities. In population genetics, one of the central questions focuses on whether each generation is more or less diverse than its predecessor. One theoretically compelling result is known as genetic drift. Genetic drift—the complete takeover of a particular part of the genetic code by one particular trait—happens over the long run if there is random interaction among individuals and reproduction follows the standard genetic laws. The homogenization predicted by the population geneticist corresponds closely to the pattern of homogenization observed in the culture model, although the logic of individual interaction and adjustment in the two models is not exactly the same.

If genetic drift (or cultural drift?) is to be expected when interactions occur among paired individuals, then perhaps a more significant conceptual departure is needed if diversity is to be preserved. We now propose to reconsider the assumptions about the outcome of the interaction.

We propose a solution that relies on the social context of political interaction. This new model implements the concept of autoregressive influence, discussed in this volume (Huckfeldt, Johnson, and Sprague). The main idea is that people who interact in a one-on-one relationship bring a context with them that moderates their reactions to one another. Agents do not copy features from each other in a "willy nilly" fashion. Rather, they change only when there is "good reason" to do so. Good reason is found when a majority of existing "friendly contacts" also support the proposed new opinion. The networks of interpersonal influence form on their own, as agents accumulate one-on-one experiences. Perhaps the original culture model is too individualistic, in the sense that individual agents interact in an isolated dyad.

This avenue is promising. We have found conditions under which diversity inside the local networks is preserved and, as a result, aggregate diversity is preserved as well. We believe it is especially deserving of further consideration because the assumptions that lie within it are extremely mild. We do not, for example, suppose that some people are, by nature, completely impervious to persuasion. We do not invoke exogenous forces that randomly change personal attitudes. We do not foreclose the possibility that such phenomena can occur, but we want to contend that such strong assumptions are not necessary to sustain diversity.

Our motivation for this approach shares a good deal with the idea that lies behind the social-impact model (Nowak, Szamrej, and Latané 1990). There are differences, however, on a number of levels. Our current approach allows for the formation of endogenous personal networks of arbitrary size. Dyadic interactions have impacts that depend on these personalized networks. In contrast, the SIM has neither dyadic interaction nor selective networks. Furthermore, our approach is asynchronic and bottom-up. In the SIM each cell is subjected to the simultaneous influence emitted by all cells and the value of the cell is adjusted in response to the net positive and negative influence (as in physics). It is a synchronous model, one in which a "snapshot" of the grid is taken and all cells are updated against that snapshot.

The detail of our modeling strategy is as follows. The agents come in contact with one another and they keep records on the opinions of the other agents. An agent records the observation that another agent is agreeable, or is a "friend," if they agree on half or more of the features. As in the original ACM, agents interact with probability equal to their similarity. When two agents interact, then a feature on which they differ is randomly selected, and the agent who initiated the contact considers adopting the other's point of view. When the agent is presented with a contradictory opinion, it can conduct a "small poll" of the other agents it has met in the past to find out if the new opinion is good one. (We have two variants of this model. The agent can base its decision on its recollections of their friends' attitudes when they last met, or the agent can actively conduct a new survey of people who are listed as friends.) If more than one-half of the contacts who are recorded as agreeable support the new point of view, then it will be adopted. As far as we can tell, this new adjustment rule works to maintain diversity with any interaction model as long as the agent is exposed to a relatively large number of other agents.

In Table 13.3 we present summary statistics for this "Networks of Autoregressive Influence" model in a couple of contexts. Part A shows the impact of this change on the original Axelrod culture model. Recall that the original model has a 10×10 grid, discussants are selected at random from the four-sided neighborhood, and interaction occurs with probability equal to the similarity of the agents. The only difference in this model is that agents adopt new points of view when there is support for that view among a majority of their friends. As in the previous cases, we stop the simulation when ten passes are made through the list of agents without a single agent changing a single feature. In each of the hundred runs of the model, the level of entropy is in the middle ranges and feature variance is far from zero. The agents believe (correctly) that they are in a mixed environment.

Part B of Table 13.3 presents the summary results for the model with five home grids and three work grids. These summary results are not substantially different from the one-neighborhood model represented by Part A of 13.3. We have selected (at random) one of the runs of this model for presentation in Figure 13.5. Note how entropy settles down into a steady state while perceptions of homogeneity rise. Agents think they agree about two-thirds of the time with the people with whom they interact, and they expect less than a third of their discussants to be identical with them.

We do not hold out this simulation exercise as a model of reality. Drawing a line between a "time step" in a simulation and a "day" in the real world is a dicey

TABLE 13.3. Networks Based on Autoregressive Influence

	Mean	Std. Dev.
A. AUTOREGRESSIVE INFLUENCE IN THE STANDARD AXELROD CULTURE MODEL (10 × 10 GRID)		
Iterations at end	71.5	13.82
Variance for each feature		
Feature 0	0.64	0.11
Feature 1	0.64	0.056
Feature 2	0.64	0.061
Feature 3	0.64	0.062
Feature 4	0.63	0.062
Total entropy	0.71	0.016
Average of perceptions		
Acquaintance	0.44	0.031
Harmony	0.60	0.030
Identical	0.36	0.046
B. AUTOREGRESSIVE INFLUENCE IN THE FIVE-HOME GRID, THREE-WORKPLACE MODEL		
Iterations at end	7,871.3	29.01
Variance for each feature		
Feature 0	0.61	0.12
Feature 1	0.64	0.13
Feature 2	0.64	0.12
Feature 3	0.61	0.11
Feature 4	0.61	0.12
Total entropy	0.65	0.054
Average of perceptions		
Acquaintance	0.49	0.025
Harmony	0.68	0.023
Identical	0.37	0.043

Note: Values represent a summary of 100 simulations with 5 features and 3 traits.

proposition. Rather, as Axelrod (1997b) argues, a simulation is a "thought experiment" through which we investigate the implications of our ideas. However, we hasten to add that we think we are in the right empirical "ballpark." First, our survey-based studies of discussion partners generally unearth diversity within the networks of discussants. Furthermore, there is evidence that individuals who are presented with views that contradict their own are more likely to change their minds when there is a high level of support for the new view within their network of political discussants (see Huckfeldt, Johnson, and Sprague 2002, 2004).

The model we have presented can be revised to take into account a variety of empirically relevant features. Husbands and wives influence each other in a way that is likely to differ from other relationships (in this volume, see Stoker and Jennings; and Zuckerman, Fitzgerald, and Dasović). In addition, it would probably also be more empirically accurate to introduce different weights for the opinions of various discussants (Levine, this volume), possibly taking into account expert-

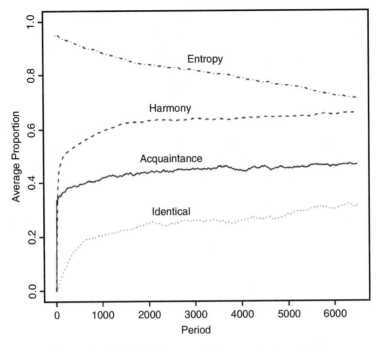

<figure>Figure 13.5. Network-embedded Resistance to Homogenization of Culture</figure>

ise and other personal characteristics. We have not pursued these avenues yet, but we may in the future. Furthermore, we encourage interested researchers to consider implementing variations of their own. The computer code for our model is available.

CONCLUSION

The tendency of repeated social interaction to squeeze out cultural diversity appears to be pervasive when opinion adjustment occurs according to the model originally specified by Axelrod. A number of efforts to adjust the logic through which agents are "put together" did not change that basic tendency. The phenomenon we have dubbed "cultural drift" indeed appears pervasive in models of dyadic interaction.

A change in the way that agents decide whether they should adopt new cultural features can change the model's fundamental tendencies, however. If agents view new information within the context of their political experience, taking into account information from other discussion partners, then the tendency toward homogenization is abated. While the interaction process does result in homogenization to a degree, it appears that, across a relatively wide range of initial conditions and within a number of interaction environments, the use of the network-embedded adjustment will preserve a measurable amount of diversity.

On the face of it, there does not seem to be any necessary reason why the network-embedded model of decision should preserve diversity. After all, if a society were completely homogeneous, then interaction would sustain that pattern, and sprinkling in minority points of view here and there would not change that. Furthermore, we acknowledge that it is possible to design starting positions for the simulation that would cause diversity to be eradicated. A carefully crafted chain of networks could be constructed, no doubt, that would fold under the pressure of repeated interaction. However, when preferences are assigned in a random way, we have found that individuals tend to build up networks of personal contacts that form the basis for a diverse political society.

The ironic aspect of this outcome is, of course, that the agents themselves are not seeking diversity in any sense of the word. Individuals are simply adjusting their opinions in light of the prevailing opinions among their most trusted associates, responding to input from any single associate in an informational context created by all of their associates. As a consequence, we are inclined to call the resulting diversity an emergent property of the complex system.

Finally, in conclusion, we would like to mention that we have considered many minor adjustments in this model that we have not reported here. We considered a model in which agents were spread unevenly on the grid. We considered a change in the interaction process so that either agent might copy a feature from the other, or that both might do so. We have considered variations on the way agents decide how appealing strangers might be. None of these changes caused results that differ from the ones presented here.

James H. Fowler

14   Turnout in a Small World

How does the turnout decision of a single person affect an election? Decision-theoretic models of voting show that the probability of one vote being pivotal in a large electorate is extremely small (Beck 1974; Ferejohn and Fiorina 1974; Fischer 1999; Fowler and Smirnov 2002; Riker and Ordeshook 1968; Tullock 1967). Empirical models use election returns to confirm this finding (Gelman, King, and Boscardin 1998; Mulligan and Hunter 2001). Because the number of individuals in modern electorates is quite large and interactions between individuals are complex and unobserved, these models of turnout assume that voters are independent of one another. In other words, a single decision to vote affects no other decisions to vote in the electorate.

Game-theoretic models relax the independence assumption, showing that strategic interaction can play a significant role in the decision to vote (Ledyard 1982, 1984; Palfrey and Rosenthal 1983, 1985). However, turnout in these models is typically quite low because the cost of voting (gathering and processing information, waiting in line at the polls, and so on) induces most people to free-ride on the efforts of a handful of voters. In equilibrium, the impact of an extra person voting is to *reduce* the incentive for others to vote.

This outcome contrasts with a growing body of empirical evidence suggesting that a single decision to vote *increases* the likelihood that others will vote. Turnout is highly correlated among friends, family members, and co-workers even when controlling for socioeconomic status and selection effects (Beck et al. 2002; Berelson et al. 1954; Campbell et al. 1954; Glaser 1959; Huckfeldt and Sprague 1995; Kenny 1992, 1993a; Knack 1992; Lazarsfeld et al. 1944; Mutz and Mondak 1998; Straits 1990). This literature illustrates the importance of social interactions for political activity (see Zuckerman, in this volume), but unlike the other literatures on voting it does not consider the impact of these interactions on aggregate turnout, election results, or the incentive to vote.

This article bridges the gap between these literatures by exploring the impact of a single decision to vote on a socially connected electorate. If people decide whether to vote based in part on the turnout decisions of their friends and acquaintances, then a single person may affect not only her own acquaintances, but her acquaintances' acquaintances, her acquaintances' acquaintances' acquaintances, and so on throughout the population. Depending on characteristics of the social network, even a small conditional correlation between acquaintances can cause a chain reaction that leads to large aggregate changes in turnout. I call this chain reaction a "turnout cascade."

Several features of real-world social networks might affect the size of a turnout cascade. In particular, I am interested in the small-world property. This is the idea that in spite of the large size of most social networks, people can connect themselves to one another through a very small number of intermediaries. Using a small-world network, I develop a model of turnout that suggests a single person's decision to vote can affect the turnout decision of several other people. Moreover, this increase in turnout tends to benefit the candidate preferred by the person initiating a turnout cascade because of the high concentration of shared interests between acquaintances in real political-discussion networks. Therefore, the incentive to vote is larger than previously thought. This incentive is increasing in several features of the social network that have elsewhere been shown to yield increases in turnout. For example, it is increasing in the number of interactions with people who vote (Ansolabehere and Snyder 2000; Brown et al. 1999; Gerber and Green 1999, 2000a, 2000b; Gray and Caul 2000; Radcliff 2001; and Radcliff and Davis 2000), the clustering of social ties (Cox et al. 1998; Monroe 1977), and the concentration of shared interests (Busch and Reinhardt 2000). It might help to explain the "duty to vote" norm expressed by many, and it implies a paradox of (not lying about) voting that I explore in the summary.

The model also predicts a feature of individual-level turnout that has previously gone unnoticed. Individuals with a mix of "strong" ties to people in their social clique and "weak" ties to people outside their clique (Granovetter 1973) can initiate larger turnout cascades than people with all weak or all strong ties. This gives them a greater incentive to vote and to influence others to do the same. Data from Huckfeldt and Sprague's Indianapolis–St. Louis Election Study (ISLES) confirms this effect on both turnout and the likelihood that an individual will try to influence an acquaintance. This finding has important implications for the literature on social capital (e.g. Putnam 2000) because it suggests that increasing the density of social networks helps encourage civic engagement up to a point, but if they are too dense then civic engagement may actually decline.

This chapter proceeds as follows. I identify several important characteristics of large-scale social networks and describe a model developed by Watts and Strogatz (1998) that features these characteristics. I then develop a small-world model of turnout in which people have a small chance of influencing the voting behavior of their acquaintances. I then measure characteristics of real political-discussion networks from Huckfeldt and Sprague's ISLES and the South Bend Election Study (SBES) in order to define features of the model. This allows me to generate a realistic estimate of the size of turnout cascades. I report the results of the model when it is tuned to look like the network implied by the ISLES, and I also study the impact of changes in social-network characteristics on turnout. Individual-level data from the model is then used to show that the density of relationships among one's acquaintances has a curvilinear impact on turnout cascades and therefore the incentive to vote. This prediction is confirmed by empirical models of turnout and influence in the ISLES. Finally, I reflect on the importance of turnout cascades for revising traditional models of voting and summarize the results with implications for future research.

Large-Scale Social Networks

Watts and Strogatz (1998) identify three main features of real large-scale social networks that should be captured in any attempt to model them. First, these networks tend to be sparse, with an average degree (the number of ties a person has to other people in the network) that is much smaller than the size (the number of people) of the network. Second, social connections are highly clustered. That is, people tend to form social connections in tightly knit cliques in which everyone is tied to everyone else. The clustering coefficient is a measure of this property, giving the probability that any two individuals to whom a person is tied also have a link between them. (In other words, the coefficient states how likely it is that your friend's friend is also your friend.) Third, large-scale social networks tend to exhibit the small-world phenomenon. In spite of the large number of people in the network, on average there is a relatively short path connecting any two people through intermediaries.

Computer databases have recently made it possible to confirm that a wide variety of large-scale social networks are sparse, clustered, and have low average path lengths. For example, Newman (2001a,b,c) and Barabasi et al. (2001) show that academic co-authorship networks in a wide variety of disciplines are sparse, clustered, and have low average path lengths. Newman et al. (2002) also document these properties for directors of the Fortune 1,000 companies and for Hollywood actors (see also Watts and Strogatz 1998).

Although networks of academics and actors suggest what a network relevant for turnout would look like, there is no guarantee that they would all exhibit the same features. Fortunately, several studies of political-discussion networks have been conducted in recent years that might help us to estimate these features. In particular, Huckfeldt and Sprague's Indianapolis–St. Louis Election Study and South Bend Election Study ask typical questions about political attitudes and behavior, but they also ask respondents to name people with whom they discuss politics. The discussants are then requested to take the same survey (called a "snowball" survey). While surveys like these do not provide a fully connected map of everyone in a network, statistical information about their relationships and activities can be used to estimate properties of the large-scale political-discussion network.

THE WATTS-STROGATZ (WS) MODEL

Once their features are known, how should these networks be modeled? Until recently, attempts to model large networks involved the formation of fixed random networks. These randomly connect each member to one or more other people in the network. While random networks can yield the small-world property of low average path length with a low average degree, they typically fail to produce realistically high levels of clustering. This might have a critical impact on the flow of interactions within the network since higher clustering affects the total number of paths between any two individuals. (For the mathematical proof, please contact the author.) Other attempts to model large networks place individuals on a two-dimensional square grid and connect them to their nearest neighbors on the grid (see Johnson and Huckfeldt, in this volume). This approach eases visual inspection of the model and achieves high levels of clustering, but the average path length between individuals is quite high, meaning that these networks do not have the small-world property.[1]

Watts and Strogatz (1998) develop an alternative model that combines a highly ordered underlying structure of social ties with random "rewiring" of these ties.

Each individual is placed on a lattice in which people are connected to a number of their nearest "neighbors" on the lattice.[2] Then with some probability each of these ties is deleted and reconnected to a randomly chosen individual in the graph. One can think of each of these rewired connections as a "weak tie" (Granovetter 1973) that connects an individual to another group of people outside her core set of acquaintances. As the number of these weak ties increases, the graph becomes less ordered and more like a random graph, and both the clustering coefficient and the average path length decline. However, the path length declines much more rapidly than clustering, so for a range of rewiring probabilities this procedure produces small-world graphs that are highly clustered. The rate of rewiring can be tuned to match the features of a particular social network—too low and the graph will cease to display the small-world property, too high and the level of clustering will be unrealistically low.

A SMALL-WORLD MODEL OF TURNOUT

Here I want to highlight the main features of the model and to provide a short analytical description (full details are available on request). To study turnout cascades in the context of a social network, the WS model is used to generate a small-world network with a given size, average degree, clustering coefficient, and average path length. Each citizen in the network is then assigned an ideological preference on a one-dimensional left-right scale. This procedure allows us to control the degree of correlation in preferences between neighbors. Next, each of these citizens is assigned an initial turnout behavior, and they are randomly chosen one at a time to interact with one of their neighbors. In each of these interactions, there is a small probability that a citizen will change her turnout behavior to match the behavior of her neighbor. Finally, following a given number of interactions between citizens and their neighbors, there is an election between two candidates.

Turnout in the model is deterministic and endogenous. Once citizens start interacting, cascades begin to form at each point where imitation takes place. Some of these cascades are turnout cascades, but others are abstention cascades since people are equally likely to imitate either kind of behavior. Moreover, these cascades may flow across one another, changing some citizens back and forth between a decision to abstain and a decision to vote. Picking out the net effect of a single cascade amid all these interactions could be very difficult, but I simplify the procedure with a counterfactual. I allow one citizen to remain unaffected by her neighbors. I then compare the aggregate turnout outcome when she abstains and when she votes, holding all else constant.

The model is based on several assumptions that may be unrealistic but are useful for keeping things simple. For example, unlike other authors in this volume, I assume that all social ties are equal. There are no elites and no special relationships. This assumption does not seem unreasonable since Huckfeldt and Sprague (1991) show that the likelihood of influence between acquaintances does not depend either on the degree of friendship or judgments of political competency. I also make the assumption that ties are bilateral so that influence can run equally in either direction. This is contrary to another finding by Huckfeldt and Sprague (1991). When asked to name other people with whom they discuss politics, many people do not name the people who originally named them as discussants. (This was true even of husbands and wives!) However, their survey design may be responsible in this case since discussants were not asked directly if they knew or spoke with the person who named them.

Note also that this analysis assumes that voters are not strategic. I set aside this feature for future work because I want to explore the simplest manifestation of the turnout-cascade phenomenon and how it might affect the decision to vote. Like other researchers doing decision-theoretic work on turnout (Aldrich 1993; Downs 1957; Ferejohn and Fiorina 1974; Riker and Ordeshook 1968), I assume that a rational individual is faced with a choice that depends on the choices of all other voters. However, this individual abstracts away from the strategic problem by assuming certain uniform characteristics in the population (such as the propensity to vote) in order to make her decision.

Related to this, I assume that people are sincere in their political discussions with one another. This is not an unreasonable assumption—many people say they vote because they do not want to tell their friends and family that they did not (Knack 1992). Implicit in this explanation is the assumption that they also do not want to lie. However, individual-level surveys indicate that a significant number of people who do not vote say that they did (Granberg and Holmberg 1991). Strategic lying would probably weaken the effect that political discussions have on actual turnout behavior, but I leave this feature out of the model for now to keep things simple.[3]

FEATURES OF POLITICAL-DISCUSSION NETWORKS

The next step is to use real political-discussion network data from the ISLES, SBES, and other sources to help us choose appropriate features for the model. These features include the size of the network, the average degree, the average number of interactions between acquaintances, the clustering coefficient, the average path length, the imitation rate, and the correlation of preferences between acquaintances.

Size of the Network

McDonald and Popkin (2001) note that there are currently about 186 million eligible voters in the United States. However, modeling so many voters is computationally intensive. A model with even 1 million voters takes several minutes to generate a single counterfactual, and hundreds of thousands of these are needed to do appropriate statistical analysis. Therefore, I limit the number of voters and explore the impact of the size of the electorate on turnout cascades by letting the number of voters vary between 1,000 and 100,000. This means that results for larger networks, such as the set of voting-eligible citizens in the United States, must be extrapolated, which makes stronger assumptions about the model (King 2002).

Average Degree

Sociologists note that most people have between about a hundred and a thousand significant friendship and family acquaintances (Bernard et al. 1988; Freeman and Thompson 1989; Pool and Kochen 1978). However, the number of political discussants named in the ISLES is much smaller. Of those who name discussants,

618 respondents reported one, 797 reported two, 695 reported three, 469 reported four, and 1,065 reported five or more. Unlike earlier studies (e.g., South Bend) that asked people to name a fixed number of political discussants, the ISLES used an open-ended name generator, allowing people to name as many discussants as they wanted to up to five. Since the sample is truncated, the average of 3.15 discussants named is probably too low. It is also possible that people have difficulty recalling all the people with whom they discuss politics, and privacy concerns may limit the number of discussants they are willing to name. To be conservative I will assume an average degree of four for the ISLES but I will let this vary up to twenty to explore the impact of network characteristics on turnout.

Average Path Length and the Clustering Coefficient

Very little is known about the true average path length of real political-discussion networks. However, independent control over both the average path length and the clustering coefficient in the WS model is not possible since both are determined by the rewiring rate. Thus a rewiring rate is chosen that generates a realistic clustering coefficient. There are two different estimates of the clustering coefficient using the ISLES data because respondents were asked separately if each of their discussants talked to each of their other discussants, and if each of their discussants knew each of their other discussants. The probability that two of one's discussants know one another is about 0.61, while the probability that they talk to one another is 0.47. These numbers indicate that the rate of clustering in the ISLES is consistent with other social networks, but they raise an interesting question: Which measure is more relevant for a model of imitation? Since discussion is the obvious way in which people might send and receive information about their turnout choice, the lower estimate based on talk is used. However, it is important to bear in mind that more casual relationships can have an effect on political behavior as well. As Huckfeldt (1984, 414) writes, "the less intimate interactions that I have ignored—discussions over backyard fences, casual encounters while taking walks, or standing in line at the grocery, and so on—may be politically influential even though they do not occur between intimate associates."

Number of Interactions

Many interactions might influence people's decision to vote. For example, people might be affected by merely observing their acquaintances' behavior. (Do they vote? Do they participate in community or group activities? Do they have a political sign in their yard?) They might also be affected by political discussions with their acquaintances. Political discussions are used to estimate the frequency of interactions because the information about discussions is better than information about other kinds of interactions. However, it is important to realize that this makes the estimate of the number of interactions conservative.

In the ISLES, respondents say they talk with each of their discussants about three times a week on average, but how often are these conversations about politics? Among these respondents, 21.3 percent say "often" and 51.2 percent say "sometimes" while everyone else says "rarely" or "never." These numbers are also consistent with the Comparative National Elections Study of the 1992 U.S. election (Huckfeldt et al. 1995). It is difficult to translate qualitative responses into actual frequencies, but given the stated frequencies, a conservative interpretation is that about a third of these conversations are about politics. This means that people probably have on average about one political discussion a week with each of their discussion partners. Another variable to consider is what length of time is relevant to the turnout decision. Lazarsfeld et al. (1944) and Berelson et al. (1954) note that political discussions are more frequent during campaigns. In most countries candidate selection happens several months prior to an election, but voter attention is probably increasingly focused as Election Day approaches. To form a reasonable guess for the relevant time period, note that the average primary in the U.S. presidential election is held about five months (or about twenty weeks) prior to the general election. This means that respondents would have around twenty discussions per discussant during the most salient period for their turnout decision. This number might seem low to some and high to others; but since lower numbers are conservative, I will let the number vary from one to twenty when exploring the impact of the number of discussions on turnout.

Imitation Rate

It is well known that turnout is highly correlated between friends, family, and co-workers (Beck et al. 2002; Berelson et al. 1954; Campbell et al. 1954; Huckfeldt and Sprague 1995; Lazarsfeld et al. 1944; Mutz and Mondak 1998). For example, Glaser (1959) finds a strong relationship in the turnout decision between spouses. More recently, Straits (1990) confirms Glaser's finding, and Knack (1992, 137) notes that many people vote because "my friends and relatives almost always vote and I'd feel uncomfortable telling them I hadn't."[4] The literature on mobilization also shows that asking people to vote is an effective tool for increasing turnout (e.g. Gerber and Green 1999, 2000a, 2000b; Wielhouwer and Lockerbie 1994). Even individuals who are unaffiliated with organized mobilization efforts may attempt to influence the turnout behavior of their peers. Thirty-four percent of respondents in the ISLES say they tried to convince someone to vote for their preferred candidate, indicating that many people believe there is a chance others will imitate them. These efforts might be aimed at influencing vote choice (see Huckfeldt, Johnson, and Sprague; Johnston and Pattie; Jennings and Stoker; and Levine, in this volume), but they also convey messages about the importance of an election, and this might affect the decision to turn out.

How much of this correlation in turnout behavior is due to imitation rather than individual incentives and status variables that happen to be correlated between peers? Using social network data from the SBES, Kenny (1992) develops a simultaneous regression model of respondent and discussant turnout, controlling for age, education, income, interest in politics, and strength of party identification. He finds that respondents are 15 percent more likely to turn out if one of their discussants votes, which is close to what one would estimate if one looked at the simple correlation ($\rho = 0.2$). This effect also extends two steps to one's discussants' discussants. In the SBES, validated turnout is 75 percent among respondents whose discussants reported that all *their* discussants voted, compared to 61 percent for those reporting at least one abstention. In the ISLES data, perceived turnout among discussants' discussants is 92 percent for respondents who say they will vote and 78 percent for those who say they will not.

These numbers may represent the total effect of imitation, but they do not give us the per-discussion imitation rate required by the model. One might think that the imitation rate can be inferred from the number of discussions and the total effect, but this misses the important point that imitation also occurs between a discussant and each of her other discussants. In expectation, these other relationships act to moderate the influence of a single turnout decision, so the per-discussion imitation rate should be higher than a simple probability calculation would imply (details available from the author). In principle, a realistic imitation rate can be selected by changing it until the model correlation matches real correlation in turnout. If respondents base their answers about political discussions on their past month of activity, then an imitation rate of about 5 percent is needed to generate a turnout correlation with acquaintances ($\rho = 0.23$) and with acquaintances' acquaintances ($\rho = 0.13$) consistent with the ISLES data.

Concentration of Shared Interests

A consistent finding in the social voting literature is that people tend to segregate themselves into like-minded groups. As a result, most social ties are between people who share the same interests. When people whose ideological or class-based interests are not shared by individuals in their physical neighborhoods and workplaces, they tend to withdraw and form relationships outside those environments (Berger 1960; Finifter 1974; Gans 1967; Huckfeldt and Sprague 1987, 1988; Noelle-Neumann 1984). Thus preferences between acquaintances tend to be highly correlated.

The concentration of shared interests does not affect total turnout, but it is very important for net favorable turnout. If there were no correlation in preferences, then any turnout cascade could be expected to include as many people who disagree as agree. With correlation, however, turnout cascades are more likely to affect like-minded individuals and yield net favorable changes for one's preferred candidate in expectation. This means that in environments with a high concentration of shared interests, the incentive to turn out might be magnified by the number of like-minded individuals one can motivate to go to the polls.

The model allows us to fine-tune how closely neighbors share interests with one another. Huckfeldt, Johnson, and Sprague (in this volume) show in a number of ways how concentrated interests are between discussants. Most relevant to the model here is the correlation between self-reported liberals and conservatives, which is about 0.66 in the ISLES. The correlation between Republicans and Democrats is somewhat lower at 0.54. It is worth pointing out here that these estimates are based on interviews with both the respondent and the discussant. Using the respondents' perceptions of how liberal or conservative their discussion partners are causes the concentration of shared interests to be even higher because people tend to overestimate the likelihood that their associates hold their own political preferences (Fabrigar and Krosnick 1995; Huckfeldt and Sprague 1995).

RESULTS: TURNOUT IN A SOCIAL NETWORK LIKE THE ISLES

Figure 14.1 shows the distribution of turnout results when a single person chooses to vote in a social network with features very similar to the political-discussion network in the ISLES. Notice first that the size of these turnout cascades varies widely. In the left graph total change in turnout varies between 1 and 25, indicating that small differences in local configurations can generate large differences in the size of a particular turnout cascade. The modal change in turnout is 1, but 82 percent of the time it is greater than one and the average change in turnout is about 4. This means that a citizen can expect to change the turnout decision of about three other people with her own turnout decision.

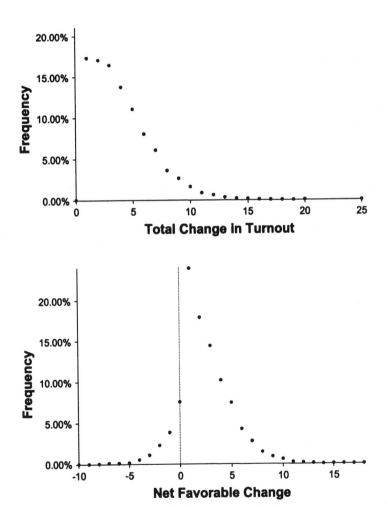

FIGURE 14.1. Turnout Cascades in a Social Network Like the ISLES

Note: Each data point represents the frequency over 10,000 trials of the change in aggregate turnout from changing a single turnout decision in a social network like the ISLES political discussion network. The simulation is based on a network with 100,000 citizens, 4 neighbors per citizen on average, 20 interactions with each neighbor on average, a 0.4 probability that neighbors know one another, an imitation rate of 0.05, a correlation in preferences of 0.66, and an average path length of about 20.

Not everyone in a turnout cascade is likely to have the same preferences, though. Some people motivated to vote will choose the left candidate and others will choose the right. How does this affect the aggregate outcome of the election? The right graph in Figure 14.1 shows the distribution for the "net favorable change" in the vote margin for the candidate preferred by the person deciding whether to turn out. Once again, the outcomes vary widely, with a substantial portion of them falling below 1. The graph shows that about 8 percent of the time the vote margin for a citizen's preferred candidate actually *decreases* because her favorite candidate's opponent gains a greater portion of the votes in the resulting turnout cascade. Another 8 percent of the time, her turnout has a net neutral impact on the vote margin. However, since citizens are embedded in networks of shared preferences, the decision to turn out usually leads to a net gain for one's preferred candidate, and this net gain ranged up to 18 votes in the simulation. Again, the modal change in the vote margin is 1, but 60 percent of the time it is greater than 1 and on average the preferred candidate gains 2.4 votes. In other words, a citizen can expect to increase the vote margin of her favorite candidate by about two to three votes with her own turnout decision.

Results: Turnout in a Variety of Social Networks

Figure 14.1 is based on features estimated with the use of political-discussion network survey data, but the true social network might be somewhat different. To characterize how features of the social network and assumptions about citizen interactions affect the expected size of a turnout cascade, I randomly search the feature space near the estimates I derived from the ISLES and run the model hundreds of thousands of times (see Table 14.1). As in the model based on ISLES, the size of individual turnout cascades varies widely, ranging up to one hundred in the 343,300 election counterfactuals simulated. However, the *expected* change in turnout only ranges up to eighteen when these counterfactuals are averaged for each unique social network.

Figure 14.2 shows the results of this exercise. Each data point in the graphs represents the expected size of a turnout cascade for a social network generated

TABLE 14.1. Summary Statistics of Social Networks Sampled

	Mean	Std. Dev.	Min.	Max.
Number of citizens (N)	50,391	28,826	1,055	99,978
Number of acquaintances (k)	12.11	5.19	4	20
Average discussions per acquaintance (D)	10.52	5.76	1	20
Imitation rate (q)	0.025	0.014	0.000	0.050
Correlation parameter (α)	0.752	0.144	0.500	0.999
Short-cuts parameter (β)	0.055	0.026	0.010	0.100
Average path length (L)	10.95	8.33	3.60	75.73
Probability acquaintances know one another (C)	0.561	0.067	0.371	0.692
Concentration of shared interests (ρ)	0.808	0.143	0.447	0.991
Expected total change in turnout (T)	3.86	2.83	1	17.94
Expected net favorable change in turnout	2.74	1.68	0.98	13.02

Note: Number of social networks sampled = 3,343.

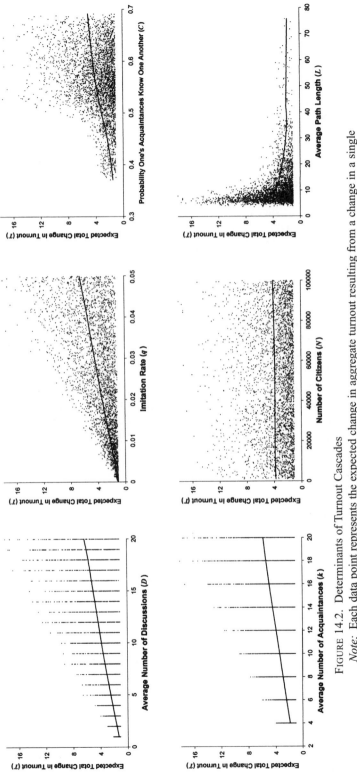

FIGURE 14.2. Determinants of Turnout Cascades

Note: Each data point represents the expected change in aggregate turnout resulting from a change in a single turnout decision for each unique social network. Solid lines indicate mean effects on turnout generated by LOESS, using a bandwidth of 0.8 (Cleveland 1979; Cleveland and Devlin 1988).

by a unique combination of features. It is difficult to conceptualize six dimensions at once, so I present six graphs, each showing how turnout changes with respect to each feature of the model. The solid lines on these graphs indicate the mean effect on expected total turnout generated by locally weighted polynomial regression (LOESS—see Cleveland 1979; Cleveland and Devlin 1988). Summary statistics for the feature space searched are presented in the chapter tables.

Notice first that turnout cascades tend to increase strongly with the number of discussions and the probability of imitation since each discussion is a new opportunity to change someone's mind and start a chain reaction in the population. This finding is consistent with studies that show mobilization efforts increase turnout (Ansolabehere and Snyder 2000; Gerber and Green 1999, 2000a,b), especially when they are carried out by unions and labor parties that have ties to their target audience (Brown et al. 1999; Gray and Caul 2000; Radcliff 2001; and Radcliff and Davis 2000).

Clustering and the average degree also have a positive effect on the turnout rate, although the effect is weaker than others previously mentioned. As the number of acquaintances or the probability that one's acquaintances know one another increases, the number of paths between individuals rises dramatically. This increases the number of ways a single turnout decision can be transmitted to other people in the population, but it also exposes each person in a turnout cascade to a larger number of external influences that might end the cascade. The cross-cutting effects cancel one another to a large degree, but the overall effect on turnout remains positive. These findings are consistent with recent empirical work on social capital and aggregate turnout. In particular, Cox et al. (1998) show that social

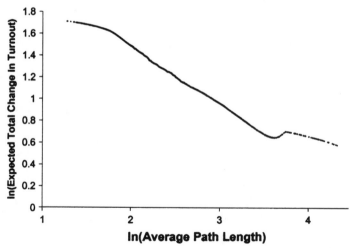

FIGURE 14.3. Power Law Relationship between Average Path Length and Turnout
    Note: Solid line indicates mean effect on turnout generated by LOESS using a bandwidth of 0.8 (Cleveland 1979; Cleveland and Devlin 1988). A regression of average path length L on the change in turnout T yields: $\ln(T) = 2.20(\pm 0.10) - 0.48(\pm 0.04)\ln(L)$ (95% confidence intervals in parentheses).

density is related to higher turnout in Japan, and Monroe (1977) shows that rural areas in the United States where social network connections are more clustered have much higher turnout than urban areas, in spite of lower levels of education and income.

The total number of citizens in a network has only a very small effect on the average size of turnout cascades. I originally believed that the size of turnout cascades would scale strongly with because of the increased number of people who might be influenced by a cascade. However, the small effect indicates that turnout cascades are primarily *local* phenomena, occurring in a smaller part of the population with short path lengths to an individual.

Finally, notice that the small-world phenomenon has a pronounced and nonlinear effect on turnout. As the average path length drops, the size of the turnout cascade rises quickly. In fact, Figure 14.3 shows that there is a power law relationship between turnout and the average path length. The size of the turnout cascade T is proportional to the inverse of the square root of the average path length L:

$$T \propto L - \tfrac{1}{2}.$$

This relationship suggests that turnout might be even higher than estimated. For example, in the model based on ISLES the average path length is about 20, but if it is dropped to the "six degrees of separation" reported by Milgram (1967), then expected turnout would be about 83 percent higher. No one knows the true average path length for a typical political-discussion network, but this result indicates that it might be very important for estimating how much influence a single individual can expect to have.

How favorable are turnout cascades to the people who initiate them? Each data point in Figure 14.4 plots the net favorable change versus the total change in turnout for a given network. For all simulations there is a strong relationship between net favorable turnout and total turnout, and nearly all of the variation in this relationship can be explained by preference correlation. To demonstrate this, the expected relationship for three different samples, those with medium ($\rho = 0.5 \pm 0.025$), medium-high ($\rho = 0.8 \pm 0.025$), and high ($\rho = 1.0 \pm 0.025$) concentrations of shared interests are plotted. Intuitively, as preference correlation approaches 1, the net favorable change approaches the total change in turnout because the turnout cascade is affecting many people with the same preferences. As it approaches 0, the net favorable change approaches 0 because the preferences of people affected will be more evenly distributed between left and right.

This implies an important finding: The high concentration of shared interests in social networks may magnify the incentive to participate. In a social network where preferences are randomly distributed, the counterfactual impact of a single vote on the outcome of the election will be just that—a single vote. However, if my turnout behavior has a positive impact on the people who surround us and they share my interests, then the counterfactual impact of a single vote on the outcome of the election may be several times a single vote. Therefore, the incentive to vote should be higher when conditions are favorable for turnout cascades, and it should be increasing where shared interests are concentrated. This helps to explain the

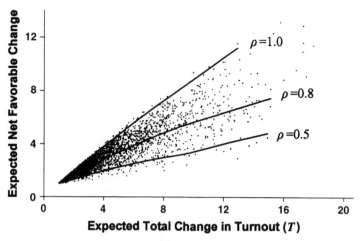

FIGURE 14.4. How Concentration of Shared Interests Affects Turnout

Note: Each data point represents the expected change in aggregate turnout from changing a single turnout decision for each unique social network. Solid lines indicate mean effects on turnout generated by LOESS using a bandwidth of 0.8 (Cleveland 1979; Cleveland and Devlin 1988). In the graph I show three of these lines, restricting the sample to networks with medium ($\rho = 0.5 \pm 0.025$), medium-high ($\rho = 0.8 \pm 0.025$), and high ($\rho = 1.0 \pm 0.025$) preference correlation.

finding by Busch and Reinhardt (2000) that geographic concentration of shared interests increases aggregate level turnout.

The Curvilinear Effect of Local Clustering

Although the small-world model of turnout produces effects that are consistent with studies of aggregate turnout, the question remains: Do turnout cascades really create individual incentives to vote? To answer this question, individual-level data on clustering from the model using the ISLES is regressed on the net favorable change in turnout (see Table 14.2). This relationship should be very noisy because it involves individual turnout cascades like those in Figure 14.1, rather than expected turnout cascades like those in Figures 14.2 and 14.4. However, in spite of the noise, Figure 14.5 shows that there is a curvilinear relationship between favorable turnout cascades and the probability one's friends know one another. Moderate levels of clustering yield more favorable turnout cascades than either very low or very high levels.

Why might this be the case? Clustering increases the number of paths available to influence other people in a network. People with acquaintances who do not know one another can only affect their acquaintances directly, but when these acquaintances know one another it opens up new paths to influence them indirectly. Moreover, this multiplies the number of connections one has to the rest of the social network via these new paths. At the extreme, however, individuals in groups that are very highly clustered may have several paths of influence within the group, but they will also have fewer connections to the rest of the social network because there are constraints on the number of relationships a person can have. In the model this is imposed by the initial choice of the average number of discussants,

TABLE 14.2. How Clustering of Relationships Affects Turnout

	Predicted: Net favorable change		Actual: Intention to vote		Actual: Influence	
	Coeff.	S.E.	Coeff.	S.E.	Coeff.	S.E.
Probability acquaintances know one another (C)	0.207	0.313	−0.018	0.098	0.094	0.080
Probability acquaintances know one another^2 (C^2)	−2.242*	0.879	−1.584*	0.772	−0.727*	0.360
Age			0.016*	0.003	−0.009*	0.002
Education			0.074*	0.017	0.014	0.011
Employed			0.074	0.092	−0.052	0.055
Group membership			0.359*	0.095	0.311*	0.077
Income			0.027	0.033	0.061*	0.019
Interest in campaign			0.969*	0.101	0.922*	0.066
Married			0.170*	0.082	−0.035	0.049
Constant	2.395*	0.150	−0.908*	0.342	−0.925*	0.202
N	10,000		4,352		4,352	
Adjusted/pseudo R^2	0.003		0.15		0.07	

Note: OLS regression for net favorable change model; probit regression for turnout and influence models. C is centered at 0.5 before squaring to reduce collinearity. Data for net favorable change model is based on a network with 100,000 citizens, 4 neighbors per citizen on average, 20 interactions with each neighbor on average, a 0.4 probability that neighbors know one another, an imitation rate of 0.05, a correlation in preferences of 0.66, and an average path length of about 20. Missing data for actual models imputed using EMis (King et al. 2001). Controls included because they correlate with C or C^2 and might be causally prior (King, Keohane, and Verba 1994).
*$p < .05$.

but one can imagine that in real life people have time to maintain only a finite set of relationships, so that tightly knit groups will tend to keep to themselves.

The model thus predicts a curvilinear relationship between clustering and turnout, but does this exist for real data? The proportion of each respondent's discussants who know one another in the ISLES is regressed on vote intention. Figure 14.4 shows that a statistically significant curvilinear relationship exists: Respondents with a mix of friends who do and do not know one another are about 1.5 percent more likely to vote than people in dispersed or highly clustered groups. To see if this difference in turnout is related to the desire to create favorable turnout cascades, clustering is also regressed on the self-expressed desire to influence others to vote for a certain candidate. Here the curvilinear relationship is even stronger: People with moderately clustered acquaintances are about 8 percent more likely to try to influence others than those in dispersed or highly clustered groups. Turnout cascades may not exist, but these findings suggest that people may believe that they do.

This finding has important implications for the literature on social capital (e.g., Putnam 2000). This literature argues that civic engagement will be higher in societies with more clustered social ties. The model suggests that this is true, but only to a point. When relationships become too clustered, individuals lose touch with the rest of the social network and are less able to influence participation beyond their circle of acquaintances. This reduces their individual incentives to be engaged

Predicted:

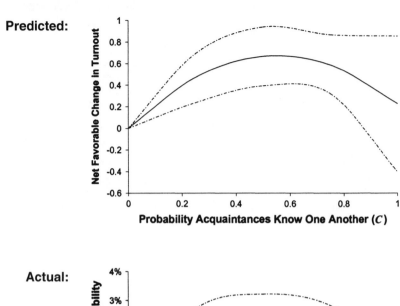

Actual:

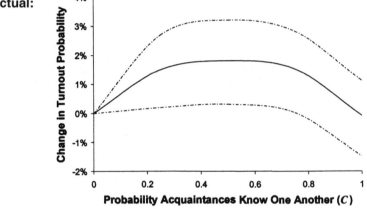

Influence:

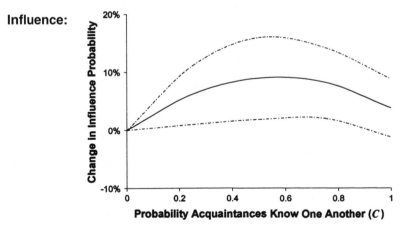

FIGURE 14.5. How Clustering of Relationships Affects Turnout

Note: Solid lines are simulated expected values of the first difference changing *C* from 0 and holding all other variables at their means (King et al. 2000). Dashed lines are simulated 95 percent confidence intervals. Estimates are based on models in Table 14.2.

in civic society and to encourage others to do the same. As Kotler-Berkowitz and Gimpel and Lay argue in this volume, diversity in one's social connections can increase the incentive to participate by opening up new paths of influence to and from the rest of the network. However, the model also suggests that too much diversity hurts participation because it increases the likelihood that participation will be stimulated among people who do not share the same interests.

TURNOUT CASCADES AND RATIONAL MODELS OF VOTING

The existence of turnout cascades suggests that previous models of turnout have underestimated the benefit of voting. Decision-theoretic and game-theoretic models assume that the expected value of voting is the benefit one would receive by having one's favorite candidate elected multiplied by the probability that one's vote matters to the outcome (Beck 1974; Downs 1957; Ferejohn and Fiorina 1974; Ledyard 1982, 1984; Palfrey and Rosenthal 1983, 1985; Riker and Ordeshook 1968; Tullock 1967). This probability is extremely small because a single vote only matters in two cases: if the election results in an exact tie, or there is a one-vote deficit for one's favorite candidate. Several variations of this argument have been put forth, but they have in common the idea that the probability of being pivotal in large electorates is inversely proportional to the number of people in the model. However, since turnout cascades mean that a single turnout decision can change the margin of victory by more than one vote, they should increase the probability of being pivotal. For example, in a large electorate the probability that a favorable cascade of two votes is pivotal is approximately twice the probability that one vote is pivotal. Three votes approximately triple the probability, and so on. Generalizing, this means that the expected benefit from being pivotal is proportional to the net favorable change in the margin of victory yielded by a turnout cascade.

Fowler and Smirnov (2002) develop an alternative "signaling" model of turnout that typically yields much higher expected utility than the pivotal model. If politicians use the margin of victory in the past election to adjust their future platforms, then each vote has a marginal impact on future policies. Therefore, people may have an incentive to signal their preferences by voting even when they would not be pivotal. Fowler and Smirnov show that the signaling benefit from voting is proportional to the change in the margin of victory, so a net favorable change in turnout of two votes would double the benefit, three would triple it, and so on. Thus the expected benefit from signaling is also proportional to the net favorable change in the margin of victory yielded by a turnout cascade.

Turnout cascades should have an effect on other kinds of benefits, too. For example, consumption models of voting assume an additional benefit derived from fulfilling one's civic duty to vote (Blais and Young 1999; Blais, Young, and Lapp 2000; Jones and Hudson 2000; Ratzinger and Kramer 1995; Riker and Ordeshook 1968). Although it is difficult to quantify how a turnout cascade would affect the duty motivation, I note that many civic-duty models emphasize the social aspect of voting and argue that people derive utility from contributing to a public good. This suggests that they might derive additional benefit from voting if they knew they were influencing others to contribute to that good. Thus, the benefit from fulfilling one's civic duty might also be in increasing the size of turnout cascades.

Thus, turnout cascades multiply the benefit associated with deciding to vote in a number of models. But can they make a rational model of turnout plausible? If we multiply the pivotal and signaling motivations by the conservative estimate of a 2.4 voter net favorable change in the margin of victory, the cost-benefit threshold at which voting yields positive expected value is no more than 1:5,000 for an electorate of one million persons.[5] In other words, "rational" voting requires that the benefit from being able personally to choose which candidate wins the election must be at least 5,000 times larger than whatever costs are incurred by voting, such as learning about the issues, waiting in line at the polls, and so on. What if we use a less conservative estimate? In a network like the ISLES, changing the average path length from twenty to seven, the number of acquaintances from four to twenty, and the probability that acquaintances know one another from 0.4 to 0.6 generates an expected change in turnout of fourteen and an expected increase in the margin of victory of 8.4 votes. This changes the cost-benefit threshold to 1:1,500, which may still be too low to explain most turnout. Thus, while turnout cascades make rational voting more plausible than previously thought, we are still left with Aldrich's (1993) conclusion that rational voting must be a "low cost–low benefit" activity.

SUMMARY AND DISCUSSION

The model of turnout in a large-scale network suggests that a single person's decision to vote affects the turnout decision of at least four people on average in a "turnout cascade." Given the high concentration of shared interests among acquaintances in real political-discussion networks, this means that a single decision to vote can increase the margin for one's preferred candidate by at least two to three votes. Therefore the incentive to vote, whether it is based on affecting the outcome of the election or some other benefit related to turnout, is larger than previously thought.

Turnout cascades and the incentive to vote are increasing in several features of social networks that have been shown to be associated with higher turnout. In particular, they are increasing in the number of interactions with people who vote (Ansolabehere and Snyder 2000; Brown et al. 1999; Gerber and Green 1999, 2000a,b; Gray and Caul 2000; Radcliff 2001; and Radcliff and Davis 2000), the clustering of social ties (Cox et al. 1998; Monroe 1977), and the concentration of shared interests (Busch and Reinhardt 2000). The model also suggests that there is a power law relationship between turnout cascades and the average distance between any two individuals in the network: As the world gets smaller, the capacity to influence others increases exponentially, and so should the incentive to participate.

At the individual level, the model predicts a feature of turnout that has previously gone unnoticed. The relationship between the size of turnout cascades and the number of one's acquaintances who talk to one another is curvilinear. In the language of Granovetter (1973), people with a mix of "weak" and "strong" ties can initiate larger turnout cascades than can people with all weak or all strong ties, and the former therefore have a greater incentive to vote and to influence others to do the same. Using data from the Indianapolis–St. Louis Election Study, I find exactly this effect on both intention to vote and the likelihood that an individual will try to influence an acquaintance. This suggests a revision to the social capital literature. Civic engagement does not increase monotonically as the density of social relationships increases. When these relationships within a group become too dense, civic engagement actually declines because people are less connected to the rest of society.

The model suggests a possible explanation for why so many people assert that there is a "duty" to vote (Blais and Young 1999; Blais, Young, and Lapp 2000; Ratzinger and Kramer 1995; Riker and Ordeshook 1968). Establishing a norm of voting with one's acquaintances is one way to influence them to go to the polls. People who do not assert such a duty miss a chance to influence people who share similar views, and this tends to lead to worse outcomes for their favorite candidates. In large electorates the net impact on the result might be too marginal to create a dynamic that would favor people who assert a duty to vote. However, arguments about the civic duty to vote originated in much smaller political settings, such as the town meetings where changing the participation behavior of a few people might make a big difference (Tocqueville 1835). In future work I plan to explore the dynamic of changing electorate size in order to see if a duty to vote emerges as a strategy in small electorates and persists as the size of the electorate increases.

The model also suggests a new paradox of (not lying about) voting. I assume that all people in the model are sincere, but in fact we know that some people lie about voting. Suppose we allow some people to be strategic in their discussions. If they believe that their political discussions can cause turnout cascades among sincere voters, they may *tell* other people that they vote in order to increase the vote margin for their favorite candidates, but never actually go to the polls themselves! In fact, as long as they know they share interests with others around them, they can do this without knowing anything about the coming election since their acquaintances are likely to vote as they would vote if they took the time to learn about the candidates and make a decision. This may help to explain over-reporting of turnout in election surveys, but it raises another question: If people were strategic, why would they ever say that they do not vote?

Finally, future research should investigate turnout cascades in alternative network models that allow for more realistic average path lengths. The literature on preferential attachment and scale-free networks notes that another feature of many real networks is a power-law distribution of the degree (Albert and Barabasi 2002). In other words, a very large number of people may have only a few acquaintances (as in the WS model), but a very small number of people may have substantially more. These "critical nodes" would help to reduce the average path length to realistic levels, but I do not know if they actually exist in political-discussion networks. The ISLES only allows people to name five discussants, and with so few data points it is hard to tell if there is actually a power law in the distribution of the degree. Future election surveys with social-network questions should ask people to estimate how many people they have political discussions with so we can get a sense of this distribution and use it to make our large-scale network models more accurate.

Notes

PREFACE

1. Some documents indicate cross-fertilization between Greek and Judaic wisdom. See especially *The Wisdom of Ben Sira* (Di Lella 1987: 249, 13:1–2 and 250, 13:15–16). For sources in the Talmud see, for example, *Mishnah Hulin*, 65, *Babylonian Talmud, Baba Metziah*, chap. 8 92A–93A, and *Babylonian Talmud, Baba Batra*, 17B.

2. "Cicero has a similar saying . . . : 'Indeed equals, according to the old proverb most easily assemble with equals'" (in Di Lella 1987, 254, whose commentary on Ben Sira I have consulted). Aquinas's argument on behalf of the importance of friends is a commentary on Aristotle. See Aquinas 1964, 2: 5, and Aquinas, 1983, 12.

CHAPTER 1: RETURNING TO THE SOCIAL LOGIC OF POLITICAL BEHAVIOR

1. There are three exceptions to this research decision. During the first two national surveys of presidential elections (1956 and 1960), respondents were asked about potential personal sources of influence on their electoral decisions. In all surveys, respondents are asked about the objective social characteristics of members of their household. Most important, as is discussed below, the studies retain questions on the political preferences of the respondents' parents.

2. Their solution does not offer a citation from Lewin, and it runs counter to the understanding that I present above of Lewin's work.

3. The British Election Studies provide information on political discussants, even as the American National Election Studies generally refrain from including these questions. See Johnston 2000; Pattie and Johnston, 2000, 2001; and Zuckerman, Kotler-Berkowitz, and Swaine 1998 for examples using these variables.

4. In a private conversation (see the Preface), Elihu Katz told me that he and Lazarsfeld considered this type of survey to be the next step for their research.

CHAPTER 2: INDIVIDUALS, DYADS, AND NETWORKS

Acknowledgments: Portions of this chapter are taken from Robert Huckfeldt, Paul Johnson, and John Sprague, *Political Disagreement: The Survival of Diverse Opinions within Communication Networks* (New York: Cambridge University Press, 2004).

1. The 2000 American National Election Study was conducted by the Center for Political Studies of the Institute for Social Research at the University of Michigan. The study entailed both a pre-election interview and a post-election re-interview. A freshly drawn cross-section of the electorate was taken to yield 1,807 cases. The 65-minute pre-election survey went into the field on September 5, nine weeks before election day. The 65-minute post-election study went into the field the day after the election, November 8, and remained in the field until December 18.

CHAPTER 3: POLITICAL SIMILARITY AND INFLUENCE BETWEEN HUSBANDS AND WIVES

This chapter draws on ongoing research that has been supported by grants from the National Science Foundation, the National Institute on Aging, and the Academic Senates of the University of California, Berkeley, and the University of California, Santa Barbara.

1. Schools were selected with probability proportionate to size. Within each school interval sampling from senior class lists was used to select respondents. The student response rate was 99 percent. For more methodological details, see Jennings and Niemi 1974 and 1981; Jennings and Markus 1984; and Jennings and Stoker 1999.

2. The few empirical studies of couples focusing on sociopolitical topics have tended to find that husband-wife similarity increases with length of marriage (Beyer and White-hurst 1976; Zuckerman and Kotler-Berkowitz 1998; Zuckerman, Fitzgerald, and Dasović in this volume).

3. The findings for the 1973–1982 and 1982–1997 spouse panels are very similar to those seen in Table 3.1. To save space, we report only the three-wave panel results here.

4. How best to express agreement between linked respondents is always a vexing problem. For an early and insightful discussion see Robinson (1957); and for a precursor to the present effort, see Niemi, Hedges, and Jennings (1977). Recent work on the subject suggests that the most appropriate measure of homogeneity within dyads is the intraclass correlation (ICC) (Gonzales and Griffin 2000; McGraw and Wong 1996). Like the product-moment correlation, the ICC measures relative rather than absolute disagreement. As such, over-time changes in the ICC are not influenced by over-time changes in the gender gap. Unlike the product-moment correlation, the intraclass correlation does not assume that the relationship between the two variables is linear. An ICC of 0 indicates no within-couple homogeneity, and an ICC of 1 indicates perfect within-couple agreement.

5. Similarity on gender equality rises between 1973 and 1982, and then plummets so that the agreement level in 1997 mirrors that seen in 1973. We have no explanation for this peculiar pattern.

6. The pattern of findings in Table 3.2 is replicated when one analyzes the two two-wave couple panels. We present only the three-wave results in the interests of conserving space.

7. The following few paragraphs are based on data from the full sample of 1973 respondents who were married at the time, not just those whose spouses completed the questionnaires. This is done to improve the estimates because of the shrinking Ns produced by the winnowing process occasioned by the question sequence.

8. Our Ns at this point are smaller but still rather reliable. Of the 163 respondents who report an early-marriage disagreement, 71 said that one person changed his or her mind, and all of these 71 designated the changer.

9. Still, at both points in time the men are more likely than the women to say that both partners changed their minds in response to the disagreement. In 1973, 43 percent of the husbands and 28 percent of the wives take this position. In 1997, 81 percent of the husbands and 65 percent of the wives express this view.

10. Some studies of influence among married couples have applied a lagged dependence model to cross-time data on marital partners (e.g., Allison and Liker 1982; Gottman 1980; Wampold 1984). In this model, one partner's influence on the other is measured by the extent to which one partner's Time 1 response helps predict the Time 1 to Time 2 change in the other's. This model is appropriate when repeated observations on each partner are made over closely spaced time intervals. But when a long time elapses between panel waves, as with our data, a model of simultaneous and reciprocal influence is preferable. On this issue see Hanushek and Jackson (1977, chapter 9).

11. That given, it is also the case that by excluding such variables we would face the risk of biasing the reciprocal influence coefficients. Spurious similarity in the attitude change of each partner might arise if each partner experiences similar changes in religiosity, for example.

12. We think of change in ideological outlook as summarizing unmodeled experiences that serve to instigate change in the specific attitudes we are examining in these models. The actual variable employed is change in liberal/conservative identification from Time 1 to Time 2 for all analyses except those explaining religiosity (where no ideological outlook predictor was used), vote choice (where both change in ideology and change in party identification were used), and liberal/conservative identification itself (where change in party identification was used). Although the causal flows between ideology and some of dependent variables may be reciprocal, we are much less worried about this than about insuring that the spousal influence coefficients are not inflated by excluding important predictors of change.

13. Specifically, we include three dummy variables: the wife is working in both Time 1 (T1) and Time 2 (T2); the wife moves into the workforce between T1 and T2; the wife moves out of the workforce between T1 and T2. Cases where the wife is out of the workforce at both T1 and T2 form the baseline category. We only include change in workforce participation for the wives because such changes were very rare among the husbands.

14. Other work on social-influence processes in politics, including some work on husbands and wives, has used characteristics of one partner to predict change in the other partner's views. Kenny (1994), for example, explains change in vote preference over time by taking into account the spouse's party identification. Such models try to account for change in only one partner's position; the process is not modeled as one that may involve mutual influence. Furthermore, the spouse attribute serving as an explanatory variable is treated as static. The model we employ overcomes both of these limitations.

15. The models are estimated using the structural equation modeling program known as AMOS. Full-information maximum-likelihood estimation has desirable statistical properties, particularly when one is working with samples that have missing-data limitations (Arbuckle and Wothke 1999). Because so many variables are involved in our models, this is particularly important. In the two-wave models, we allow the following correlations: (1) between the husband's and the wife's error terms; (2) between the husband's and the wife's education, religiosity, ideology, and/or party identification (when included as explanatory variables), political engagement, T1–T2 change in religiosity, T1–T2 change in ideology, and/or T1–T2 change in party identification; (3) between each pair of T1 and T1–T2 change variables (e.g., between T1 education and T1–T2 change in education); and (4) between the lagged dependent variable (measured at T1) and ideology and/or party identification as measured at T1.

16. Although the dependent variables in our model are T2 scores, not T1–T2 change scores, this is a model of change between T1 and T2 by virtue of the fact that the T1 score is included as a predictor. If a change-score dependent variable is instead used, then as long as the T1 score is still included as a predictor (as it must be, to account for floor and ceiling effects) only the coefficient on the T1 variable would change; the T1 variable is now predicting T1–T2 change whereas before it was predicting the T2 level.

17. If marital mortality plays this role, then over-time increases should be less visible in the analysis of the three-wave panel pairs because cases of marital failure are, by definition, not included. This turns out to be the case (results not shown), thereby providing indirect evidence in support of the compositional explanation.

18. We are inclined to take seriously any difference with a p-value less than .10, rather than the conventional .05 or less, because of the low statistical power of these analyses—low both because of the small Ns we are working with and because of the inefficiencies entailed when estimating reciprocal effects.

19. For a similar conclusion found among Australian couples but based on cross-sectional data, see Hays and Bean 1992, 1994. See also Miller, Wilfor, and Donoghue 1999.

20. The "unmarried" group includes sixty-two people who were never married across the period and twenty who were unmarried at each wave but experienced a very brief marriage or cohabitation with a partner at one point in their lives.

21. Although these crucial markers are constants across the two groups, there could be politically relevant selection effects accompanying their contemporary marital status. We address this further below.

22. Each analysis, save that for 2000, combines cases from the presidential study for the year named in the table and the midterm study that follows. For example, the 1956 results combine data from the 1956 and 1958 election study. This was done to increase the sample size for the "never married" group.

23. One might expect the gender gap to be larger among the young than among the old, and the "never married" tend to be much younger than the married. So perhaps the marital status differences in Figure 3.3 reflect age differences. To assess this rival interpretation of the results in Figure 3.3, we build a regression model that includes sex, age, marital status (married versus never married), all the two-way interaction terms, and the three-way interaction term. This specification allows the gender gap to vary by age as well as by marital status. We then compare the predicted gender gap among single and married folks, holding age constant. These results, available upon request, continue to show an attenuated gender gap among the married, relative to the single. Hence, the findings in Figure 3.3 are not an artifact of the age differences between the "never married" and married groups.

24. The separate National Election Study results for single women, single men, married women, and married men are available upon request.

Chapter 4: Do Couples Support the Same Political Parties?

Acknowledgments: Our thanks go to Rachel Friedberg, Robert Huckfeldt, Kent Jennings, Paul Johnson, Gary King, Ulrich Kohler, Jeffrey Levine, Laura Stoker, and Ezra Zuckerman for very helpful comments on various parts of this chapter. We remain responsible for the analysis and argument.

1. Because we describe the data sets in Zuckerman, Dasović, Fitzgerald, and Brynin (2002), here we present only their utility for the study of couples. Full descriptions of the surveys may be obtained from the websites of the surveys' home institutions, the Institute for Social and Economic Research at the University of Essex and Das Deutsche Institut für Wirtschaftsforschung (DIW Berlin). For the BHPS access www://iser.essex.ac.uk, and for the GSOEP in English go to www.diw.de/english/soep/index.html. We thank both institutions for making the data available; they bear no responsibility for our analyses. Many sociologists and economists have used these surveys. For examples of work by political scientists, see Johnston and Pattie (2000), Kohler (Chapter 6), Kotler-Berkowitz (2001), Sanders and Brynin (1999), Schmitt-Beck, Weick, and Christoph (2002), and Zuckerman and Kotler-Berkowitz (1998).

2. In this analysis, we examine only West Germans because only they are present for all waves of the survey. We do not include immigrants and foreigners so as to focus the analysis on persons with full voting rights, who are most likely to develop views about the political parties.

3. For reasons of technical convenience, we omit couples who leave or enter during the years of the survey, as well as those who divorce or suffer a death. We have compared the distributions of several variables among the different samples and found no significant differences. Still, the couples we analyze are more likely to offer stable and consistent responses. Hence, the location of change and inconsistent responses carries even more analytical weight.

4. This question closely resembles the one used in the German national election and other political surveys, and the marginal results match these data as well (see Green, Palmquist, and Schickler 2002, 164–203; Schickler and Green 1997, 463; and Zelle 1998, 70).

5. Most traditional measures contain wording like the following: "Generally speaking do you think of yourself as an X, Y, or Z?" where the letters indicate the names of particular political parties. This question implies identification and contributes a specific answer to the question, thereby prompting a response.

6. In both countries, examining whether both choose "no party" increases the rate of similarity, to 60 percent in Britain and 67 percent in Germany. Because explanations of picking "no party" differ from those for the selection of one of the major parties, we confine this analysis to partisan choice. In order to save space and maintain a consistent analytical focus, we examine the choice of major parties: the Conservatives and Labour in Britain, and the Christian Democratic Union/Christian Social Union (CDU/CSU) in Germany. Relatively few choose one of the smaller parties in any one year. Note as well that Huckfeldt, Johnson, and Sprague (in this volume) report that 60 percent of the dyads in the 2000 U.S. National Election Study hold the same political preference.

7. Consider a set of persons defined by social class, religion, or household membership. This measure assesses the fraction of time that they choose the same party, given the opportunities to make that choice. The BHPS provide ten opportunities, and the GSOEP offers fourteen. In order to answer these questions, we leave the couples' sample to examine all persons who were interviewed in all the waves of the two surveys.

8. We place each choice on a scale, where a Conservative (or CDU/CSU) selection is scored as $+1$, no party or another party is 0, and the Labour (or the SPD) is -1. These are more accurately taken to be ordinal, not interval, scales. Hardly any couples ever choose both of the major parties, and almost all pick two adjacent choices, $+1$ and 0 or -1 and 0. As a result, the ICC scores probably inflate the level of similarity.

9. This technique displays the responses for each year as a column in a table that includes all years. We labeled the parties as follows: in Britain, L = Labour, C = Conservatives; in Germany, S = Social Democrats, C = Christian Democrats/Socials; and in both O = Other, and N = None. Because there are so many unique paths, the results cover many pages, and so we provide only summary descriptions.

10. For the appropriate citations and a review of the literature, see Chapter 1 in this volume.

11. Here, too, see the Preface and Chapter 1 to this volume, as well as Kotler-Berkowitz's and Levine's chapters, for a discussion of the relevant literature.

12. In Zuckerman, Dasović, Fitzgerald, and Brynin (2002), we explore multiple measures of social class: Goldthorpe measure of occupation, various categories of education, as well as social class identification and membership in a trade union. The results of that analysis support our decision to simplify this presentation by looking at only two measures of social class: union membership in both countries and class identification in Britain. Problems associated with multicollinearity require that we exclude from the same analysis measures of the different social classes and religions.

13. For an early effort to address the issue of interactions between husbands and wives, see Duncan and Duncan 1978; and see also Stoker and Jennings's chapter in this volume for a full discussion. As another test of our claims, we also examined models in which the partner's class and religious identification substitute for partisanship. We found that these too have a strong impact on the respondent's partisan selection.

14. Please note that because of problems of multicollinearity, we specified separate models for the partner's partisanship: one in which the partner chose the party defined as the dependent variable in the previous year, or he or she picked no party; and another for

the case in which the partner selected the opposing major political party. All the tables are available from the authors.

15. This finding implies that the extent to which political influence between members of dyads is autoregressive depends on the nature of the relationship, a point that elaborates on Huckfeldt, Johnson, and Sprague, in this volume.

16. This applies as well among persons who run their own businesses. Writing in the Wall Street Journal, Breeden (2002) addresses the question of whom they are most likely "to rely on in a critical decision." Fifty-six percent select a family member, most often their spouse. Business partners account for 16 percent of their preferred sources of advice, and professionals 14 percent. Here too the exchange of explicit advice and cues between spouses is the modal form of influence.

CHAPTER 5: FAMILY TIES

1. Our emphasis, it ought to be noted, is on the family of origin and the process by which children are influenced in ways that affect their political activity and attitudes when they are adults. Families also have a more contemporaneous influence on adult members, as Stoker and Jennings (in this volume) show. On political socialization in general, and the role of the family in particular, see, among others, Beck and Jennings (1991); Davies (1970); Dawson and Prewitt (1969, especially chapter 7); Easton and Dennis (1969); Greenstein (1965, especially chapter 5); Hess and Torney (1967, especially chapters 5 and 7); Jaros (1973, especially chapter 4); Jennings and Niemi (1974, especially parts 1, 2, and 5); Jennings and Niemi (1981); Jennings and Stoker (2001); and Jennings, Stoker, and Bowers (1999). For reviews of the literature, see Beck (1979), Cook (1985), and Dennis (1968), as well as Jennings's (2000) thoughtful assessment of the long series of political-socialization studies that he and his associates have conducted.

2. The assumption behind the Interpersonal Transfer Model is that certain aspects of family dynamics—for example, the autonomy permitted to children, the relative emphasis placed on obedience, and the encouragement of discussion of controversial matters—have implications for the political life of future citizens. While this assumption is surely plausible, it has received very little in the way of direct empirical confirmation. For a rare test, see Chaffee, McLeod, and Wackman (1973).

3. In his literature review, Beck (1977, 122–27) concludes that, except in the case of partisan identification, parents' ability to influence their children's political choices is notably weak.

4. Related to these themes is Greenstein's (1965, 89–94) emphasis upon the advantages enjoyed by children from backgrounds of higher socioeconomic status with respect to IQ, intellectual skills, and academic achievement. However, Greenstein compares children stratified by SES, not by IQ or academic accomplishment.

5. On the intergenerational transmission of SES, see, for example, Blau and Duncan (1967); Hauser and Featherman (1977); Hout (1988); Ganzeboom, Treiman, and Ultee (1991); Solon (1992); Corcoran (1995); McMurrer and Sawhill (1998); and Smelser, Wilson, and Mitchell (1999). Nevertheless, as demonstrated by SES differences between adult siblings, the transmission of socioeconomic status from parent to child is far from assured.

6. Among the analyses of political activity that demonstrate the connection between SES and political activity are Verba and Nie (1972), Wolfinger and Rosenstone (1980), and Rosenstone and Hansen (1993). In spite of its unambiguous empirical power, the "SES Model of Participation" is commonly derided as simplistic, apolitical, and atheoretical. See Leighley (1995, 183–88) for a trenchant summary of the criticisms of the SES model. For a more theoretical presentation that explains the linkage between socioeconomic status and

activity and presents an empirical specification of the participatory consequences of education, see Verba, Schlozman, and Brady (1995, part 3).

7. On the Civic Voluntarism Model, see Verba, Schlozman, and Brady (1995); and Burns, Schlozman, and Verba (2001).

8. An additional reason for paying special attention to education is that we have better measures of parental education than of the other socioeconomic characteristics of the family of origin.

9. We use data from the Citizen Participation Study, which was conducted in 1990. For wording of all questions and information about the survey, including the oversamples of Latinos, African Americans, and those who are active in politics, and the characteristics that allow it to be treated as a national random sample, see Verba, Schlozman, and Brady (1995, appendixes A and B). These data turn upside down the usual problem with socialization studies. Ordinarily, compelling information about youthful experiences cannot be linked to adult politics. We have rich information about the lives, especially the political lives, of our respondents but are forced to rely on weaker, retrospective data about their pre-adult experiences. Because it would be preferable to have longitudinal panel data following individuals over the life cycle, we considered using the Jennings, Niemi, and Stoker data, which have the unambiguous advantage of representing multiple studies of the same individuals over time. However, the oversamples of Latinos and African Americans in the Citizen Participation sample and the measures of civic skills and recruitment in the questionnaire make these data more appropriate for the questions we ask here. See Appendix A for an explanation of why we believe that the retrospective descriptions of family patterns have a good deal of verisimilitude.

10. The division into quartiles is based on the average of both parents' educational attainment as reported by respondents. Because aggregate educational levels have risen dramatically in recent generations, education attainment is deeply influenced by birth cohort. Therefore, here and elsewhere, we have corrected the measure of parents' actual education for age by calculating the average parental education for each age group in our sample and then dividing actual parental education (as reported by the individual respondent) by the average parental education for respondents of the same age. The resultant variable measures the relationship of the respondents' parents' education to the average educational level at the time. Thus, the assignment into quartiles reflects both the average of mother's and father's education and the educational distribution in the parental age cohort.

11. The activity scale for respondents is an eight-point summary measure that includes the following political acts: voting; working in a campaign; contributing to a campaign; contacting a public official; taking part in a protest, march, or demonstration; being affiliated with an organization that takes stands on political matters; being active in the local community; and serving as a volunteer on a local board or attending meetings of such a board on a regular basis.

12. Verba, Schlozman, and Brady (1995, chapter 15) contains an analysis that has affinities to the data presented in Tables 5.1–5.3. However, those data were presented in the service of a quite different set of intellectual questions and were placed in a very different context.

13. In the regressions in Table 5.1, and in all analogous data analyses, the variables have been rescaled to vary from 0 to 1. In addition, all regressions contain controls for the respondent's race or ethnicity, gender, and age.

14. Definitions of these variables can be found in Appendix B.

15. As we have done elsewhere, we standardize the measure of overall participation to vary between 0 to 1. However, political contributions are measured in the number of dollars given.

16. We also replicated this analysis including a variable that measured participation in high school activities (student government and other clubs and activities, but not high

school sports). Not surprisingly, it is related to SES and to future educational attainment. Taking part in high school activities is a significant predictor of both overall political activity and contributions when added at Step 2, although the magnitude of the coefficient is smaller than for the respondent's education. With all the variables in the full model in Step 4, high school activity remains significant for overall activity; however, it is positive, but insignificant, for contributions. All other relationships shown in Table 5.3 are undisturbed. Because we are unsure whether high school activity is a measure of some underlying predisposition to volunteer or an alternate measure of civic skills developed in nonpolitical activity, we have not included it in our analysis.

17. In measuring strength of partisanship, a strong Republican and a strong Democrat have the same score and the direction of partisanship is lost.

18. We conducted a parallel analysis of the impact of parental religiosity on the respondent's financial contributions to religious institutions, with results that mirror those for political contributions. Once again, the single most powerful predictor of the *amount* contributed to religious institutions is family income. When it comes to the *proportion* of all contributions that is targeted at religious institutions—a measure that is, by definition, inversely related to the proportion allocated to politics—parental religious attendance is a significant predictor that retains its significance even when the analysis includes a measure of how important religion is to the respondent. The importance of religion to the respondent is, not surprisingly, the single strongest predictor of the percentage of total contributions that flow to religious institutions.

19. On this theme, see Verba, Nie, and Kim (1978).

20. For the groundbreaking statement of generational theory, see Karl Mannheim's essay "The Problem of Generations," in Mannheim (1952).

21. In Figure 5.3, we define the civil rights generation as African Americans who were sixteen years old during the Kennedy, Johnson, or Nixon administrations (1961–74). We experimented with alternative definitions, beginning as early as the *Brown* decision (1954) and ending as early as the assassination of Martin Luther King, Jr. (1968). These alternatives produced minor variations, but no real change, in the result report in Figure 5.3.

22. Even within this group, however, the stratifying impact of education is manifest. Among African-Americans who were adolescents during the civil rights era, those whose parents were more highly educated were more likely to report having been brought up in a politically stimulating home than those whose parents were less well educated. For the two groups, the scores on the political stimulation scale are .31 and .24 respectively. However, for both groups, these scores are higher than the scores for their counterparts in other cohorts.

23. In order to have enough cases of African Americans from the civil rights generation for analysis, we use the Screener data from the Citizen Participation Study, which had a truncated questionnaire. Therefore, we do not have access to the range of participatory factors used in earlier models predicting participation. We replicated the data analysis using separate equations for Anglo white and African American respondents with the same results.

24. Our findings are supported by Jennings and Niemi (1981, 316–18), who found extraordinarily high rates of political activity for nonwhite college students during the 1965–73 period.

CHAPTER 6: CHANGING CLASS LOCATIONS AND PARTISAN CHOICE IN GERMANY

This chapter is based on a paper presented at the twenty-third biennial conference of the Society for Multivariate Analysis in the Behavioral Sciences (SMABS), July 1–3, 2002, Tilburg, The Netherlands. Thanks to Josef Brüderl, Frauke Kreuter, Walter Müller, and

Reinhard Pollak for useful comments, and to Jennifer Fitzgerald and Alan S. Zuckerman for comments and editorial assistance. Thanks to the SMABS for letting me present this paper and for useful comments.

1. A related data set is the British Household Panel Survey (BHPS). For a discussion of its features, see Zuckerman, Fitzgerald, and Dasović, in this volume.

2. See also Haisken-De New and Frick (1998), which is downloadable from the web site of DIW-The German Institute for Economic Research, http://www.diw.de/english/soep/.

3. The term "unbalanced panel design" refers to data that are used for all respondents who are interviewed at least once.

4. Exclusion of respondents from the former GDR has been done via the variable for the actual sampling region (qsampreg). As a result, almost all respondents socialized in the former GDR or living with such a person are excluded and only those who move together with a respondent from the sampling region West Germany remain. Foreign workers who do not have the right to vote are also excluded from the sample, although a handful of them remain as well.

5. See Long (1997) for a description of these measurements.

6. Weighting is necessary due to the complex survey design of the GSOEP.

7. A model for cross-sectional data calculated for comparison reasons (see below) has a pseudo R2 of about .08

8. Another way to assess the model is to look at the significance level. Using the traditional method of significance testing, most of the coefficients presented in this chapter are significant. However, the traditional approach to significance testing is not valid for GSOEP data. In the analysis I have therefore applied the random group-variance estimator proposed by Wolter (1985). This procedure leads to a much more conservative estimation of standard errors, yielding many insignificant effects in the model above as well as in all other models. However, throughout this analysis I discuss the coefficients along with their theoretically expected direction instead of testing for significance. In any case, the Stata do-files used to calculate the standard errors for the models are downloadable from the Internet, and the Stata program to calculate the random group-variance estimator, written by myself, can be installed from inside Stata with the command "ssc install rgroup."

9. The dotted line represents the coefficients of usual logit models for each of the two different dependent variables on the following independent variables: class position, occupational category, education, vocational training, marital status, children, gender, year of birth, country, year of observation. The data for those models are the same as for the fixed-effects model, except that a random observation for each respondent is drawn. Clearly, the between-respondent model cannot be entirely the same as the fixed-effects model since the latter controls for time-invariate variables by definition. The nuts and bolts of the between-respondent model can be studied in the Stata do-file crbe.do.

10. Some respondents are lost due to missing values in the variable for political interest.

Chapter 7: Choosing Alone?

1. Respondents were first asked, "Looking back over the last six months, I'd like to know the people you talked with about matters that are important to you. Can you think of anyone?" Once the respondent provided four names or could offer no more names, a follow-up question was asked: "Aside from anyone you have already mentioned, who is the person you talked with most about the events of the recent presidential election campaign?" This study is one part of a five-nation comparative effort undertaken in Britain, Germany, Japan, Spain, and the United States during the early 1990s. The Amerian study was conducted using computer-assisted telephone interviewing by the Polimetrics Laboratory at Ohio State University and the Center for Survey Research at Indiana University.

2. That only a portion of discussants named were ultimately interviewed can be attributed to the reluctance of about 50 percent of main respondents to provide contact information for their named discussants. As Appendix B indicates, respondents who were most interested in politics and more partisan were particularly willing to release contact information.

3. Several points must be made about this analysis. First, although only logit results are presented here, similar results were obtained when the models were estimated using probit. Second, these results hold even when a variety of other variables are included as controls (e.g., discussant opinion on various issues). Third, although the analysis is based on a sample of all network members who are not married to the main respondent, the results hold when the sample consists of various subsets of this population (i.e., those network members who are and are not related to the main respondent).

4. Although some may argue that several other attitudinal and social-group variables (e.g., opinions on affirmative action; race) should have been included in the final models, preliminary analyses indicated that the substantive findings changed very little when such variables were included. Thus, in order to maintain a fairly large N, only the most significant variables were included in the final model. See Appendix D for coding and wording of the variables.

5. For this strategy, the discussant candidate instrument is calculated first by running a logistic regression of main-respondent candidate choice on various predictors of main-respondent candidate choice. Then, another logistic regression is run, this time with discussant candidate choice as the dependent variable and several discussant variables, variables that are weighted with the coefficients obtained in the first step, as the explanatory variables. The end product of these two steps is a discussant candidate instrument that is the estimated probability of support for a candidate for each discussant that is detached from the effects of the main respondent's influence. This instrument is then inserted as an explanatory variable into a final logit model, with main-respondent candidate choice as the dependent variable.

6. The models are estimated using LIMDEP (7.0) (Greene 1995, 664).

7. The models are estimated using Stata 4.0. A two-stage probit model was also estimated, but the pattern of results was very similar. Given the greater ease with which logit results can be interpreted, therefore, only the two-stage logit bootstrap results are presented.

8. The models are estimated using SYSTAT 5.0.

9. The percentage change in the odds is calculated in the following manner: percentage change = (factor change in odds − 1)(100).

10. Since, as Table 7.2 demonstrates, the various ways of estimating the impact of networks on choice produce similar patterns of results, the results of only one method are presented for the remainder of the analysis: Huckfeldt and Sprague's (1991) modified two-stage logit procedure.

11. Support for Ross Perot, however, is another matter. Analyses demonstrate that discussants have only a small impact on main-respondent Perot support. Indeed, nonmarried network members exert an influence on main-respondent Perot preference that only reaches significance at the .1 level, while nonrelative discussants do not have a statistically significant influence on main-respondent Perot choice. More detailed findings can be provided upon request.

12. In several contexts, scholars have found that intimate family members as well as friends exert a strong influence on political choice, one often rivaling that of more casual acquaintances (e.g., Berelson et al. 1954; Katz and Lazarsfeld 1955; Lazarsfeld et al. 1944).

13. For wording and coding of variables, see Appendix E.

14. Accuracy of perception, as measured here, is whether the main respondent accurately names the vote choice of his/her network members in the 1984 presidential election.

15. Although the analyses presented here are conducted using the 1984 South Bend Study, it is important to note that these results hold when similar analyses are run using the

1996 Political Network Study, a survey of St. Louis and Indianapolis residents, thus lending even greater credibility to the results.

16. A number of factors have been found to correlate with the various dependent variables of interest (i.e., partisanship, abortion, school prayer, women's rights, government aid for minorities, and economic trade barriers) (Abramowitz 1995; Alvarez and Brehm, 1995; Alvarez and Nagler 1995; Dalton and Wattenberg 1993; Franklin and Kosaki 1989; Kenny 1993b; Page and Shapiro 1992; Plutzer 1988; Stanley and Niemi 1991). The explanatory variables included in the analyses are gathered from this literature. See Appendix G for wording and coding of the variables.

17. These data have been described elsewhere (Huckfeldt and Sprague 1995; Huckfeldt et al. 1999) and so will be described only briefly here. The 1984 South Bend Study is a three-wave election study of approximately 1,500 South Bend area residents and a one-stage snowball survey of 900 of their discussion partners. The snowball sample was obtained during the post-election portion of the survey, when respondents were asked to provide information regarding three discussants whom "they talked with most about the events of the past year," including their last names and street addresses. The 1996 Political Network Study was conducted over a ten-month period beginning in late February 1996 and ending in early January 1997. Similar to the South Bend Study, this study included two separate samples: the main respondents ($N = 2,174$) and a one-stage snowball sample of the main respondents' discussion partners ($N = 1,475$). Respondents in the 1996 study, however, were asked to provide information on up to five discussion partners.

18. It is important to note that the coefficients of the control variables in each of the models are all in the expected direction.

19. It is important to note that, consistent with Huckfeldt and Sprague's (1991) findings, these results also held when the analyses were conducted only for discussion pairs in which the discussant's vote choice was accurately perceived.

20. Frequency of interaction, as measured here, is the amount of time main respondents report talking about politics with their discussants (see Appendix E for coding).

21. The exception, of course, is partisanship in 1992. In this case, increased frequency of contact does significantly increase the likelihood that discussant partisanship will affect main respondent partisanship. An explanation for why partisanship is the only opinion that exhibits this effect is beyond the scope of this chapter, but the fact that none of the other opinions has the effect allows me to conclude that frequency of contact, in general, does not have an impact on social influence.

CHAPTER 8: FRIENDS AND POLITICS

1. Also see Lin in this volume. For other analyses linking social contexts and networks to political behavior, see Huckfeldt (1979) and Giles and Dantico (1982) on neighborhood contexts; Kenny (1992, 1993a) and Knoke (1990a) on political discussants; and Zuckerman and Kotler-Berkowitz (1998) and Verba, Schlozman, and Burns, in this volume, on family and household members.

2. Verba, Schlozman, and Brady (1995, chapter 5) provide empirical evidence showing that family members as well as friends are an important source of political recruitment.

3. See Nie, Junn, and Stehlik-Barry (1996) for an alternative causal argument: that citizens, especially those with high levels of education, take advantage of their access to social and political elites in order to protect their political interests through participation.

4. Verba, Schlozman, and Burns's analysis in this volume examines how both family socioeconomic resources and the political environment of the family household independently influence the intergenerational transmission of political participation.

5. See Leighley 1995 for a critique of theoretical efforts to connect socioeconomic resources and participation and an effort to develop an alternative mobilization model.

6. Education and organizational participation have often been conceptualized as competing explanations of political activity, and are presented here as alternative explanations to social and political networks for conceptual and empirical clarity. In contrast, Nie, Junn, and Stehlik-Barry (1996) present a causal model and empirical path analysis with education as the master variable, the first source of a causal chain that works through occupational status, family income, nonpolitical participation, and proximity to central social and political networks to promote political participation.

7. Leighley and Vedlitz (1999) refer conceptually to social connectedness rather than social stability but use the same empirical indicators.

8. The Social Capital Benchmark Study 2000 was sponsored by the Saguaro Seminar at the John F. Kennedy School of Government, Harvard University. The study's field phase was conducted by TNS Intersearch. The data file and study documentation, which contain information about the study's methodology, are publicly available through the Internet from the Roper Center for Public Opinion Research (http://www.ropercenter.uconn.edu/). None of the organizations associated with the study design, data collection, or data distribution bears any responsibility for the analysis reported here.

9. The scale was submitted to a reliability analysis, with a resulting standardized Cronbach's alpha of .64.

10. Initially, consideration was given to including electoral participation as part of the dependent variable. However, in a factor analysis of seven variables, the five nonelectoral measures loaded together on one factor, while two electoral measures—vote turnout in 1996 and current voter registration—loaded separately on another factor. In addition, voter turnout referred to the 1996 election, an event that occurred four years prior to the respondents' current characteristics that were used to construct independent variables. As a result, only a scale of nonelectoral participation is utilized in this analysis. For a theoretical discussion of the distinction between voting and other forms of political participation, see Verba, Schlozman, and Brady 1995, especially chapters 2 and 6.

11. Cronbach's alpha for the scale equals .73.

12. Though the indicator of community leader does not specify or imply a particular social group, as the other indicators do, community leaders are an important component of diverse friendship networks that provide information about and recruitment into political participation.

13. "No close friends" is set to a value of 1, rather than zero, so that the variable can be used as a denominator to standardize friendship diversity.

14. Non-Hispanic whites, mainline Protestants, and males are the respective reference categories.

15. A total of 284 respondents who were not part of the ethnic and religious groups referenced by the dummy variables, or could not be classified as either working or middle class as described above, were excluded from the multivariate analysis.

16. For a nominal, multi-category dependent variable with response categories 1, 2, . . . , n, the probability of nonreference category 1 occurring, relative to all other categories, is equal to:

$$\exp(xB_1)/[1 + \exp(xB_1) + \exp(xB_2) + \ldots \exp(xB_n)],$$

where exp is the exponential function, x is the set of all independent variables, and B_1, B_2, . . ., B_n are the set of regression coefficients for the explanatory variables corresponding to the dependent response categories. The probability of the reference category is equal to $1/[1 + \exp(xB_1) + \exp(xB_2) + \ldots \exp(xB_n)]$.

17. The exception is employment status, held constant at currently working, a nonreference category.

CHAPTER 9: NETWORKS, GENDER, AND THE USE OF STATE AUTHORITY

Acknowledgments: The data collection and analysis for this chapter were made possible by the University of Michigan Rackham Graduate School and the University of Michigan Institute for Research on Women and Gender. I am also grateful to the Russell Sage Foundation for the year I spent as a Visiting Scholar, 1999–2000. Amaney Jamal and I collaborated on the data collection. All conclusions expressed in the chapter are my own and should not be attributed to Amaney Jamal, the University of Michigan, or the Russell Sage Foundation.

1. In order to protect our interviewees' privacy, all names are pseudonyms and some identifying details have been changed. Amaney Jamal and Ann Chih Lin conducted all of the interviews, in Arabic or English as the respondent preferred. Interviews were conducted privately, in person, at locations the respondents chose. They lasted between one and two hours and followed a structured, open-ended questionnaire. Ann Chih Lin is solely responsible for the interpretation and analysis of the interview data.

2. Calculations are available from the author.

3. This raises the possibility that men simply find it easier to identify with authority than women—unsurprising, given the gendered nature of political authority and its representatives. This is an intriguing explanation, but it loses some force given that, in answer to another question in this battery, men and women were equally likely to condemn police behavior in the Middle East. It is not just authority, but American authority, with which these men are casting their lot. Thus it seems more likely that their identification with American law is tied to their efforts to make a place for themselves in American society.

4. The role of personal experience is a complicated question that I can only touch upon here. But it is interesting that reports of personal experience with discrimination fall into three non-overlapping categories. Among those who saw police actions as ethnic harassment and said that it should be protested, 35 percent reported that the police had mistreated them or someone they knew. Like Ikhlas, they spoke of the experience in terms of righteous indignation, and that indignation seemed to empower them. Interestingly, however, they did not report being vindicated when they complained, so it was not the experience of victory that created empowerment. Twenty-seven percent of those who identified with the police also reported personal experiences. Their stories, however, were all about good treatment. Faruq, for example, mentioned how friendly the police were when they stopped him to let him know that his taillight was broken. Finally, there are the stories of mistreatment told by those who fear the police. Here it is interesting that a conviction that one should complain coexists with a fear of complaining. It is not clear whether people are selectively remembering experiences that fit their preferred identification or whether those experiences "caused" their beliefs.

CHAPTER 10: PUTTING VOTERS IN THEIR PLACES

1. Scotland was omitted from the study because of difficulties in compiling the data sets.

2. For this reason, governments seek to convince voters that they are improving services in their local areas, even if this means manipulating data to show that "everything is getting better, everywhere" (Dorling et al. 2002).

3. This project was funded by the U.K. Economic and Social Research Council (Grant R000222649) and involved Danny Dorling, David Rossiter, Ian MacAllister, and Helena Tunstall as well as the current authors.

4. The class schema used is that devised by Goldthorpe and modified by Heath. It is widely applied in British voting studies.

5. By using two standard deviations around the mean as the limits for the horizontal axes in these graphs, we incorporate 95 percent of all neighborhood observations.

6. This apparently counterfactual finding was typical of the 1992 and 2001 elections as well.

7. Not surprisingly, those who have an owner-occupied home are more likely to live in areas with high levels of owner occupancy, one of the variables that loads heavily on the first component.

8. The lack of a relationship with the age-structure component sustains the earlier argument regarding age and voting Conservative.

9. Recently, the validity of some of these studies has been challenged because they have not taken into account the likelihood of endogeneity—that is, people's perceptions of a government's economic performance are likely to be influenced by whether they voted for it (Evans and Andersen 2001).

CHAPTER 11: PARTY IDENTIFICATION, LOCAL PARTISAN CONTEXTS, AND THE ACQUISITION OF PARTICIPATORY ATTITUDES

1. With respect to the important matter of external validity, we are more cautious. On one hand, external-validity concerns can never be resolved in any firm, conclusive way, given that generalization always involves extrapolating to a realm not represented in one's survey (Campbell and Stanley 1963, 17). On the other hand, believing that nature exhibits order and regularity, we make comparisons with the findings of researchers working with previous generations of adolescents. We do not claim that our results will stand as truth for all generations. Nor do we assume that our findings neatly generalize to all other geographic settings, even within the current time frame. But one of the great values of this study is that it represents the views of adolescents in geographic settings and a temporal context that have not been widely studied. We think that our work presents some useful findings and is clearly replicable, even if unrepresentative of other settings. Ultimately, however, it is the return of similar or dissimilar findings from related research that will yield a definitive judgment on the important external-validity issue (Campbell and Stanley 1963).

CHAPTER 12: MACRO-POLITICS AND MICRO-BEHAVIOR

Acknowledgments: An earlier version of this chapter was presented at the annual meeting of the American Political Science Association, Boston, Mass., August 29–September 1, 2002. We are grateful to Kay Schlozman and Alan Zuckerman for their comments. We also thank Michael McDonald for providing the Comparative Manifestos Project (CMP) and electoral data used in the analysis. This research was supported by National Science Foundation grant SES-9818525 to Chris Anderson. The survey data are available as the Inter-university Consortium for Political and Social Research (ICPSR) Study no. 2790. The original collector of the data, ICPSR, and the relevant funding agency bear no responsibility for uses of this collection or for interpretations or inferences based upon such uses. The data were analyzed with the MLwiN, version 1.10, statistical software.

1. Several studies have pointed to the importance of considering political discussion as a crucial variable in connection with electoral behavior (e.g., Zuckerman, Valentino, and Zuckerman 1994).

2. A major exception is the literature on the spiral of silence, first advocated by Noelle-Neumann (1974, 1993). This theory suggests that people are less likely to express their political views as they perceive themselves to occupy a more extreme minority position in the population. While there appears to be a relationship between the degree to which a person believes others hold similar opinions and the willingness to express one's own opinions, a meta-analysis of the existing evidence reports that support of the theory is weak

at best (Glynn, Hayes, and Shanahan 1997). It also is unclear what dimension of majority beliefs—issue attitudes, support for the government—is most relevant for inhibiting
political discussion.

3. This assumes that the space of political contestation is single peaked and normally
distributed; this turns out to be the case in most democracies and all countries included in
our study.

4. This is consistent with Noelle-Neumann's argument that the hard core are "not prepared to conform, to change their opinions, or even be silent in the face of public opinion"
(Noelle-Neumann 1974, 48). As a result, individuals with extreme beliefs should not be
influenced by the prevailing climate of opinion in the same way that other individuals are.
(See also Glynn and McLeod 1984.)

5. These may but do not have to coincide. That is, the median voter may or may not be
represented in the government.

6. The idea that the macro-political environment, conceptualized in the form of the
left-right continuum, matters to political discussions among democratic mass publics
presumes that individuals think of themselves and their political environment in terms
of left and right. While this may be a safe assumption, in light of the empirical literature
on the topic, our approach further assumes that people are aware of their own location
relative to the wider political community. Whether this is indeed the case is, in the end,
an empirical question. However, we believe it to be a reasonable assumption, given that
information about national politics is likely to be available through a variety of channels,
including mass media.

7. In contrast to networks, contexts are structurally imposed rather than individually constructed (Huckfeldt and Sprague 1995).

8. It should be noted, however, that political heterogeneity may encourage political discussions only when diverse attitudes are evenly balanced in a society (MacKuen 1990). The
emergence of asymmetry may easily result in a "silenced majority" (Glynn and McLeod
1984; Noelle-Neumann 1974, 1977). In other words, a skewed political balance tends to
produce false social consensus and may discourage those who believe they are in a minority from political conversations, even when others are willing to encounter contrary views
(MacKuen 1990, 84–85).

9. In the German case, the data were drawn only from the population of West Germany,
which, at the time of the survey, was still a separate state.

10. The national differences reported in Figure 12.1 may be surprising in light of
national stereotypes. Generally speaking, northern Europeans tend to talk about politics
more frequently with their friends than southern Europeans, for example (with the exception of Greece; see Topf 1995, 62). It is worth noting, though, that the object of interest
here is political discussion rather than the frequency of informal conversations more generally or simply loquaciousness.

11. Because the individual variable of primary interest—distance from the median—is
constructed on the basis of the left-right self-placement scale, we also control for respondents' left-right placement to ensure that the effect of distance from the median variable is
not driven by the average left-right placement in each country.

12. It is, of course, possible that better educated people simply claim to speak about
politics more frequently than other people, without actually doing so.

13. Please note that we thus do not have direct measures of immediate social contexts,
but we include organizational memberships, which can be seen as an indirect measure.

14. These policy categories include external-relations categories (e.g., anti-imperialism), freedom and democracy categories (e.g., human rights), political-system categories
(e.g., governmental and administrative efficiency), economic categories (e.g., nationalization), welfare and quality-of-life categories (e.g., environmental protection), fabric-of-

society categories (e.g., multiculturalism), and social-group categories (e.g., underprivileged minority groups). For each document the data represent the percentage of all statements comprised by each category. This, in effect, standardizes the data with respect to document length, yielding a measure of party emphasis that is comparable (McDonald and Mendes 2001).

15. Additional analyses revealed that, because the data are distributed approximately normally, the standard deviation is highly correlated with other indicators that measure the nature of distributions, such as kurtosis and skewness.

16. An example may help make this clear: If we were scoring four parties and those (hypothetical) parties' positions and vote percentages were -15 and 5 percent (Party A), -10 and 40 percent (Party B), $+3$ and 8 percent (Party C), and $+12$ and 40 percent (Party D), then we would weight the party scores, sum them, and divide by the sum of the weights: $\{(-75) + (-400) + (24) + (480)\} / 93$. This would give the mean position for a country. The standard deviation calculation follows the same procedure.

17. The reason the sum of the weights in the above example is not 100 is that 7 percent of the (hypothetical) votes went to parties that the CMP did not score.

18. To be sure, given that discussion networks tend to be relatively homogeneous, the important question here is to assess the relative homogeneity of political identity from one country to another. On average, discussion networks in more heterogeneous countries should be more heterogeneous than those in more homogeneous countries.

19. We used MLwiN 1.10.0006 (2000) to estimate these models (see also Rasbash et al. 1999).

20. A way to capture variable intercepts would be to introduce a series of dummy variables for fourteen of the fifteen countries in the data set. In our case, however, this solution is impossible because of perfect multicollinearity among the macro-level variables and the set of country dummies.

21. These calculations are based on the ratios of each variance component relative to the total variance in system support (Bryk and Raudenbush 1992; Snijders and Bosker 1999).

22. Note also that greater macro-political heterogeneity is not synonymous with a greater number of political parties. The correlation between the two measures is negative and weak ($r = -.22$).

23. Regarding the remaining individual-level control variables, the results are largely consistent with those reported for the individual country analyses. Given the increase in the number of cases and the associated statistical power, it should not be surprising that most variables achieve statistical significance. The only major difference is the result for the age variable. While increased age is still associated with more political discussion, the relationship no longer appears to be curvilinear. That is, in the pooled analyses, we do not find evidence that political discussion tapers off with advanced age.

24. Having said this, we would add that, maybe precisely because the wider community is potentially much less threatening than one's immediate social environment, these findings are not necessarily inconsistent with the literature on the micro-environment of political discussion, although they do warrant further investigation. In the end, although we make no claims about the effects of the immediate social and political environment, our findings suggest, at the very least, that homogeneity of discussion partners and heterogeneity in the larger political community may jointly increase the frequency of political discussion.

25. Naturally, this conclusion is tempered by the fact that our sample is composed of highly stable and highly democratic countries. Whether these findings would hold in countries with only brief histories of democratic governance or where it is lacking is, of course, another empirical question.

CHAPTER 13: AGENT-BASED EXPLANATIONS FOR THE SURVIVAL OF DISAGREEMENT IN SOCIAL NETWORKS

Acknowledgments: Earlier versions of this paper were presented at the Brown University conference "Social Context of Politics," Providence, R.I., June 2–4, 2002, and at the annual meetings of the American Political Science Association, San Francisco, Calif., August 30–Sept. 2, 2001. Special thanks go to Rick Riolo of the University of Michigan, Marcus Daniels of the Santa Fe Institute, Michael Craw of the University of Indiana, and Howard Lavine of Stony Brook University.

1. The computer code and documentation for these models are available. For the latest versions, please check http://lark.cc.ukans.edu/~pauljohn/Swarm/MySwarmCode. Look for the SIM under SocialImpact and ACM under OpinionFormation.

2. The simulation model can be run interactively (with graphical displays of the grid and various conditions in the model), or it can be run as a batch mode. Interactive runs allow parameters to be adjusted "on the fly" and various on-screen displays can be used. Runs in batch mode are calibrated to assure that only changes in model design and parameters can be responsible for difference in outcomes. (The ith run of the model under one set of conditions is seeded with the same random numbers as the ith run under any other set of conditions.) As a result, any difference between two runs can be attributed to changes that occur according to the logic of the model itself.

3. In order to implement this version of the model, we have developed a general-purpose multi-agent grid called MultiGrid2d, which allows us to create containers in the grid into which many agents can be inserted and removed.

CHAPTER 14: TURNOUT IN A SMALL WORLD

Acknowledgments: I thank Robert Bates, Lars-Erik Cederman, Eric Dickson, Paul E. Johnson, Orit Kedar, Gary King, Ferran Martinez I Coma, and Ken Shepsle for valuable feedback on earlier drafts. Supporting programs can be found at the author's web site.

1. It is worth noting here that the small-world property might dramatically affect the results in Johnson and Huckfeldt (in this volume) since information tends to flow more quickly through small-world networks.

2. The term "neighbor" is not restricted to someone who is physically proximate. In the context of a social network, the term simply means someone with whom a person has a connection.

3. A wide variety of threshold models do incorporate strategic behavior, especially those used to explain spontaneous collective action like mass protests (e.g., Birchoux and Johnson 2002; Kuran 1989, 1991, 1995; Lohmann 1994). However, they do not attempt to use empirical data to generate predictions for real networks, nor do they consider the impact of changes in the network structures on the flow of information and resulting behaviors.

4. This quote raises the important point that costs and benefits may be associated with voting that explain why people imitate their acquaintances. For example, there may be a benefit to conforming with one's peers or a cost associated with lying to them. In this chapter I set aside the important question of why people imitate one another in order to focus on how imitation affects aggregate turnout.

5. Figure 14.2 in Fowler and Smirnov (2002) shows that the cost-benefit threshold implied by both the signaling and pivotal motivations ranges up to about 1:13,000.

References

Abelson, Robert P. 1964. "Mathematical Models of the Distribution of Attributes under Controversy." In *Contributions to Mathematical Psychology*, ed. Norman Fredriksen and Harold Gulliksen. New York: Holt, Rinehart, and Winston.

Abelson, Robert P. 1979. "Social Clusters and Opinion Clusters." In *Perspectives on Social Network Research*, ed. Paul W. Holland and Samuel Leinhardt. New York: Academic Press.

Abramowitz, Alan I. 1995. "It's Abortion Stupid: Policy Voting in the 1992 Presidential Election." *Journal of Politics* 57:176–186.

Achen, Christopher. 1975. "Mass Political Attitudes and the Survey Response." *American Political Science Review* 69:1218–1231.

Achen, Christopher. 1986. The *Statistical Analysis of Quasi-Experiments*. Berkeley: University of California Press.

Agnew, John A. 1990. "From Political Methodology to Geographical Social Theory? A Critical Review of Electoral Geography, 1960–1987." In *Developments in Electoral Geography*, ed. Ron J. Johnston, Fred M. Shelley, and Peter J. Taylor, 15–21. London: Croom Helm.

Albert, Réka, and Albert-László Barabasi. 2002. "Statistical Mechanics of Complex Networks." *Reviews of Modern Physics* 74:1, 47–97.

Aldrich, John H. 1993. "Rational Choice and Turnout." *American Journal of Political Science* 37:246–278.

Allison, Paul D. 1994. "Using Panel Data to Estimate the Effects of Events." *Sociological Methods and Research* 23:174–199.

Allison, Paul D., and J. K. Liker. 1982. "Analyzing Sequential Categorical Data on Dyadic Interaction: A Comment on Gottman." *Psychological Bulletin* 91:2, 393–403.

Alvarez, R. Michael, and John Brehm. 1995. "American Ambivalence towards Abortion Policy: Development of a Heteroskedastic Probit Model of Competing Values." *American Journal of Political Science* 39:1055–1082.

Alvarez, R. Michael, and Jonathan Nagler. 1995. "Economics, Issues and the Perot Candidacy: Voter Choice in the 1992 Presidential Election." *American Journal of Political Science* 39:714–44.

Andersen, Kristi. 1997. "Gender and Public Opinion." In *Understanding Public Opinion*, ed. Barbara Norrander and Clyde Wilcox. Washington D.C.: CQ Press.

Anderson, Christopher J., and Christine A. Guillory. 1997. "Political Institutions and Satisfaction with Democracy: A Cross-National Analysis of Consensus and Majoritarian Systems." *American Political Science Review* 91:1, 66–82.

Anderson, Christopher J., and Andrew J. LoTempio. 2002. "Winning, Losing, and Political Trust in America." *British Journal of Political Science* 32, 335–351.

Anderson, Christopher J., and Yuliya V. Tverdova. 2001. "Winners, Losers, and Attitudes toward Government in Contemporary Democracies." *International Political Science Review* 22:4, 321–338.

Anselin, Luc. 1988. *Spatial Econometrics: Methods and Models*. Dordrecht: Kluwer Academic.

Ansolabehere, Stephen, and Shanto Iyengar. 1994. "Of Horseshoes and Horse Races—Experimental Studies of the Impact of Poll Results on Electoral-Behavior." *Political Communication* 11:4, 413–430.

Ansolabehere, Stephen, and James Snyder. 2000. "Soft Money, Hard Money, Strong Parties." *Columbia Law Review* 100:3, 598–619.

Aquilino, William S., and L. Lo Sciuto. 1990. "Effect of Interview Mode on Self-reported Drug Use." *Public Opinion Quarterly* 54:3, 362–395.

Aquinas, Thomas. 1964. *Commentary on the Nichomechean Ethics,* trans. C. I. Litzinger. O. P. Library of Living Catholic Thought 2: 855. Chicago: Henry Regnery.

Aquinas, Thomas. 1983. *Treatise on Happiness. Question 4, Article 8.* Notre Dame, Ind.: University of Notre Dame Press.

Arbuckle, James L., and Werner Wothke. 1999. *AMOS 4.0 User's Guide.* Chicago: SmallWaters Corporation.

Aristotle. 1962. *Nichomechean Ethics,* trans. Martin Oswald. New York: Bobbs-Merrill.

Asch, Solomon E. 1963. "Effects of Group Pressure upon the Modification and Distortion of Judgments." In *Groups, Leadership, and Men: Research in Human Relations,* ed. Harold Guetzkow, 177–190. New York: Russell and Russell.

Axelrod, Robert. 1997a . "The Dissemination of Culture: A Model with Local Convergence and Global Polarization." *Journal of Conflict Resolution* 41:203–226.

Axelrod, Robert. 1997b. *The Complexity of Cooperation: Agent-Based Models of Competition and Collaboration.* Princeton, N.J.: Princeton University Press.

Axtell, Robert, Robert Axelrod, Joshua M. Epstein, and Michael D. Cohen. 1996. "Aligning Simulation Models: A Case Study and Results." *Computational and Mathematical Organization Theory* 1:123–141.

Balch, Tucker. 2000. "Hierarchic Social Entropy: An Information Theoretic Measure of Robot Team Diversity." *Autonomous Robots* 8:3, 209–238.

Balestra, Pietro. 1992. "Fixed Effect Models and Fixed Coefficient Models." In *The Econometrics of Panel Data: Handbook of Theory and Applications,* ed. László Mátyás and Patrick Sevestre, 30–45. Dordrecht: Kluwer Academic Publishers.

Barabasi, Albert-László, Hawoong Jeong, Erzsebet Ravasz, Zoltan Néda, Andras Schubert, and Tamas Vicsek. 2001. "On the Topology of the Scientific Collaboration Networks." *Physica A* 311, 590–614 (2002).

Bartle, John. 2001. "The Measurement of Party Identification in Britain: Where Do We Stand Now?" In *British Elections and Parties Review,* ed. Jonathan Tonge, Lynn Bennie, David Denver and Lisa Harrison, 11:9–22. London: Frank Cass.

Baybeck, Brady, and Robert Huckfeldt. 2002a. "Spatially Dispersed Ties among Independent Citizens: Connecting Individuals and Aggregates." *Political Analysis* 10: 261–275.

Baybeck, Brady, and Robert Huckfeldt. 2002b. "Urban Contexts, Spatially Dispersed Networks, and the Diffusion of Political Information." *Political Geography* 21:195–220.

Beck, Nathaniel. 1974. "A Note on the Probability of a Tied Election." *Public Choice* 23:75–80.

Beck, Paul Allen. 1977. "The Role of Agents in Political Socialization." In *Handbook of Political Socialization,* ed. Stanley Allen Renshon. New York: Free Press.

Beck, Paul Allen. 1991. "Voters' Intermediation Environments in the 1988 Presidential Contest." *Public Opinion Quarterly* 55:3, 371–395.

Beck, Paul Allen, Russell J. Dalton, Steven Greene, and Robert Huckfeldt. 2002. "The Social Calculus of Voting: Interpersonal, Media, and Organizational Influences on Presidential Choices." *American Political Science Review* 96:1, 57–73.

Beck, Paul Allen, and M. Kent Jennings. 1975. "Parents as 'Middlepersons' in Political Socialization." *Journal of Politics* 37:1, 83–107.

Beck, Paul Allen, and M. Kent Jennings. 1991. "Family Traditions, Political Periods, and the Development of Political Orientations." *Journal of Politics* 53: 742–763.

Bendix, Reinard, and Seymour M. Lipset. 1967. "The Field of Political Sociology." In *Political Sociology: Selected Essays,* ed. Lewis A. Coser, 9–47. Harper and Row.

Bennett, Stephen Earl. 1990. "The Educational Turnout 'Puzzle' in Recent U.S. National Elections." *Electoral Studies* 9:1, 51–58.

Bennett, Stephen Earl, Richard S. Flickinger, and Stacy L. Rhine. 2000. "Political Talk Over Here, Over There, Over Time." *British Journal of Political Science* 30:1, 99–119.

Berelson, Bernard R. 1952. "Democratic Theory and Public Opinion." *Public Opinion Quarterly* 16:313–330.

Berelson, Bernard R., Paul F. Lazarsfeld, and William N. McPhee. 1954. *Voting: A Study of Opinion Formation in a Presidential Campaign.* Chicago: University of Chicago Press.

Berger, Bennett M. 1960. *Working-Class Suburb: A Study of Auto Workers in Suburbia.* Berkeley: University of California Press.

Bernard, H. Russel, Peter D. Kilworth, Michael J. Evans, Christopher McCarty, and Gene A. Selley. 1988. "Studying Social Relations Cross-culturally." *Ethnology* 2: 155.

Beyer, Mary Alice, and Robert Whitehurst. 1976. "Value Change with Length of Marriage: Some Correlates of Consonance and Dissonance." *International Journal of Marriage and the Family* 6:109–120.

Blais, Andre, and Robert Young. 1999. "Why Do People Vote? An Experiment in Rationality." *Public Choice* 99:1–2, 39–55.

Blais, Andre, Robert Young, and Miriam Lapp. 2000. "The Calculus of Voting: An Empirical Test." *European Journal of Political Research* 37:2, 181–201.

Blau, Peter M. 1960. "Structural Effects." *American Sociological Review* 25:178–193.

Blau, Peter M., and Otis D. Duncan. 1967. *The American Occupational Structure.* New York: Wiley.

Bobo, Lawrence, and Franklin D. Gilliam, Jr. 1990. "Race, Sociopolitical Participation, and Black Empowerment." *American Political Science Review* 84:2, 377–393.

Bohman, James. 1996. *Public Deliberation: Pluralism, Complexity, and Democracy.* Cambridge, Mass.: MIT Press.

Bollen, Kenneth A. 1989. *Structural Equations with Latent Variables.* New York: John Wiley.

Bollen, Kenneth A. 1995. "Structural Equation Models That Are Nonlinear in Latent Variables: A Least Squares Estimator." *Sociological Methodology* 25:223–251.

Books, Charles. L., and John W. Prysby. 1991. *Political Behavior and the Local Context.* New York: Praeger.

Bottomore, T. B., and Maximilien Rubel, eds. 1956. *Karl Marx: Selected Writings in Sociology and Social Philosophy.* New York: McGraw-Hill.

Bowler, Shaun. 1990. "Voter Perceptions and Party Strategies: An Empirical Approach." *Comparative Politics* 23:1, 61–83.

Bowler, Shaun, and Todd Donovan. 2002. "Democracy, Institutions, and Attitudes about Citizen Influence on Government." *British Journal of Political Science* 32:2, 371–90.

Boyd, Lawrence H., and Gudmund R. Iversen. 1979. *Contextual Analysis: Concepts and Statistical Techniques.* Belmont, Calif.: Wadsworth.

Bradburn, Norman M. 1983. "Response Effects." In *Handbook of Survey Research*, ed. Peter D. Rossi, James D. Wright, and Andy B. Anderson. New York: Academic Press.

Breeden, Richard. 2002. "Small Talk: The Big Decision." *Wall Street Journal,* September 24, 2002: B6.

Brichoux, David, and Paul E. Johnson. 2002. "The Power of Commitment in Cooperative Social Action." *Journal of Artificial Societies and Social Simulation* 9:1.1–5.4.

Bronfenbrenner, Urie. 1979. *The Ecology of Human Development.* Cambridge, Mass.: Harvard University Press.

Brooks, Clem, and Jeff Manza. 1997. "The Social and Ideological Bases of Middle-Class Political Realignment in the United States, 1972–1992." *American Sociological Review* 62:191–208.

Brown, Robert D., Robert A. Jackson, and Gerald C.Wright. 1999. "Registration, Turnout, and State Party Systems." *Political Research Quarterly* 52:3, 463–479.

Bryk, Anthony S., and Stephen W. Raudenbush. 1992. *Hierarchical Linear Models: Applications and Data Analysis Methods*. Newbury Park, Calif.: Sage.

Buck, Nick. 2001. "Identifying Neighbourhood Effects on Social Exclusion." *Urban Studies* 38:2251–2276.

Budge, Ian, and Michael Laver. 1993. "The Policy Basis of Government Coalitions: A Comparative Investigation." *British Journal of Political Science* 23:4, 499–519.

Budge, Ian, David Robertson, and Derek Hearl, eds. 1987. *Ideology, Strategy, and Party Change: Spatial Analyses of Post-War Election Programmes in Nineteen Democracies*. New York: Cambridge University Press.

Burns, Nancy, Kay L. Schlozman, and Sidney Verba. 2001. *The Private Roots of Public Action: Gender, Equality, and Political Participation*. Cambridge, Mass.: Harvard University Press.

Burr, Jeffrey A., and John R. Nesselroade. 1990. "Change Measurement." In *Statistical Methods in Longitudinal Research*, vol. 1, *Principles and Structuring Change*, ed. Alexander von Eye, 3–125. Boston: Academic Press.

Burt, Ronald S. 1983. "Range." In *Applied Network Analysis: A Methodological Introduction*, ed. Ronald S. Burt and Michael J. Minor, 176–194. Beverly Hills, Calif.: Sage Publications.

Burt, Ronald S. 1992. *Structural Holes: The Social Structure of Competition*. Cambridge, Mass.: Harvard University Press.

Busch, Marc, and Eric Reinhardt. 2000. "Geography, International Trade, and Political Mobilization in U.S. Industries." *American Journal of Political Science* 44:4, 703–719.

Busemeyer, J. R., and L. E. Jones. 1983. "An Analysis of Multiplicative Combination Rules When the Causal Variables are Measured With Error." *Psychological Bulletin* 93:549–563.

Butler, David E., and Donald Stokes. 1969. *Political Change in Britain: The Evolution of Party Choice*. London: Macmillan

Butler, David E., and Donald Stokes. 1974. *Political Change in Britain: The Evolution of Electoral Choice*. New York: St. Martin's Press.

Cacioppo, John T., and Richard R. Petty. 1979. "Effects of Message Repetition and Position on Cognitive Responses, Recall, and Persuasion." *Journal of Personality and Social Psychology* 37:97–109.

Campbell, Angus, Philip E. Converse, Warren E. Miller, and Donald E. Stokes. 1960. *The American Voter*. New York: Wiley.

Campbell, Angus, Philip E. Converse, Warren E. Miller, and Donald E. Stokes. 1966. *Elections and the Political Order*. New York: Wiley.

Campbell, Angus, Gerald Gurin, and Warren E. Miller. 1954. *The Voter Decides*. Evanston, Ill.: Row, Peterson.

Campbell, David E. 2002. "Getting Along Versus Getting Ahead: Why the Absence of Party Competition Leads to High Voter Turnout." Paper presented at the annual meeting of the Midwest Political Science Association, Chicago, April 25–28.

Campbell, Donald T., and Julian C. Stanley. 1963. *Experimental and Quasi-Experimental Designs for Research*. Boston, Mass.: Houghton Mifflin.

Cassel, Carol A. 1999. "Voluntary Associations, Churches, and Social Participation Theories of Turnout." *Social Science Quarterly* 80:3, 504–517.

Chaffee, Steven H., Jack M. McLeod, and Daniel Wackman. 1973. "Mass Communication and Socialization." In *Socialization to Politics: A Reader*, ed. Jack Dennis. New York: John Wiley.

Chamberlain, Gary. 1980. "Analysis of Covariance with Qualitative Data." *Review of Economic Studies* 47:225–238.

Chaney, Carol Kennedy, R. Michael Alvarez, and Jonathan Nagler. 1998. "Explaining the Gender Gap in United States Presidential Elections, 1980–1992." *Political Research Quarterly* 51:2, 311–340.

Chavez, Leo. 1992. *Shadowed Lives: Undocumented Immigrants in American Society.* Fort Worth: Harcourt Brace Jovanovich.

Cleveland, William S. 1979. "Robust Locally Weighted Regression and Smoothing Scatterplots." *Journal of the American Statistical Association* 74, 829–836.

Cleveland, William S., and Susan J. Devlin. 1988. "Locally Weighted Regression: An Approach to Regression Analysis by Local Fitting." *Journal of the American Statistical Association* 83, 596–610.

Cohen, Sheldon, Lynn G. Underwood, and Benjamin A. Gottlieb, eds. 2000. *Social Support Measurement and Intervention: A Guide for Health and Social Scientists*. New York: Oxford University Press.

Coleman, James S. 1964. *Introduction to Mathematical Sociology.* New York: Free Press.

Conover, Pamela J., Donald D. Searing, and Ivor M. Crewe. 2002. "The Deliberative Potential of Political Discussion." *British Journal of Political Science* 32:1, 21–62.

Converse, Philip E. 1964. "The Nature of Belief Systems in Mass Publics." In *Ideology and Discontent,* ed. David Apter, 206–261. New York: Free Press.

Converse, Philip E. 1969. "Of Time and Partisan Stability." *Comparative Political Studies* 2:139–171.

Converse, Philip E. 1976. *The Dynamics of Party Support: Cohort Analyzing Party Identification.* Beverly Hills, Calif.: Sage.

Conway, M. Margaret, A. Jay Stevens, and Robert Smith. 1975. "The Relation between Media Use and Children's Civic Awareness." *Journalism Quarterly* 57:1, 45–54.

Cook, Timothy E. 1985. "The Bear Market in Political Socialization and the Costs of Misunderstood Psychological Theories." *American Political Science Review* 79: 1079–1093.

Corcoran, Mary. 1995. "Rags to Rags: Poverty and Mobility in the United States." *Annual Review of Sociology* 21:237–267.

Cox, Gary W., Frances M. Rosenbluth, and Michael F. Thies. 1998. "Mobilization, Social Networks, and Turnout—Evidence from Japan." *World Politics* 50:3, 447–474.

Cross, Rob. 2001. "Beyond Answers: Dimensions of the Advice Network." *Social Networks* 23:3, 215–235.

Dalton, Russell J., and Martin P. Wattenberg. 1993. "The Not So Simple Act of Voting." In *Political Science: The State of the Discipline II*, ed. Ada W. Finifter. Washington, D.C.: American Political Science Association.

Davies, James C. 1970. "The Family's Role in Political Socialization." In *Learning about Politics*, ed. Roberta S. Sigel. New York: Random House.

Davis, James A., Joe L. Spaeth, and Carolyn Huson. 1961. "Analyzing Effects of Group Composition," *American Sociological Review* 26:215–225.

Dawson, Richard E., and Kenneth Prewitt. 1969. *Political Socialization.* Boston: Little, Brown.

DeBono, Kenneth G., and Richard J. Harnish. 1988. "Source Expertise, Source Attractiveness, and the Processing of Persuasive Information: A Functional Approach." *Journal of Personality and Social Psychology* 55:541–546.

De Graaf, Nan Dirk, and Anthony Heath. 1992. "Husbands' and Wives' Voting Behaviour in Britain: Class-dependent Mutual Influence of Spouses." *Acta Sociologica* 35:4, 311–322.

De Graaf, Nan Dirk, and Bram Steijn. 1996. "The Service Class in a Post-industrial Society: Attitudes and Behaviour of the Social and Cultural Specialists in the Public Sector." Paper presented at the meeting of the International Sociological Association in Stockholm, May 30–June 2, 1996.

De Leeuw, Edith D. 1992. *Data Quality in Mail, Telephone, and Face to Face Surveys: A Mode Comparison in the Netherlands.* Amsterdam: TT-Publiaties.

Delli Carpini, Michael X., and Scott Keeter. 1996. *What Americans Know about Politics and Why It Matters.* New Haven: Yale University Press.

Dennis, Jack. 1968. "Major Problems of Political Socialization Research." *Midwest Journal of Political Science* 12:85–114.

Denver, David T., and Gordon Hands. 1997. *Modern Constituency Electioneering: The 1992 General Election.* London: Frank Cass.

Di Lella, Alexander A, ed. 1987. *The Wisdom of Ben Sira,* trans. Patrick W. Skehan. New York: Doubleday.

Dorling, Daniel F. L., Heather Eyre, Ron J. Johnston, and Charles J. Pattie. 2002. "A Good Place to Bury Bad News? Hiding the Detail in the Geography on the Labour Party's Website." *Political Quarterly* 73:476–492.

Downs, Anthony. 1957. *An Economic Theory of Democracy.* New York: Harper and Row.

Duncan, Beverly, and Otis D. Duncan. 1978. *Sex Typing and Social Roles: A Research Report.* New York: Academic Press.

Dunleavy, Patrick. 1979. "The Urban Bases of Political Alignment: Social Class, Domestic Property Ownership and State Intervention in Consumption Processes." *British Journal of Political Science* 9:403–443.

Durkheim, Émile. 1964 [1933]. *The Division of Labor in Society,* trans. George Simpson. New York: Free Press.

Easton, David. 1953. *The Political System: An Inquiry into the State of Political Science.* New York: Knopf.

Easton, David, and Jack Dennis. 1969. *Children and the Political System: Origins of Political Legitimacy.* New York: McGraw Hill.

Elster, Jon, ed. 1998. *Deliberative Democracy.* New York: Cambridge University Press.

Erbring, Lutz, and Alice A. Young. 1979. "Individuals and Social Structure: Contextual Effects as Endogenous Feedback." *Sociological Methods and Research* 7:396–430.

Erickson, Bonnie. 2003. "Social Networks: The Value of Variety." *Contexts* 2:1, 25–31.

Erikson, Robert. 1984. "Social Class of Men, Women and Families." *Sociology* 18:500–514.

Erikson, Robert, and John H. Goldthorpe. 1992. *The Constant Flux: A Study of Class Mobility in Industrial Societies.* Oxford: Clarendon Press.

Eulau, Heinz. 1962. *Class and Party in the Eisenhower Years: Class Roles and Perspectives in the 1952 and 1956 Elections.* New York: Free Press of Glencoe.

Eulau, Heinz. 1980. "The Columbia Studies of Personal Influence." *Social Science History* 4:207–228.

Eulau, Heinz. 1986. *Politics, Self, and Society.* Cambridge: Harvard University Press.

Evans, Geoffrey, ed. 1999. *The End of Class Politics? Class Voting in Comparative Context.* New York: Oxford University Press.

Evans, Geoffrey, and Robert Andersen. 2001. "Endogenizing the Economy: Political Preferences and Economic Perceptions across the Electoral Cycle." CREST Working Paper 88. Oxford University: Centre for Research into Elections and Social Trends. (Available on http://www.crest.ox.ac.uk).

Fabrigar, Leandre R., and Jon A. Krosnick. 1995. "Attitude Importance and the False Consensus Effect." *Personality and Social Psychology Bulletin* 21:468–479.

Falter, Jürgen, Harald Schoen, and Claudio Caballero. 2000. "Zur Validierung des Konzepts 'Parteiidentifikation' in der Bundesrepublik" [On the validity of the concept of "party identification" in the Federal Republic of Germany]. In *50 Jahre empirische Wahlforschung in Deutschland. Entwicklung, Befunde, Perspektiven, Daten* [50 years of the empirical study of electoral behavior in Germany: Developments, findings, and data], ed. Markus Klein, Wolfgang Jagodzinski, Ekkehard Mochmann, and Dieter Ohr, 235–271. Wiesbaden: Westdeutscher Verlag,.

Fazio, Russell H. 1995. "Attitudes as Object-Evaluation Associations: Determinants, Consequences, and Correlates of Attitude Accessibility." In *Attitude Strength: Antecedents and Consequences,* ed. R. E. Petty and J. A. Krosnick. Mahwah, N.J.: Erlbaum.

Fearon, James. 1998. "Deliberation and Discussion." In *Deliberative Democracy,* ed. Jon Elster. New York: Cambridge University Press.

Ferejohn, John, and Morris Fiorina. 1974. "The Paradox of Not Voting: A Decision Theoretic Analysis." *American Political Science Review* 68:525–536.

Festinger, Leon. 1957. *A Theory of Cognitive Dissonance.* Palo Alto, Calif.: Stanford University Press.

Fine, Michelle, and Lois Weis. 1998. "Crime Stories: A Critical Look through Race, Ethnicity, and Gender." *Qualitative Studies in Education* 3:435–459.

Finifter, Ada W. 1974. "The Friendship Group as a Protective Environment for Political Deviants." *American Political Science Review* 68:607–625.

Fiorina, Morris P. 1981. *Retrospective Voting in American National Elections.* New Haven: Yale University Press.

Fischer, A. J. 1999. "The Probability of Being Decisive." *Public Choice* 101:267–283.

Fishkin, James S. 1991. *Democracy and Deliberation.* New Haven: Yale University Press.

Foner, Nancy. 1997. "The Immigrant Family: Cultural Legacies and Cultural Changes." *International Migration Review* 31:4 (Winter), 961–974.

Fowler, James, and Oleg Smirnov. 2004. "A Dynamic Calculus of Voting." Working paper. Davis: University of California. Available: http://jhfowler.ucdavis.edu (accessed July 16, 2004).

Fowler, Robert Booth, and Allen D. Hertzke. 1995. *Religion and Politics in America: Faith, Culture, and Strategic Choices.* Boulder, Colo.: Westview Press.

Franklin, Charles H. 1984. "Issue Preferences, Socialization, and the Evolution of Party Identification." *American Journal of Political Science* 28:459–478.

Franklin, Charles H., and John E. Jackson. 1983. "The Dynamics of Party Identification." *American Political Science Review* 77:957–973.

Franklin, Charles H., and Liane C. Kosaki. 1989. "Republican Schoolmaster: The U.S. Supreme Court, Public Opinion, and Abortion." *American Political Science Review* 83:751–771.

Franklin, Mark N. 1985. *The Decline of Class Voting in Britain.* Oxford: Clarendon Press.

Freeman, Lin C., and Claire R. Thompson. 1989. "Estimating Acquaintance Volume." In *The Small World,* ed. Manfred Kochen, 147–158. Norwood, N.J.: Ablex Publishing.

Fuchs, Dieter, and Hans-Dieter Klingemann. 1989. "The Left-Right Schema." In *Continuities in Political Action,* ed. M. Kent Jennings and Jan W. van Deth, 203–234. New York: De Gruyter.

Fuchs, Lawrence H. 1955. "American Jews and the Presidential Vote," *American Political Science Review* 49:385–401.

Gabel, Matthew J., and John D. Huber. 2000. "Putting Parties in Their Place: Inferring Party Left-Right Ideological Positions from Party Manifestos Data." *American Journal of Political Science* 44:1, 94–103.

Gamson, William A. 1992. *Talking Politics.* New York: Cambridge University Press.

Gans, Herbert J. 1967. "Levittown and America." In *The City Reader,* ed. Richard T. LeGates and Frederic Stout, 63–69. New York: Routledge.

Ganzeboom, Harry B.G., Donald J. Treiman, and Wout C. Ultee. 1991. "Comparative Intergenerational Stratification Research." *Annual Review of Sociology* 17:277–302.

Gastil, John, and James P. Dillard. 1999. "Increasing Political Sophistication through Public Deliberation." *Political Communication* 16:1, 3–23.

Gelman, Andrew, John B. Carlin, Hal S. Stern, and Donald B. Rubin. 1995. *Bayesian Data Analysis*. London: Chapman and Hall.

Gelman, Andrew, Gary King, and W. John Boscardin. 1998. "Estimating the Probability of Events That Have Never Occurred: When Is Your Vote Decisive?" *Journal of the American Statistical Association*, 93:441, 1–9.

Gerber, Alan S., and Donald P. Green. 1999. "Does Canvassing Increase Voter Turnout? A Field Experiment." *Proceedings of The National Academy of Sciences of The United States of America* 96:19, 10939–10942.

Gerber, Alan S., and Donald P. Green. 2000a. "The Effect of a Nonpartisan Get-Out-the-Vote Drive: An Experimental Study of Leafletting." *Journal of Politics* 62:3, 846–857.

Gerber, Alan S., and Donald P. Green. 2000b. "The Effects of Canvassing, Telephone Calls, and Direct Mail on Voter Turnout: A Field Experiment." *American Political Science Review* 94:3, 653–663.

Gibson, James L. 1992. "The Political Consequences of Intolerance: Cultural Conformity and Political Freedom." *American Political Science Review* 86:2, 338–356.

Giles, Micheal W., and Marilyn K. Dantico. 1982. "Political Participation and Neighborhood Social Context Revisited." *American Journal of Political Science* 26:144–150.

Gill, Jeff. 2002. *Bayesian Methods: A Social and Behavioral Sciences Approach*. Boca Raton, Fla.: Chapman and Hall.

Gillespie, John H. 1998. *Population Genetics*. Baltimore, Md.: Johns Hopkins University Press.

Gimpel, James G., J. Celeste Lay, and Jason E. Schuknecht. 2003. *Cultivating Democracy: Civic Environments and Political Socialization in America*. Washington, D.C.: Brookings Institution Press.

Gimpel, James G., and Jason E. Schuknecht. 2003. *Patchwork Nation: Sectionalism and Political Change in American Politics*. Ann Arbor: University of Michigan Press.

Glaser, William A. 1959. "The Family and Voting Turnout." *Public Opinion Quarterly* 23:4, 563–570.

Glynn, Carroll J., Andrew F. Hayes, and James Shanahan. 1997. "Perceived Support for One's Opinions and Willingness to Speak Out: A Meta-Analysis of Survey Studies on the 'Spiral of Silence.'" *Public Opinion Quarterly* 61:3, 452–463.

Glynn, Carroll J., and Jack M. McLeod. 1984. "Public Opinion du Jour: An Examination of the Spiral of Silence." *Public Opinion Quarterly* 46:4, 731–740.

Godwin, Deborah D., and John Scanzoni. 1989. "Couple Decision Making: Commonalities and Differences across Issues and Spouses." *Journal of Family Issues* 10:3, 291–310.

Goldthorpe, John H. 1982. "On the Service Class, Its Formation and Future." In *Social Class and the Division of Labour: Essays in Honour of Ilya Neustadt*, ed. Anthony Giddens and Gavin MacKenzie, 162–185. Cambridge: Cambridge University Press.

Goldthorpe, John H. 1983. "Women and Class Analysis: In Defence of the Conventional View." *Sociology* 17:465–488.

Gonzalez, Richard, and Dale Griffin. 2000. "On the Statistics of Interdependence: Treating Dyadic Data with Respect." In *The Social Psychology of Personal Relationships*, ed. William Ickes and Steve Duck, 181–213. New York: Wiley.

Goodsell, Charles, ed. 1981. *The Public Encounter: Where State and Citizen Meet*. Bloomington: Indiana University Press.

Granberg, Donald, and Soren Holmberg. 1991. "Self-Reported Turnout and Voter Validation." *American Journal of Political Science* 35:2, 448–459.

Granovetter, Mark. 1973. "The Strength of Weak Ties." *American Journal of Sociology* 78:1360–1380.

Granovetter, Mark. 1974. *Getting a Job: A Study of Contacts and Careers.* Cambridge: Harvard University Press.

Gray, Mark, and Miki Caul. 2000. "Declining Voter Turnout in Advanced Industrial Democracies, 1950 to 1997: The Effects of Declining Group Mobilization." *Comparative Political Studies* 33:9, 1091–1122.

Green, Donald Philip, and Bradley Palmquist. 1990. "Of Artifacts and Partisan Instability." *American Journal of Political Science* 34:872–902.

Green, Donald Philip, and Bradley Palmquist. 1994. "How Stable Is Party Identification?" *Political Behavior* 43:437–466.

Green, Donald, Bradley Palmquist, and Eric Schickler. 2002. *Partisan Hearts and Minds: Political Parties and the Social Identities of Voters.* New Haven: Yale University Press.

Greene, William H. 1995. *LIMDEP Version 7.0 User's Manual.* New York: Econometrics Software.

Greenstein, Fred I. 1965. *Children and Politics.* New Haven: Yale University Press.

Greig, J. Michael. 2002. "The End of Geography? Globalization, Communications, and Culture in the International System." *Journal of Conflict Resolution* 46:2, 225–243.

Habermas, Jürgen. 1989. *The Structural Transformation of the Public Sphere.* Cambridge, Mass.: MIT Press.

Haisken–De New, John, and Joachim R. Frick, eds. 1998. *Desktop Companion to the German Socio-Economic Panel Study (GSOEP).* Version 2.0. Berlin: DIW.

Hansen, Susan B. 1997. "Talking about Politics: Gender and Contextual Effects on Political Proselytizing." *Journal of Politics* 59:1, 73–103.

Hanushek, Eric A., and John E. Jackson. 1977. *Statistical Methods for Social Scientists.* New York: Academic Press.

Hauser, Rita M., and David L. Featherman. 1977. *The Process of Stratification.* New York: Academic Press.

Hays, Bernadette D., and Clive S. Bean. 1992. "The Impact of Spousal Characteristics on Political Attitudes in Australia." *Public Opinion Quarterly* 56:4, 524–529.

Hays, Bernadette D., and Clive S. Bean. 1994. "Political Attitudes and Partisanship among Australian Couples: Do Wives Matter?" *Women and Politics* 14:1, 53–80.

Heath, Anthony, Roger Jowell, and John Curtice. 1985. *How Britain Votes.* Oxford: Pergamon Press.

Heath, Anthony, and Mike Savage. 1995. "Political Alignments within the Middle Classes, 1972–1989." In *Social Change and the Middle Classes*, ed. Tim Butler and Mike Savage, 275–292. London: UCL.

Hedström, Peter, and Richard Swedberg, eds. 1998. *Social Mechanisms: An Analytical Approach to Social Theory.* New York: Cambridge University Press.

Hess, Robert D., and Judith V. Torney. 1968. *The Development of Political Attitudes in Children.* Garden City, N.Y.: Doubleday, Anchor Books.

Hippler, Hans-J., and Norbert Schwarz. 1987. "Response Effects in Surveys." In *Social Information Processing and Survey Methodology*, ed. Hans-J. Hippler, Norbert Schwarz, and Seymour Sudman. New York: Springer-Verlag.

Hochschild, Jennifer. 1981. *What's Fair: American Beliefs about Distributive Justice.* Cambridge: Harvard University Press.

Hondagneu-Sotelo, Pierrette. 1994. *Gendered Transitions: Mexican Experiences of Immigration.* Berkeley: University of California Press.

Hout, Michael. 1988. "More Universalism, Less Structural Mobility." *American Journal of Sociology* 93:1358–1400.

Hout, Michael, Clem Brooks, and Jeff Manza. 1995. "The Democratic Class Struggle in the United States, 1948–1992." *American Sociological Review* 60:805–828.

Huber, John. 1989. "Values and Partisanship in Left-Right Orientations: Measuring Ideology." *European Journal of Political Research* 17:5, 599–621.

Huckfeldt, Robert. 1979. "Political Participation and the Neighborhood Social Context." *American Journal of Political Science* 23:579–592.

Huckfeldt, Robert. 1984. "Political Loyalties and Social Class Ties: The Mechanisms of Contextual Influence." *American Journal of Political Science* 28:2, 399–417.

Huckfeldt, Robert. 1986. *Politics in Context: Assimilation and Conflict in Urban Neighborhoods.* New York: Agathon.

Huckfeldt, Robert. 2001. "The Social Communication of Political Expertise." *American Journal of Political Science* 45:2, 425–438.

Huckfeldt, Robert, Paul Allen Beck, Russell J. Dalton, and Jeffrey Levine. 1995. "Political Environments, Cohesive Social Groups, and the Communication of Public Opinion." *American Journal of Political Science*, 39:4, 1025–1054.

Huckfeldt, Robert, Paul Allen Beck, Russell J. Dalton, Jeffrey Levine, and William Morgan. 1998. "Ambiguity, Distorted Messages, and Nested Environmental Effects on Political Communication." *Journal of Politics* 60:4, 996–1030.

Huckfeldt, Robert, and Carol Weitzel Kohfeld. 1989. *Race and the Decline of Class in American Politics.* Urbana: University of Illinois Press.

Huckfeldt, Robert, Paul E. Johnson, and John Sprague. 2002. "Political Environments, Political Dynamics, and the Survival of Disagreement." *Journal of Politics* 64:1, 1–21.

Huckfeldt, Robert, Paul E. Johnson, and John Sprague. 2004. *Political Disagreement: The Survival of Diverse Opinions within Communication Networks.* New York: Cambridge University Press.

Huckfeldt, Robert, Eric Plutzer, and John Sprague. 1993. "Alternative Contexts of Political Behavior: Churches, Neighborhoods, and Individuals." *Journal of Politics* 55: 365–381.

Huckfeldt, Robert, and John Sprague. 1987. "Networks in Context: The Social Flow of Political Information." *American Political Science Review* 81:4, 1197–1216.

Huckfeldt, Robert, and John Sprague. 1990. "Social Order and Political Chaos: The Structural Setting of Political Information." In *Information and Democratic Processes,* ed. John A. Ferejohn and James H. Kuklinski. Urbana: University of Illinois Press.

Huckfeldt, Robert, and John Sprague. 1991. "Discussant Effects on Vote Choice: Intimacy, Structure, and Interdependence." *Journal of Politics,* 53:1, 122–158.

Huckfeldt, Robert, and John Sprague. 1993. "Citizens, Contexts and Politics." In *The State of the Discipline II*, ed. Ada W. Finifter, 281–303. Washington, D.C.: American Political Science Association.

Huckfeldt, Robert, and John Sprague. 1995. *Citizens, Politics, and Social Communication: Information and Influence in an Election Campaign.* New York: Cambridge University Press.

Huckfeldt, Robert, John Sprague, and Jeffrey Levine. 2000. "The Dynamics of Collective Deliberation in the 1996 Election: Campaign Effects on Accessibility, Certainty, and Accuracy." *American Political Science Review* 94:641–651.

Inglehart, Ronald. 1977. *The Silent Revolution.* Princeton: Princeton University Press.

Inglehart, Ronald, et al. 2000. World Values Surveys and European Values Surveys, 1981–1984, 1990–1993, and 1995–1997 (computer file, ICPSR version). Ann Arbor, Mich.: Institute for Social Research (producer) / Inter-university Consortium for Political and Social Research (distributor).

Iyengar, Shanto. 1980. "Subjective Political Efficacy as a Measure of Diffuse Support." *Public Opinion Quarterly* 44:2, 249–256.

Jackson, John E. 1975. "Issues, Party Choices, and Presidential Votes." *American Journal of Political Science* 19:161–185.

Jaros, Dean. 1973. *Socialization to Politics*. New York: Praeger.

Jennings, M. Kent. 1979. "Another Look at the Life Cycle and Political Participation." *American Journal of Political Science* 73:755–771.

Jennings, M. Kent. 1996. "Political Knowledge over Time and across Generations." *Public Opinion Quarterly* 65:1, 228–252.

Jennings, M. Kent. 2000. "Participation as Seen through the Lens of the Political Socialization Project." Paper presented at the "Conference on Participation: Building a Research Agenda," Center for the Study of Democratic Politics, Princeton University, October 12–14.

Jennings, M. Kent, and Gregory B. Markus. 1984. "Partisan Orientations over the Long Haul: Results from the Three-Wave Political Socialization Panel Study." *American Political Science Review* 78:4, 1000–1018.

Jennings, M. Kent, and Richard G. Niemi. 1974. *The Political Character of Adolescence: The Influence of Families and Schools*. Princeton, N.J.: Princeton University Press.

Jennings, M. Kent, and Richard G. Niemi. 1981. *Generations and Politics: A Panel Study of Young Adults and Their Parents*. Princeton, N.J.: Princeton University Press.

Jennings, M. Kent, and Laura Stoker. 1999. "The Persistence of the Past: The Class of 1965 Turns Fifty." Paper presented at the annual meeting of the Midwest Political Science Association, Chicago, April 15–17.

Jennings, M. Kent, and Laura Stoker. 2001. "Generations and Civic Engagement: A Longitudinal Multi-Generation Analysis." Paper presented at the annual meeting of the American Political Science Association, San Francisco, August 30–September 2.

Jennings, M. Kent, Laura Stoker, and Jake Bowers. 1999. "Politics across Generations: Family Transmission Reexamined." Paper presented at the annual meeting of the American Political Science Association, Atlanta, September 2–5.

Johnson, Martin, W. Phillips Shively, and Robert M. Stein. 2002. "Contextual Data and the Study of Elections and Voting Behavior: Connecting Individuals to Environments." *Electoral Studies* 21:219–233.

Johnson, Paul E. 1996. "Unraveling in a Variety of Institutional Settings." *Journal of Theoretical Politics* 8:3, 299–330.

Johnson, Paul E. 1999. "Simulation Modeling in Political Science." *American Behavioral Scientist* 42:10, 1509–1530.

Johnson, Paul E., and Alex Lancaster. 2000. *The Swarm User Guide*. Santa Fe, New Mexico: Swarm Development Group. Available http://www.santafe.edu/projects/swarm/swarmdocs/userbook/userbook.html (accessed July 6, 2004).

Johnston, Ron J. 1982. "The Changing Geography of Voting in the United States: 1946–1980." *Transactions, Institute of British Geographers* 7:187–204.

Johnston, Ron J. 1986. "Places and Votes: The Role of Location in the Creation of Political Attitudes." *Urban Geography* 7:2, 103–117.

Johnston, Ron J. 1987a. *Money and Votes*. London: Croom Helm.

Johnston, Ron J. 1987b. "The Rural Milieu and Voting in Britain." *Journal of Rural Studies* 3:2, 95–103.

Johnston, Ron J. 1999. "Context, Conversation and Conviction: Social Networks and Voting at the 1997 British General Election." *Political Studies* 47:877–889.

Johnston, Ron J., and Charles J. Pattie. 1997a. "Where's the Difference? Decomposing the Impact of Local Election Campaigns in Great Britain." *Electoral Studies* 16:165–174.

Johnston, Ron J., and Charles J. Pattie. 1997b. "Anchors Aweigh: Variations in Strength of Party Identification and in Socio-Political Attitudes among the British Electorate 1991–1994." In *British Elections and Parties Review*, ed. Charles J. Pattie, David T. Denver, Justin Fisher, and Steve Ludlam, 7:42–56. London: Frank Cass.

Johnston, Ron J., and Charles J. Pattie. 1999. "Aspects of the Interrelationships of Attitudes and Behaviour as Illustrated by a Longitudinal Study of British Adults: 2. Predicting

Voting Intention, Strength of Party Identification and Change in Both." *Environment and Planning A* 31:1279–1294.

Johnston, Ron J., and Charles Pattie. 2000. "Inconsistent Individual Attitudes within Consistent Attitudinal Structures: Comments on an Important Issue Raised by John Bartle's Paper on Causal Modeling of Voting in Britain." *British Journal of Political Science* 30:361–373.

Johnston, Ron J., and Charles J. Pattie. 2001a. "Dimensions of Retrospective Voting: Economic Performance, Public Service Standards, and Conservative Party Support at the 1997 British General Election." *Party Politics* 7:469–490.

Johnston, Ron J., and Charles J. Pattie. 2001b. "It's the Economy Stupid—But Which Economy?" *Regional Studies* 35:309–320.

Johnston, Ron J., and Charles J. Pattie. 2002. "Geographical Scale, the Attribution of Credit/Blame, Local Economic Circumstances, and Retrospective Economic Voting in Great Britain, 1997." *Environment and Planning C: Government and Policy* 20:421–438.

Johnston, Ron J., Charles J. Pattie, Daniel F. L. Dorling, Iain MacAllister, Helena Tunstall, and David J. Rossiter. 2000a. "The Neighbourhood Effect and Voting in England and Wales: Real or Imagined?" In *British Elections and Parties Review,* vol. 10, ed. Philip J. Cowley, David T. Denver, Andrew T. Russell, and Lisa Harrison, 47–63. London: Frank Cass.

Johnston, Ron J., Charles J. Pattie, Daniel F. L. Dorling, Iain MacAllister, Helena Tunstall, and David J. Rossiter. 2000b. "Local Context, Retrospective Economic Evaluations, and Voting: The 1997 General Election in England and Wales." *Political Behavior* 22:121–143.

Jones, Philip, and John Hudson. 1998. "The Role of Political Parties: An Analysis Based on Transaction Costs." *Public Choice* 94:1–2, 175–189.

Katz, Elihu. 1957. "The Two-Step Flow of Communication: An Up-to-Date Report on a Hypothesis." *Public Opinion Quarterly* 21:61–78.

Katz, Elihu, and Paul F. Lazarsfeld. 1955. *Personal Influence: The Part Played by People in the Flow of Mass Communications.* Glencoe, Ill.: Free Press.

Katznelson, Ira. 1986. "Working Class Formation: Constructing Cases and Comparisons." In *Working-Class Formation: Nineteenth Century Patterns in Western Europe and the United States,* ed. Ira Katznelson and Aristide Zolberg, 3–44. Princeton: Princeton University Press.

Kelley, Jonathan, and Ian McAllister. 1985. "Social Context and Electoral Behavior in Britain." *American Journal of Political Science* 29:3: 564–586.

Kenny, Christopher B. 1992. "Political Participation and Effects from the Social Environment." *American Journal of Political Science* 36:1, 259–267.

Kenny, Christopher B. 1993a. "The Microenvironment of Political Participation." *American Politics Quarterly* 21:2, 223–238.

Kenny, Christopher B. 1993b. "Social Influence and Opinion on Abortion." *Social Science Quarterly* 74:298–310.

Kenny, Christopher B. 1994. "The Microenvironment of Attitude Change." *Journal of Politics* 56:3, 715–728.

Kenny, Christopher B. 1998. "The Behavioral Consequences of Political Discussion: Another Look at Discussant Effects on Vote Choice." *Journal of Politics* 60:231–244.

Kenny, David A., and Charles M. Judd. 1984. "Estimating the Nonlinear and Interactive Effects of Latent Variables." *Psychological Bulletin* 96:201–210.

Key, V. O., Jr. 1949. *Southern Politics in State and Nation.* New York: Knopf.

Key, V. O., Jr. 1955. "A Theory of Critical Elections." *Journal of Politics* 17:3–18.

Key, V. O., Jr. 1961. *Public Opinion and American Democracy.* New York: Knopf.

Key, V. O., Jr. 1966. *The Responsible Electorate: Rationality and Presidential Voting 1936–60.* Cambridge: Harvard University Press.

Key, V. O., Jr., and Frank Munger. 1959. "Social Determinism and Electoral Decision: The Case of Indiana." In *American Voting Behavior,* ed. Eugene Burdick and Arthur Brodbeck, 281–299. Glencoe, Ill.: The Free Press.

Kinder, Donald R. 1986. "Presidential Character Revisited." In *Political Cognition,* ed. Richard R. Lau and David O. Sears. Hillsdale, N.J.: Lawrence Erlbaum Associates.

King, Gary. 1996. "Why Context Should Not Count." *Political Geography* 15:2, 159–164.

King, Gary. 2002. "When Can History Be My Guide? The Pitfalls of Counterfactual Inference." Cambridge, Mass.: Harvard University. Available http://gking.harvard.edu/files/counterf.pdf (accessed July 16, 2004).

King, Gary, James Honaker, Anne Joseph, and Kenneth Scheve. 2001. "Analyzing Incomplete Political Science Data: An Alternative Algorithm for Multiple Imputation." *American Political Science Review* 95:1, 49–69.

King, Gary, Robert Keohane, and Sidney Verba. 1994. *Designing Social Inquiry: Scientific Inference in Qualitative Research.* Princeton, N.J.: Princeton University Press.

King, Gary, Michael Tomz, and Jason Wittenberg. 2000. "Making the Most of Statistical Analyses: Improving Interpretation and Presentation." *American Journal of Political Science* 44:2, 347–361.

Kingston, Paul William, and Steven E. Finkel. 1987. "Is There a Marriage Gap in Politics?" *Journal of Marriage and the Family* 49:1, 57–64.

Klingemann, Hans-Dieter. 1979. "Ideological Conceptualization and Political Action." In *Political Action: Mass Participation in Five Western Democracies,* ed. Samuel Barnes and Max Kaase, 279–304. Beverly Hills, Calif.: Sage.

Knack, Stephen. 1992. "Civic Norms, Social Sanctions, and Voter Turnout." *Rationality and Society* 4:133–156.

Knight, Jack. 1992. *Institutions and Social Conflict.* New York: Cambridge University Press.

Knight, Jack, and James Johnson. 1994. "Aggregation and Deliberation: On the Possibility of Democratic Legitimacy." *Political Theory* 22:277–296.

Knoke, David. 1990a. "Networks of Political Action: Toward Theory Construction." *Social Forces* 68:4, 1041–1063.

Knoke, David. 1990b. *Political Networks: The Structural Perspective.* Cambridge: Cambridge University Press.

Kochen, Manfred, ed. 1989. The Small World: A Volume of Recent Research Advances Commemorating Ithiel de Sola Pool, Stanley Milgram, and Theodore Newcomb. Norwood, N.J.: Ablex Publishing.

Kotler-Berkowitz, Laurence. 2001. "Religion and Voting Behaviour in Great Britain: A Reassessment." *British Journal of Political Science* 31:523–554.

Krassa, Michael A. 1990. "Political Information, Social Environments, and Deviants." *Political Behavior* 12:4, 315–330.

Kriesi, Hanspeter. 1989. "New Social Movements and the New Class in the Netherlands." *American Journal of Sociology* 94:1078–1116.

Kuran, Timur. 1989. "Sparks and Prairie Fires: A Theory of Unanticipated Political Revolution." *Public Choice* 61:1, 41–74.

Kuran, Timur. 1991. "Now Out of Never: The Element of Surprise in the Eastern European Revolution of 1989." *World Politics* 44:1, 7–48.

Kuran, Timur. 1995. *Private Truths, Public Lies: The Social Consequences of Preference Falsification.* Cambridge, Mass.: Harvard University Press.

Laakso, Markku, and Rein Taagepera. 1979. "Effective Number of Parties: A Measure with Application to West Europe." *Comparative Political Studies* 12:3–27.

Lane, Robert E. 1959. *Political Life: Why People Get Involved in Politics.* Glencoe, Ill.: Free Press.

Langton, Kenneth P., and Ronald Rapoport. 1975. "Social Structure, Social Context, and Partisan Mobilization: Urban Workers in Chile." *Comparative Political Studies* 8:318–344.

Lasswell, Harold. 1953. *Politics: Who Gets What When and How.* New York: McGraw Hill.

Latané, Bibb, Andrzej Nowak, and James H. Liu. 1994. "Measuring Emergent Social Phenomena: Dynamism, Polarization, and Clustering as Order Parameters of Dynamic Social Systems." *Behavioral Science,* 39:1–24.

Lazarsfeld, Paul F., Bernard Berelson, and Hazel Gaudet. 1968 [1944]. *The People's Choice: How the Voter Makes Up His Mind in a Presidential Campaign.* New York: Columbia University Press.

Ledyard, John D. 1982. "The Paradox of Voting and Party Competition." In *Essays in Contemporary Fields of Economics,* ed. George Horwich and James Quirk. West Lafayette, Ind.: Purdue University Press.

Ledyard, John D. 1984. "The Pure Theory of Large Two-Party Elections." *Public Choice* 44:7–41.

Leighley, Jan. 1990. "Social Interaction and Contextual Influences on Political Participation." *American Politics Quarterly* 18:4, 459–475.

Leighley, Jan. 1995. "Attitudes, Opportunities, and Incentives: A Field Essay on Political Participation." *Political Research Quarterly* 48:1, 181–209.

Leighley, Jan. 1996. "Group Membership and the Mobilization of Political Participation." *Journal of Politics* 58:447–463.

Leighley, Jan, and Jonathan Nagler. 1992. "Individual and Systemic Influences on Turnout: Who Votes? 1984." *Journal of Politics* 54:718–740.

Leighley, Jan, and Arnold Vedlitz. 1999. "Race, Ethnicity and Political Participation: Competing Models and Contrasting Expectations." *Journal of Politics* 61:1092–1114.

Lewin, Kurt. 1948. *Resolving Social Conflicts: Selected Papers in Group Dynamics.* New York: Harper and Brothers.

Lewin, Kurt. 1964 [1951]. *Field Theory in Social Science: Selected Theoretical Papers of Kurt Lewin.* Ed. Dorwin Cartwright. New York: Harper and Row.

Lewis-Beck, Michael S., and Mary Stegmaier. 2000. "Economic Determinants of Electoral Outcomes." *Annual Review of Political Science* 3:183–219.

Lieberson, Stanley. 1969. "Measuring Population Diversity." *American Sociological Review* 34:850–862.

Lijphart, Arend. 1984. *Democracies.* New Haven: Yale University Press.

Liker, Jeffrey, Sue Augustyniak, and Greg J. Duncan. 1985. "Panel Data and Models of Change: A Comparison of First Difference and Conventional Two-Wave Models." *Social Science Research* 14:80–101.

Lin, Ann Chih. 1998. "Bridging Positivist and Interpretivist Approaches to Qualitative Methods." *Policy Studies Journal* 26:1, 162–180.

Lin, Ann Chih, Amaney Jamal, and Abigail Stewart. 2000. "Patriarchy, Connection, and Individualism: Immigration and the Experience of Gender in Arab Immigrant Families." Gerald R. Ford School of Public Policy, University of Michigan.

Lipset, Seymour Martin, and Earl Raab. 1995. *Jews and the New American Scene.* Cambridge: Harvard University Press.

Lipset, Seymour Martin, and Stein Rokkan, eds. 1967. *Party Systems and Voter Alignments.* New York: Free Press.

Lodge, Milton. 1995. "Toward a Procedural Model of Candidate Evaluation." In *Political Judgment: Structure and Process,* ed. Milton Lodge and Kathleen M. McGraw, 111–139. Ann Arbor: University of Michigan Press.

Lodge, Milton, and Ruth Hamill. 1986. "A Partisan Schema for Political Information Processing." *American Political Science Review* 80:2, 505–519.

Lodge, Milton, and Charles Taber. 2000. "Three Steps toward a Theory of Motivated Political Reasoning." In *Elements of Reason,* ed. Arthur Lupia, Mathew D. McCubbins, and Samuel L. Popkin. New York: Cambridge University Press.

Lohmann, Susanne. 1994. "The Dynamics of Informational Cascades: The Monday Demonstrations in Leipzig, East Germany, 1989–91." *World Politics* 47:42–101.

Long, Scott J. 1997. *Regression Models for Categorical and Limited Dependent Variables.* Thousand Oaks, Calif.: Sage.

MacAllister, Ian, Ronald J. Johnston, Charles J. Pattie, Helena Tunstall, Daniel F. L. Dorling, and David J. Rossiter. 2001. "Class Dealignment and the Neighbourhood Effect: Miller Revisited." *British Journal of Political Science* 31:41–60.

Macedo, Stephen, ed. 1999. *Deliberative Politics: Essays on Democracy and Disagreement.* New York: Oxford University Press.

MacKuen, Michael. 1990. "Speaking of Politics: Individual Conversational Choice, Public Opinion, and the Prospects for Deliberative Democracy." In *Information and Democratic Processes,* ed. John A. Ferejohn and James H. Kuklinski. Urbana and Chicago: University of Illinois Press.

MacKuen, Michael, and Courtney Brown. 1987. "Political Context and Attitude Change." *American Political Science Review* 81:2, 471–490.

Maddala, G. S. 1983. *Limited-Dependent and Qualitative Variables in Econometrics.* New York: Cambridge University Press.

Maimonides. 1972 [c. 1190]. *Mishnah Torah. Sefer Mada. Hilchot Deot.* [The book of knowledge. Laws of beliefs]. Jerusalem: Hotzaat Makor.

Manin, Bernard, Elly Stein, and Jane Mansbridge. 1987. "On Legitimacy and Political Deliberation." *Political Theory* 15:3, 338–368.

Mannheim, Karl. 1952. "The Problem of Generations." In *Essays on the Sociology of Knowledge,* ed. Paul Keskemeti. London: Routledge and Kegan Paul.

March, James G. 1953–54. "Husband and Wife Interaction over Political Issues." *Public Opinion Quarterly* 17:4, 461–470.

Markus, Gregory B. 1979. *Analyzing Panel Data.* Beverly Hills, Calif.: Sage.

Markus, Gregory B. 1983. "Dynamic Modeling of Cohort Change: The Case of Political Partisanship." *British Journal of Political Science* 27:717–739.

Marsden, Peter V. 1987. "Core Discussion Networks of Americans." *American Sociological Review* 52:1, 122–131.

Marsden, Peter V., and Noah E. Friedkin. 1994. "Network Studies of Social Influence." In *Advances in Social Network Analysis,* ed. Stanley Wasserman and Joseph Galaskiewicz, 3–25. Thousand Oaks, Calif.: Sage.

Marsh, Michael. 2002. "Local Context." *Electoral Studies* 21:207–217.

McAdams, James. 1987. "Testing the Theory of the New Class." *Sociological Quarterly* 28:23–49.

McAllister, Ian, and Donley T. Studlar. 1992. "Region and Voting in Britain: Territorial Polarization or Artifact?" *American Journal of Political Science* 36:168–199.

McClosky, Herbert, John Zaller, and Dennis Chong. 1985. "Social Learning and the Acquisition of Political Norms." In *American Ethos,* ed. Herbert McClosky and John Zaller. Cambridge, Mass.: Harvard University Press.

McDonald, Michael D., and Myunghee Kim. 2002. "Cross-National Comparisons of Party Left-Right Positions." Binghamton, N.Y.: Department of Political Science, Binghamton University.

McDonald, Michael D., and Silvia M. Mendes. 2001. "The Policy Space of Party Manifestoes." In *The Policy Space of Political Actors,* ed. Michael Laver. London: Routledge.

McDonald, Michael P., and Samuel L. Popkin. 2001. "The Myth of the Vanishing Voter." *American Political Science Review* 95:963–974.

McGraw, Kenneth O., and S. P. Wong. 1996. "Forming Inferences about Some Intraclass Correlation Coefficients." *Psychological Methods* 1:30–46.

McGuire, William J. 1985. "Attitudes and Attitude Change." In *The Handbook of Social Psychology,* 3rd ed., ed. G. Lindzey and E. Aronson, 2:233–246. Reading, Mass.: Addison-Wesley.

McMurrer, Daniel P., and Isabel Sawhill. 1998. *Getting Ahead: Economic and Social Mobility in America.* Washington, D.C.: Urban Institute Press.

McPhee, William N., with Robert B. Smith and Jack Ferguson. 1963. "A Theory of Informal Social Influence." In *Formal Theories of Mass Behavior*, ed. William N. McPhee, 74–203. New York: Free Press.

Merton, Robert K. 1957. *Social Theory and Social Structure,* rev. ed. New York: Free Press.

Milburn, Michael A. 1991. *Persuasion and Politics.* Pacific Grove, Calif.: Brooks/Cole Publishing.

Milgram, Stanley. 1967. "The Small World Problem." *Psychology Today* 2 (May), 60–67.

Miller, Robert L., Rick Wilfor, and Freda Donoghue. 1999. "Personal Dynamics as Political Participation." *Political Research Quarterly* 52:2, 269–292.

Miller, Warren E. 1956. "One-Party Politics and the Voter." *American Political Science Review* 50:707–725.

Miller, Warren E., and J. Merrill Shanks. 1996. *The New American Voter.* Cambridge, Mass.: Harvard University Press.

Minar, Nelson, Roger Burkhart, Chris Langton, and Manor Askenazi. 1996. The Swarm Simulation System: A Toolkit for Building Multi-agent Simulations. Santa Fe Institute Working Paper 96-06-042, Santa Fe, NM. (available at http://www.swarm.org/archive/overview.ps)

Mondak, Jeffrey J. 1995. "Media Exposure and Political Discussion in U.S. Elections." *Journal of Politics* 57:62–85.

Monroe, Alan D. 1977. "Urbanism and Voter Turnout: A Note on Some Unexpected Findings." *American Journal of Political Science* 21:1, 71–78.

Mooney, Christopher Z. 1996. "Bootstrap Statistical Inference: Examples and Evaluations for Political Science." *American Journal of Political Science* 40:570–602.

Mooney, Christopher Z., and Robert D. Duval. 1993. *Bootstrapping: A Nonparametric Approach to Statistical Inference.* Newbury Park, Calif.: Sage.

Mosca, Gaetano. 1939. *The Ruling Class: Elementi di Scienza Politics.* Ed. and rev. Arthur Livingson; trans. Hannah D. Kahn. New York: McGraw-Hill.

Müller, Walter. 1998. "Klassenstrukur und Parteiensystem. Zum Wandel der Klassenspaltung im Wahlverhalten." *Kölner Zeitschrift für Soziologie und Sozialpsychologie* 50:3–47.

Mulligan, Casey B., and Charles G. Hunter. 2001. "The Empirical Frequency of a Pivotal Vote." NBER Working Papers W8590 (November). Cambridge, Mass.: National Bureau of Economic Research.

Mutz, Diana C. 1998. *Impersonal Influence: How Perceptions of Mass Collectives Affect Political Attitudes.* New York: Cambridge University Press.

Mutz, Diana C. 2002a. "Cross-cutting Social Networks: Testing Democratic Theory in Practice." *American Political Science Review* 96:1, 111–126.

Mutz, Diana C. 2002b. "The Consequences of Cross-Cutting Networks for Political Participation." *American Journal of Political Science* 46:4, 838–855.

Mutz, Diana C., and Jeffrey Mondak. 1997. "Dimensions of Sociotropic Behavior: Group-Based Judgments of Fairness and Well-Being." *American Journal of Political Science* 41:1, 284–308.

Mutz, Diana, and Jeffrey Mondak. 1998. "Democracy at Work: Contributions of the Workplace toward a Public Sphere." Paper presented at the annual meeting of the Midwest Political Science Association, Chicago, April 23–25.

Newcomb, Theodore M., Ralph H. Turner, and Philip E. Converse. 1964. *Social Psychology: The Study of Human Interaction.* New York: Holt, Rinehart, and Winston.

Newman, Mark E. J. 2001a. "The Structure of Scientific Collaboration Networks." *Proceedings of the National Academy of Sciences U.S.A.* 98:404–409.

Newman, Mark E. J. 2001b. "Scientific Collaboration Networks: I. Network Construction and Fundamental Results." *Physical Review E* 64:016131.

Newman, Mark E. J. 2001c. "Scientific Collaboration Networks: II. Shortest Paths, Weighted Networks, and Centrality." *Physical Review E* 64:016132.

Newman, Mark E. J. 2002. "Random Graph Models of Social Networks." *Proceedings of the National Academy of Science USA* 99:2566–2572.

Nie, Norman H., Jane Junn, and Kenneth Stehlik-Barry. 1996. *Education and Democratic Citizenship in America.* Chicago: University of Chicago Press.

Niemi, Richard G., and Jane Junn. 1998. *Civic Education: What Makes Students Learn?* New Haven: Yale University Press.

Niemi, Richard G., Roman Hedges, and M. Kent Jennings. 1977. "The Similarity of Husbands' and Wives' Political Views." *American Politics Quarterly* 5:2, 133–148.

Niemi, Richard G., and Barbara I. Sobieszek. 1977. "Political Socialization." *Annual Review of Sociology* 3:209–233.

Niemi, Richard G., and Herbert F. Weisberg. 1993. "Is Party Idenification Stable?" In *Controversies in Voting Behavior*, ed. Richard Niemi and Herbert F. Weisberg, 268–382. Washington, D.C.: Congressional Quarterly Press.

Noelle-Neumann, Elisabeth. 1974. "The Spiral of Silence: A Theory of Public Opinion." *Journal of Communication* 24:2, 43–51.

Noelle-Neumann, Elisabeth. 1984. *The Spiral of Silence: Public Opinion—My Social Skin.* Chicago: University of Chicago Press.

Noelle-Neumann, Elisabeth. 1993. *The Spiral of Silence: Public Opinion, Our Social Skin.* 2nd ed. Chicago: University of Chicago Press.

Norrander, Barbara. 1997. "Is the Gender Gap Growing?" In *Reelection 1996*, ed. Herbert F. Weisberg and Janet M. Box-Steffensmeier. New York: Chatham House.

Nowak, Andrzej, and Maciej Lewenstein, "Modeling Social Change with Cellular Automata." In *Modeling and Simulation in the Social Sciences from a Philosophy of Science Point of View*, ed. R. Hegselmann et al., 249–285. Amsterdam: Kluwer.

Nowak, Andrzej, Jacek Szamrej, and Bibb Latané. 1990. "From Private Attitude to Public Opinion: A Dynamic Theory of Social Impact." *Psychological Review* 97:362–376.

Olsen, Marvin E. 1972. "Social Participation and Voting Turnout: A Multivariate Analysis." *American Sociological Review*, 37:3, 317–333.

Page, Benjamin I., and Robert Y. Shapiro. 1992. *The Rational Public: Fifty Years of Trends in Americans' Policy Preferences.* Chicago: University of Chicago Press.

Palfrey, Thomas R., and Howard Rosenthal. 1983. "A Strategic Calculus of Voting." *Public Choice* 41:7–53.

Palfrey, Thomas R., and Howard Rosenthal. 1985. "Voter Participation and Strategic Uncertainty." *American Political Science Review* 79:62–78.

Pattie, Charles J., and Ron J. Johnston. 1995. "'It's Not Like that Round Here': Region, Economic Evaluations and Voting at the 1992 British General Election." *European Journal of Political Research* 28:1–32.

Pattie, Charles J., and Ron J. Johnston. 1999. "Context, Conversation and Conviction: Social Networks and Voting in the 1992 British General Election." *Political Studies* 47:877–889.

Pattie, Charles J., and Ron J. Johnston. 2000. "People Who Talk Together Vote Together: An Exploration of the Neighbourhood Effect in Great Britain." *Annals, Association of American Geographers* 90:41–66.

Pattie, Charles J., and Ron J. Johnston. 2001. "Talk As a Political Context: Conversation and Electoral Change in British Elections, 1992–1997." *Electoral Studies* 20:1, 17–40.

Pattie, Charles J., Ron J. Johnston, and Edward A. Fieldhouse. 1995. "Winning the Local Vote: The Effectiveness of Constituency Campaign Spending in Great Britain, 1983–1992." *American Political Science Review* 89:969–986.

Plutzer, Eric. 1988. "Work Life, Family Life, and Women's Support of Feminism." *American Sociological Review* 53:4, 640–649.

Plutzer, Eric, and Michael McBurnett. 1991. "Family Life and American Politics Reconsidered." *Public Opinion Quarterly* 55:1, 113–127.

Pool, Ithiel De Sola, and Manfred Kochen. 1978. "Contacts and Influence." *Social Networks* 1:1, 1–48.

Popkin, Samuel L. 1991. *The Reasoning Voter: Communication and Persuasion in Presidential Campaigns*. Chicago: University of Chicago Press.

Pozzetta, George E., ed. 1991. *Immigrant Family Patterns: Demography, Fertility, Housing, Kinship, and Urban Life*. New York: Garland.

Price, Vincent, Joseph N. Cappella, and Lilach Nir. 2002. "Does Disagreement Contribute to More Deliberative Opinion?" *Political Communication* 19:1, 95–112.

Putnam, Robert D. 1966. "Political Attitudes and the Local Community." *American Political Science Review* 60:640–654.

Putnam, Robert D. 2000. *Bowling Alone: The Collapse and Revival of American Community*. New York: Simon and Schuster.

Radcliff, Benjamin. 2001. "Organized Labor and Electoral Participation in American National Elections." *Journal of Labor Research* 22:2, 405–414.

Radcliff, Benjamin, and Patricia Davis. 2000. "Labor Organization and Electoral Participation in Industrial Democracies." *American Journal of Political Science* 44:1, 132–141.

Raftery, Adrian E. 1995. "Bayesian Model Selection in Social Research." In *Sociological Methodology,* vol. 25, ed. Peter V. Marsden, 111–163. Oxford: Blackwell.

Rasbash, Jon, William Browne, Harvey Goldstein, M. Yang, Ian Plewis, Michael Healy, G. Woodhouse, David Draper. 1999. *A User's Guide to MLwiN*. London: Institute of Education.

Ratzinger, Hans, and Jürgen Kramer. 1995. "Wahlnorm und Wahlbeteiligung in der Bundesrepublik Deutschland: Eine Kausalanalyse" [Values to vote and voting turnout in Germany: A causal analysis]. *Politische Vierteljahresschrift* 36:2, 267–285.

Renshon, Stanley Allen. 1973. "The Role of Personality Development in Political Socialization." In *New Directions in Political Socialization*, ed. David C. Schwartz and Sandra Kenyon Schwartz. New York: Free Press.

Riesman, David. 1961 [1951]. *The Lonely Crowd: A Study of the Changing American Character.* New Haven: Yale University Press.

Riker, William H. 1982. "The Two-Party System and Duverger's Law: An Essay on the History of Political Science." *American Political Science Review* 76:4, 753–766.

Riker, William H. 1983. "Political Theory and the Art of Heresthetics." In *Political Science: The State of the Discipline*, ed. Ada W. Finifter. Washington: American Political Science Association.

Riker, William H., and Peter C. Ordeshook. 1968. "A Theory of the Calculus of Voting." *American Political Science Review* 62:25–42.

Rinehart, Sue Tolleson. 1992. *Gender Consciousness and Politics*. New York: Routledge.

Robinson, W. S. 1957. "The Statistical Measurement of Agreement." *American Sociological Review* 22:1, 17–25.

Roch, Christine H., John T. Scholz, and Kathleen M. McGraw. 2000. "Social Networks and Citizen Responses to Legal Change." *American Journal of Political Science* 44:4, 777–791.

Rodgers, Willard L. 1989. "Comparisons of Alternative Approaches to the Estimation of Simple Causal Models from Panel Data." In *Panel Surveys*, eds. Daniel Kasprzyk, Greg J. Duncan, Graham Kalton, and M. P. Singh, 432–456. New York: Wiley.

Rogers, William. 1993. "Regression Standard Errors in Clustered Samples." *Stata Technical Bulletin* 13:19–23.

Rose, Richard, and Ian McAllister. 1990. *The Loyalties of Voters: A Lifetime Learning Model*. London: Sage.

Rosenstone, Steven J., and John Mark Hansen. 1993. *Mobilization, Participation, and Democracy in America*. New York: Macmillan.

Ross, Lee. 1990. "Recognizing the Role of Construal Processes." In *The Legacy of Solomon Asch: Essays in Cognition and Social Psychology*, ed. Irvin Rock, 77–96. Hillsdale, N.J.: Lawrence Erlbaum Associates.

Ross, Lee, Gunter Bierbrauer, and Susan Hoffman. 1976. "The Role of Attribution Processes in Conformity and Dissent." *American Psychologist* 31:2, 148–157.

Roth, Guenther, and Claus Wittich, eds. 1978. *Max Weber: Economy and Society*. Berkeley: University of California Press.

Sanders, David. 1996. "Economic Performance, Management Competence, and the Outcome of the Next General Election." *Political Studies* 44:203–231.

Sanders, David. 2000. "The Real Economy and the Perceived Economy in Popularity Functions: How Much Do the Electorate Need to Know?" *Electoral Studies* 19:275–294.

Sanders, David, and Malcolm Brynin. 1999. "The Dynamics of Party Preference Change in Britain, 1991–96." *Political Studies* 47:219–239.

Sanders, David, Harold Clarke, Marianne Stewart, and Paul Whiteley. 2001. "The Economy and Voting." In *Britain Votes 2001,* ed. Pippa Norris, 224–238. Oxford: Oxford University Press.

Sapiro, Virginia. 2002. "It's the Context, Situation, and Question, Stupid: The Gender Basis of Public Opinion." In *Understanding Public Opinion*, 2nd ed., ed. Barbara Norrander and Clyde Wilcox. Washington, D.C.: CQ Press.

Särlvik, Bo, and Ivor Crewe. 1983. *Decade of Dealignment: The Conservative Victory of 1979 and Electoral Trends in the 1970s*. Cambridge: Cambridge University Press.

Savage, Mike. 1991. "Making Sense of Middle-Class Politics: A Secondary Analysis of the 1987 British General Election Survey." *Sociological Review* 39:26–54.

Scarbrough, Elinor. 1984. *Political Ideology and Voting*. Oxford: Clarendon Press.

Schachter, Stanley, and Michael Gazzaniga, eds. 1989. *Extending Psychological Frontiers: Selected Works of Leon Festinger*. New York: Russell Sage Foundation.

Scheufele, Dietram A. 1999. "Deliberation or Dispute? An Exploratory Study Examining Dimensions of Public Opinion Expression." *International Journal of Public Opinion Research* 11:1, 25–58.

Schickler, Eric, and Donald Philip Green. 1993–94. "Issue Preferences and the Dynamics of Party Identification: A Methodological Critique." *Political Analysis* 5:151–180.

Schickler, Eric, and Donald Philip Green. 1997. "The Stability of Party Identification in Western Democracies." *Comparative Political Studies* 30:4, 450–483.

Schmitt-Beck, Rüdiger, Stefan Weick, and Bernhard Christoph. 2002. "The Influence of Life-Cycle Events on Partisanship: Long-term Evidence from the German Socio-Economic Panel." Paper presented at the 98th annual meeting of the American Political Science Association, August 29–September 1, Boston, Mass.

Schneider, Mark, Paul Teske, Christine Roch, and Melissa Marschall. 1997. "Networks to Nowhere: Segregation and Stratification in Networks of Information about Schools." *American Journal of Political Science* 41:4, 1201–1223.

Scorza, Jason A. 1998. "Uncivil Friendship: Emersonian Lessons for Democratic Disagreement." Presented at the annual meeting of the American Political Science Association, Boston, Mass.

Shannon. C. E. 1949. *The Mathematical Theory of Communication*. Champaign-Urbana: University of Illinois Press.

Shapiro, Robert Y., and Harpreet Mahajan. 1986. "Gender Differences in Policy Preferences: A Summary of Trends from the 1960s to the 1980s." *Public Opinion Quarterly* 50:1, 42–61.

Shibanai, Yasufumi, Satoko Yasuno, Itaru Ishiguro. 2001. Effects of Global Information Feedback on Diversity. *Journal of Conflict Resolution*, 45:1, 80–96.

Shils, Edward A. 1951. "The Study of the Primary Group." In *The Policy Sciences*, ed. Daniel Lerner and Harold D. Lasswell, 44–69. Stanford: Stanford University Press.

Shryock, Andrew. 2000. "Family Resemblances: Kinship and Community in Arab Detroit." In *Arab Detroit: From Margin to Mainstream*, ed. Nabeel Abraham and Andrew Shryock. Detroit: Wayne State University Press.

Sigel, Roberta S., and Marilyn B. Hoskin. 1981. *The Political Involvement of Adolescents*. New Brunswick, N.J.: Rutgers University Press.

Simmel, Georg. 1955. *Conflict and the Web of Group-Affiliations*. Trans. Kurt H. Wolf and Reinhard Bendix. New York: Free Press.

Simon, Herbert A. 1965 [1957]. *Administrative Behavior: A Study of Decision-Making in Administrative Organization*. New York: Free Press.

Simon, Herbert A. 1999. "Comments on Remarks of James Buchanan and Douglass C. North." In *Competition and Cooperation: Conversations with Nobelists on Economics and Politics*, ed. James Alt, Margaret Levi, and Elinor Ostrom. New York: Sage Foundation.

Singer, Eleanor, and Stanley Presser. 1989. "Mode of Administration." In *Survey Research Methods: A Reader*, ed. Eleanor Singer and Stanley Presser. Chicago: University of Chicago Press.

Singerman, Diane. 1995. *Avenues of Participation: Family, Politics, and Networks in Urban Quarters of Cairo*. Princeton: Princeton University Press.

Smelser, Neil J., William Julius Wilson, and Faith Mitchell, eds. 2001. *America Becoming: Racial Trends and Their Consequences*. Washington, D.C.: National Academy Press.

Smith, Tom W. 1985. "Working Wives and Women's Rights: The Connection between the Employment Status of Wives and the Feminist Attitudes of Husbands." *Sex Roles* 12:5–6, 501–508.

Sniderman, Paul M., Richard A. Brody, and Philip E. Tetlock. 1991. *Reasoning and Choice*. New York: Cambridge University Press.

Sniderman, Paul M., Philip E. Tetlock, and Laurel Elms. 2001. "Public Opinion and Democratic Politics: The Problem of Nonattitudes and Social Construction of Political Judgments." In *Citizens and Politics: Perspectives from Political Psychology*, ed. James H. Kuklinski, 254–288. New York: Cambridge University Press.

Snijders, Tom A. B., and Roel J. Bosker. 1999. *Multilevel Analysis: An Introduction to Basic and Advanced Multilevel Modeling*. London: Sage.

SOEP Group. 2001. "The German Socio-Economic Panel (GSOEP) after More Than Fifteen Years: Overview." *Vierteljahreshefte zur Wirtschaftsforschung* (Quarterly Journal of Economic Research) 70:7–14.

Solon, Gary. 1992. "Intergenerational Income Mobility in the United States." *American Economic Review* 82:393–408.

Soss, Joe. 2000. *Unwanted Claims: The Politics of Participation in the U.S. Welfare System*. Ann Arbor: University of Michigan Press.

Sprague, John. 1982. "Is There a Micro Theory Consistent with Contextual Analysis?" In *Strategies of Political Inquiry*, ed. Elinor Ostrom, 99–121. Beverly Hills: Sage.

Stanley, Harold W., and Richard G. Niemi. 1991. "Partisanship and Group Support, 1952–1988." *American Politics Quarterly* 19:189–210.

Steenbergen, Marco R., and Bradford S. Jones. 2002. "Modeling Multilevel Data Structures." *American Journal of Political Science* 46:1, 218–237.

Stoker, Laura, and M. Kent Jennings. 1995. "Life Cycle Transitions and Political Participation: the Case of Marriage." *American Political Science Review* 89:2, 421–433.

Stoloff, Jennifer A., Jennifer L. Glanville, and Elisa Jayne Bienenstock. 1999. "Women's Participation in the Labor Force: The Role of Social Networks." *Social Networks* 21:91–108.

Straits, Bruce C. 1990. "The Social Context of Voter Turnout." *Public Opinion Quarterly* 54:1, 64–73.

Straits, Bruce C. 1991. "Bringing Strong Ties Back In: Interpersonal Gateways to Political Information and Influence." *Public Opinion Quarterly* 55:3, 432–448.

Sullivan, John L. 1973. "Political Correlates of Social, Economic, and Religious Diversity in the American States." *Journal of Politics* 35:1, 70–84.

Tate, Katherine. 1991. "Black Political Participation in the 1984 and 1988 Presidential Elections." *American Political Science Review* 85:4, 1159–1176.

Tedin, Kent L. 1974. "The Influence of Parents on the Political Attitudes of Adolescents." *American Political Science Review* 68:1579–1592.

Tocqueville, Alexis de. 2000 [1835]. *Democracy in America.* Ed. Harvey C. Mansfield and Delba Winthrop. Chicago: University of Chicago Press.

Tocqueville, Alexis de. 1969 [1835]. *Democracy in America.* Ed. J. P. Mayer; trans. George Lawrence. New York: Doubleday-Anchor.

Topf, Richard. 1995. "Beyond Electoral Participation." In *Citizens and the State*, ed. Hans-Dieter Klingemann and Dieter Fuchs. New York: Oxford University Press.

Tullock, Gordon. 1967. *Towards a Mathematics of Politics.* Ann Arbor: University of Michigan.

Tyler, Tom R., and Yuen J. Huo. 2002. *Trust in the Law: Encouraging Cooperation with Police and the Courts.* New York: Russell Sage Foundation.

Uhlaner, Carole J. 1995. "What the Downsian Voter Weighs: A Reassessment of the Costs and Benefits of Action." In *Information, Participation, and Choice*, ed. Bernard Grofman. Ann Arbor: University of Michigan Press.

U.S. Bureau of the Census. 1996. *Statistical Abstract of the United States.* Washington, D.C.: U.S. Bureau of the Census.

van Deth, Jan W. 1991. "Politicization and Political Interest." In *Eurobarometer: The Dynamics of European Public Opinion*, ed. Karlheinz Reif and Ronald Inglehart. New York: St. Martin's Press.

Vaux, Alan. 1988. *Social Support: Theory, Research, and Intervention.* New York: Praeger.

Verba, Sidney. 1961. *Small Groups and Political Behavior: A Study of Leadership.* Princeton: Princeton University Press.

Verba, Sidney, Nancy Burns, and Kay L. Schlozman. 2002. "Unequal at the Starting Line: Creating Participatory Inequalities across Generations and among Groups." Paper presented at the conference "The Social Context of Politics," Brown University, Providence, R.I., June 2–4.

Verba, Sidney, and Norman H. Nie. 1972. *Participation in America.* New York: Harper Row.

Verba, Sidney, Norman H. Nie, and Jae-On Kim. 1978. *Participation and Political Equality.* Cambridge: Cambridge University Press.

Verba, Sidney, Kay L. Schlozman, and Henry Brady. 1995. *Voice and Equality: Civic Voluntarism in American Politics.* Cambridge: Harvard University Press.

Verba, Sidney, Kay L. Schlozman, Henry E. Brady, and Norman H. Nie. 1993. "Race, Ethnicity and Political Resources: Participation in the United States." *British Journal of Political Science* 23:453–497.

Wald, Kenneth D. 1997. *Religion and Politics in the United States,* 3rd ed. Washington, D.C.: CQ Press.

Wampold. B. E. 1984. "Tests of Dominance in Sequential Categorical Data." *Psychological Bulletin* 96:424–429.

Warren, Donald I. 1981. *Helping Networks: How People Cope with Problems in the Urban Community.* Notre Dame, Ind.: University of Notre Dame Press.

Warwick, Paul. 1992. "Ideological Diversity and Government Survival in Western-European Parliamentary Democracies." *Comparative Political Studies* 25:3, 332–361.

Watts, Duncan J. 1999. *Small Worlds: The Dynamics of Networks between Order and Randomness.* Princeton, N.J.: Princeton University Press.

Watts, Duncan J., and Steven H. Strogatz. 1998. "Collective Dynamics of Small-World Networks." *Nature* 393:440–442.

Weatherford, M. Stephen. 1982. "Interpersonal Networks and Political Behavior." *American Journal of Political Science* 26:117–143.

Weisberg, Herbert. 1987. "The Demographics of a New Voting Gap: Marital Differences in American Voting." *Public Opinion Quarterly* 51:3, 335–343.

Weissberg, Robert. 1975. "Political Efficacy and Political Illusion." *Journal of Politics* 37:2, 469–487.

Wielhouwer, Peter W., and Brad Lockerbie. 1994. "Party Contacting and Political-Participation, 1952–90." *American Journal of Political Science* 38:1, 211–229.

Winkelmann, Rainer. 2000. *Econometric Analysis of Count Data.* New York: Springer.

Wolfinger, Raymond E., and Steven J. Rosenstone. 1980. *Who Votes?* New Haven: Yale University Press.

Wolter, Kirk M. 1985. *Introduction to Variance Estimation.* New York: Springer.

Worcester, Robert, and Robert Mortimore. 2001. *Explaining Labour's Second Landslide.* London: Politico's.

World Bank. 2000. *World Development Indicators.* CD-ROM. Washington, D.C.: World Bank.

Wuthnow, Robert. 1983. "The Political Rebirth of American Evangelicals." In *The New Christian Right: Mobilization and Legitimation,* ed. Robert C. Liebman and Robert Wuthnow, 168–185. New York: Aldine Publishing Company.

Wyatt, Robert O., Elihu Katz, and Joohan Kim. 2000. "Bridging the Spheres: Political and Personal Conversation in Public and Private Spaces." *Journal of Communication* 50:1, 71–92.

Zaller, John. 1992. *The Nature and Origins of Mass Opinion.* New York: Cambridge University Press.

Zelle, Carsten. 1998. "A Third Face of Dealignment? An Update on Party Identification in Germany, 1971–94." In *Stability and Change in German Elections: How Electorates Merge, Converge, or Collide,* ed. Christopher J. Anderson and Carsten Zelle, 55–70. Westport Conn.: Praeger.

Zorn, Christopher J. W. 2001. "Generalized Estimating Equation Models for Correlated Data: A Review with Applications." *American Journal of Political Science* 45:2, 470–490.

Zuckerman, Alan S. 1982. "New Approaches to Political Cleavage: A Theoretical Introduction." *Comparative Political Studies* 15:131–144.

Zuckerman, Alan S. 1989. "The Bases of Political Cohesion: Applying and Reconstructing Crumbling Theories." *Comparative Politics* 21:4473–4496.

Zuckerman, Alan S., Josip Dasović, Jennifer Fitzgerald, and Malcolm Brynin. 2002. "The Dynamics of Partisan Support: Simple and Complex Patterns in British and German Electorates." Paper presented at the 2002 annual meeting of the American Political Science Association, August 29–Sept. 1, Boston, Mass.

Zuckerman, Alan S., and Laurence A. Kotler-Berkowitz. 1998. "Politics and Society: Political Diversity and Uniformity in Households as a Theoretical Puzzle." *Comparative Political Studies* 31:4, 464–497.

Zuckerman, Alan S., Laurence A. Kotler-Berkowitz, and Lucas A. Swaine. 1998. "Anchoring Political Preferences: The Importance of Social and Political Contexts and Networks in Britain." *European Journal of Political Research* 33:3, 285–321.

Zuckerman, Alan S., Nicholas A. Valentino, and Ezra W. Zuckerman. 1994. "A Structural Theory of Vote Choice: Social and Political Networks and Electoral Flows in Britain and the United States." *Journal of Politics* 56:4, 1008–1033.

Index

Abelson, Robert P., 256–57
access: to political information, 152, 168; to political resources, and socioeconomic status, 96
accommodation in marriages, 51–53
Accumulation Model of political socialization, 96
ACM. *See* Axelrod culture model (ACM)
acquaintance measure (agent-based modeling), 255–59, 262, 267
acquaintances: impact on political choice, 132; impact on turnout decisions, 269, 280, 282–83, 286; interactions among, 269; learning activism from, 182; low-density networks, 46; numbers of, 273; political influence, 274–75, 279, 287; political information from, 132; relationships among, 272; shared interests, 270, 276; social influence, 147; strong-tie versus weak-tie, 175. *See also* turnout cascades
action, social and political: class, and partisanship, 117–18; and diversity of social networks, 168; factors that influence, xvi, xviii, 103–5, 176–77, 181–82; gender differences, 172–73, 180, 182; measuring, 117–18; political activism, 178, 182, 220; social context, 10. *See also* political efficacy
Administrative Behavior: A Study of Decision-Making Processes in Administrative Organizations (Simon), 10
administrative services classes (EG class scheme), 122
adolescents: partisanship, 212, 217–18; political socialization, 211, 220, 225–26, 245
African Americans: in diverse friendship networks, 157–58, 160–64, 166; influence of Civil Rights movement, 108–12; political efficacy, 213; political participation, 155, 213; political stimulation at home, 108–9
age: and electoral choices, 135, 137–39; in fixed-effects models, 122; impact on political discussion frequency, 238; neighborhood age structures, 189; and political activity, 98–99; and political attitudes, 187; and susceptibility to outside influence, 66; as variable in Citizen Participation Study, 114
agent-based modeling: advantages of, 251, 257; approaches to, 19; autoregressive influence, 264; cellular automata, 251; culture arrays,

264; identity-based selection of discussants, 262–64; multi-agent villages, 258–59; multiple neighborhoods and workplaces, 260–62; network-embedded model of decision, 265–67; parochialism, 258; and political discussion frequency, 238; self-selection, 259–60. *See also* Axelrod culture model (ACM); social impact model (SIM)
aggregate analysis, 7, 16, 208
Agnew, John A., 187
agreement, political: among social intimates, 16; among spouses and couples, 56, 80–83, 85; applying social logic approaches to, 16–17, 19–20, 22–23; and duration of cohabitation, 82; within dyads, 36–39, 43, 87–88; false assumptions of, 22; and social network structures, 27
Aldrich, John H., 286
Allison, Paul D., 120
American national elections: 1944, 12; 1948, 5, 12, 22; 1952, 12; 1984, 23, 133, 141–47; 1992, 134–39, 146–51, 274–75; 1996, 71; 2000, 24–27, 37–39, 45–46
American National Election surveys: reinterpretation and reanalysis of data from, 17; underlying premises, 11–13
American Voter, The (Campbell, Converse, Miller, Stokes), 3–4, 8, 10, 11–14, 133
analysis of variance (ANOVA), 240–41
Anglo whites, political stimulation at home, 108–9
ANOVA (analysis of variance), 240–41
Aquinas, xvii
Aristotle, xvii
Asch, Solomon (Asch experiments), 32
asocial model of political choice, 132
associative (assortative) mating (marital homophily): assumptions about, xvii, 17, 20, 82; and class identification, 82–83; and partisan agreement, 82; and political preferences, 76; shared interests and experience, 53, 60
asymmetrical influence among spouses, 60–61, 68
asymmetrical relationships, 24
atomized individuals (autonomous agents), 8, 168, 184, 257
autoregressive influence of social networks: defined, 31–32; modeling, 264–66